CLASSICAL RHETORIC
AND ITS CHRISTIAN
AND SECULAR TRADITION
FROM ANCIENT TO
MODERN TIMES

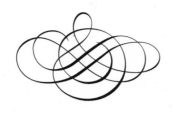

CLASSICAL RHETORIC

& Its Christian *&* Secular Tradition *from* Ancient *to* Modern Times

SECOND EDITION, REVISED AND ENLARGED

GEORGE A. KENNEDY

The University of North Carolina Press

Chapel Hill and London

© 1999

The University of North Carolina Press

All rights reserved

Manufactured in the United States of America

The paper in this book meets the guidelines for
permanence and durability of the Committee on
Production Guidelines for Book Longevity of the
Council on Library Resources.

Library of Congress Cataloging-in-Publication Data

Kennedy, George Alexander, 1928–

Classical rhetoric and its Christian and secular tradition from
ancient to modern times / by George A. Kennedy. — 2nd ed.,
rev. and enl.

p. cm.

Includes bibliographical references and index.

ISBN 0-8078-2467-4 (cloth : alk. paper).

ISBN 0-8078-4769-0 (pbk. : alk. paper)

1. Rhetoric—History.   I. Title.

PN183.K4   1999

808—dc21   98-34331

CIP

03   02   01   00   99   5   4   3   2   1

CONTENTS

WK 12
11/11 - 63

WK 12
WK 13
11/18 - 20
WK 14 - TG.
11/25-27
draft final
papers
WK 15 - 12/2-4
peer review final
papers
WK 16
12/9 - 11
Edit & submit
final papers

PREFACE TO THE SECOND EDITION

For twenty years this book has been a popular and useful introduction to the history of the rhetorical tradition in the West for students in colleges and universities and for general readers. In thoroughly revising it, I have taken account of much new scholarship that has appeared since the original publication, changed some of my own views as the result of further study, given greater attention to rhetorical study in Spain, and added discussion of women who have contributed to the history of rhetoric, a subject that had been little studied at the time of the first edition. I am grateful to the readers of the first edition who encouraged me to make this revision, to The University of North Carolina Press for its willingness to undertake a new edition, and to members of the Press staff who have assisted in preparing it.

George A. Kennedy
Fort Collins, Colorado
March 9, 1998

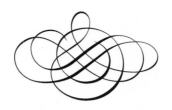

CLASSICAL RHETORIC
AND ITS CHRISTIAN
AND SECULAR TRADITION
FROM ANCIENT TO
MODERN TIMES

The lyvelie pithe of Platoes witte and Aristots ingeine

The pleasant vayne of Cicero, and of Quintiliane

The judment high, here thou maiest see: therefor if thou be wise,

No farther seeke but in this booke thy self doe exercise.

—Roland M'Kilwein,

The Logike of the Most Excellent Philosopher, P. Ramus Martyr

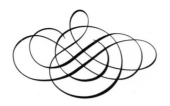

CHAPTER 1

Traditional and Conceptual Rhetoric

"Rhetoric," and its cognates in other languages, is derived from the Greek word *rhêkorikê*, the art or technique of a *rhêtôr*, or public speaker. The word first appears in Plato's dialogue *Gorgias*, written in the second decade of the fourth century B.C., but dramatically set a generation earlier. In conversation with Socrates (453a2), Gorgias defines *rhêkorikê* as "the worker of persuasion." "Persuasion" (*peithô*) was used in earlier Greek to describe what came to be called "rhetoric."[1] Another Greek word often used of rhetoric is *logos*, literally "word," but also meaning "speech, argument, reason."

Rhetoric in Greece was specifically the civic art of public speaking as it developed under constitutional government, especially in Athenian democracy of the fifth and fourth centuries. This art was described and discussed in handbooks, speeches, dialogues, treatises, and lectures and was expanded and developed by teachers of public speaking, philosophers, and practicing orators to produce what we call "classical rhetoric," social and political practices and a body of texts that describe or illustrate that practice. Classical rhetoric, in turn, was transmitted to the Middle Ages, the Renaissance, and the modern period, adapted to the needs of each era, but repeatedly drawing new inspiration from the major classical sources, especially from writings of Cicero, but at times from readings of Plato, Aristotle, Quintilian, or other Greek or Latin sources.

Rhetoric in the sense of techniques of persuasion is a phenomenon of all human cultures, and analogies to it are also found in animal communication.[2] All communication involves rhetoric. A speaker or writer has some kind of purpose, and rhetoric includes the ways of accomplishing, or attempting to accomplish, that purpose within a given culture. The Greeks and Romans thought of this purpose as persuasion, but by that they meant something more general than persuasion as understood by a modern social scientist. Purposes cover a spectrum from converting hearers to a view opposed to that previously held, to implanting a conviction or belief not otherwise entertained, to teaching or exposition, to entertainment and demonstration of the cleverness of the speaker. Persuasion can be accomplished by *direct* means, such as force, threats, or bribes, or it can be done *symbolically* by the use of signs, of which the most important are spoken and written words or gestures.

Every communication is rhetorical because it uses some technique to affect the beliefs, actions, or emotions of an audience. The simplest verbal techniques are pitch, volume, and repetition, as in "help, Help, HELP!" The white pages of the telephone directory show a relatively low degree of rhetoric. Their main rhetorical technique is alphabetization, which accomplishes the purpose of allowing a reader to find a particular name easily, and except for occasional flashes of bold type their author does not seek to influence a reader to call one number rather than another. The yellow pages are distinctly more rhetorical, seeking to make an effect upon the reader and using visualization of products and other typographical devices to influence a decision.

Some definitions will help to trace the influence and adaptations of classical rhetoric through western history. One is the concept of *primary* rhetoric. Primary rhetoric is the conception of rhetoric held by the Greeks when artistic techniques were first described in the fifth century B.C. Rhetoric was primarily an art of persuasion; it was primarily something used in civic life; it was primarily oral. Primary rhetoric involves utterance on a specific occasion; it is an act not a text, though subsequently it can be treated as a text. The primacy of primary rhetoric is a fundamental fact in the classical tradition: through the time of the Roman Empire teachers of rhetoric, whatever was the real situation of their students, took as their nominal goal the training of persuasive public speakers; even in the early Middle Ages, when there was reduced practical opportunity to exercise civic rhetoric, the definition and content of rhetorical theory as set forth by Isidore and Alcuin, for example, show the same civic assumption; the revival of classical rhetoric in

Renaissance Italy was foreshadowed by renewed need for civic rhetoric in the cities of the twelfth and thirteenth centuries; and the great period of neoclassical rhetoric was the time when public speaking emerged as a major force in church and state in France, England, and America.

Secondary rhetoric, on the other hand, refers to rhetorical techniques as found in discourse, literature, and art forms when those techniques are not being used for an oral, persuasive purpose. In secondary rhetoric the speech act is not of central importance; that role is taken over by a text. Frequent manifestations of secondary rhetoric are commonplaces, figures of speech, and tropes in written works. Much literature, art, and informal discourse is decorated by secondary rhetoric, which may be a mannerism of the historical period in which it is composed. Secondary rhetoric, however, contributes to accomplishing the purpose of the speaker or writer, but indirectly or at a secondary level. It provides ways of emphasizing ideas or making them vivid. It enlivens the page and relieves the tedium of the reader. It may demonstrate the writer's education, eloquence, or skill, and it thus often makes the writer more acceptable to an audience.

It has been a persistent characteristic of classical rhetoric in almost every stage of its history to move from primary to secondary forms, occasionally then reversing the pattern. For this phenomenon the Italian term *letteraturizzazione* has been coined. *Letteraturizzazione* is the tendency of rhetoric to shift focus from persuasion to narration, from civic to personal contexts, and from speech to literature, including poetry. Such slippage can be observed in Greece in the Hellenistic period, in the time of the Roman Empire, in medieval France, and from the sixteenth to the eighteenth centuries in Europe, and still occurs to today: rhetoric as understood in English departments of colleges and universities is largely secondary rhetoric. The primary cause of the *letteraturizzazione* of rhetoric was probably the place given rhetoric in education through the centuries, combined with limited opportunities for public speaking and an increased role for writing in society.

There is also a secondary rhetoric in arts other than literature. In antiquity, the analogy between rhetoric and painting or sculpture was repeatedly noticed—by Aristotle, Cicero, and Quintilian among others—and an analogy to architecture is occasionally mentioned as well. Writers on the arts sometimes borrowed terminology from rhetoric. In the

Renaissance and later, treatises on music, painting, and other arts borrowed the structure and categories of classical rhetoric. Rhetorical techniques are also evident in political propaganda throughout history, in which forms of speech, writing (inscriptions, for example), drama, ritual, art, architecture, and public works and largess were combined to strengthen or impose the power of the regime.

Traditional rhetoric is rhetorical practice as found in traditional cultures that do not use writing and have been relatively untouched by western civilization. The forms and functions of rhetoric in societies without writing are discussed in a recent book by George A. Kennedy, entitled *Comparative Rhetoric*, published by Oxford University Press. Among the themes of that book are that rhetoric in traditional societies is primarily a means of attaining consensus, and the existence all over the world of levels of *formal language* required for serious discourse. The book also discusses rhetoric in ancient societies in the Near East, India, and China where writing was introduced. Although oral societies generally have words for an "orator," for various speech genres, and sometimes for rhetorical devices, and many accord high honor to eloquence, conceptualized theories of rhetoric are found only in societies that use writing, and even there full conceptualization is slow to emerge. Speakers cannot explain well how they do what they do, and skill is learned by imitation, not by rule. This includes the early history of rhetoric in Greece. In *The Apology* (21e) Plato makes Socrates ridicule the inability of fifth-century Athenian politicians and poets to describe what they were nevertheless often able to do well.

Conceptualization of rhetorical techniques, the synthesis of a *metarhetoric*, as it is sometimes now called, has taken place in sophisticated, literate societies in varying degrees depending on the practical need for rhetorical instruction, the extent to which the society is introspective, and the rhetorical values the society holds. *The Instruction of Ptahhotep*, written in Egypt in the early second millennium B.C., is sometimes regarded as the earliest handbook of public speaking.[3] In third-century B.C. China, Han Fei-tzu wrote a work on power politics that includes discussion of ways to persuade,[4] and about the same time Kautilya in India wrote an extensive discussion of politics and rhetoric that has features in common with Greek rhetorical theory.[5] A major difference between metarhetoric in Greece and in other literate cultures is that in

Greece theories of rhetoric were developed largely for speakers in the lawcourts, whereas elsewhere judicial rhetoric is not a major consideration; and only in Greece, and thus in western Europe, was rhetoric separated from political and ethical philosophy to form a specific discipline that became a feature of formal education. Isocrates and Aristotle, despite great differences in their thinking, were largely responsible for this second development.

In an attempt to understand the nature of rhetoric and its historical manifestations we are fortunate to have on record descriptions of the circumstances and contents of speeches, and thus of traditional rhetoric, that were composed before the conceptualization of a metarhetoric. Such records exist in the Near East, China, and India. In the West, early Greek literature, and in particular the Homeric poems *Iliad* and *Odyssey*, give a vivid picture of speech in a society that did not yet use writing. The poems are the artistic result of a tradition of oral composition describing great events of the end of the second millennium B.C. They probably attained approximately the form in which we read them in the eighth century and were written down, perhaps from dictation, in the following century. It is true, of course, that neither of these works is a verbatim account of what someone actually said. What matters is that speech as found in the poems provides a detailed picture of what and how someone might have spoken under the conditions imagined, and they contain also observations about the nature and functions of speech of a traditional nature. Additional evidence comes from two other early Greek poems, *Theogony* and *Works and Days* by Hesiod.[6]

Rhetoric in the Homeric Poems

The Homeric poems portray Greek society before the introduction of writing. This society had its own oral poetry, the songs of bards on heroic or mythological subjects. How such poetry can be created and transmitted is now reasonably well understood from study of modern oral poets in the Balkans and other areas.[7] Oral bards do not memorize songs as a whole but recreate them on each delivery from common elements: the structure of folktales; themes or incidents useful in the telling of many stories, such as festivals, banquets, sacrifices, duels, councils, or journeys, adapted to the needs of the context; and formulas or verbatim repetitions consisting of whole passages, single lines, phrases, or epithets useful as building blocks in the narrative. A bard learned the craft by listening to other bards, trying to imitate them, and accumulating a reservoir of structures, themes, and formulas. In the singing of a really successful bard there is also an element that neither the bard nor the audience fully understands: "inspiration." The bard feels a god, in Greek poems a "muse," singing to and through him.

In the society described in the Homeric poems and in other traditional societies the world over, to a degree also in literate societies, public speaking is learned the same way. A would-be orator listens to older speakers and acquires knowledge of past precedent, as well as a sense of rhetorical conventions, formal styles, and what is effective. Through imitation and practice the speaker builds self-assurance in speaking and acquires techniques and a collection of examples, stock phrases, and themes. The Homeric orator is always understood as speaking extempore, and sometimes with inspiration from a god.

Achilles, the hero of the *Iliad*, is said to have been taught by Phoenix to be "a speaker of words and a doer of deeds" (*Iliad* 9.443). These are the two great areas of distinction for the Homeric hero, and Achilles and Odysseus excel at both. Because the Homeric poems, after being written down in the seventh century B.C., became the textbooks out of which Greek students learned to read and were venerated as the bibles of the culture, the attitude toward speech in the *Iliad* strongly influenced the conception of the orator in Greco-Roman civilization. As in most other cultures, an eloquent speaker is greatly admired, but unlike most other cultures, where harmony and consensus are valued, the Greeks not only tolerated but admired open contention. The Greek male orator, like the Greek male athlete, seeks to win and gains honor from defeating an opponent.[8] Anger, retribution, and personal attacks were acceptable in public. This is evident in the spirited debates, even mud-slinging, between Agamemnon and Achilles beginning in the first book of the *Iliad*, and acceptance of contentious debate remained a distinctive feature of Greek culture and has remained a characteristic of western rhetoric except when constrained by autocratic government or religious authority.

Unlike Achilles, Telemachus, the son of Odysseus, has been left at home, and in the opening books of the *Odyssey* he is faced with the difficult situation of how to deal with the suitors besetting his mother. He has had no model in oratory. In the second book he succeeds in summoning an assembly of the men of Ithaca, before whom he presents his complaints, but he lacks adequate authority to prevail, even though the goddess Athene gives him a physical charisma beyond his years. The effective Homeric orator must have authority. It comes partly from a position in society by birth, but must be bolstered by what he has done, by how he carries himself, by what sanctions he can bring to support his words. Because personality is important, different styles of delivery emerge. Menelaus is described as speaking rapidly, clearly, and simply, while Odysseus bursts out in a veritable storm of oratory (*Iliad* 3.212–24). Nestor, oldest of the orators, is garrulous, but his words are compared to honey (*Iliad* 1.247–52). Such differences become important in defining the characters of style and delivery in classical rhetoric.

Classical rhetoricians later became interested in defining the species of oratory: When are speeches employed and how do they differ with different functions? Beginning with Aristotle, the usual classification is into deliberative, judicial, and epideictic forms. Deliberative rhetoric was viewed as concerned with determination of the advantages of some future action; judicial rhetoric with the determination of the justice or legality of a past action; epideictic with praise or blame of what was honorable or dishonorable. The Homeric poems do not reveal any perception of different kinds of oratory or any indication that, as in some traditional societies, different dialects or levels of formality were regarded as appropriate for different settings, but oratory is used in a variety of contexts. Many of the occasions for speech in the Homeric poems are personal encounters, more appropriate for conversation than for oratory, but when Odysseus is asked in the *Odyssey* to tell who he is, he regularly replies with a formal speech—and regularly the contents are totally fictitious. Lying was endemic in western oratory from its beginning and produced the repeated, if ineffective, protests of Plato and other philosophers that the only valid rhetoric was that speaking the truth. In addition to casual encounters, oratory in the Homeric poems is engendered by formal deliberative occasions, often with open clash of opinions and allegations. These include meetings of the council of leaders of the army; the assembly of the soldiers in the *Iliad* or of the citizens of cities in the *Odyssey*; and embassies, both official such as that to

Achilles in *Iliad*, Book 9, or unofficial as in Book 24. Some speeches in councils, in assemblies, or on embassies are declarative, in that a person with some power or authority simply announces what he is going to do—for example, Agamemnon's announcement to the council in Book 2 of the *Iliad* that he will test the army; others are debates about what should be done in a particular situation. The only trial in the Homeric poems is that carved on the shield of Achilles described in Book 18 of the *Iliad*, but some speeches are calls for justice and resemble judicial occasions, as, for example, the debate between Agamemnon and Achilles in the first book of the *Iliad* or Telemachus's complaints in the second book of the *Odyssey*. There are also some speeches that anticipate the occasions of later epideictic oratory, such as the speeches of lament for Hector in the eighteenth and twenty-fourth books of the *Iliad* and Achilles' speech of consolation to Priam in *Iliad*, Book 24 (599–620).[9]

The ninth book of the *Iliad* contains perhaps the finest set of speeches in the poem and is interesting for study because it shows differences in technique of three different orators and the reply of Achilles to each. Some of the techniques employed anticipate categories of classical rhetoric. The occasion is the embassy sent by the Greek army with the consent of its commander-in-chief, Agamemnon, to try to persuade Achilles to return to battle after he has withdrawn in anger at his treatment by Agamemnon. There are three ambassadors, Odysseus, Phoenix, and Ajax, chosen for their potential influence on Achilles. He acknowledges (9.204) that they are the men he loves most.

Odysseus speaks first, and his address is the most carefully organized in the group. It falls into five parts. First he addresses Achilles and expresses thanks for his hospitality (225–28), establishing a cordial tone. This corresponds to the *proemium*, or introduction, of a classical oration, which seeks the attention and goodwill of an audience. Second, he states a *proposition* (228–31): the Greek ships will be destroyed unless Achilles returns to help the army. The contrast between the pleasant setting beside the campfire and the realities of the military situation is a startling note. Odysseus may be thought to exaggerate the danger slightly, for his own purposes, but only slightly. In any event, his description of the situation is direct, clear, and brief. He then moves on to a third part, a *narration* of how the situation developed (232–46). This too is clear and rapid, and predominance is given to actions of Achilles' rival

Hector, leader of the Trojans. At the end of the narration Hector's threat to the ships is amplified in three clauses ("tricolon," in the terminology of later rhetoric): he threatens "to cut off the stern tops of the ships," "to torch the ships themselves with ravening fire," and "to cut down the Greeks as they rush from the smoke." The clauses are arranged in a "climax" both in meaning and in length; in the Greek there are four words plus four words plus seven words. The fourth part of Odysseus's speech is his exhortation, "Up! If, late as it is, you want to rescue the Greeks" (247–48). This introduces the *proof*, the reasons that Achilles should return to battle (249–306). There are five reasons given. The first is ethical: he will regret it later if he fails to help the Greeks. The second is an appeal to authority: Achilles' father, Odysseus says, had advised him to control his anger and avoid quarrels. Achilles' father's words are directly quoted as though he were speaking. This is a dramatic device that is given development in classical rhetoric as the figure *prosopopoeia*. The third reason is nonartistic; that is, it is not an idea originating in the speaker's art but a list of specific inducements offered by Agamemnon to Achilles if he will come back. Some of these are available immediately, including seven tripods and ten talents of gold, along with return of Achilles' concubine Briseis, whom Agamemnon claims not to have touched. Other inducements are promises of prizes when Troy has been taken, including twenty Trojan women and Agamemnon's daughter as wife. These two lists are the largest element in the speech. The fourth reason that Achilles should return is pity for the Achaeans and the glory he will gain from them if he comes. Such an appeal to emotions could be described by the rhetorical term *pathos*. Emotional appeal is often a feature of the *epilogue* or conclusion of a classical speech. The final reason is also emotional: the present circumstances offer Achilles a chance to kill Hector, who now boasts that no one is his equal.

Odysseus's argument is based on an attempt to identify the interests of Achilles with those of the other Greeks. The attempt to arouse emotion is rather obvious, and the psychological devices are rather flagrant, particularly waving the red flag of Hector's vaunting victory in proud Achilles' face. Odysseus's remarks in fact prove counterproductive.

In contrast to Odysseus's formal and carefully ordered speech, Achilles' reply is personal and rather digressive, though it has some structural framework beneath the surface. After a polite introductory apology at being so negative, his remarks fall into three groups: his view of the situation, his reaction to the specific offers of Agamemnon, and his advice to the ambassadors. His general reaction is that fighting gets one nowhere: "Fate is the same for one who does nothing and one who fights" (318). Such general statements become a feature of classical rhetoric under the label "maxims" or *sententiae*. He introduces a *simile*, comparing himself to a mother bird (323). He uses *irony*: "Let Agamemnon sleep with Briseis and enjoy himself" (336–37). Lines repeatedly begin with the same words, a device known as *anaphora*: "Not even" or "not even if." As for Hector, he has shown his fear of Achilles. Achilles will now fight no more and says he plans to sail home the next morning. This threat has not previously been mentioned and apparently results from Odysseus's reference to Hector at the end of his speech. Achilles takes a more extreme position in defense than he would have otherwise, for under the force of the following discourses he will gradually retreat from what he says here.

In the next part of his speech Achilles proceeds to reject Agamemnon's offers in detail. The character (*êthos*) of Agamemnon, which he regards as evil, is to him a more important factor than the gifts offered or the emotional appeals that have been made. His own character, even personality, emerges clearly: he is moody, sensitive, offended, but idealistic and principled in his way. If Odysseus's appeal can be called generally "pathetical," Achilles' response is generally "ethical," that is, based on the character of himself and Agamemnon. He makes no mention of his father, but does cite the tragic choice offered him by his mother: a short life made glorious by victory at Troy, or an inglorious return to a long life at home. The last part of Achilles' speech is his advice to the ambassadors (421–29). They should go back to the Greek camp and find some other solution to the problem. Let Phoenix stay with Achilles and decide if he wants to go home with him to Greece.

Phoenix then takes up the appeal to Achilles with a long and very personal speech. His remarks have two special features. The first is an extended account of his own early life and his relationship to Achilles (434–96). Its object is to establish Phoenix in the role and with the authority of a parent to Achilles. This is followed (497–528) by an appeal on religious ground to Achilles to give up his anger. The second special feature of Phoenix's speech is the story of Meleager (529–99), which provides a parallel to Achilles' situation: What happens to a hero who withdraws from his duty? This is analogous to the use of examples by later orators. At the end, Phoenix briefly sums up his main points: If you wait you will eventually have to come, but without gifts and honor.

Achilles' reply to Phoenix is brief: I have enough honor; it does not become you to take Agamemnon's side; stay and share my life. But Achilles is not unaffected by Phoenix's appeal, and the latter's speech is not counterproductive in the way Odysseus's was. Achilles no longer says that he will leave in the morning. Rather, he will decide in the morning whether to leave or not. It is difficult of course to say specifically what produced this change of heart, but the general nature of Phoenix's speech would suggest that Achilles has been touched by his personal appeal. He finds it harder to say no to Phoenix, and he may have been impressed by the example of Meleager.

The third ambassador is Ajax, who throughout the *Iliad* is presented as a blunt soldier. His short speech here does not begin by addressing Achilles. Instead, he turns aside (*apostrophê* in classical rhetoric) to speak to Odysseus, saying essentially, "let's go home—we are wasting our time." But he obviously intends for Achilles to hear and easily slips into the second person, referring to Achilles (636), reminds him of the inducements offered to him, and concludes with a protestation of love and honor from Achilles' friends. This appeal, added to Phoenix's, has an effect on Achilles. He further retreats from his declared intention to go home and tells Ajax that though his anger at Agamemnon remains great, he will stay in the Troad, and if Hector breaks through to his own camp, he will fight him.

Much can be learned about classical rhetorical traditions from the ninth book of the *Iliad*. Many devices of invention, arrangement, and style were clearly in use long before they were identified and named. The role of ethos, or character, is particularly strong and results in quite different presentations by the three orators, but there are instances of statements with supporting reasons, what in classical rhetoric came to be called *enthymemes*. Individually, the speeches show a sense of structure, and as a group there are balances between the speeches: Phoenix and Achilles in the center, framed by Odysseus and Ajax. Classical literature, including Greek oratory, has a predilection for balance, symmetry, and framing.

For all the artistic quality of the speeches, the ninth book of the *Iliad* is a picture of the failure of rhetoric in dealing with a highly personal situation. Arguments based on practical expediencies are not persuasive, and the attempt to awaken passions is here counterproductive. Personal loyalty and friendships are what make the greatest impression. In the first work of European literature we are brought face to face with some of the limitations of rhetoric.

The Literate Revolution

A syllabic script known as Linear B was used in Greece for commercial record keeping in the late second millennium, the Mycenaean Age. Widespread destruction took place in the twelfth and eleventh centuries, and knowledge of writing was lost. With improved conditions by the eighth century, the Greeks adapted to the needs of their own language a form of Phoenician alphabetic writing. By the seventh century, traditional oral poetry was being preserved in writing on papyrus imported from Egypt, and by the sixth century new works were being published in written form; that is, handwritten copies were made and circulated. Books and readers, however, were few until the second half of the fifth century, when there was a marked increase in literacy in Athens and some other cities, and bookstores and personal libraries are known to have existed.[10] The increased use of writing in the fifth and fourth centuries is known as the "literate revolution" in Greece and has been compared to changes resulting from the introduction of printing in Europe in the fifteenth century and of electronic technology in the twentieth century.[11] The reasons for the literate revolution are not easily specified; it probably resulted from a combination of influences. The Greeks had become aware of the extensive use of writing in the Near East for commercial, administrative, religious, and literary purposes and saw its utility. For some individual Greeks, opportunities for education and study increased with increased wealth. The needs of Athens's military and commercial empire led to increased use of writing for communication over distances. An increase in literacy was encouraged by democracy and participation in public affairs by a growing number of people.

Opposition to reliance on written texts was occasionally voiced. The sophist Alcidamas wrote a short work entitled *Against Those Writing*

Written Texts,[12] and Plato criticizes writing at the end of *Phaedrus* on the ground that it destroys memory and that a written text cannot defend itself in dialogue. The effect of writing on the history of rhetoric was, however, largely positive. Writing made possible the circulation of the early handbooks of rhetoric, to be discussed in the Chapter 2, and the publication of speeches by orators and sophists that could be read, studied, and imitated at leisure. It also encouraged precision in the use of words and facilitated revision and polishing of a text. It may have contributed to the use of longer, more complex sentences. For the audience, writing made it possible to reread a text, to compare statements made in one passage with those in another, to quote passages accurately, and to study the style and artistry of the text. Generally, writing facilitated collection of facts, study of science, and research on many subjects. Finally, writing preserved knowledge of the past; without written texts we would know little of Greek civilization.[13]

Technical, Sophistic, and Philosophical Rhetoric

The sixth, fifth, and fourth centuries in Greece constituted one of the greatest creative periods in history. It marked the development of the intellectual and artistic basis for western civilization that featured the emergence of philosophy, science, literature, and art as those subjects have been defined and studied ever since. Greek thinkers sought to give a nonmythological account of why things are as they are; they attempted to make generalizations and define the relationship of universals to particulars, employing abstract language as never before. A consciousness of both natural and social forces began to be felt for the first time, and attempts were made to define and describe them. Rhetoric was one of the things the Greeks sought to describe, and as in other areas of humanistic consciousness, description of rhetoric involved movement in two directions: toward general statements of rules applicable in all situations, and toward a breaking down of universals into categories and subcategories that better define the particulars.

Out of this intellectual fervor there emerged three approaches to rhetoric that are continuing strands in its tradition throughout the history of western Europe. The first and most conceptualized of these strands may be called *technical* rhetoric in that it is the rhetorical theory of a *technê*, or rhetorical handbook. Technical rhetoric grew out of the needs of democracies in Syracuse and Athens, and it remained primarily concerned with public address. Of the three factors in the speech situation identified by Aristotle (*Rhetoric* 1.3.1)—speaker, speech, and audience—technical rhetoric concentrates on the speech at the expense of the other two. It is pragmatic; it shows how to present a subject efficiently and effectively but makes no attempt to judge the morality of the speaker and pays little attention to the audience. The characteristic definition of rhetoric in this technical tradition is "the art of persuasion." Technical rhetoric of the fifth and fourth centuries in Greece is the ancestor of Latin manuals of rhetoric, including Cicero's *On Invention* and *Rhetoric for Herennius*. Its focus on public life, and especially on speech in the lawcourts, made it attractive to Romans, who transmitted it in turn to the western Middle Ages and thus to later times. Technical rhetoric repeatedly experienced *letteraturizzazione* and was often reduced to guides to composition and style.

The second strand, also a development of the fifth century B.C., is *sophistic* rhetoric, rhetoric as understood by Gorgias and other sophists, carried to full development by Isocrates in the fourth century, revived in the Second Sophistic of Roman times, and converted to Christianity by preachers like Gregory of Nazianzus in later antiquity. Sophistic rhetoric was a stronger strand in the Byzantine tradition than in the western Middle Ages but reemerged as a powerful force in the Renaissance. It emphasizes the speaker rather than the speech or audience and is responsible for the image of the ideal orator leading society to noble fulfillment of national ideals. Some sophistic rhetoric is deliberative, some epideictic. It is often ceremonial and cultural rather than active and political, and though moral in tone, it tends not to press for difficult decisions or immediate action. Sophistic rhetoric is a natural spawning ground for amplification, elaborate conceits, and stylistic refinement, and thus is often criticized, but it has positive qualities that have ensured its survival. Like technical rhetoric, the sophistic strand often has experienced *letteraturizzazione*, seen in large-scale works of literature that are intended to be read and enjoyed for their eloquence.

The third strand, *philosophical* rhetoric, began with Socrates' objections to technical and sophistical rhetoric in dialogues by Plato. It tended to deemphasize the speaker and to stress the validity of the message and the effect on an audience. Philosophical rhetoric has close ties to dialectic or logic, to ethics and political theory, and sometimes to psychology. Its natural topic is deliberation about the best interests of the audience, but the philosophical strand in discussions of rhetoric is often found in combination with technical or sophistic rhetoric. Aristotle's *Rhetoric* is a classic work in the philosophical tradition, but it also contains much technical rhetoric. Cicero's dialogue *On the Orator* attempts a synthesis of all three traditions. In the Middle Ages, the chief manifestation of philosophical rhetoric is in dialectic. In the Renaissance the philosophical view of rhetoric inspired the transfer of invention from rhetoric to dialectic, but a purer strain reappeared in the work of Bacon and Fénelon in the seventeenth century.

Women in Classical Rhetoric

Women rarely spoke in public in classical Greece, but there is some evidence of their rhetorical skills and of their voices in ancient society. The ancient Greek woman who is best known directly from her own words is Sappho of Lesbos.[14] She wrote lyric poetry on themes of love and marriage in the first half of the sixth century B.C., over a century before the first writing about rhetoric, and she may have directed a kind of finishing school for young girls. Her poetry was greatly admired in antiquity. The grammarians of Alexandria included her works in their canons of classical poetry, and extensive fragments of it have been recovered in modern times from papyri written in the Hellenistic and Roman periods. Her works, however, were not copied into codex manuscripts in the early Middle Ages, perhaps because of Christian distaste for homosexual love, and thus are known to us only from the chance survival of papyri and from quotations by male authors of the Roman period. The author of *On Sublimity*, known as Longinus, who was perhaps writing in the second century after Christ, quotes (10.2) one short poem and praises it for its vividness. Dionysius of Halicarnassus, a rhetorician of the late first century B.C., quotes (*On Composition* 23) Sappho's "Prayer to Aphrodite" as an example of elegance of style. In this poem, Sappho prays to the goddess of love to come to her again and describes her previous manifestation in a golden chariot pulled by fluttering sparrows: "Whom now," Aphrodite says, "do you long for Peitho to bring to your love? Who, Sappho, wrongs you?" Peitho, goddess of persuasion, appears elsewhere in Sappho's poetry, and indeed, much of her writing deals directly or indirectly with the emotional basis of amatory persuasion. Her poetic and rhetorical skills, like those of other early Greek poets, can be attributed to her own genius, experience, and observation, and to imitation and adaptation of earlier poetry, especially the Homeric epics. Fragments of the poetry of one other woman, Corinna of Tanagra, have been found on papyri. They include parts of a poem describing a song contest between mountain gods and of another poem foretelling the destiny of the daughters of Aesopus who married gods.[15]

Speeches attributed to women in Greek literature were written by men, but they often portray women as skillful artisans of speech. They include the divine and human women speakers in the *Iliad* and *Odyssey* and in the tragedies of Aeschylus, Sophocles, and Euripides. Sophocles' Antigone, in the play of that name, is especially adept at argument in her debates with Creon and Ismene over her right to bury her brother, and characters in Euripides' plays—Medea, Hecuba, Helen, Andromache, and others—are shown utilizing techniques of contemporary sophistry. These women characters are all imagined as living and speaking in the heroic past, when aristocratic women may have enjoyed a fuller participation in society than was true in Athens in the classical period. Respectable Athenian women and girls were largely secluded at home. Many learned to read and write, and some may have exercised great influence through husbands, sons, and brothers, but their primary responsibilities were those of wives and mothers; ordinarily they did not take meals with men or have much opportunity for intellectual engagement with men. They did attend public religious festivals, including theatrical productions (the female roles were, however, played by men in costume). There were some athletic games for girls, but women did not participate in meetings of the political assembly or hold any offices, except as priestesses, and there, like nuns, they were under the control of male superiors. Their sworn depositions could be entered into evidence, but they could not speak or even appear in the lawcourts. When Aristophanes, in *Lysistrata* and *Thesmophoriazusae*, imagines contemporary women engaging in a strike and holding political debates, this is intended to be outrageously funny. The comedies of Menander, describing

Athenian society in the second half of the fourth century, seem to suggest that by that time women had some greater freedom of action than had been true earlier, and this was probably also true in Greek-speaking Hellenistic cities.[16]

Exceptions to the closeted life of Athenian women were found in the class of *hetairai*, members of which were largely foreign born. These ranged from persons of great influence like Aspasia of Miletus, who lived for many years with Pericles and bore him a son, to skilled female musicians and dancers who performed at festivals and symposia, noncitizen concubines in permanent relationships with a man, and prostitutes.

There is no record of any woman student of the sophists, but some women studied in the greater privacy of philosophical schools, and a few wrote works on philosophical subjects.[17] A short piece, "On Human Nature" by Aesara of Lucania, an early Pythagorian, has survived.[18] Two women are named among the students in Plato's Academy, Lastheneia of Mantinea and Axiothea of Phliasa, both non-Athenians (see Diogenes Laertius 3.46). Nothing is known of them except their names. A woman named Leontium was a member of the philosophical school of Epicurus in the late fourth century and wrote a work, now lost, on the nature of the gods, attacking the views of Theophrastus (Cicero *On the Nature of the Gods* 1.93). The sixty-first oration of the philosopher-sophist Dio Chrysostom is a dialogue between Dio and a woman friend about the representation of women in the *Iliad*. The most famous woman philosopher, Hypatia, lived at the end of antiquity. She taught Neoplatonic philosophy in Alexandria in the fifth century after Christ, wrote commentaries, now lost, on philosophical texts, and was murdered by Christians at the instigation of Bishop Cyril.[19]

The women who had the greatest opportunity to influence public affairs and who would have had some occasion to speak in public were those few women who became queens of Greek cities. For example, Artemisia, Queen of Caria, accompanied Xerxes on his invasion of Greece in 480 B.C. and commanded a naval contingent at the battle of Salamis. Herodotus, who clearly admired her, attributes to her two short speeches in which she gives frank, practical advice to the king (Herodotus 8.68 and 102). A second Artemisia succeeded her husband, Mausolus, as Queen of Caria in 353 B.C. In her husband's memory she built the Mausoleum, one of the Seven Wonders of the World, and sponsored a rhetorical contest in which leading sophists of the time participated (Aulus Gellius 10.18). Later Greek queens include Cleopatra in Egypt in the first century B.C., described in Plutarch's life of Antony, and Zenobia, Queen of Palmyra in the third century after Christ, who brought the famous rhetorician Cassius Longinus to live at her court to advise her. The most famous woman writer of the Byzantine period in Greece was the royal princess Anna Comnena, who lived in the twelfth century. She is the author of *The Alexiad*, a history of her own time, and the preface speaks of her education in grammar, rhetoric, and philosophy.[20]

Plato's attitude toward women seems to have been ambiguous. References to women in his dialogues are sometimes negative, but in *Laws*, one of his last works, he describes an ideal constitution in which women are to be educated, are to participate in politics, and are even to hold public offices (*Laws* 785b). No women appear directly in the Platonic dialogues, where emotional relationships are those of male homosexuality, but in *Symposium* (201d–212c) Socrates reports an extended conversation on philosophical love with a priestess named Diotima.[21] She may well have been a real person, though the speech is certainly Plato's dramatic creation. In *Menexenus* (236b–c) Socrates speaks of a conversation with Aspasia, attributes to her the famous funeral oration of Pericles, and claims to have learned from her the funeral oration that he subsequently recites. Plato's objective in *Menexenus* and the interpretation of "Aspasia" are very controversial. One reading of the dialogue suggests that Plato's attribution of an Athenian funeral oration to the non-Athenian Aspasia is directed at those naive enough to listen to the words of an outsider.[22]

Aristotle did not regard rhetoric as a faculty limited only to men. In his treatise on the subject he quotes examples of rhetorical techniques attributed to women, and in 1.5.6 he says that happiness is only half present in states where the condition of women is poor. On the other hand, in *Politics* 1.13.11 he quotes with approval Sophocles' line "A modest silence is a woman's crown," and in general he seems to have had a negative opinion of women's intellectual abilities.

There are many good recent publications on women in Greece and Rome.[23] Women played a somewhat more public role in Roman society than in Greek, which will be discussed in Chapter 5. Reference to women and rhetoric will also be found in later chapters.[24] In the Renaissance and Neoclassical periods texts by women begin to be numerous enough to be the basis of description of a women's rhetoric. As later chapters will explain, there are records of public speeches by women, including epideictic orations in the Renaissance, but most women's rhetoric is to be found in other genres, especially in lyric poetry, novels, dramas, and letters.

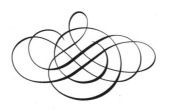

CHAPTER 2

Technical Rhetoric

The needs of democracy in Greece prompted the composition of the first classical handbooks of public speaking. Democratic government existed in a number of Greek cities but most fully in Athens in the fifth and fourth centuries B.C. A series of political changes took place over a period of more than two hundred years from monarchical to aristocratic and finally to democratic government. Athenian democracy assumed the active participation of adult male citizens in the deliberative assembly and the lawcourts. Any male citizen could speak in the assembly, which resembled a very large town meeting, but there was no requirement that anyone speak there. In the lawcourts, however, men involved in litigation or accused of a crime were normally expected to speak on their own behalf. Women were represented in court by a male relative. If for any reason, such as illness, a man could not speak on his own behalf, a relative or friend could speak for him. It became possible to buy a speech from a logographer, or speechwriter, which the party involved would try to memorize, but there were no lawyers or others with a special knowledge of law and procedure. Furthermore, there was no public prosecutor; criminal prosecutions had to be conducted by the injured party or a relative or some interested person.

The minimum size of an Athenian jury was 201 members, in important cases, 501, and even more in some cases. The procedure in court consisted primarily of a speech by the plaintiff and a reply by the defendant, each in the form of a continuous address to the jury. Sometimes there were two speeches by each. Evidence of witnesses was taken down in writing before the trial and read out in court. The whole procedure assumed that an ordinary citizen was competent to prosecute or defend a case, but a person with no previous experience in public speaking might find it difficult to address a large jury, explain the case clearly, and persuade the jury of the justice of the speaker's side of the issue. As noted in Chapter 1, Greek society tolerated and even encouraged contention and rivalry to an extent not commonly found outside the West, and Athenians were particularly prone to engage in litigation. At times, the lawcourts became a kind of public entertainment in Athens.

According to reports derived from a lost work by Aristotle, the first attempt to provide an unskilled speaker with some guidelines about how to prepare and deliver a speech in court seems to have occurred in Syracuse in Sicily, where democracy on the Athenian pattern was introduced suddenly in 467 B.C.[1] Citizens found themselves involved in disputes over the ownership of property or other matters and forced to take up their own cases before the courts. A clever Syracusan, for a fee, taught simple techniques for effective presentation and argumentation. Later Greek writers refer to two Sicilian "inventors of rhetoric" named Corax and Tisias, but they are probably the same person.[2] Corax means "crow" and is an unusual personal name for a Greek. It is probably a nickname, and the inventor of a system of rhetoric should be known as "Tisias the Crow," since the rhetorical teaching attributed to Tisias by Plato seems identical to that attributed to Corax by Aristotle.

The art of Tisias was originally taught orally for a fee but then written down by him or one of his students, and copies were made and sold. Copies reached Athens, where their utility was recognized, and various people there also began to write *Technai logôn*, "Arts of Speech." By the end of the fifth century a handbook or technical literature existed to which anyone could turn to secure basic principles and topics of public speaking. The best picture of the contents of these early "Arts" is to be found in Plato's dialogue *Phaedrus*, written in the second quarter of the fourth century, when they still existed and were still studied. In discussing the nature of rhetoric Phaedrus reminds Socrates that there are books on the subject, and Socrates surveys their contents (*Phaedrus* 266–267d). He says that they indicate that a speaker should begin with a *prooemion*, or introduction, and should then continue with a *diêgêsis*, or narration, followed by witnesses, evidence, and probabilities. Theodorus of Byzantium was one of the writers of handbooks, and Socrates says his divisions included a *pistis* and *epipistis,* or proof and supplementary proof, followed by a refutation (*elenchos*) and supplementary refutation (*epexelenchos*). Socrates ironically claims that Tisias and Gorgias showed how much more important probabilities were than facts and could make small things great, great things small, new things old, old things new, and discuss anything for any length. Such amplification suggests matters of style, and Socrates goes on to note categories of diction identified by Polus, Licymnius, and Protagoras. Included are "proper" words, figurative words, poetic words, and devices for securing pathos that were illustrated by Thrasymachus. Finally, we are told that a speech is supposed to have an *epilogos,* or conclusion, in which there is a recapitulation of the argument.

From Plato's account we should not conclude that the early handbooks were theoretical discussions of the nature and uses of rhetoric.[3] They only suggested an outline of a speech into four or more parts that could give a clear organization to the subject, and they probably consisted largely of examples of what one might say in each of the parts: how to win the audience's good will and interest in the proemium; how to give a clear and brief statement of a case in the narration; how to construct or refute an argument in the proof; or how to recapitulate the argument in the epilogue. It is clear that the handbooks were intended to be used as preparation for speaking in courts of law, though some of the procedures could be applied to deliberative speeches in the assembly. They probably did not treat word choice or aspects of style. For that, one went to the works by Polus, Licymnius, or Protagoras, as noted by Plato, and these were probably simple lists of different kinds of words that might be useful in some context.

The most important part of a speech is usually the argument, and the technique taught by the early handbooks focused on what is called *eikos* in Greek, argument from "probability." A few pages later in the *Phaedrus* (273a–c) Socrates says that by *eikos* Tisias meant that which "seems" true to the multitude, and he quotes the following example:

If a weak and brave man, having beaten up a strong and cowardly man, is brought into court, neither must tell the truth. The coward must claim that he was not beaten by a single brave man: that is, he must claim to have been attacked by two or more; whereas the other must refute this, insisting that the two of them were alone, in order to use the argument "How could a little one like me have attacked a big one like him?" (273b4–c1).

There is thus the possibility of using probabilities on either side of the case. Far from discrediting the technique as immoral, this adaptability seems to have recommended it to the Greeks of the fifth century, who delighted in subtleties of argument and in the demonstration that one probability was more probable than another probability. Conversely, they distrusted direct evidence, such as that of documents and eyewitnesses, because of their experience that these could be faked or bribed. Now, of course, most oratory deals with matters of probability, not certainty, and most evidence is in the realm of the probable, not the scientifically demonstrable; but later orators usually prefer to construct a complex fabric of argumentation in which probable conclusions are drawn on the basis of more or less hard evidence, including witnesses, using the personality of those involved and their motivations as important factors. Fifth-century orators as known from extant texts, and the speeches in fifth-century dramatic and historical writing make less use of either direct evidence or the specific character or personality of those involved and prefer to rest their case on the probability of basic human action: What would anybody have believed or done under the circumstances?

Handbooks of public speaking first appeared in fifth-century Greece and have continued to be written and published ever since. At first, such a work was called a *technê logôn*, an "art of words," later a *technê rhêtorikê*. *Ars rhetorica* became the usual title in Latin for such a work. Rhetoric as described in such handbooks is generally easy to distinguish from rhetoric as understood in other forms of the classical tradition: They set out precepts for public speaking, often accompanied by examples, with primary focus on judicial rhetoric, though in the Middle Ages and Renaissance focus shifts to letter writing, verse composition, and preaching. Writers of handbooks usually have not regarded it as part of their task to tell a prospective speaker what cases to undertake or what should be the limits of legitimate appeal to an audience. They imply success if the rules are followed and usually do not insist on truthfulness. It is often easy to recognize their characteristically prescriptive language: "You should. . . ." The qualifications "usually" and "often" are needed in the previous sentences since some important writings on rhetoric, Quintilian's *Institutio Oratoria*, for example, contain extensive material from the handbook tradition, but combine it with a wider view of the subject. Even Aristotle, as we shall see in Chapter 4, occasionally uses prescriptive language (e.g., in *Rhetoric* 1.9), and in the second half of the third book he expounds a revised version of handbook rhetoric in discussion of the parts of an oration. Aristotle was writing lectures on rhetoric for students in his philosophical school and laying out the subject systematically as a discipline. His inquiring mind, however, tended to draw everything he found into the picture, and this included the rhetoric of the handbooks, which he had summarized in a lost study, *Synagôgê Technôn* ("Collection of the Arts") and which he both criticizes and uses in his extant treatise.

The only surviving Greek handbook of rhetoric from the classical period (other than portions of Aristotle's work just mentioned) is what is known as the *Rhetoric for Alexander*.[4] It shows a development from discussion only of judicial rhetoric to include precepts for deliberative and epideictic oratory as well. Probably originally the work of Anaximenes of Lampsacus (ca. 380–320 B.C.) and written a little earlier than Aristotle's *Rhetoric*, it has an introductory letter purporting to be by Aristotle, who is sending the treatise to Alexander the Great. Aristotle was indeed Alexander's teacher, but this letter is a later forgery, perhaps intended to give greater authority to the work, and Anaximenes' original treatise seems to have been altered in some other ways as well to make it seem more Aristotelian. Although the author identifies three kinds of rhetoric—deliberative, epideictic, and judicial—as does Aristotle, he treats oratory as falling into seven species: exhortation and dissuasion; encomium and vituperation; prosecution and defense; and examination, which includes the questioning of an opponent. These are discussed in chapters 2 through 5. The author then treats at length (chs. 6–28) matters common to all species, which include common topics, amplification, proofs, anticipation of the opponent, irony, choice and arrangement of words, and a few devices of style. What he has to say about proof includes argument from probability. Finally, the parts of the oration are taken up in terms of the seven species of oratory (chs. 29–37), with a miscellaneous discussion at the end.

The structure of *Rhetoric for Alexander* is not entirely satisfactory, and the question of how to integrate discussion of the parts of rhetoric with the kinds of oratory and the parts of the oration remained a problem for handbook writers throughout antiquity.[5] Fourth-century theorists— Plato, Isocrates, Aristotle, and Anaximenes—clearly thought of rhetoric as concerned with the three subjects of invention, arrangement, and style, and Aristotle (3.1) proposed that delivery might be added as a fourth part of the subject. The problem of how to treat invention was compounded by the development of *stasis* theory by Hermagoras in the second century B.C. Various solutions were found, but the parts of the oration, which we saw in the *Phaedrus* providing the fundamental struc- ture of the earliest handbooks, remained important elements. In the fullest ancient treatise on rhetoric, Quintilian's *Institutio Oratoria*, most material relating to the content and argument of a speech is inserted into a discussion of eight parts of a judicial oration that runs from Books 4 through 6, treating in order exordium, narration, digression, proposi- tion, partition, proof, refutation, and conclusion (in Latin *peroratio*). This is then followed in books 8–10 by discussion of style and in book 11 by discussion of memory and delivery. As in most Latin handbooks, judicial rhetoric is given by far the greatest attention, with brief mention of deliberative and epideictic species.

Rhetorical handbooks came into existence to meet the needs of Greek city-states in which citizens were deemed equal and expected to be able to speak on their own behalf. In origin they are to be associated with freedom of speech and with amateurism, first in the lawcourts, but also in democratic political assemblies. Freedom of speech on political issues received major setbacks with the defeat of the Greek states by Macedon in 338 B.C. and with the establishment of the Roman Empire by Au- gustus after the battle of Actium in 31 B.C., though considerable freedom of speech existed in courts of law throughout the Roman period. Ama- teurism survived in local courts in Greece even in the Roman period; in Rome, however, professional advocates, or "patrons," usually repre- sented "clients" in court, and public speaking in Rome, in the lawcourts, the senate, and assemblies, was practiced chiefly by a relatively small number of professional orators who were highly conscious of tech- niques and of their own roles.[6] Rhetorical handbooks like *Rhetoric for Herennius* were studied by young men aspiring to a public career, or, as in the case of Cicero's *On Invention*, are a compilation of their own studies written for themselves. These works will be discussed in detail in Chapter 5.

Handbooks and technical treatises were written on a variety of other subjects in antiquity. The earliest are medical works, originating in the school of Hippocrates in the fifth century; some, for example *On Airs, Waters, and Places*, are theoretical, but others, for example *On Wounds to the Head*, are practical handbooks for physicians and surgeons. Fourth-century technical handbooks include Xenophon's works *On Horsemanship* and *On the Duties of a Cavalry Commander*. Greek works on geometry and grammar appeared in the third and second centuries B.C.; the most famous, Euclid's *Elements of Geometry*, dates from around 300. The earliest grammar book to have survived is that by Dionysius Thrax, written in the middle of the second century and used in Greek schools for over fifteen hundred years. There were also technical works on agriculture, astronomy, architecture, military tactics, music, the interpretation of dreams, and other subjects. For the history of rhetoric, however, the most important handbooks other than those directly concerned with public speaking were the *progymnasmata*, which describe the system of teaching prose composition that developed in the Hellenistic period and continued in use until early modern times.

Progymnasmata

The Greek word *progymnasmata* means "preliminary exercises," preliminary, that is, to declamation as practiced in schools of rhetoric. The word occurs once in *Rhetoric for Alexander* (28.1436a25), suggesting that some exercises in written composition were already in use in the fourth century, and two of the common exercises are mentioned in *Rhetoric for Herennius*, written in the early first century B.C. (narrative in 1.12 and maxim in 4.56–57). Four Greek handbooks on composition survive, and there is a Latin discussion of the subject in Quintilian's rhetorical treatise (2.4). Practice in composition began in grammar schools with the simplest narrative exercises, followed by gradually more difficult assignments involving proving or disproving something, and were sometimes continued in the early years of the study of rhetoric.[7]

The earliest surviving treatment of *progymnasmata* is the work of Aelius Theon, a teacher in Alexandria in the middle of the first century after Christ.[8] In Theon's method of teaching a passage was read aloud and students were first required to listen and try to write it out from memory; after gaining skill in doing this they were given a short passage and asked to paraphrase it and to develop and amplify it, or seek to refute it. Theon describes and gives examples of the treatment of ten exercises: chria (or anecdote), fable (such as those attributed to Aesop), narrative, commonplace (dealing with virtues or vices), ecphrasis (or description of something), prosopopoeia (or speech in character), encomium, syncrisis (or comparison), thesis (first refutation of a proposition, then arguing a proposition), and an argument supporting or opposing a law.

A short account of exercises in composition is attributed, probably wrongly, to the second-century rhetorician Hermogenes of Tarsus and was the basis of a Latin account, entitled *praeexercitamina*, by the grammarian Prisician, written about 500 A.D.[9] The most influential of the compositional handbooks was the work of Aphthonius, who was writing in the late fourth century.[10] His treatise was used throughout the Byzantine period and was popular in the Renaissance, when it was translated into Latin by Rudolph Agricola. There is also a treatment of the subject by Nicolaus, dating from the fifth century after Christ.

By at least the first century B.C., virtually all Greek and Roman students were practiced in progymnasmatic exercises in grammar or rhetorical schools. They learned a highly structured, approved way of narrating, amplifying, describing, praising, criticizing, comparing, proving, and refuting something. These skills could then be combined in different ways to compose a speech. The subjects for treatment were assigned by the teacher; free composition was not a feature of Greek and Roman education. *Progymnasmata* are important for the study of Greek and Latin literature of the Hellenistic and Roman periods in that the exercises often supplied writers with structural units in their works and with techniques of amplification. Among the best examples are the *Heroides* by the Latin poet Ovid, which are versified prosopopoeia. Practice of encomium was particularly important, since epideictic oratory became an important rhetorical genre in the imperial period and was not treated in detail in most rhetorical handbooks.

Scholarly research and the writing of technical handbooks originated in Greece. Cato the Elder, Varro, Celsus, and other Romans compiled short Latin encyclopedias that summarized information on several subjects, including rhetoric. These were the ancestors of encyclopedias of the liberal arts by Martianus Capella, Cassiodorus, and Isidore of Seville, major sources for some knowledge of rhetorical theory in the western Middle Ages. Teachers and students could amplify these accounts by study of Cicero's handbook *On Invention* and the *Rhetoric for Herennius* (which was regarded as also by Cicero). In the Greek-speaking East, technical discussions of rhetoric by Hermogenes and of *progymnasmata* by Aphthonius performed a similar function. Both in the East and the West, the pedestrian handbooks, with their simplified and easily memorized rules, were often preferred as school texts over the more profound accounts of the subject, such as Aristotle's *Rhetoric* and Cicero's *On the Orator*. New handbooks, often adapted for very elementary students and treating either rhetoric as a whole or only the ornaments of style, appeared in the Renaissance but continued strongly indebted to classical sources. Lectures on rhetoric in medieval and Renaissance universities usually took the form of commentaries on Cicero's *On Invention* or *Rhetoric for Herennius*, but eventually professors began to restate classical theory in their own words, to take a more philosophical approach to the subject, and to refer students to the classics for additional study.

In the nineteenth century, as part of the romantic movement in literature and the arts, there was a reaction against the highly structured nature of handbook rhetoric with its rules for argument, arrangement, and style. Rhetoric as a discipline lost its central role in education. The twentieth century has seen a recovery of rhetoric, both that of the classical tradition and a variety of "new" rhetorics. Aristotle's *Rhetoric*, with its philosophical approach to the subject, has regained great authority. Classical handbooks, which long dominated rhetorical teaching, have been replaced by introductory texts in public speaking and written composition. These texts often adapt concepts, terminology, organization, and precepts from classical sources, consciously or unconsciously, but they have abandoned the focus on judicial rhetoric that characterized earlier handbooks. Judicial rhetoric became the exclusive province of lawyers.

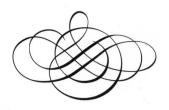

CHAPTER 3

Sophistic Rhetoric

Handbooks were not the only source of skill for one who wished to learn speaking and argumentation in classical Greece. The older tradition of imitating a successful orator, without necessarily any conceptualization of the techniques involved, continued to be followed and became the characteristic form of rhetorical study in what may be called the "schools" of sophists.

The word *sophist* is derived from the adjective *sophos*, meaning "wise," and might be translated "expert." In the fifth century the term was used for anyone who gave lessons in grammar, rhetoric, politics, ethics, or other subjects for pay (see Plato *Protagoras* 313c). Among the most famous were Protagoras, Gorgias, Prodicus, and Hippias. Sophists were professors of how to succeed in the civic life of the Greek states. Most were not Athenians, but the young men of Athens constituted their chief clientele. A vivid, though rather negative picture of sophists can be found in several dialogues of Plato, including *Protagoras, Gorgias, Hippias Major* and *Minor*, and *The Sophist*. Sophists taught primarily by public or private *epideixis*, oral demonstrations that presented in a striking style their ideas and techniques of proof. Their presentations were sometimes dramatic, as when Hippias appeared at Olympia in a costume of his own making (Plato *Hippias Minor* 368b).

Some of the sophists, Protagoras in particular, may rightly be thought of as philosophers who developed ideas and published treatises on what we might call epistemology, anthropology, linguistics, and almost anything involving human life and belief. Before the time of Aristotle, however, what we think of as separate disciplines of the arts and sciences had not been defined or differentiated except in the case of medicine.[1] The sophists of the fifth century were generalists with wide and overlapping interests, they projected great self-confidence, and they sometimes claimed knowledge of all subjects.[2] A crucial issue in their *epideixis* was often the antithesis between what the Greeks called *physis*, or nature (i.e., that which is objectively true), and *nomos*, which means "law," but that included institutions, conventions, and beliefs, often viewed in relativistic terms. Since *nomos* is a human creation, transmitted by education, the *physis/nomos* contrast is sometimes referred to as "nature vs. nurture." Vigorous presentation of paradoxes and controversial moral views by sophists illustrated the potential of rhetoric for social change and provided an opening for self-aggrandizement. Good examples of the latter are the arguments of Callicles in Plato's *Gorgias* or of Thrasymachus in the first book of the *Republic* that justice is the right of the stronger over the weaker. Sophistry seems to be a characteristic development in "sophisticated" literate societies at times of change and conflicting philosophical teachings, and it appeared in India and in China as well as in Greece.[3]

Sophists are said to have "schools" in the sense that they attracted followers who paid fees for instruction. Exactly what went on in these schools is not well-known, but a central activity was certainly listening to the sophist speak or reading versions of his speeches, followed by memorization or imitation of these works as models of argument and style, which the sophist may have criticized. Some sophists engaged in question-and-answer dialogue resembling dialectic as developed by Plato. Their model speeches furnished examples of topics, forms of argument, and style that could be useful in public address.

The *Tetralogies* Attributed to Antiphon

The best illustration of how judicial oratory could be learned from sophistic examples are the *Tetralogies* attributed to Antiphon. Antiphon is known to history as a sophist and oligarchic politician who was executed as a result of the failure of the revolution of 411 B.C. in Athens. He was also a logographer, that is, a person who, for pay, wrote speeches for others to deliver in court; three of these survive, all dealing with homicide cases.[4] Whether he was also the author of the *Tetralogies* has been much debated; recent research suggests they may have been written a generation after his death and have been attributed to him because they concern homicide cases and resemble his techniques.[5] Both in the *Tetralogies* and in the genuine speeches the speaker relies on argument from probability, and the few fragments of Antiphon's speech in his own defense when he was tried for treason argue that it was improbable that he would have plotted to overthrow the government for his own advantage.[6] Whoever was the author, the *Tetralogies* were clearly intended to serve as models of techniques in judicial oratory and consist of three sets of four speeches, two for the prosecution and two for the defense in imaginary murder trials. No names are given to any of the persons involved in the cases.

The situation imagined in the first *Tetralogy* is as follows. A man has been killed in a deserted spot. The slave accompanying him was also attacked and has died, but not before stating that the defendant was the aggressor. The trial in a case like this would have been held before the Areopagus, an ancient council with jurisdiction over cases of premeditated murder and made up of former holders of high office in the city. It is difficult to estimate the number who would have served on such a jury but it might well be a hundred or more. Since there was no public prosecutor, criminal actions were brought by anyone who felt injured. In this case, the prosecutor claims to be concerned about the religious pollution that will infect the city if a murderer is allowed to go free. The prosecutor opens his speech with the following proemium. It could easily be adapted by other speakers to open any case dependent on circumstantial evidence and argument from probability.

Whatever actions result from plots by ordinary citizens are not difficult to prove, but if people of considerable ability are the perpetrators, experienced in the business, and at a time of life when they are at the peak of their mental powers, they are difficult to discover and convict. Through the greatness of the risk, they pay much attention to the safety of their schemes, and they take no action until they have provided against every suspicion. Knowing this, it is necessary for you [the jury] to put great trust in any probability you perceive. . . . It is improbable that muggers killed the man, for no one who ran the risk of his life would have abandoned the object of his robbery when he had it in his hands. Yet the victims were found with all their property intact. Nor did someone kill them in a drunken frenzy, for we would have information from fellow drinkers. Nor did the murder result from an argument, for they wouldn't have been arguing in the middle of the night in a deserted spot. Nor did the murderer kill the victim in mistake for somebody else, for he would not have killed both him and his slave. Since these possibilities are dismissed, the fact of the death points to the man having died as a result of premeditation. And who is more likely to have set upon him than one who had suffered great wrongs at his hands and was expecting to suffer still more? That man is the defendant. (1.1.4–5)

The speaker continues his development of probabilities, then adds the deathbed evidence of the slave as corroboration of them, and finally summarizes what he has said and stresses the importance of removing the pollution from the city. A speech in a real case would have included a narration, describing the persons involved and the circumstances; here we have only proemium, proof from probabilities, evidence, and epilogue. In the second speech in the same *Tetralogy* we see how the defendant might deal with the argument just quoted. Under Athenian law, he is required to defend himself, and he responds: "It is not improbable, as they say, but probable that a person wandering around in the middle of the night should be killed for his property. That he was not robbed is a sign of nothing. But if the assailants had not yet stripped him, but left in fear of somebody who was coming, they were sensible and not at all mad to prefer safety to profit" (1.2.5).

The *Tetralogies* are examples of a form of rhetorical teaching that flourished in Athens. They are not accompanied by any generalized rules and were presumably to be studied in written form and imitated. In the opening pages of Plato's *Phaedrus* we find young Phaedrus studying a speech by Lysias; impressed with it on first hearing, he claims to have made Lysias repeat it, borrowed the manuscript, and is now learning it by heart (*Phaedrus* 228a–b). It is obvious in this case, which perhaps is imaginary, that there was no discussion of the technique until Phaedrus encountered Socrates. Other evidence that indicates a lack of conceptualization of technique and the formation of rules includes Aristotle's complaint in his treatise *On Sophistical Refutations* (183b–84a) that the pragmatic method of Gorgias consisted only of furnishing speeches to be memorized by students, much as if one tried to teach shoemaking by giving the student a collection of shoes.

Students of sophists did not necessarily memorize and reproduce only whole speeches. Just as the composition of oral poetry and the oratory in it was built up with blocks of memorized material adapted to a variety of situations, so sophistic oratory was to a considerable extent a pastiche, or piecing together of commonplaces, long or short. Some of these commonplaces even appear in actual judicial speeches given in Athens, especially in the introductions and in treatment of stock issues such as the reliability of witnesses. We have a collection of proemia by Demosthenes, which he and others drew on as needed, and the references to style, amplification, and emotional appeal in the account of the handbooks in the *Phaedrus* seem to suggest that these included collections of material made by a sophist whose students could then incorporate parts in their speeches at will. In the fragmentary speech *Against the Sophists* (12–13) Isocrates compares the teaching of rhetoric by some sophists to teaching the alphabet. Students memorized passages as they would letters and made up a speech out of these elements as they would words out of letters. Except, says Isocrates, that the sophists neither knew nor could teach their students how to combine the passages in a useful or appropriate way, for composition is a creative process and not something with definite rules, like spelling. The use of commonplaces remained characteristic of sophistic oratory and of some other genres of rhetoric as well. In the Middle Ages handbooks of letter writing often contained formulas, such as salutations and exordia, that a writer could insert in a letter, and in the Renaissance a whole series of formulary rhetorics existed. A modern successor is a collection of anecdotes and after-dinner stories for the use of speakers.

The sophists introduced a revolution in education, one resisted by conservative thinkers in the fifth century, as we can see from the satire of sophists in Aristophanes' *Clouds*. In Greek schools before this time, after acquisition of simple reading and writing skills, the principal activity seems to have been the memorization and recitation of epic and lyric poetry. There was no provision for practice in original composition and no encouragement of original thinking. Students of the sophists, for the first time, were encouraged to engage in original composition and in argument and to question traditional values. Much of what the students produced was probably imitative, shallow, or even silly, but it represented their own attempt to enter actively into the culture of their time, a period that has been called "the Greek Enlightenment."[7]

Gorgias

The most famous of the older Greek sophists is Gorgias, whose long life stretched from sometime around 480 to around 375 B.C. Gorgias was a native of Leontini in Sicily, near Syracuse. He is supposed to have been a student of the philosopher Empedocles and may have known Tisias. In 427 he was sent by his native city as an ambassador to Athens, and he visited the city frequently for much of the rest of his life. His remarkable oratorical style and dramatic presentations attracted much attention. Although the devices he used were largely drawn from Greek poetry and can individually be found in some earlier Greek prose, he exploited them to an unprecedented degree. On Gorgias's lips oratory became a tintinnabulation of rhyming words and echoing rhythms. Antithetical structure, which is native to Greek syntax, became an obsession. Clauses were constructed with persistent parallelism and attention to corresponding length, even the number of syllables in each clause was equalized. The sound effects are difficult to convey in English, but the following translation of Gorgias's description of Helen of Troy might suggest something of the style:

> Born from such parents, she possessed godlike beauty, which getting and not forgetting she preserved. On many did she work the greatest passions of love, and by her one body she brought together many bodies of men greatly minded for great deeds. Some had the greatness of wealth, some the glory of ancient noblesse, some the vigor of personal prowess, some the power of acquired knowledge. And all came because of a passion that loved conquest and a love of honor that was unconquered. (§ 4)[8]

This is called the Gorgianic style. The particular devices on which it is based were among the first to be given descriptive names, perhaps by Gorgias's students, and later were called *schêmata* in Greek, or *figurae* in Latin, or "schemes" or "figures" in English. Reference to Gorgianic figures such as *homoeoteleuton* (rhyme at the ends of successive phrases) or *parison* (equal length of phrases) is already found in fourth-century rhetorical treatises, and the figures continued to be treated as a group by later writers, though often regarded as somewhat gauche.[9] In Gorgias's own time they were imitated widely, by Thucydides the historian, Lysias the orator, and Isocrates, for example, but with greater restraint than their orginator showed.

What was the point of the Gorgianic figures? This is the period of the first experiments in artistic prose and the beginning of the acceptance of prose as having literary merit. It is thus not surprising that poetry furnished the stylistic model. Gorgias can be regarded as having sought to create an elevated oratorical style for formal speech, distinct from conversational language, though at the risk of drawing attention away from what he was saying to how he was saying it. In addition, as Jacqueline de Romilly has argued,[10] Gorgias saw magic in speech, the same kind of magic that appeared in religious poetry or in the healing incantations of medicine men. In his *Encomium of Helen* (§ 8) he speaks of the power of speech: "Speech is a powerful lord that with the smallest and most invisible body accomplishes most godlike works. It can banish fear and remove grief and instill pleasure and enhance pity." The Gorgianic figures probably should be regarded as the devices by which Gorgias sought to work his magic. They are the techniques that stir the passions or obsess the mind and perhaps draw the listener to unconscious agreement with the speaker. The view of Gorgias as a magician seems supported by the general reaction to him in antiquity. He was more often thought of as a clever rhetorician than as a philosopher. When he appears in Plato's dialogue *Gorgias*, he seems quite incapable of conceptualizing or analyzing what he does.

Gorgias's speeches were not only studied as examples of style; they also illustrated arrangement and logical argument. His *Encomium of Helen*, for example, is divided into proemium, narration, proof, and epilogue, as taught in the handbooks of his time. He argues that Helen deserted Menelaus and went off with Paris to Troy for one of four possible reasons: it was the will of the gods; she was taken by force; she was seduced by words; or she was overcome by love. He then tries to show that whichever of these was the reason, she should be held blameless.

Some scholars have argued that Gorgias was a serious philosopher who speculated about the nature of being and the limitations of knowledge and was influenced by the Pythagoreans and Empedocles.[11] Gorgias shares with these philosophers an interest in oppositions, antitheses, and paradox. His treatise *On the Nonexistent, or On Nature*, which survives in outline form, can be read as a serious effort at logical argument.[12] Here Gorgias proposes that nothing exists, that even if anything does exist it is inapprehensible by human beings, and even it were apprehensible it would be impossible for one person to communicate knowledge to another. The argument is supported through the identification and elimination of alternative possibilities. In consequence, it can be argued, since the truth cannot be known rationally, the function of an orator is not logical demonstration so much as emotional presentation that will stir the audience's will to believe. Thus, the power of persuasion involves deceiving "the emotional and mental state of listeners by artificially stimulating sensory reactions through words."[13]

The philosophical approach to Gorgias, valuable as it is in relating his work to other intellectual developments of the fifth century, probably exaggerates his sophistication and credits him with an uncharacteristic power of conceptualization. Gorgias imitated what he found in the philosophers as he did what he found in the poets, not so much as contributions to a theory of knowledge as to a technique of speech. Although, like most other sophists of his time, he was probably a relativist about the truth and moral values, it is not clear that he cared very much about philosophical implications. What was important to him, and what remains characteristic of the sophistic strand in rhetoric, is a sense of the power of the orator to accomplish whatever he wishes, to make great things small, small things great, and even the worse seem the better cause. It is the claim to do this that opens the discussion of rhetoric in Plato's *Gorgias*, and this is the technique Gorgias illustrated and taught to others by furnishing, orally and in writing, models for imitation. To many followers of the sophist, rhetoric was an exhilarating game, with no necessary relation to reality or truth.

Sophistry as Play

At the end of his *Encomium of Helen* Gorgias refers to that speech as a *paignion*, "childish sport, a game." Anecdotes about him suggest a good sense of humor. Other sophists were more serious or even self-important, but a recurrent feature of sophistic rhetoric is a love of paradox and of playing with words and ideas. Isocrates (*Helen* 12) mentions encomia of salt or bumble bees, and from later times we have Dio Chrysostom's *Encomium of Hair*, Synesius's *Encomium of Baldness*, from the Renaissance Erasmus's *Encomium of Folly*, and other discourses that are either openly playful or disguise their serious intent. The two sophistic speeches in Plato's *Phaedrus*, arguing that a nonlover should be preferred to a lover, are playful exercises, not serious attempts at persuasion, though Socrates becomes alarmed at their inherent immorality.

Some of the playful element in sophistry derives from an effort to teach rhetorical methods by using subjects that will interest students to whom more serious subjects might seem tiresome. An effort to engage young minds in rhetorical exercises by unrealistic but exciting themes is also a feature of declamation as it developed in the Hellenistic and Roman periods. Playfulness in sophistry also sometimes reflects a disillusion with a seemingly self-righteous and complacent religious or political establishment that refuses to question traditional values and practices. Sophistry uses satire to bring about change. An outrageous example of sophistic rhetoric in this mode in English is Jonathan Swift's *Modest Proposal*, arguing that Irish babies should be killed and eaten in time of famine. Satire or playfulness on the part of the early sophists can also be associated with their relativism, implicit in Gorgias's works and most famously stated in the words of his older contemporary, Protagoras: "Man is the measure of all things, of things that are in so far as they are and of things that are not in so far as they are not" and "Concerning the gods, I cannot know either that they exist or that they do not exist; for there is much to prevent one's knowing: the obscurity of the subject and the shortness of man's life" (Diogenes Laertius 9.51). Skeptical schools of philosophy existed throughout antiquity. Some individuals concluded that life is a game and should not be taken too seriously. The view was consistent with the great interest of the Greeks in athletics, something unique in ancient societies. An analogy between the Greek games and public life is drawn in the opening of Isocrates' *Panegyricus* and found often in later writing.

The playfulness, relativism, and skepticism of the early sophists has appealed to some modern thinkers, and has similarities to some postmodern intellectual movements, especially to "deconstruction."[14] In rejecting logocentrism, the belief in absolute truth, postmodern thinkers open up a new realm for rhetoric that resembles some of the experiments of the early sophists.[15] In addition, the sophists' ways of challenging students and encouraging self-expression have some application to the teaching of composition to modern students, although other features of their teaching, such as their great use of commonplaces, may be less applicable. As we shall see, however, the questioning of values associated with the early sophists has not consistently characterized the sophistic strand in rhetoric. Sophistry has often been a tool of conservatism and defense of cultural values of the past. The earliest example is the teaching of Isocrates.

Isocrates

Various trends and influences of philosophy and sophistic rhetoric were brought together and further developed in the work of Isocrates (436–338 B.C.). He helped make rhetoric a central subject in the educational system of the Greek and Roman world and thus of many later centuries as well, and he established oratory as a literary form. His speeches are often characterized as epideictic, but this needs some qualification. A few, including his *Evagoras, Helen, Busiris,* and *Archedemus,* are rhetorical exercises or speeches of praise and are purely epideictic. Six early speeches were written for clients to deliver in the lawcourts and are judicial. His long major works, *Panegyricus, Antidosis, Philippus,* and *Panathenaicus,* include epideictic passages but are attempts to influence public policy and are thus deliberative in intent. He never delivered any of his speeches in public, though he did read them to his students and invite their criticism.

Isocrates was a native Athenian who knew Socrates and Plato, but his thought did not move in the dialectical and metaphysical direction of Plato's. Having lost his family wealth in the Peloponnesian War, he subsisted for a time as a logographer, a writer of judicial speeches for others to deliver, but about 393 or 392, several years before Plato founded the Academy, he opened a school for advanced students, the first of its kind in Europe, to deepen their liberal education and prepare them for careers of leadership in various cities of the Greek world. Among the most famous individuals to study with him were Nicocles, son of the king of Cyprus, and Timotheus, the most important Athenian general of the second quarter of the fourth century. Isocrates' school was a development of the schools of sophists, but unlike the older sophists he did not travel: he required students to come to him and to stay for an extended period of time. This gave his school a stability that the demonstrations of the sophists lacked. To judge from what he says in *Antidosis* (§§ 287–90), he also took a personal interest in the students and their development of self-discipline, which as far as we know the sophists had not done. Finally, his school had clearly stated goals and a consistent curriculum that he maintained for over fifty years.

An understanding of Isocrates' goals and methods can be gained from reading three of his speeches, *Against the Sophists*, *Panegyricus*, and *Antidosis*, though a full understanding of his career, his significance to his contemporaries, and his political ideas requires extensive reading in his other works.[16] *Against the Sophists* is a program-speech composed and published by Isocrates soon after he opened his school. He here seeks to differentiate his teaching from that of others, both those who taught tricks of argumentation and those who taught public speaking through models and commonplaces. He agreed with others that one must start with native ability, which training can sharpen but not create. There are in fact three elements in successful oratory—and these remain permanent features of classical rhetorical theory—nature, training, and practice. It is the function of the teacher to explain the principles of public address and also to set an example of rhetorical composition on which students can pattern themselves. Isocrates does not use the noun "rhetoric," perhaps because of Socratic criticisms (though he does use the adjective *rhêtorikos* to describe public speakers), preferring to speak instead of *logos*, "speech," and he calls the training he gives "philosophy," or love of wisdom. By that he means a practical rather than theoretical form of knowledge. A very important factor, in his judgment, was moral character; it cannot be taught, he says, but the study of speech and politics can help to encourage and develop moral consciousness. Unfortunately, the extant text of the speech ends at this point.

To continue consideration of Isocrates' ideas on education it is necessary to turn to *Antidosis*, a long speech that he published about 353 B.C. to justify his life's work and to answer mounting criticism of him. It takes the form of a judicial defense in an *antidosis* trial, a legal procedure in which a defendant was challenged to undertake an expensive public service or else exchange property with another citizen who had been assigned the obligation to pay for the service in question. Athenian citizens did not pay personal taxes, but the state required wealthy individuals to pay for dramatic productions, the construction of warships, and other public needs. An individual called upon to contribute could challenge somebody else and attempt to prove that that person was better able to bear the expense. Here the claim is imagined that Isocrates has made great sums from his school, but the charge is extended into one of corrupting the young by teaching them to speak and thus to gain an advantage in contests contrary to justice. Isocrates means his readers to think of the charges made against Socrates over forty years before and presents himself throughout the speech as a Socrates-like figure.

The *Antidosis* is exceedingly wordy and becomes rather tiresome, though it is interesting to see how Isocrates introduces passages from three of his earlier speeches as "witnesses" on his behalf, as well as naming his leading students and discussing in considerable detail the activities of one of them, Timotheus. He denies (§§ 32–34) that he has been active in the courts or that he has taught techniques of judicial oratory, and he claims (§ 67) that all his writings have tended toward virtue and justice. In the later part of the speech he turns to the question of the arts and his method of instruction and takes up some of the matters touched on in his speech *Against the Sophists*. He divides art into that of the mind and that of the body (§§ 180–85): the former is philosophy, which teaches forms of discourse; the latter is gymnastic, which teaches postures of the body. Each is an *antistrophos*, or counterpart, of the other (§ 182). This concept will be of interest in contrast to remarks by Plato and Aristotle on the relationship of the arts. Isocrates glorifies the art of discourse (§§ 253– 57) in a passage he borrows from his *Nicocles* (§§ 5–9); he warns against the moral and intellectual dangers of dialectic and abstruse philosophy, and he elaborates his conception of how the study and practice of speech can improve human beings. The argument is that the truly ambitious orator, the kind trained in Isocrates' school, will first of all choose as subjects only great themes for the good of all rather than for personal ambition. Second, the orator will select examples of noble actions of the past as proof or illustration of what he is discussing. In so doing, the fledgling orator will become accustomed to contemplating virtue and will feel its influence, not only in the planning of a particular speech, but throughout life, "so that eloquence and wisdom will become the possession of those who are philosophically and honorably disposed toward speech" (§ 277).[17]

By the time Isocrates wrote these words Plato had published the dialogues *Gorgias*, in which rhetoric is denigrated, and *Phaedrus*, in which a philosophical rhetoric is outlined (to be discussed in Chapter 4). Isocrates never mentions Plato by name, but it is clear that in many of his works he is responding to Plato's distrust of rhetoric. Isocrates and Plato held very different views of politics and education, and there was apparently a sharp rivalry between them. Isocrates' response to Plato's moral objections is to focus on the speaker rather than on the nature of the art. The technique of a speech is neither morally good nor bad; only individuals are good and bad, and Isocrates would start with a young man who is good, developing that potential by the contemplation of great models. This view becomes a permanent feature of classical rhetoric, taken up in ensuing centuries by Cicero and by Quintilian, who claims that only a good man can be a good orator. In response to Plato's claims that rhetoric lacks knowledge and a distinct subject matter, Isocrates seeks to provide knowledge of ethics, politics, and history, and he repeatedly says that speech should concern the "highest" subjects, by which he means international affairs and policies.

Isocrates says (*Antidosis* 295–96) that Athens is the school of orators because Athens holds out the greatest prizes to their ability, offers the largest number and greatest variety of opportunities, provides the most practical opportunities to speak, and has the best of the Greek dialects as its native speech; thus it is not unjust that all great speakers should be pupils of Athens. This view is tenable in terms of the role that Athenian democracy and intellectual history played in the development of rhetoric and eloquence, though it glosses over the oppressive and sometimes cruel actions of Athenian imperialism and the self-serving actions of some famous Athenian leaders; it is not a view that was acceptable to Plato.

It would be interesting to know details about the actual curriculum of Isocrates' school and his conceptualization of rhetoric. A passage in *Against the Sophists* (16–18) seems to indicate that he taught composition in terms of what later came to be called invention, arrangement, and style, and he may have been the first to distinguish these fundamental parts of rhetoric. He also says that the teacher "should go over these matters so carefully as to leave out nothing that can be taught and otherwise should himself provide such an example that those who are being formed and are able to imitate him will, from the start, shine in their speaking in a more flowery and graceful way than others." This statement suggests that he may have given lectures about rhetoric and laid down rules for rhetorical composition. Certainly he offered many examples of how to write and speak. Some later Greek and Latin writers mention a rhetorical handbook, either composed by Isocrates for the use of students or by students from his oral teaching. Quintilian, for example, says (3.4.11) that the followers of Isocrates required the narration in a speech to be clear, brief, and probable (an idea with which many later rhetoricians agreed) and that Aristotle is referring to Isocrates when he objects to the rule of brevity (*Rhetoric* 3.16.4). Isocrates' contributions to rhetorical technique were probably largely in the area of style. Seeking a medium for the expression of noble if somewhat bland ideas, he developed an extraordinarily smooth prose, in contrast to the jerky style of Gorgias. His diction is pure, unusual or poetic words being generally avoided. Taking advantage of the fact that he was writing and not speaking, Isocrates weaves these words together into very long periodic sentences. Antithesis, causal and result clauses, and an inclination not only to make a positive statement but to deny its contrary keep the thoughts remarkably clear. His works are among the easiest to read in Greek, despite the long sentences, because he never leaves anything unsaid and never makes abrupt jumps of thought. Characteristic of his concern for smoothness is his obsession with avoiding *hiatus*, or the gap that results from juxtaposing words ending and beginning with vowels. These stylistic features were permanently influential on Greek prose.

Also permanently influential was the creation of a rhetorical school.[18] Successors flourished not only in Athens but in all Greek-speaking cities in the coming centuries, and the institution was eventually exported to Rome, survived in Byzantium, and reappeared in Renaissance Italy. After Isocrates' time a regular pattern evolved consisting of roughly seven years of instruction for boys and girls in a primary or grammar school, followed, for boys only, by several years studying rhetoric. Beyond that might come advanced study in rhetoric or philosophy. In late antiquity and the Middle Ages this system developed into the trivium—grammar, rhetoric, and dialectic. Although Greek and Roman students learned some arithmetic at the elementary level, and picked up a fair amount of mythology, religion, geography, history, and politics incidentally in their reading, and though Greek students, but not Romans, regularly studied geometry, music, and gymnastics, ancient, medieval, and Renaissance education was largely verbal and rhetorical. Isocrates' view that speech was the basis of leadership in society made it the study par excellence of the *free* citizen, and thus the primary *liberal* art. Only in the eighteenth century was the curriculum broadened to include higher mathematics and science; and the social sciences, including history, were not systematically taught in schools or colleges until the nineteenth century.

Isocrates' greatest speech is *Panegyricus*, published about 380 B.C., relatively early in his long career as a teacher. A number of later speeches, including *Areopagiticus* and *Panathenaicus*, resemble it, but are less successful. *Panegyricus* is the finest and most carefully crafted example of Isocrates' prose style as just described; it has greater unity of theme, structure, and imagery than any of his other long works, and it well illustrates his goal of dealing with only the greatest issues and adorning them with accounts of the noblest actions. His proposal is "pan-Hellenism," the proposition that all Greeks should unite against the barbarians, as they had against Persian invaders in the early fifth century, and that the leadership in such a union belongs morally and historically to Athens. Gorgias and Lysias had spoken on pan-Hellenism at Olympia earlier, and Isocrates here imagines himself doing the same. The unity of Greek culture and Greek traditions remained for centuries a rallying cry that was effectively used by orators and kept Hellenism alive through the time of the Roman Empire. Among the proofs of Athens's greatness Isocrates cites the role of "philosophy" there as he understood it, and more particularly of speech, in a splendid period (47–50), a translation of which appears in the diagram on p. 44. The translation attempts to show how some of the Gorgianic figures were utilized. There is a pervasive antithesis or balancing of concepts, two or more clauses or phrases are often given approximately the same shape and length, and in the original Greek there is a considerable amount of similarity of sound at the beginning or end of sense units. In the translation some of these sound effects

Love of wisdom, then,

    which has helped us *to discover*

    and helped *to establish* all that makes Athens great,

    which *has educated* us *for practical affairs*

    and made gentle our relations *with each other*,

    which *has distinguished* misfortunes of ignorance from those of necessity

    and *taught* us to guard against the former and bear up against the latter,

[this love of wisdom] OUR CITY *made manifest*,

    and honored Speech,

    which all *desire*

        and *envy* those who know,

    recognizing, on the one hand,

        that this is the natural feature distinguishing us from all animals,

       and that through the advantage it gives us we excel them in all other things,

    and seeing, on the other hand,

        that in other areas fortune is troublesome

          so that in those areas the wise fail

            and the ignorant succeed,

        and that there is no share of noble and artistic speech to the wicked,

          but *it is* the produce of a well-knowing soul,

        and that the wise and those seemingly unlearned

          most *differ* from each other in this,

        and that those *educated* liberally, from the start, are not *recognized*

          by courage and wealth and such benefits,

          but most by what has been said,

        and that those who *use* speech well are

          not only *powerful* in their own cities,

          but also honored among other men;

and to such an extent has OUR CITY outstripped the rest of mankind in wisdom and speech

    that her students have become the teachers of others,

    and she has made the name of the Hellenes seem no longer that of a people,

        but that of an intelligence,

    and that those rather are called Greeks who share our education

        than those who share our blood.

are identified by italics. The rhythm of the concluding words in Greek is that of the end of a line of heroic verse: dactyl plus spondee.

A final contribution of Isocrates to the rhetorical tradition that should not be overlook is that he was the first major "orator" who did not deliver his speeches orally. They were carefully edited, polished, and published in written (but, of course, not printed) form. He is thus a major figure in the literate revolution mentioned in Chapter 1, and by his action speech was converted into literature, an influence toward the *letteraturizzazione* of rhetoric.

Modern scholars often distinguish an Isocratean tradition in classical rhetoric, contrasted with an Aristotelian tradition. The distinction specifically derives from a passage in Cicero's *On Invention* (2.8), that speaks of two "families" of teachers in the period after Aristotle and Isocrates, one primarily interested in philosophy but giving some attention to rhetoric, the other entirely devoted to the study of speech. The Isocratean tradition is thought of as emphasizing written rather than spoken discourse, epideictic rather than deliberative or judicial speech, style rather than argument, amplification rather than forcefulness. To this it should be added that the Isocratean tradition in its purest form is a continuation of sophistry and that its main instructional method, like that of the older sophists, was listening to or reading speeches and imitating their invention, arrangement, and style. In contrast to the Aristotelian tradition, followers of Isocrates put less emphasis on theory and the learning of abstract rules and precepts.

Declamation

The term "sophist" is regularly used throughout antiquity to mean a teacher of rhetoric. Although some teachers gave lectures on rhetoric or wrote rhetorical handbooks for the use of their students, their primary method of teaching was to give speeches on imaginary subjects, often pointing out features of their treatment of the theme, and to require their students to write, memorize, and deliver speeches on similar subjects. In Greek, such a speech was called a *meletê*, in Latin a *declamatio*, from which is derived the English word "declamation." Declamation is a hybrid of handbook and sophistic rhetoric. It is related to handbook rhetoric in that the students had been taught precepts of invention, arrangement, and style to apply in their speeches, and in that the assigned speeches were often imagined as delivered before a court of law and regarded as preparation for judicial oratory. Declamation is, however, part of the sophistic tradition in that the students learned method by imitating famous speeches of the past or the speeches of the teacher, and in that their speeches were exercises, not real attempts at persuasion, in which they were often judged more for the cleverness or novelty of what they said or the ornamentation of their style than for the cogency of their argument. Public demonstrations of declamation attracted large audiences on some occasions and became an important form of entertainment in Greece and Rome.

According to Quintilian (2.4.41), the use of fictitious cases in imitation of the lawcourts began in the time of Demetrius of Phaleron, who ruled Athens from 317 to 307 B.C. Declamation was introduced into Roman schools by the early first century B.C. and was divided into *suasoriae*, deliberative speeches in which the student was to imagine giving advice to a mythological or historical character—e.g., persuading Agamemnon not to sacrifice Iphigenia, or advising Alexander the Great whether to continue his conquests in India—or the commoner form of the *controversiae*, in which the instructor posited a law, real or imaginary, and then constructed a special case to tax the student's ingenuity. For example, a law requires that a woman who has been raped choose whether her assailant is to be put to death or required to marry her; the special case: a man rapes two women in one night; the first woman demands his death; the second demands marriage. Declamation was not practiced as debate; several speakers might contend on the same theme, in which case they might all argue on the same side of the case and not be matched against each other. Our best information about Roman declamation comes from a work by Seneca the Elder, written in the second quarter of the first century after Christ, in which he recalls the activities of the schools in his youth.[19] There are also collections of declamations attributed to Quintilian and to Calpurnius Flaccus, dating from later centuries.[20] Declamation often exploited themes of sex, violence, tyrants, pirates, and problems between parents and children, presumably as a way of interesting teenage boys, but the result was the creation of an imaginary world remote from the concerns of the actual courts of law.[21] Declamation had a marked influence on Latin literature, where speeches in epic, elegiac, and dramatic poetry draw on skills learned in the schools. Good examples can be found in the works of Ovid and the tragedies of Seneca the Younger.

Our best information about declamation in Greek is found in the rhetorical handbook of Apsines,[22] in speeches of Libanius, and in the work of Sopatros in late antiquity. Greek teachers seem to have preferred historical themes to a greater extent than their Roman counterparts. The practice of declamation continued in the East intermittently through the Byzantine period. In the West it declined in the early Middle Ages, or was absorbed into dialectic, but reappeared later in medieval and Renaissance schools, and a version of it was practiced in early American colleges. Most American colleges of the early nineteenth century still provided for declamation in the formal curriculum and at commencement, as well as through the programs of debating societies.

The Second Sophistic

In the first century after Christ a movement began, primarily in Greek but with some imitation in Latin, that was later given the name "Second Sophistic" by the sophist Philostratus, who wrote a history of it up to around A.D. 230.[23] Philostratus distinguished two kinds of sophists: the pure sophist and the philosophical sophist. Pure sophists were teachers of rhetoric who taught their students some theory, but from Philostratus's account and other sources their emphasis seems clearly to have been on declamation. The sophist's own declamation before his class was the chief form of instruction. In a typical case he imagined himself in some situation in classical Greek history and composed an appropriate speech for the occasion. He might, for example, reply to a famous speech by Demosthenes or he might even try to outdo a speech by Demosthenes by composing one on the same subject and in Demosthenes' style.[24]

The other kind of sophist according to Philostratus was the philosophical sophist, who used oratory to expound views on political, moral, or aesthetic subjects. Dio Chrysostom (ca. A.D. 40–115) is an early example of the type. These sophists might also teach declamation, but they became famous orators and often served as ambassadors of their native cities or spoke on civic occasions, and like the earlier sophists they traveled widely, giving dramatic demonstrations of their art. In the second century of the Christian era this art form became extraordinarily popular as a form of public entertainment, and some sophists became very rich; but sophists also performed an important cultural function. Their commonest themes were the cultural values of Greek civilization and their manifestation in the Roman Empire; unlike the early Greek sophists, they were traditionalists and conservatives. They can be thought of as fashionable preachers who encouraged belief in inherited values of religion and morality in the most polished and elegant form, and they contributed significantly to the stability of a society whose major goal was preservation of the status quo in the face of barbarian attack and new religious movements, of which Christianity became the most threatening. The greatest of the second-century Greek sophists was Aelius Aristides, in whose work reemerges the magical element celebrated by Gorgias.[25] Sophists existed throughout the third century, but wars and economic crisis made life difficult for them as for others. In the fourth century, with more stable conditions, there was another flowering of sophists, described in Eunapius's *Lives of the Philosophers*.[26] Major orators of that time include Libanius in Antioch, Themistius in Constantinople, Himerius in Athens, and Synesius in North Africa. Although most of these sophists actually delivered speeches, like Isocrates they also wrote, edited, and published their greatest efforts as works of literature, and many of these survive.

During the Hellenistic period, when Greek became the international language of the eastern Mediterranean and Asia Minor, the spoken language underwent changes in pronunciation and vocabulary and a simplification of grammar and syntax, leading to what is called Koine Greek, best known as the language of the Greek New Testament. At the same time, teachers of rhetoric indulged in various forms of a highly artificial style called "Asianism," somewhat reminiscent of the technique of Gorgias. Toward the end of the first century B.C. a reaction took place, canonizing the prose style of the Attic orators of the fourth century as the approved model for imitation in public address and academic discourse. This is known as the Atticism movement, and its effects can be seen in the language of the Second Sophistic. Atticism, in varying degrees of purity, characterizes serious composition throughout the time of the Roman Empire, and a version of it persisted as a formal language throughout the Byzantine period, even though the language of everyday Greek continued to depart more and more from classical Greek, eventually becoming Modern Greek. Attic Greek as a formal language can be compared to the continued use of Latin in the West during late antiquity and the Middle Ages when early forms of the romance languages were replacing it in ordinary speech.

Sophistry filled an intellectual, emotional, and ceremonial role in later antiquity. In particular, the orations of the Second Sophistic fall into a number of formal genres, each with a technical name and certain conventions of structure and content. These include *panegyric*, which is, technically, a speech at a festival; *gamelion*, a speech at a marriage; *genethliac*, a speech on a birthday; *prosphonetic*, an address to a ruler; *epitaphios*, a funeral oration; and many other forms. These forms are discussed and exemplified in two handbooks by a rhetorician named Menander, who lived in the late third century after Christ.[27] They have in common the topic of praise or blame and thus are subdivisions of what Aristotle had called epideictic.

The Second Sophistic was primarily a Greek movement, but it was imitated in Latin, and Latin encomia of Roman emperors have survived, beginning with the *Panegyric* of Trajan by Pliny the Younger. Sophistry was also pagan in origin and spirit, and was often criticized by Christians because of its celebration of the beauties of pagan mythology or because of the emphasis it gave to style, ornament, and the cleverness of the orator. But the Second Sophistic also influenced some Christian writing and preaching as early as the second century, as will be discussed in Chapter 7. In the fourth century, when Christianity was granted toleration and then became the official religion of the state, both the emperors and the orators who celebrated them were usually Christians, and a Christian sophistry was created by Fathers of the Church. This tradition of Christian sophistry remained strong throughout the Byzantine period in the East. It can be found in the western Middle Ages as well, and it was embraced with enthusiasm by the humanists of the Renaissance both as a way of ingratiating an orator or writer with the rich or powerful and for the sheer joy of unrestrained artistic expression. French ecclesiastical oratory of the seventeenth century, especially its funeral oratory, is part of the sophistic tradition, and so is the American Memorial Day or Fourth of July oration and commencement oratory.

Sophistry has had a bad name with many critics. Plato's objections to the relativism of early sophists began this attitude, and the distaste of austere Christians for meretricious adornment perpetuated it. There is often an empty verbosity and self-indulgence evident in the vast orations of Isocrates and Aelius Aristides, for all their impeccable standards of language and expression. But sophistry, like rhetoric itself, is not necessarily depraved, decadent, or in poor taste. It is a natural development of sophisticated, literate societies, found in India and China as well as in Greece. In its western history it has emphasized the role of the speaker and the process of learning to speak or to write primarily by imitation of models. Imitation is a subject to which we shall return in discussion of literary rhetoric. Sophistry is also one place within the rhetorical system where allowance is made for genius and inspiration, something that technical handbooks cannot create. In this sense, the great critical work of the sophistic movement is the treatise *On Sublimity*, attributed to Longinus and written in the time of the Second Sophistic. The rediscovery of "Longinus" in the Renaissance was to have important implications for neoclassical rhetoric.

If sophists have sometimes liked to shock or indulge conceits, it should be remembered that most sophists have believed that the orator should be morally good, and their most consistent theme has not been how to make the worse seem the better cause, but celebration of enlightened government, the love of the gods, the beauty of classical cities, the values of friendship, the meaning of patriotism, the triumph of reason, and the artistry of speech.

Sophists and Politics

Greek sophists of the classical period sometimes attempted to influence international or domestic policy. Protagoras drew up the law code for the Athenian colony at Thurii; Gorgias urged the unity of the Greek states at a speech at the Olympic games; and Isocrates published a series of speeches designed to influence events of his time. His *Panegyricus* of 380 B.C. probably contributed to the formation of the Second Athenian

Confederacy in 377. Otherwise it is difficult to trace direct influence of the classical sophists on public policy, but their indirect influence, through the training they gave their students in history, political theory, and rhetoric, was significant.

In the time of the Roman Empire, sophists who had gained fame in Greek cities were sent on embassies to plead local causes with the emperor or governors and sometimes succeeded in obtaining favors for their constituents. Dio Chrysostom, Aelius Aristides, and other second-century sophists delivered major addresses to emperors that were flattering in tone but were also public expressions of the qualities expected in Greek rulers; they exercised a subtle influence on how the ruler should govern.[28] Although the emperors had great power, through control of the army, finances, and administration, they needed support, especially from the upper classes throughout the empire. Sophists helped them get and keep this support, while sponsorship of games, distribution of food or money, and the building of baths, theaters, or other public buildings helped attract the support of the masses. The more successful emperors all made use of art and architecture as propaganda tools; this was particularly true of Hadrian, who was also the emperor with the closest connections to the Second Sophistic.

The later Roman Empire was an undisguised military autocracy, but it continued to need the adherence, or at least not open opposition, from the populace, especially the upper socio-economic class of society throughout the empire. Sophists continued to fulfill this need through public speeches, primarily in the Greek-speaking East, and this function continued into the Byzantine period. Although the later Roman Empire suppressed freedom of speech generally, sophists and philosophers had a traditional independence, perhaps sometimes reflecting the rulers' respect for their learning and eloquence, sometimes their amused contempt for sophists' impracticality. Libanius, Themistius, and Synesius were able to speak rather frankly about the duties of the ruler without incurring punishment, and with the victory of Christianity in the fourth century Christian bishops, who took up some of the function of sophists and philosophers, acquired great authority to influence Christian rulers, holding over them the threat of excommunication and damnation. Ambrose, bishop of Milan, repeatedly intervened in actions of the emperors of the second half of the fourth century and in 390 excommunicated Theodosius for ordering a massacre at Thessalonica. An excellent discussion of the influence of sophists, philosophers, and bishops on public affairs in late antiquity can be found in Peter Brown's book *Power and Persuasion in Late Antiquity: Towards a Christian Empire.*

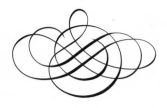

CHAPTER 4

Philosophical Rhetoric

There is little expressed distrust of rhetoric in traditional societies, and this seems to have been the case in Greece before conceptualization, but the creation of rhetorical handbooks and the claims of sophists to teach the art of speech made rhetoric vulnerable to criticism. Bold claims about the role of the orator and the power of speech replaced tacit assumptions, and rhetorical techniques could now be learned by anyone motivated to speak in public. Intimately involved with democracy and new ideas, rhetoric awakened the hostility of oligarchs and conservatives. Because of its newness, it tended to overdo experiments in argument and style. Not only did it easily seem vulgar or tasteless, it could seem to treat the truth with indifference and to make the worse seem the better cause. Aristophanes found sophistic rhetoric a fertile source of comic satire in *Clouds* and other plays. More serious reaction also occurred, and that reaction produced what may conveniently be termed "philosophical" rhetoric, the view of rhetoric expounded by Socrates, Plato, and Aristotle.

Socrates (469–399 B.C.) resembled the sophists superficially. He had little interest in physics or astronomy as studied by earlier philosophers and was deeply concerned with human life and human judgment, as were Protagoras and the more thoughtful sophists. Like them, he contributed to the conceptualization of abstractions; like them he taught orally, was interested in words, and showed a fondness for paradox. He is distinguished from many sophists by a preference for the question-and-answer discussion to expound his views rather than lectures or speeches; by a rejection of the claims of *nomos*, or convention, as the basis of thought and action; by the fact that he did not accept fees from his followers; and perhaps most of all by his rejection of the rhetorical and assertive role of a sophist. In addition, he believed that little good had been accomplished by the debates of the Athenian democracy and doubted that justice was being achieved by the rhetoric of the lawcourts. Whereas the rhetoric of the handbooks was democratic in origin, and sophistic rhetoric was politically ambiguous, philosophical rhetoric was in origin antidemocratic. In speaking of Socrates' views on any subject, however, caution is needed, for in common with several other great teachers of antiquity, he left no writings expounding his views. We know him only from the reports of his followers or the reactions of his critics.

By far the most important of these followers was Plato (ca. 429–347 B.C.), who took up many of Socrates' views and developed them over a period of fifty years in a series of dialogues, most of which are represented as Socrates' conversations. What is often called the "Socratic question" is the problem of the extent to which these dialogues represent actual views of Socrates and the extent to which they are vehicles for Plato's own philosophical speculations. The commonest view today is that the historical Socrates stressed the need to examine assumptions and make definitions, and that although the seeds of many Platonic doctrines such as the "forms," recollection, and imitation were perhaps implicit in Socrates' interests, Plato felt free to develop his own beliefs, retaining Socrates as a dramatic figure in the exposition.[1] If this is the case, the earlier Platonic writings are likely to be more Socratic than later ones.

Plato is the greatest Greek prose writer, a master of structure, characterization, and style, as well as one of the most original thinkers of all time; he is perhaps also one of the most dangerous as an influential "enemy of the open society."[2] He was a consummate rhetorician and a literary artist of so many dimensions that any analysis of his work is likely to fall far short of appreciating its full meaning or art. No dialogue of Plato is untouched by rhetoric—*Republic*, *Symposium*, and *Menexenus*, in particular, contain interesting applications of the art—but the *Apology* provides the best example of the Socratic orator, and *Gorgias* and *Phaedrus* most specifically discuss the nature of rhetoric, so discussion here can be limited to these three works.

Plato's *Apology of Socrates*

The *Apology* is Plato's after-the-fact version of a speech for Socrates at the trial in 399 B.C. that led to his conviction on charges of atheism and corrupting the young and to his eventual execution.[3] A majority of critics have preferred to think that it was composed in the first year or two after the trial, which Plato attended (*Apology* 38b6),[4] but it is possible that the work was written sometime around 390 B.C. in reply to the publication of an *Accusation against Socrates* (now lost) by the sophist Polycrates. In any event, the *Apology* is one of the earliest works of Plato and is thus one of the closest in time and thought to the actual Socrates. If Socrates did not say what is here attributed to him, the discourse is at least something that, within ten years of his death, he was regarded as capable of having said.

The opening lines of the *Apology* make clear not only the premise on which philosophical rhetoric was developed but also the ambivalence of the philosophical orator in regard to conventional rhetoric. Socrates is represented as trying to counteract a warning by the prosecutors that the jury should beware of him as a clever speaker. He says that he will soon reveal how lacking in cleverness he is, "unless they label clever one who speaks the truth" (17b4–5). He goes on to say that he will tell the whole truth, that there will be no flowery language, that he is confident in the justice of his cause, that he will speak in his usual way, without affectation, and that since he has never been in court before, the jury should excuse his inexperience and consider only whether he says what is just or not, "for this is the excellence of a juryman, and of an orator it is to speak the truth" (18a5–6). This is a vignette of the philosophical orator consistent with what is pictured elsewhere. As it happens, however, it is also largely consistent with the conventional claims of a litigant in a Greek court of law as seen in the introductions of judicial speeches—for example, in Antiphon's speech *On the Murder of Herodes* (1–3). Similarly, at the end of his defense (34c–d) Socrates rejects the kind of emotional appeal by relatives and friends that was commonly introduced into the epilogue of a Greek judicial speech, but even in so doing he manages to include pathetic reference to his three sons, two of them still children. The reason given by Socrates for including the reference here is to prevent resentment by a juryman who might think Socrates arrogant; but in a perfectly philosophical speech all this would be irrelevant.

What intervenes between proemium and epilogue in Socrates' speech falls into three main parts: a statement of the case, which is Socrates' denial of the charges (19a–20d); an explanation of the prejudice that has arisen against him over a period of many years (20d–24b); and finally, refutation of the specific charges made against him now. The second of these parts constitutes a narration, since the technique followed is a vivid narrative of Socrates' way of life in Athens and his encounters with others. The technique in the refutation, by contrast, is basically dialectical. Meletus, one of the prosecutors, is interrogated in a way characteristic of Socrates in Plato's other writings, and his claims that Socrates has misled the youths and is an atheist are reduced to absurdities. Although the terminology of argument from probability is not paraded, Socrates in fact claims that it is improbable that he would intentionally have an evil influence in the city in which he lives (25d–26a) and that it is improbable that anyone would believe in supernatural activities, as Meletus admits Socrates does, and not also believe in supernatural beings (27b–e). Socrates then returns to the topics of the hostility to himself and his situation before the court and introduces an excursus in which he reveals his philosophy of life and explains why he cannot abandon it now, even to save himself from death (28a–34b). From the point of view of the legal charges this excursus is a digression (*parekbasis*), but a digression in support of a deeper understanding of the ethical situation. Such "relevant" digressions are characteristic of classical oratory. Antiphon's speech *On the Murder of Herodes* has one (64–73), and the "ethical digression," in particular, is a feature of the greatest speeches of Lysias, Aeschines, Demosthenes, Lycurgus, and, in Latin, Cicero.[5]

Plato's *Apology* includes three speeches. The first, which we have been considering, is Socrates' defense. The jurors then cast their ballots and found him guilty, probably by a vote of 280 to 221 (36a–b). Since the law provided no specific penalty, each side next made a proposal about what punishment Socrates should be given. The prosecution proposed death. Socrates would probably have escaped death if he had proposed exile instead, but he regarded that as a betrayal of his philosophy of life; initially he proposes that he be given a feast in the town hall, but that was obviously not going to be accepted, and he finally proposes a fine. This speech contains a passage relevant to Plato's later picture of philosophical rhetoric. Socrates refers to his rejection of ordinary political life in the city, with its assemblies and other meetings, and to his choice instead to address citizens on an individual basis, "trying to persuade each of you not to have a greater concern for anything you have than for yourselves, that each of you may be the best and wisest person possible, nor to consider the affairs of the city in preference to the well-being of the city itself" (36c5–9). Socrates has thus been engaged in rhetoric, but on a one-to-one basis and not in oratory to the masses.

The jury then voted on the two proposals and chose death by 360 to 141, some of the jurymen who had earlier voted for acquittal having been antagonized by Socrates' intransigent attitude. Before being taken off to prison—the actual building has been identified in the excavations near the Athenian agora—Socrates is presented as delivering his thoughts on death, which make up a third speech in the *Apology*. Among other things he says:

> Perhaps, gentlemen of the jury, you think that I have been convicted because of a lack of the kind of words by which I would have persuaded you if I had thought it right to do and say everything so as to escape the charge. Far from it. I have been convicted by a lack of daring and shamelessness and of wanting to say to you the kinds of things that you most like to hear: you would have liked me to wail and carry on and do and say lots of things unworthy of me in my own judgment. This is what others have accustomed you to hear. But during the trial I didn't think I should do anything slavish and I have no regrets now at the nature of my defense; indeed, I much prefer to die after a defense like this rather than to live after another kind of defense. Neither in court nor in battle should I, nor anyone else, fight in order to avoid death at any cost. . . . Avoiding death, gentlemen, is probably not very difficult; it is much more difficult to avoid doing wrong. . . . Now having been condemned to death I leave you, but my opponents leave having been convicted by the truth of wickedness and injustice. I stick with my punishment and they can have theirs. (38d–39b)

It should be noted that Socrates blames orators and not jurors or others for the vitiated form of rhetoric that so widely prevailed. Jurors are easily satisfied by hearing what they want to hear, and this form of flattery works on the weaker aspects of human nature, but the orator who uses such flattery is demeaning himself and destroying justice in the state of which he is a part.

Plato's *Gorgias*

Gorgias is one of the earlier dialogues, thus perhaps relatively close to the thought of Socrates; it was probably written soon after Plato's visit to Sicily in 387 B.C.[6] It is a dramatic presentation of a discussion between Socrates, Gorgias, Polus, and Callicles, imagined to have taken place in Athens in the late fifth century. Although the interlocutors in most of Plato's dialogues were dead by the time he portrayed them, Gorgias was still alive in the 380s and is reported by Athenaeus (9.505d) to have remarked, "How well Plato knows how to satirize!"

The dialogue has three main parts. The first is a conversation between Socrates and Gorgias that is concerned with the definition of rhetoric; in the second part, the conversation between Socrates and Gorgias's follower Polus, the focus shifts to the question of whether it is better to do or to suffer wrong, and thus how rhetoric should be used; in the third part, the conversation with Callicles, the still broader topic of how one should live is the context in which rhetoric is given treatment. Dramatically, the dialogue as a whole is a confrontation between the dialectician Socrates and three rhetoricians, each in turn more sophistic and further removed from sympathy with Socrates. Polarization thus increases as the dialogue progresses. Socrates seeks to carry on the discussion as dialectic; that is, he asks questions to which the respondent can be expected to give an answer. From argument based on the answer he then can lead his opponent, and the audience in general, along a path to greater understanding. As in other dialogues, for example *Meno*, false knowledge must be destroyed or refuted before a better hypothesis can be advanced and tested. This process can then lead to what Plato calls "true opinion" and at its best to philosophical knowledge.

Dialectic is a faculty of discovering available arguments to answer proposed questions, and in Plato it is the only acceptable form of philosophical reasoning. It follows a method of division of the question and definition of the factors involved, testing hypotheses as they are advanced. In theory, the leader of the discussion does not know, at least not with any certainty, what the conclusion will be (see, for example, the words of Socrates in *Republic* 3.394d8–9), but the Platonic Socrates certainly has predilections, and his hypotheses often work out with a feeling of inevitability. Plato would say that this is not because new truth is discovered, but rather old truth is recollected: we all existed before birth and we know much more than we can immediately remember.

In contrast to dialectic, rhetoric involves a preselected arbitrary conclusion: that a defendant is guilty or that the assembly should follow a particular policy or that a certain proposal is feasible. The orator chooses those arguments that prove or seem to prove the conclusion, whether or not it is true. Plato had little confidence in the democratic process, partly as a result of having witnessed the worst excesses of the late fifth century B.C., and he was unwilling to consider debate in the assembly or the speeches of litigants before a court as potentially a larger-scale form of dialectic in which conflicting hypotheses are tried before an audience and justice or wise policy determined by clarification and compromise. (Demosthenes and other Greek orators, in contrast, saw clearly the strength of debate and the dynamics contained within it.) On the other hand, Plato does seem to recognize that there are situations in which dialectic will not work and where recourse to rhetoric may be the only alternative. This happens in *Gorgias* (505b–509c) when Callicles becomes so angry that for a while he will not continue the conversation and Socrates is forced to expound some of his argument in a continuous speech.

In the following discussion many philosophically important features of the dialogue are ignored; the objective here is to state as clearly as possible what the dialogue has to say about rhetoric.

Socrates asks Gorgias what art he knows and what he should be called (449a3). Gorgias replies that he knows *rhêtorikê* and should be called a *rhêtôr*. *Rhêtôr* was in common use in the fifth century to mean a public speaker or politician; *rhêtorikê*, however, is not found in any earlier text.[7] Socrates then, following his method of definition and division, asks what class of objects is included in the knowledge that constitutes rhetoric (449d8–9). Gorgias replies that it is knowledge about words. Socrates next wants to know what kind of words: for example, does it include knowledge of words that explain to the ill how they can get well? Gorgias says that it does not. If this were the report of an actual discussion between Socrates and Gorgias, we should label Gorgias's answer a mistake. As he appears in the dialogue he has not clearly conceptualized what rhetoric is, but his general view is that rhetoric is an art or faculty that can take any subject matter and present it persuasively. Somewhat later (456b) he describes how he himself has accompanied his brother, a physician, on his rounds and used rhetoric for the very purposes about which Socrates here asks. Gorgias's dialectical position would be stronger throughout if Plato had allowed him to compare rhetoric to logic or dialectic and other arts that cut across disciplines, but it is likely that this was not clearly recognized before being stated by Aristotle. The Platonic Socrates has no interest in helping Gorgias to such a definition because it runs counter to his philosophical views. Since knowledge in Socrates' view is something grounded in nature and not in convention, only those arts built on knowledge have validity. The verbal faculty that fulfills that requirement most generally is dialectic, though the dialogue eventually isolates a small valid function for rhetoric in the scheme of things.

Under Socrates' questioning Gorgias explains that he understands rhetoric to be an art productive of persuasion by means of words and that its sphere is the lawcourts, the council, the assembly, and other public meetings (452e). He subsequently concedes that it deals with justice and injustice (454b7) and that it is the kind of persuasion that produces belief, not knowledge (454e8). Both points, again, would have been a mistake in a real debate: rhetoric may deal with other subjects than justice, as Aristotle will show, and the orator deals with both knowledge and belief, depending on the evidence available or the nature of the subject. It subsequently emerges that Gorgias has a low estimate of knowledge (459c), which is consistent with the views of the real Gorgias as expounded in the treatise *On the Nonexistent or On Nature*. He rather casually asserts (460a) that if one of his students lacks knowledge of a subject he will teach it to him. Conversely, Socrates' very high opinion of knowledge leads him to what may be called the fallacy of the expert, in which the generally educated citizen is seen to be incapable of making any determination of good public policy. Socrates unrealistically distinguishes the expert and the orator. He says, for example, that if the city is considering building a wall, the rhetor will keep silent and the master builder will give advice (455b). Gorgias fails to take up this issue and to point out the existence in the same human being of a rhetorical function and the knowledge of a builder, a point that Aristotle will later clarify. Plato portrays Gorgias as very enthusiastic about rhetoric and more interested in making claims for its greatness than in understanding its nature, which may well be true historically, but he does allow him one good speech (456a7–457c3) in which Gorgias distinguishes clearly between rhetoric as an amoral force and the morality of the orator. It is not fair, in Gorgias's view, to blame the teacher of rhetoric if a pupil makes an unjust use of the art he has learned. The speaker must bear moral responsibility for what he says.

Socrates is not very satisfied with the direction the conversation has begun to take and asks Gorgias whether he can make anyone into a rhetor. Gorgias says "yes," but rather gratuitously points out that the orator's ability will be evident "in a crowd" (459aa3). Socrates then asks if that does not in fact mean "among the ignorant," and Gorgias says "yes." The functional role of rhetoric is once again obscured because of Socrates' (or Plato's) insistence on the necessity of knowledge. Rhetoric, Socrates claims, has no need of facts and is a tool of persuasion that makes the unknowing seem to know more than the knowing (459b8–c2). This point is then applied specifically to knowledge of justice and injustice. Socrates asserts that since it has been agreed that rhetoric deals with justice, it is inconsistent to say that the orator might use rhetoric for unjust purposes (460e5–461b2). This is an application of the general Socratic paradox that if a person knows what is good he or she will do it. Thus, an orator who knows what is just will not seek to persuade what is unjust.

At this point Polus breaks in with some irritation, claiming that Gorgias has been too polite to Socrates and has been embarrassed to insist that he has a knowledge of justice and other subjects and could teach this to his students as they need it (though in fact Gorgias earlier indicated this). Polus tries to take the lead in the dialectical process and sets out to grill Socrates on his personal views of rhetoric. The attempt leads to the celebrated comparison of rhetoric and the art of cooking (462b–466a). The passage is probably intended to startle and amuse; it is somewhat tongue-in-cheek in tone and is provoked by the brash personality of Polus, whose name means "colt." Socrates might not have expounded the image to Gorgias, whom he seems to treat with some respect. On the other hand, the comparison, like other images in Plato, is seriously intended as a way of getting at the truth and vividly presents Socrates' deep distrust of rhetoric.

Rhetoric, Socrates says, is not *technê* in any true sense; that is, it is not based on knowledge and rule, but is *empeiria*, a matter of experience, a facility gained from trial and error, or *tribê*, a knack, an empirically acquired cleverness at something. Three other *empeiriai* in this sense are sophistic argument (which is the acquired skill of seeming to prove an argument by verbal trickery), cosmetics (which is the skill to make the flesh look young and healthy by application of paints and powders), and cookery (which is the skill of producing temporary pleasure through spicing up food). These four *empeiriai* are forms of flattery (*kolakeia*) and images or reflections (*eidôla*) of four true arts. The true arts are divided into two groups: those that work upon the soul (*psychê*), or politics, and those working on the body, which have no collective name in Greek but might be labeled physical culture in English. (*Psychê* literally means "breath" and refers to the life force in an individual; in Plato's writings it is often best translated "soul" and is regarded as immortal; in other writers it often means "mind.") Politics, in turn, is subdivided into two parts, the art of making laws, or legislation, and the art of administering justice (i.e., the politics of the assembly and that of the lawcourts respectively). Similarly, physical culture is divided into two parts, gymnastics, or the art of training the body, and medicine, or the art of curing bodily illness. These constitute a proportion: as legislation is to the administration of justice, gymnastics is to medicine. The first member of each pair is normative and looks toward the future; the second is corrective, setting right what has gone wrong in the past. Plato describes each (464b8) as the *antistrophos*, or counterpart, of the other, a term we have seen in Isocrates.

The True Arts

Of the Soul: Politics		*Of the Body: Physical Culture*	
Legislation	Justice	Gymnastics	Medicine
(Normative)	(Corrective)	(Normative)	(Corrective)

Forms of Flattery

Of the Soul		*Of the Body*	
Sophistic	Rhetoric	Cosmetics	Cookery
(Normative)	(Corrective)	(Normative)	(Corrective)

In Socrates' view, set against the four true arts are the "arts" of flattery, also involving soul and body. The two knacks of flattery of the soul are sophistic, which he arbitrarily defines as a sham form of inducing belief in some fake principles or norms for conduct or action, and rhetoric, which is a sham form of persuading an audience by flattery that something is just. The former, being normative, can be compared with legislation; the latter, a corrective technique, with the administration of justice. The two arts of flattery of the body are cosmetics, corresponding to gymnastics, which makes the body seem to be healthy and strong when it is not, and cookery, which corresponds to medicine and tries to correct weakness or illness by pleasurable feelings of well-being. The true arts are always based on knowledge and aim at the good; the sham arts or flatteries are based on experience and aim at producing pleasure. The diagram above outlines these relationships and may help to make clear how the arts are counterparts to each other, a concept also important for Aristotle's description of rhetoric as an *antistrophos* to dialectic.

The long discussion that follows (466b–479e) takes its start from the sophistic theme of the power of the orator in the community and leads to Socrates' conclusions that it is more wretched to do injustice than to suffer injustice and that a person who is not punished for crimes is more wretched than one who is. Under those circumstances, Socrates asks (480a2), what great use is there for rhetoric? A person who has really done wrong will only become more miserable by using rhetoric in self-defense. It would be better for the guilty person to use techniques of rhetoric to make the crime clear and thus to be rid of injustice (480d)! (A literary example of this form of self-deprecatory rhetoric is Saint Augustine's *Confessions*.) Socrates also suggests using rhetoric to prevent an enemy from being punished, thus forcing the opponent to languish in the wretchedness of injustice (480e–481b).

The third and longest part of *Gorgias* is the conversation with Callicles, who is the most violent of the three interlocutors. He expounds his view that justice is a matter of convention rather than nature (482d5–6), makes fun of philosophy as childish inanity, cites the authority of Homer for the importance of speech, and regards speech as a tool of self-advancement and self-defense (486a–c). In general, Callicles admires drive, energy, acquisitiveness, hardheadedness, lack of concern for others, self-confidence, the attainment of luxuries, and, above all, success. He is an ambitious Athenian of the fifth century who would also have been at home in Renaissance Italy and in the executive offices of some modern corporations. Rhetoric is important to him in meeting his goals. Socrates, in contrast, admires justice, philosophy, restraint, self-examination, and simplicity. Rhetoric is not an acceptable way to attain his goals, at least not in its common forms. Of course, Socrates does have a "rhetoric" of his own; he attains his purposes not only by logical argument, but also by using irony, by subtly appealing to better instincts in his listeners, and elsewhere sometimes by using a mystical pathos, and he is not always fair to his opponents.

In the course of the discussion Socrates asks Callicles if there are not forms of flattery that aim at pleasure without consideration of what is better or worse (501b5). Callicles is already incredulous about the entire discussion, but he admits there are such forms and also that it is possible to play upon the souls of not just one or two, but many people at the same time. This leads to consideration of poetry, which Socrates describes as a form of rhetorical public address. "Or," he asks, "don't poets seem to you to use rhetoric in their plays?" (502d2–3). If public address is a form of flattery, it is not very admirable, but Callicles observes that some orators speak with a concern for the citizens (503a3), and Socrates almost unexpectedly agrees. There is, he says, the rhetoric of flattery and shameless address to the public, but there is another kind of rhetoric too, "and this other is beautiful, making provision that the souls of citizens will be the best possible, striving to say what is best, whether this is more pleasant or more unpleasant to the audience. But you have never seen this rhetoric. Or if you are able to name any such orator, why have you not told me who he is?" (503a7–b3). This orator will be morally good, will speak nothing at random, and will always keep to a single purpose (503d–e).

> Will not that orator, artist and good man that he is, look to justice and temperance? And will he not apply his words to the souls of those to whom he speaks, and his actions too, and whether he gives something to someone or takes something away from someone, will he not do it with his mind always on this purpose: how justice may come into being in the souls of his citizens and how injustice may be

removed, and how temperance may be engendered and intemperance be removed, and every other virtue be brought in and vice depart? (504d5–e3)

This is the primary statement of philosophical rhetoric found in *Gorgias*. It represents an advance over the description of rhetoric as flattery in the conversation with Polus and over the acceptance of a kind of rhetoric by which repentant sinners may lay open their sins.

In answer to Socrates' inquiry as to whether there have been any good orators, Callicles suggests Themistocles, Cimon, Miltiades, and Pericles (503c1–2), all statesmen of the fifth-century Athenian democracy. Socrates does not reply at the time, but he later (515c–517a) returns to the subject and concludes that there has not been a single good politician in the state of Athens. The test he imposes is whether the statesman made the citizens better than they were when he entered office, and all are rejected—somewhat illogically—because of the way the people turned against them. But the statesman must not fear death and judgment, and the final pages of the dialogue present the myth of Minos, Rhadamanthus, and Aeacus, judges in the underworld.

The conclusion of *Gorgias* is that one must study to be good. The bad must be punished; flattery of all sorts should be avoided; and rhetoric, like other things, must only be used for the sake of justice (527c3–4). The main strength of the dialogue is the insistence on knowledge as the basis of valid communication. Its main logical flaw is Socrates' unwillingness to separate those arts like politics that have a specific subject matter from those like rhetoric that are reasoning faculties applicable to many subjects. The need for an orator to be morally good was recognized by Isocrates and the more responsible sophists, but they often regarded the truth as relative to the situation and their standards were more flexible than Plato's in this dialogue, which projects a somewhat impractical ideal. Socrates was executed on a charge of which he was innocent, whereas rhetoric perhaps could have secured his escape at the cost of some flattery of the jury. Philosophical rhetoric was beyond the possibilities of the Greek city. Plato's recognition of this fact is shown in the *Republic*, which takes up many of the moral concepts of *Gorgias*, but it proves necessary in the later dialogue to construct an ideal state in order to discover justice. The *Republic* also has much to say about the proper forms and functions of poetry, which turns out to be very similar to philosophical rhetoric.

Plato's *Gorgias* is the earliest example of the identification of rhetoric with flattery and deceit, a view that has recurred throughout western history.[8] Plato was a widely revered thinker throughout antiquity, and his attack on rhetoric was a problem for many readers. Plato's successors in the Academic School took a skeptical turn against his apparent dogmatism and interpreted the dialogues, including *Gorgias*, as dramatic explorations of issues that did not necessarily imply belief on the part of either Socrates or Plato in their apparent, often extreme, propositions. The commonest interpretation of *Gorgias* by teachers of rhetoric was that Plato was attacking rhetoric as practiced in the time of the radical democracy of the late fifth century and the oligarchic revolution it provoked and that he was holding out the possibility of improvement. This was the view of Quintilian, who says (2.15.30) that it was against the class of men who used their facility of speech for evil purposes that Plato directed his denunciations. In the second century after Christ, the great sophist Aelius Aristides composed three long works seeking to answer Plato's indictment of rhetoric in detail, including a defense of the four fifth-century statesmen criticized by Socrates, from the point of view of the Second Sophistic.

Plato's *Phaedrus*

Phaedrus is one of the middle group of Platonic dialogues, probably composed ten or fifteen years after *Gorgias*.[9] It is possible to see a relationship between the development of views on rhetoric in Plato's Academy and the works of Isocrates and their students, in which case a probable sequence can be drawn beginning with Isocrates' *Against the Sophists*, followed by Plato's *Gorgias*, then Isocrates' *Helen*, followed by Plato's *Phaedrus*, then Isocrates' *Antidosis*, and followed by early works of Aristotle in the Academy. Aristotle is said to have begun his teaching of rhetoric with the remark that it was shameful to keep silent and allow Isocrates to teach (Cicero *On the Orator* 3.141). This sequence would put the composition of *Phaedrus* in the late 370s or early 360s B.C. *Phaedrus* is among the most complex of Plato's dialogues in a literary sense. Although the view of rhetoric that emerges from it is relatively clear, that

PHILOSOPHICAL RHETORIC

subject is subtly connected with the theme of love and complicated by the question of the relative value of the spoken and the written word.[10] Here Plato goes significantly beyond the suggestions of *Gorgias* about the positive role of rhetoric; he lays the foundation for basic features of Aristotle's *Rhetoric*, and he integrates rhetoric into his other philosophical ideas in a way not attempted elsewhere.

From the outset, the tone of the dialogue is vastly different from *Gorgias*. Instead of a conversation with three sophists with whom Socrates is personally at odds, we find here a conversation with a young man to whom Socrates is strongly attracted and who responds to him warmly. The first half of the dialogue has a pervasive erotic tone. Not only is homosexual love discussed, but the dialogue is set in an almost voluptuous vale of rustic beauty, unique in Plato. Were anyone other than Socrates involved it would not be difficult to imagine the scene developing into a physical intimacy. Homosexual relationships between men and adolescent boys were a common feature of upper-class society in classical Greece, resulting not so much from sexual orientation as from segregation of the sexes and the cult of the male body in Greek athletics. Phaedrus entices Socrates, partially seduces him to the pleasures of sophistic rhetoric, and even threatens rape (236c8–d1). Socrates flirts with him in turn, but in the course of the dialogue converts the relationship into a higher level of philosophical, or what has come to be called "Platonic," love.

The dialogue falls into two parts. The first part is made up of an introduction and three speeches about love. Phaedrus is said to have attended a demonstration by Lysias in which that orator, known to us chiefly as the writer of speeches for clients in the lawcourts, argued that an imaginary young man should accept the attentions of another who does not love him but is physically attracted to him. The result would be a pleasant relationship in which neither would be emotionally hurt. Phaedrus is much impressed with the cleverness of the paradox and the eloquence of the speech, and he has secured a copy of it to memorize. He is prevailed upon to read it to Socrates. We do not know whether this speech is an actual work by Lysias or whether it is a creation of Plato in the style of erotic sophistry. The latter is probable on analogy to the homoerotic speeches in Plato's *Symposium*. Plato clearly delighted in imitating the style of sophists, including Protagoras and Gorgias, and may have tried his hand with the simple style of Lysias, whom he had known personally. Lysias was dead before the dialogue was composed.

The speech is exciting to both Phaedrus and Socrates, but it represents the antithesis of Socrates' view of what rhetoric should be. It is deceitful and untrue; if successful, it will adversely affect the soul of both speaker and addressee, and it is philosophically unacceptable. Socrates does not begin with that objection, however; what he finds wanting in the speech is its method, for it is repetitive and lacks structure. He is thus led to compose a better speech on the same theme, but he veils his head to avoid the embarrassment of catching Phaedrus's eye, and he makes one small change in the situation: he imagines the speaker as secretly in love with the boy he is addressing; pretending not to love him is a ploy to secure his attention (237b4). Socrates' speech is characterized by a definition of love and by a logical division of the subject, both lacking in Lysias's version, but many of the arguments are necessarily similar to those in the first speech.

After speaking, Socrates prepares to leave before he is led into doing anything more immoral (242a1–2). As he is about to cross the stream on the way home, and thus to escape from the incident, the divine voice, mentioned also in the *Apology*, tells him not to leave. He turns back and confesses to Phaedrus that his speech has been dreadful, for it represents love as an evil, whereas love is in fact divine. A recantation is necessary, for the boy should accept the love of a true lover. "Where is that boy to whom I was speaking?" he asks. "Here he is, very close beside you, whenever you want him," replies Phaedrus (243e).

Socrates then begins a second, longer speech. Love may be a form of madness (*mania*), he grants, but madness is not necessarily an evil. Beneficent madness has at least four forms: the inspiration of prophets like the Delphic oracle; rites of purification such as those of Dionysus; poetic inspiration from the Muses; and the madness of love. To understand the last we must understand the soul, which Socrates describes mythically in terms of a charioteer and two winged horses. One horse is spiritual and noble, one physical and evil. It is natural for the soul to rise, and in the intervals between its lives on earth the soul rises up through the heavens to a glimpse of the reality of beauty and truth. When the soul is born in a human being it loses much of its vision, but it continues to be drawn to beauty, and when it sees beauty in a boy it is moved to love. The great danger is that the vicious horse of physical passion will pull the lovers down to sordid hedonism, but if the better element can prevail, the two can mount to a philosophical and orderly life together that is the greatest human experience. Socrates' speech is vibrant with a mystical intensity and a beauty of image that inspires Phaedrus and has enchanted readers for twenty-five hundred years. The tone of the dialogue is thus changed from the sensual cleverness of the sophists to the vision of a religious philosopher.

Socrates' second speech is not specifically foreshadowed by the description of good rhetoric in *Gorgias*, in the sense that the latter was chiefly limited to public address, but it is consistent with the objectives foreseen in *Gorgias*, reflecting the need to address the soul of the hearer, to seek to make the soul better, and to move it toward temperance and virtue. This is largely accomplished not by dialectic, for all Socrates' definitions and divisions of love, but by the ethical force of the speaker and by the emotional impact of the myth. Such a use of myth is an important part of Plato's own rhetoric in many dialogues, the most famous example being the somewhat similar myth of Er at the end of the *Republic*.

The first half of *Phaedrus* is a drama of the rhetorical encounter between good and evil on the field of love. The speech of Lysias scores a point for evil; the first speech of Socrates is a more significant victory for evil in that it is not merely sophistic cleverness that prevails but a use of the dialectic of definition and division for evil purposes. The situation is then dramatically turned around by intervention of the divine voice that leads to the delivery of the second speech of Socrates and the victory of the true and philosophical rhetoric. This sudden inspiration is interesting historically, since outside of Platonism the other great field for philosophical rhetoric is that of religion and there too the impulse to valid rhetoric is often represented as dependent on an act of God in warming the heart so that truth can be revealed, as we shall see in Chapter 7. In Greek and Latin civic oratory this feature is lacking. Its counterpart is a living sense of tradition, seen in Isocrates' philosophy of Hellenism, shared also by orators of the Second Sophistic, and in the patriotism of Demosthenes or of Cicero. These traditions furnish the orator with an outside test of the consistency and value of ideas in the way that philosophy did to Plato and religion did to Christian orators.

The first half of *Phaedrus* illustrates forms of rhetoric and utilizes examples of sophistic oratory and the tradition of composition by imitation. The second half conceptualizes rhetorical composition and appropriately considers the contents of the rhetorical handbooks of the time. The first subject mentioned is that of writing speeches (257c–258e). Lysias is a speechwriter. Is that disgraceful? Not necessarily, Socrates says; disgrace comes from speaking or writing badly. A more important question is how we are able to distinguish these qualities. A brief digression (258e–259d) then reminds us of the physical setting of the dialogue and of the Muses who combine attention to heavenly things with an interest in human discourse, thus symbolizing philosophical rhetoric. The question of the standards of good speech is then discussed at length (259d–274b). This discussion first raises briefly the matter of the orator's knowledge (259d–261a). Can a speaker be content with what *seems* to be true? Is there need to know the good and the beautiful or only what *seems* good and beautiful? It is quickly agreed that knowledge is required, and the subject is put aside for the moment in favor of a second question: granted that the orator needs knowledge, is that adequate or is an art of rhetoric needed, and if so what does it include?

Socrates gives a preliminary definition of the rhetorical art as "a kind of leading the soul (*psychagôgia*) by means of words, not only in lawcourts and public assemblies but in individual encounters" (261a7–9). Socrates' two speeches in the first half of the dialogue and his view of the relationship of the speaker to the hearer certainly indicate that a one-to-one relationship can be as rhetorical as public address. Even though private applications can be found in all periods and all literary forms (for instance, the epistle eventually emerges as a specific manifestation of private rhetoric), classical rhetorical theory consistently limited the scope of formal rhetoric to public speaking. It is perhaps regrettable that Plato's suggestions of a wider application were not taken up by Aristotle, since the result might have been greater attention to the nature of the rhetorical act and less to the conventions of public address. Socrates here points out that debate can occur in a public assembly, but also between two individuals, and he describes the art involved as one by which a person can make everything similar to everything or refute another speaker who seeks to do so. Similarities or dissimilarities are often matters of very small differences, and the conclusion is, therefore, that the orator needs knowledge adequate to make such distinctions. Particularly, the speaker must be able to make definitions (as Socrates did in both his speeches) and to divide the subject into logical categories (263b6–9). Lysias's speech illustrates the failure to do this and also the failure to order the material and create unity of related parts: "It is necessary for every speech to cohere like a living thing having its own body so that nothing is lacking in head or foot, but to have a middle and extremities suitable to each other, sketched as part of a whole" (264c6–9).

This is probably the single most influential principle of literary criticism in Plato, reflected in Aristotle's requirement that tragedy have a beginning, middle, and end, and important for the critical method of the Neoplatonists of late antiquity, who insisted on approaching the Platonic dialogues and other major works of literature as absolutely consistent wholes. The idea was partially anticipated in *Gorgias* (505d1–2), where Socrates does not want to break off the argument "without a head," that is, without a proper conclusion. These abilities to structure the argument and achieve a unity are restated by Socrates as two contrasting faculties: that of bringing widely scattered material together into a single "idea," and that of dividing material into species on the basis of its natural articulation (265d–e). Those who can do this, he says (266c1), he has been accustomed to call "dialecticians," but he does not insist on that word. That is, a true "rhetorician" would do the same, and both dialectic and rhetoric have the same logical structure.

The subject then turns to consideration of existing handbooks to see what features of the subject they omit. As we saw in Chapter 2, the handbooks turn out to be devoted to the parts of a judicial oration, to types of diction, and to lists of commonplaces. Phaedrus is quickly led to see that they fail to provide understanding of when it is appropriate to use these materials. Their authors deal only with preliminaries; they lack the dialectic necessary to understand rhetoric; and they leave it up to their students to achieve organization and unity in speech (269b–c). Rhetorical ability, like everything else, is a combined result of nature, knowledge, and practice (269d), a view shared by Isocrates and other rhetoricians. For great oratory one additional requirement looms large, a loftiness of mind striving always for perfection (270a). This comes from philosophy and in particular involves a knowledge of the soul.

It is clear then, Socrates concludes, that Thrasymachus and anyone else who seriously publishes an art of rhetoric will first, with all possible accuracy, describe and make us see the soul, whether it is one thing and uniform or multiple like the nature of the body. And second, he will describe what the soul does to what other thing or has done to it by something else, in accordance with its nature. And third, arranging in order the kinds of speeches and the kinds of souls and their various states, he will describe all the causes of change in the soul, fitting each kind of speech to each state and teaching what soul is necessarily persuaded by what speech through what cause and what is unpersuaded (271a4–b5). This is the outline of what Plato conceives to be a true art of rhetoric. Although Socrates restates the description in slightly fuller terms (271c10–272b4), Plato never worked out the theory in detail. Discussion of emotions and characters takes up a considerable part of Aristotle's *Rhetoric*, and foreshadows the interest in psychology of the British rhetoricians of the eighteenth century. One importance of the concept is that it puts the audience on a full equality with the speaker and the speech in the rhetorical act. As is often the case in evaluating Plato's theories, the major problem it raises is the practical one. How can a speaker know the souls of an audience in any full sense? How can a speaker fit a speech to the variety of souls likely to be found in an audience, even granting that a Greek audience was more homogeneous than a modern American audience? There is danger of enflaming some at the same time others are calmed. Plato shows a preference for rhetoric in a one-to-one situation: Socrates can perhaps know the soul of Phaedrus, but he regularly speaks of souls in terms of genera and species, which suggests they are to be viewed as types rather than individuals. Such stereotyping was a common feature of Greek thought, well exemplified in Theophrastus's *Characters*. Aristotle's solution was to deal with psychology in terms of the stages of life and the dominant passions and thus to carry through the study in terms of group psychology.

The discussion in *Phaedrus* of what would constitute a true art of rhetoric was preceded by remarks about the orator's need for knowledge. It is followed, and thus framed, by a return to that subject. In the lawcourts, we are told, it is commonly believed that the speaker must prove what is plausible and probable, not what is true (272d7–32), and Socrates goes on to describe argument from probability as expounded by Tisias. But just as small differences in similarity cannot be detected except by a person with full knowledge, so the probable is a semblance of the true and can only be known by knowing truth (273d–e).

Finally, the entire discussion of knowledge and art is framed by a return to the first issue raised in the second half of *Phaedrus*, that of the relative value of speaking and writing.[11] Here the view of writing is more negative than in the earlier passage. An Egyptian tale about Theuth and Thamus is told, with the conclusion that writing encourages forgetfulness. We know from Socrates' second speech what a bad thing forgetfulness is, since it separates us from the good and beautiful. Socrates makes the additional point here that a written work is like a painting and cannot speak. It can fall into the hands of those who do not understand it, and if so has no way of explaining itself, or if it is ill-treated it has no way to answer back. Writing is in fact an illegitimate brother of true, or oral discourse (275d–276a). If a person who knows truth and beauty uses writing, it will be as a kind of plaything for personal amusement (276d). The major thrust of the passage is to assert the superiority of dialectic again, this time not in the sense of definition and division, but of the question-and-answer process of exploring an hypothesis. Rhetoric, in contrast, is like writing, being frozen into the form of a continuous speech with a thesis stated and proved and with no opportunity for questioning. In a literary sense, the passage helps to unify the dialogue, for it takes the reader back, not only to the beginning of the second part, but to the beginning of the whole dialogue, where Phaedrus appeared with a written text of Lysias's speech, a text that proved singularly unable to defend itself.[12] Finally, the passage helps to restore the ironically playful tone with which the dialogue opened. Socrates, after all, did not commit his discourses to writing; Plato did, and suggests that he viewed them only as a kind of game for his own amusement. We see again the paradoxical side of Plato: the rhetorician who distrusted rhetoric, the poet who abolished traditional poetry from the ideal state, and the admirer of oral dialectic who published dialogues worked out with extraordinary care.

Two other passages in the concluding pages of *Phaedrus* deserve mention. One is the ostensibly complimentary reference to Isocrates as a promising young orator at the time the dialogue is imagined to take place (278e8). It is difficult not to take this statement as somewhat ironic in the context, for no Greek orator more developed the written forms of oratory and was less at home in dialectic. The other passage is Socrates' final picture of philosophical rhetoric as it emerges from all that has been said before. The passage contains nothing new, but it is a convenient summary of Plato's view. Although most translators chop it up into a series of short sentences, what Plato wrote was a long periodic sentence in which a true art of rhetoric is made dependent on the fulfillment of a series of previous steps:

> Until someone knows the truth of each thing about which he speaks or writes and is able to define everything in its own genus, and having defined it knows how to break the genus down into species and subspecies to the point of indivisibility, discerning the nature of the soul in accordance with the same method, while discovering the logical category which fits with each nature, and until in a similar way he composes and adorns speech, furnishing variegated and complex speech to a variegated soul and simple speech to a simple soul—not until then will it be possible for speech to exist in an artistic form in so far as the nature of speech is capable of such treatment, neither for instruction nor for persuasion, as has been shown by our entire past discussion. (277b5–c6)

Among the implications of this passage is that there are various styles of discourse, appropriate in various settings and with different audiences. This idea, briefly touched on by Aristotle, was taken up by Theophrastus and developed by later writers into the "characters" of style, largely under the influence of the versatile successes of orators like Demosthenes and Cicero.

Aristotle

Aristotle was born in Stagira, a northern Greek city bordering on Macedonia, in 384 B.C. His father, Nicomachus, was the doctor to the rulers of Macedon, and throughout his life Aristotle had friendly connections with the court. He went to Athens to study with Plato in 367 and remained as member of the Academy for twenty years. In many areas of study Aristotle may have begun with questions as Plato viewed them, but he lacked Plato's mystical side and was far more pragmatic than his master. He found it impossible to accept the Platonic theory of "ideas" as separate reality, and he was not attracted by the interest in mathematics that characterized Plato's later years. Doubtless realizing that he could not expect to succeed Plato as head of the school, and perhaps nervous at the growing hostility between Athens and Macedon, Aristotle left Athens shortly before Plato's death in 347 and moved to Assos, near Troy in Asia Minor, and then in 345 to the island of Lesbos. In 343 he was invited to become the tutor of the thirteen-year-old Alexander, heir to the throne of Macedon. He continued in this capacity until 340, when he probably returned to Stagira. The Macedonians defeated the Greek city-states at the battle of Chaeronea in 338, and in 336 Alexander became king. In 335 Aristotle returned to Athens and opened a school in a covered walk or *peripatos* (hence the term "Peripatetic School") of the public gymnasium known as the Lyceum. Here he taught until 323, when he retired to Chalcis in Euboea to avoid the hostility to Macedon that followed the death of Alexander, and he died there in 322. Theophrastus succeeded him as head of the school in Athens.

Early in his career Aristotle wrote dialogues in the style of Plato, none of which has survived. The earliest of these was *Gryllus*, which dealt with rhetoric and was named for Xenophon's son who was killed in 362 B.C. and was the subject of several encomia.[13] Little is known for certain about the content of the dialogue. Quintilian (2.17.14) says it presented arguments against viewing rhetoric as an art, which suggests a resemblance to Plato's *Gorgias*. Aristotle may have discussed encomia of Gryllus in a preface and then constructed a dialogue, set in the recent past, in which Gryllus and his friends discussed the extent to which rhetoric should be regarded as an art.

The surviving works of Aristotle, including his *Rhetoric*, are systematic accounts of the natural sciences, metaphysics, ethical and political philosophy, and other subjects, apparently composed as notes for lectures to his students or for their study within his school and not for publication. They are lacking in literary adornment, and most seem to have been revised on several occasions as he developed or changed his views. They lack final revisions, and there remain gaps and inconsistencies. Although the texts thus present problems of interpretation, they are all the more interesting as living documents in which the reader can see the philosopher's mind at work. The spirit of the Peripatetic School was one of on-going cooperative research; with Aristotle's encouragement,

Theophrastus and other students further developed or revised some of his theories, including his views of rhetoric.

Aristotle's earliest draft of lectures on rhetoric was probably written about 350 B.C. While still a member of Plato's Academy, and probably with Plato's encouragement, he began to offer a public course on rhetoric in the afternoons in reaction to the teaching of Isocrates (Cicero, *On the Orator* 3.141; Quintilian 3.1.14). *Synagôgê Technôn*, his summary of earlier rhetorical handbooks mentioned in Chapter 2, was perhaps put together during his preparation of these lectures. Rhetoric was probably one of the subjects Aristotle taught young Alexander, and he may have revised his notes then. The text as we have it seems to have had its last revision about 336 B.C. when he was preparing to return to Athens. We do not know for certain that the text was ever used as the basis of lectures after he opened his new school, but it seems likely, and in any event it was available for study in the library of the school.[14]

Aristotle's works, despite many inconsistencies resulting from composition at different times, are part of an evolving system or network of thought,[15] and it is desirable for a reader of the *Rhetoric* to have some understanding of this system and the place of rhetoric in it. Before Aristotle's time, what we think of as the academic disciplines had not been clearly defined and organized. One of his great contributions was the creation of a "map of learning" in which each discipline was given a name ("politics," "ethics," "rhetoric," "poetics," "physics," "metaphysics," etc.), a subject, and a method. A second important contribution of Aristotle was the earliest detailed description of logic, and connected with this the recognition that there are "tool" disciplines (*organa*) that have no specific subject matter of their own but are methods for dealing with many subjects. This contribution was especially valuable in the case of rhetoric, where, as we saw in discussing Plato's *Gorgias*, there was much confusion about the function of the art. Aristotle discusses "tools" in his works known collectively as the *Organon*; they include formal logic, scientific demonstration (*apodeixis*), and dialectic (discussed in the *Topics*).

In *Metaphysics* (6.1) Aristotle says that all intellectual activity is divided into three categories: theoretical, practical, and productive. Theoretical intellectual activity is directed toward subjects like mathematics, where the objective is to know; practical intellectual activity is directed

PHILOSOPHICAL RHETORIC

toward subjects like ethics and politics, where the objective is doing something in a certain way; productive intellectual activity is directed toward making something, like creating a poem or a work of art. The sciences differ from the arts in that the former deal with things that cannot be other than they are: in studying mathematics or physics, for example, we seek to learn what is necessarily true, not what is probable. Art, on the other hand, is a capacity to realize a potential by reasoning and operates in the realm of the probable. It is not concerned with things that exist by nature or by necessity, but rather with "the coming into being of something which is capable of being or not being" (*Nicomachean Ethics* 6.4.4). "Coming into being" results from the operation of causes, of which there are four kinds, according to Aristotle. A simple statement of the concept of the four causes, or ways things are said to be caused, can be found in the *Physics* (2.3). First is the material cause, such as metal as a cause of metal objects. Second is the formal cause, the pattern or genus that causes the form a product takes. Third is the efficient cause, the maker as cause of the product. Fourth is the final cause, that for the sake of which something is done or made, as the cause of exercise is health.

Aristotle does not specifically discuss how the four causes are to be applied to rhetoric, but he does seem to apply the theory in his discussion. The material cause of a speech is, at one level, the words of which it is composed, and he discusses the use of different kinds of words, but more generally he regards the material of rhetoric as the arguments and topics that the words construct, and these are discussed in detail. The formal cause in the most general sense is the species to which a speech belongs, and Aristotle comes to the conclusion that there are three species of rhetoric: judicial, deliberative, and epideictic. The efficient cause is the speaker, whose projection of moral character turns out to be an important factor in rhetoric. The final cause of rhetoric as a whole is persuasion to right judgment, action, or belief, but each species of rhetoric has its own final cause: justice in the case of judicial rhetoric; what is advantageous in deliberative rhetoric; what is honorable in epideictic rhetoric.

What kind of an art is rhetoric: theoretical, practical, or productive? Aristotle begins his treatise with the statement that rhetoric is a counterpart of dialectic, and he stresses that connection in other passages. From that point of view, rhetoric is one of the tool disciplines, capable of dealing with many subjects. Tool disciplines, however, have theoretical, practical, and productive levels of activity. When Aristotle gives a definition of rhetoric at the beginning of the second chapter, he proposes that rhetoric be regarded as "an ability, in each case, *to see* the available means of persuasion." The word translated as "to see" is *theorêsai*, and here and in other passages Aristotle is considering rhetoric as a theory of persuasion. Later in the same chapter, however, (1.2.7) he describes rhetoric as an "offshoot" of dialectic and the ethical part of politics, and in *Nicomachean Ethics* (1.2.4–6) he refers to rhetoric as a part of the larger discipline of politics, thus a practical art. Quintilian (2.18.2) reviewed the problem with reference to Aristotle's discussion and concluded that rhetoric is best regarded as a practical art. Aristotle, however, also sometimes regards rhetoric as a productive art, especially in Book 3, where he compares it to poetics.

The question of what kind of art rhetoric is relates to the audience Aristotle is addressing. His school attracted not only young men who might become philosophers but also others who hoped for political careers in Athens or elsewhere and individuals who might be called upon to evaluate the speeches of others. In different passages in the treatise he seems to have different audiences in mind. The beginning of Book 1 seems to be addressed to students who have been studying dialectic and are given a transition to the related subject of rhetoric. Other passages, especially those containing practical precepts on composing a speech, may reflect the audience of his early public lectures, students anxious to improve their rhetorical skills. Those planning public careers would benefit from instruction in composing a speech, but it might have been even more important that they have an understanding of rhetoric as it was being used by others and be able to make sound judgments about speeches they heard. Aristotle's theory of rhetoric also provides an excellent basis for criticism and evaluation of spoken and written persuasive discourse.[16]

Aristotle's *Rhetoric* as we have it consists of three books.[17] It is convenient here to discuss the contents in terms of chapters, but the reader should understand that chapter numbers were first introduced into the text by George Trebizond in the fifteenth century; originally the text of each book (each papyrus scroll) was continuous. The first three chapters of the first book present in outline Aristotle's view of a philosophical rhetoric. Although there is no reference to Plato, they provide an answer to the objections found in *Gorgias* regarding rhetoric as an art and develop suggestions found in *Phaedrus* about what constitutes a valid rhetoric. The rest of Book 1 and all of Book 2 work out a system of rhetorical invention in detail. In Book 3, perhaps originally a separate work, Aristotle adds discussion of delivery, style, and arrangement. Recognizing that the work, like most of Aristotle's treatises, was written at different times, we should not impose an artificial consistency on it. Aristotle never finally revised the whole, so words, even technical terms, are not always used with the same meaning, and he has not always reconciled material developed in detail in one part of the treatise with references in other parts. In addition to the problem of classification of the art just mentioned, three major inconsistencies are as follows: (1) the inconsistency between Aristotle's complaints in the first chapter of Book 1 about earlier writings on rhetoric and the material he himself discusses in Book 2 on the emotions and in Book 3 on style and arrangement; (2) his use or omission of the term *topos*, and especially his failure to make clear the difference between the "topics" described in Book 2, chapter 23, and other "topics"; and (3) varying degrees of emphasis on the enthymeme, or the enthymeme and the example, as the basis of proof and its relationship to ethical and pathetical modes of persuasion. Inconsistencies in the text certainly result from composition at different times and perhaps for different audiences. Some scholars believe a development can be traced from an early, Platonic view limiting rhetoric to logical argument and best seen in the opening chapters, to a later view incorporating ethical and emotional persuasion and matters of style.[18]

Aristotle begins Book 1 with the relationship of rhetoric to dialectic. "Rhetoric," he says in the first sentence, "is an *antistrophos* to dialectic." *Antistrophos* means "counterpart." We have seen that Plato and Isocrates also regarded rhetoric as a counterpart or correlative to some other art. The functions of rhetoric and dialectic, Aristotle means, are comparable methods. Both deal with matters that are common subjects of knowledge; neither falls within any distinct discipline. All people have occasion to question or support an argument, to defend themselves or accuse others, and the issues relate to a variety of subjects. The relationship of rhetoric to dialectic will continue to be a subject of debate throughout the history of western rhetoric.

What does Aristotle mean by "dialectic"? Dialectic to him is a somewhat more limited form of intellectual activity than it was to Plato. Superior to it is *apodeixis*, or demonstration, which is reasoning from scientifically true premises. Dialectic, in contrast, is the form of reasoning built on premises that are generally accepted, whether by everybody, by most people, or by those with some authority on a matter (see *Topics* 1.1). Aristotle says that dialectic is useful in three ways: as an intellectual training in argumentation; in unstructured discussions with others for the sake of determining the truth of some issue; and in connection with study of the various intellectual disciplines (*Topics* 1.2). The first use took the form of exercises practiced in Aristotle's school in which one student stated a proposition, such as "pleasure is the only good," and another student sought to refute it by asking questions that could be answered yes or no. The second use resembles argumentation in a Socratic dialogue. The third involves the ability of a reasoner to raise difficulties on two sides of an issue, thus clarifying a problem, and it also facilitates the development of premises on which disciplines can be constructed. Aristotle's *Politics*, for example, begins with the premises that every state is a community, that a community is established for some good, and that citizens act in order to obtain what they regard as good. These premises are based on general agreement; they are not developed within the science of politics, and they can be demonstrated only by a process of showing that they are probably true. It is characteristic of Aristotle's system that dialectic, like rhetoric, is more an art of communication than of the discovery of new truth; in the *Topics*, for instance, the student, like an orator, is usually assumed to have a hypothesis to prove rather than to be engaged in an open-ended discussion. This feature of Aristotelian dialectic contributed to its rejection from the scientific method in the seventeenth century.[19]

Aristotle is at pains to explain how rhetoric is similar to dialectic but says virtually nothing about how the two differ. He takes up rhetoric as commonly understood by the sophists and Isocrates and initially largely reduces it to dialectic, but certain differences remain. One is formal: rhetoric is found in continuous discourse, whereas dialectic takes the form of question-and-answer debate. Rhetoric usually addresses a large audience, and the orator needs to pay attention to the reactions of hearers; dialectic usually involves one-to-one argument and explicit agreement or refutation. There is also some difference in subject matter. Dialectic usually deals with philosophical or at least general questions, rhetoric with concrete or practical ones. Dialectic is rigorous and constructs chains of argument; rhetoric is popular and expansive. Zeno the Stoic compared dialectic to a closed fist, rhetoric to an open hand (Cicero, *Orator* 113), an analogy cited by many later writers. As treated in the *Rhetoric*, rhetoric is limited to civic life and to three kinds of speeches: judicial, deliberative, and epideictic. Because Gorgias and Isocrates had treated rhetoric as an art of political discourse, Aristotle is at pains to show that it is a tool and not a substantive art of politics, but he does view it as a tool whose application is political. In *Poetics* (chapter 19) rhetoric is found in the speeches of tragedy and epic as well as in oratory, but these are analogous to political discourse. Finally, and perhaps most importantly, in oratory and poetry rhetoric arouses emotion, rightly or wrongly, which dialectic does not do, and the good character of the speaker has a vital role in rhetoric, whereas in dialectic only the argument matters.

If rhetoric is a form of dialectic, the handbooks were sadly lacking in Aristotle's judgment. Existing handbooks were inadequate because of their preoccupation with judicial oratory to the exclusion of the nobler form of political oratory, their emphasis on the parts of the oration and the emotions, and most of all their neglect of the essence of rhetoric: *pisteis*, which can be translated as "forms of proof" or "modes of persuasion." Rhetoric, rightly understood, is useful, for the audience cannot be expected to come to the right conclusion if the truth is not presented so people can understand it, and there are those whom it is difficult to instruct. Ability to argue on two sides of an issue makes it easier for a speaker to understand the strength and weakness of a case. Also, one ought to be able to defend oneself with speech, which is something characteristic of human society. Speech can do great harm, but so can most good things.

After the introductory remarks of chapter 1, Aristotle begins chapter 2 with his definition of rhetoric as "a *dynamis*, in each case, to see the available means of persuasion." *Dynamis* is Aristotle's philosophical term for a "potentiality," but it also means "power" or "ability" and has often been translated as "faculty." The phrase "in each case" distinguishes rhetoric, which deals with particular people, occasions, and facts, from dialectic, which deals with universals. Means or modes of persuasion, Aristotle says, are of two sorts, *atechnoi* and *entechnoi* (1.2.2). *Atechnoi*—atechnic, nonartistic, or external modes—are outside the art of the orator to create and are used rather than invented by the orator. They include the evidence given by free witnesses, the evidence extracted from slaves under torture, written contracts, and other direct evidence discussed in detail in chapter 15 of Book 1. Under the influence of the technical handbooks, with their judicial focus, Aristotle fails to consider external proofs available to deliberative or epideictic speakers, such as the matter of the occasion on which they speak. *Entechnoi*—entechnic, artistic, or internal modes of persuasion—are of three sorts, which we may call *ethos*, *pathos*, and *logos*. They derive from the three constituents of the speech-act: speaker, audience, and speech respectively.

Ethos is the personal character of the speaker as projected in the speech: the orator should seem trustworthy. In Aristotle's view, ethos should be established by what is said and should not be a matter of authority or the previous reputation of the orator (1.2.4). The reason for this is that only ethos projected in this way is artistic. The authority of the speaker would be analogous to the role of a witness and would thus be *atechnos*, something not created but used, though Aristotle fails to point this out. It may have seemed unnecessary because of the common situation in Greek lawcourts, where the litigants were often persons of no particular reputation, some of whom had purchased speeches from logographers, the professional speechwriters. A logographer's duties came to include the artistic creation of a credible ethos for the client.

Pathos occurs as a mode of artistic proof when the minds of the audience are moved to emotion: they will come to a different conclusion, for example, when they are angry than when pleased. Aristotle acknowledges that this is the same subject that he criticized writers of handbooks for treating to the exclusion of anything else and promises to discuss it in detail later in the work, which he does in Book 2.

He then takes up, for the rest of chapter 2, what we have called *logos*, or that mode of proof found in the argument and most characteristic of rhetoric as he understands it. In chapter 1 this was said to be a matter of enthymemes, but here a twofold classification is made, parallel to that in dialectic. We are referred to the *Topics* for additional information. Argumentation, Aristotle says, can be inductive, based on the use of *paradeigmata*, or "examples," or deductive, in the form of an enthymeme. An instance of argument from example would be to cite occasions in Greek history in which a popular leader demanded a bodyguard in order to make himself tyrant, which the orator than can compare to the demand of a contemporary leader for a bodyguard. The generalized conclusion "thus anyone who seeks a bodyguard seeks tyranny" might be expressed or only assumed. We are told later (1.9.39) that proof by example is more suitable to deliberative than to judicial oratory, since we must predict the future on the basis of knowledge of the past. In chapter 20 of Book 2 the subject of the use of examples is taken up again and they are classified into "historical" and "invented" examples. The instance just given would serve for the historical type. Invented examples are of two sorts: the parable, or comparison, as when Socrates ridiculed the choosing of public officials by lot by comparing the process to choosing athletes or pilots by lot; and the fable, which is an imaginary example such as one of Aesop's animal fables. Aristotle says that he favors using enthymemes where possible, and then adding an example as a kind of witness to the point. If the speaker puts examples first, a number of them are needed to establish their general implication. But the orator might say, "Dionyius should not be given a bodyguard, for one who seeks a bodyguard seeks tyranny. If you don't believe me, look at the example of Pisistratus." Here a general observation, which could have been established by induction, is stated as an enthymeme, its premises being regarded as generally accepted, and then a specific example is added to clinch the point. In a passage in *Prior Analytics* (2.23) Aristotle recognizes that proof from example can take syllogistic form, and elsewhere in the *Rhetoric* (2.25.8) he lists example as one of the kinds of premise on which enthymemes are built. It may be that his view on this subject differed at different times or that he used the term *paradeigma* in two different senses.[20]

The term *enthymeme* was used by Isocrates (e.g., *Evagoras* 10) to mean a thought or idea uttered by an orator. In *Prior Analytics* (2.27) Aristotle gives the word the technical meaning of a syllogism based on probabilities or signs. One thus might expect it to be commonly used in dialectic, which deals with probabilities; but in the *Topics*, Aristotle's discussion of dialectic, enthymeme is only used to refer to an argument in rhetoric (8.14.164a6) and dialectical arguments are called syllogisms. Aristotle seems to have thought that though argumentation in rhetoric, as in dialectic, rested in large part on the use of syllogisms, it was desirable to call rhetorical arguments by a different name to suggest the less rigorous logical context of oratory. Enthymemes are certainly reducible to syllogistic argument but are not usually presented as a formal argument. In particular, the orator often suppresses one of the premises (*Rhetoric* 1.2.13). For example, "Doreus has been victor in a contest where the prize is a crown, for he has won the Olympic games" is an enthymeme that, in its full form, would consist of the major premise, "The prize in the Olympic games is a crown"; the minor premise, "Doreus has won the Olympic games"; and the conclusion, "Doreus has been victor in a contest where the prize is a crown." In 2.22.3 Aristotle says that it is not necessary "to include everything" in an enthymeme and conclusions do not need to be drawn only from what is "necessarily valid." Any syllogistic argument in a rhetorical context is, in Aristotelian terms, an enthymeme whether the premises are certain or only probable and whether all are expressed or not. Most commonly, enthymemes take the form of a statement followed by a reason or are cast in the form of *if* something is so, *then* so is something else. Omission of one premise can have the psychological effect of pleasing listeners by appealing to their intelligence and can help to bring listeners into identification with the speaker.[21]

Aristotle categorizes enthymemes in two different ways: one way is in terms of the source of their premises, whether probabilities or signs; the other way is in terms of the subject discussed. Many of the enthymemes in a speech concern politics, economics, military strategy, or the like. He usually avoids calling these "topics" and refers to them as *idia*, "specificities," though they are often known today as "specific topics" or sometimes just "topics." Rhetoric, of course, makes use of them, but more characteristically rhetorical are what Aristotle initially calls *koinoi topoi*, "common topics," which have no specific subject matter and do not make the listener knowledgeable about any one class of things. In 1.2.21 only one is identified, the topic of the more and the less, but in 1.3 and 2.18–19, four *koina*, "commonalities," are identified: the possible and the

Forms of Proof in Aristotle's *Rhetoric*

I. Scientific Demonstration (*apodeixis*).

II. Probable Demonstration (*dialektikê*):

RHETORIC (an offshoot of Dialectic and the Ethical Part of Politics):

    A. Artistic Modes of Persuasion (1.2):

        1. Ethos of the Speaker (2.1);

        2. Pathos or Emotion of the Audience (2.2–17);

        3. Logos or Argument of the Speech (1.2):

            a. Deductive: Enthymemes (2.22):

                i. Sources: Probabilities and Signs (Infallible; Fallible)(1.2);

                ii. Topics: a. Special Topics (*idia*)(1.2);

                        b. Common Topics (*koina*)(1.2; 2.18–19);

                        c. Dialectical Topics (*topoi*)(2.23);

            b. Inductive: Examples (2.20):

                i. Historical;

                ii. Invented: Parable; Fable.

    B. Non-Artistic Modes of Persuasion (1.15):

        1. Laws; 2. Evidence of Witnesses; 3. Contracts;

        4. Evidence of Slaves under Torture; 5. Oaths.

Species of Rhetoric

Distinguished by the Function of the Audience (1.3):

I. Judges:

    A. Of the Past: Judicial: Issue of Justice (1.10–14);

    B. Of the Future: Deliberative: Issue of Advantage (1.4–8):

        1. Subjects (1.4):

            Ways and Means; War and Peace; Defense; Imports and Exports; Legislation;

        2. Goal (1.6–7): Happiness; the Good;

        3. Context (1.8):

            Democracy; Oligarchy; Aristocracy; Monarchy.

II. Spectators: Epideictic: Issue of Honor; Praise and Blame (1.9) impossible, past fact, future fact, and magnitude (the more and the less, the great and the small). An example of the last is what later came to be known as *a fortiori* argument: if the harder of two things is possible, so is the easier; similarly, if the less likely of two things occurred in the past, the more likely probably occurred as well. In addition, a third kind of "topic" will be discussed in chapter 23 of Book 2. This kind involves strategies of argument, including argument from opposites, from definition, from division, and many others and have come to be known as "dialectical topics."

The third chapter begins with identification of the elements in the speech-act as speaker, speech, and audience. Modern rhetoricians would add other factors, including the occasion, which might have proved useful to Aristotle in his subsequent discussion but which he would apparently regard, like the speaker's authority, as nonartistic. Here he next defines three species of rhetoric on the basis of three kinds of audience that a speaker can address in a speech: judges of past action, judges of future action, and spectators. This is the most influential of all his divisions. Before Aristotle's time various species of oratory had been recognized, including prosecutions, defenses, funeral orations, and others, but these had not been classified into genres. That he intended the classification to be a universal one can be seen in the universal terms in which it is first laid out. A hearer of a speech, he says, must be a judge or not a judge. In the latter case the hearer is described as a *theôros*, a spectator. If the hearer is a judge, the hearer is being asked either to judge past fact (Did X perform this act? Was this act illegal?) or to make a judgment about what should be done in the future (Will the proposed policy be advantageous? Should it be adopted?). These two possibilities are the situations of judicial (*dikanika*) and deliberative (*symbouleutika*) rhetoric, respectively, and each has its final cause: litigants seek to establish what is just or unjust; the deliberative speaker is fundamentally concerned with establishing that a course of action will be advantageous for the audience, or at least not harmful. The speaker might have something to say about justice, but that would be a secondary consideration. All this is incisively sketched. In chapters 4 through 8 of Book 1 the various subjects, objectives, and contents of deliberative rhetoric are examined in detail, and in chapters 10 through 15 the materials of judicial oratory are considered: incentives for wrongdoing (10–11), the states of mind of wrongdoers (12), the kinds of persons wronged (12), the classification of just and unjust actions (13), and the comparative evaluation of unjust actions (14). In these chapters Aristotle summarizes a great deal of specifics (*idia*), chiefly from politics and ethics, of which he believes the orator needs knowledge. Indeed, one is reminded of the sophist's claim in Plato's *Gorgias* that if a student did not know enough about a subject, Gorgias would teach him.

The treatment of the situation when the hearer is not a judge is less satisfactory. Aristotle calls such a speech "epideictic," that is, "demonstrative," and says it refers to the present time, in contrast with the focus on the past seen in judicial oratory, and on the future in deliberative, though the speaker may remind the audience of the past and project events into the future. In a later passage (2.18.1), however, he admits that the spectator of epideictic is, in a sense, a judge of the effectiveness of a speech. Generally, he thinks of epideictic as praise or blame of a person and says that the final cause of such a speech is demonstration of the honorable or shameful. The category is thus descriptive of funeral oratory or of that kind of sophistic speech exemplified by encomia by Gorgias and Isocrates. In the consideration of epideictic in chapter 9 the subject is somewhat enlarged to include praise of gods, animals, and inanimate objects (1.9.2). Slippage of the moral tone of philosophical rhetoric is first clearly evident in this chapter as Aristotle reaches out to include practical advice on how to praise the subject. For example, he says that when praising "one should always take each of the attendant terms in the best sense; for example, one should call an irascible and excitable person 'straightforward' and an arrogant person 'highminded,'" etc. (1.9.29). It is also in this chapter that the prescriptive tone associated with rhetorical handbooks becomes evident, including use of the verb in the second person; for example, "If you do not have enough to say about your subject himself, compare him to others, as Isocrates used to do." (1.9.38).

Aristotle admits (1.9.35) that epideictic and deliberative rhetoric overlap and suggests that the difference is often one of style. This is further confirmed by his discussion of epideictic style in Book 3, chapter 12. A great deal of what is commonly called epideictic oratory is deliberative, written in an epideictic style. In many speeches of Isocrates, for example, the objective of the speech is to get an audience (in Isocrates' case, readers) to make judgments about future policies for Athens or Greece. Conversely, both judicial and deliberative speeches often contain epideictic passages—for example, Demosthenes' personal attacks on Aeschines in the Greek lawcourts and Cicero's praise of Pompey in the Roman assembly to secure passage of the Manilian law. Some Christian oratory is deliberative, often with epideictic passages praising God, some is predominantly epideictic: the missionary sermon seeks to convert the heathen to a new faith to the end that the audience's actions will be consistent with Christian teaching; but a Christian homily, addressed to believers, seeking to deepen their understanding and faith rather than urging them to specific actions, may be regarded as epideictic. A speech of greeting to a visiting dignitary, a speech of thanks, such as Cicero's to the senate on his return from exile, or speeches of congratulation at birthdays or weddings, which were common in later antiquity, fall within Aristotle's concept of epideictic, as do modern ceremonial speeches—on Memorial Day, the Fourth of July, and at graduations, as well as at funerals. At many times in history, praise or blame has been the chief form of speech under autocratic government, allowing an orator to accomplish some other purposes. Such speeches, including encomia of public officials, are often intended, or partly intended, to urge the addressee to some future action or at least to a point of view about possible action. To that extent they logically fall into Aristotle's concept of deliberative oratory, but his classification recognizes the fact that such speeches are distinctly different in structure and in style from the oratory of political debate. Perelman and Olbrechts-Tyteca in *The New Rhetoric* (pp. 47–57) suggested that epideictic is noncontroversial and aims at increased adherence to an accepted value. Another way to view it is as "performance rhetoric," characterized by its association with formal occasions.[22] Aristotle's concept of epideictic is derived from speech genres common in his own society and needs to be generalized to include the rituals, performances, and occasional rhetoric found in cultures all over the world. Much traditional oral poetry is epideictic, and many genres of literary poetry are as well, especially lyric poetry in the form of odes and sonnets celebrating an occasion, describing a work of art, praising a lover, or attacking vice or an enemy.

At the beginning of the second book Aristotle resumes the discussion in 1.2.3–5 of the character of the speaker and the emotions of the au-

dience as artistic modes of persuasion.²³ Chapters 2–11 detail propositions about the emotions useful to a speaker in all species of rhetoric,
and are the earliest surviving systematic account of human psychology.
The discussions of emotions are arranged in contrasting pairs: anger
and calmness, friendship and enmity, etc. Chapters 12–17 discuss ethos
or character, approaching it in terms of stages in life—young, old,
prime—and as affected by birth, wealth, and power. Although in 1.3 and
2.1 Aristotle identified ethos with the projection of the character of the
speaker, ethos here is viewed abstractly with no application to rhetoric.
Apparently all of chapters 2–17 were written originally in some context
not concerned with rhetoric and then incorporated into the *Rhetoric* as
a kind of appendix to the account of ethos and pathos.²⁴ Chapter 18 then
resumes consideration of dialectical features of rhetoric, including further discussion of subjects mentioned in 1.2–3: the "commonalities" of
the possible and impossible, past and future fact, and magnitude in
chapter 19; the example in chapter 20; the maxim as a form of enthymeme in chapter 21; enthymemes in chapter 22; and a list of twenty-
eight *topoi* of enthymemes, that is, dialectical strategies in chapter 23.
This chapter contains historical references to events in the late 340s and
early 330s and was probably written later than any other part of the
work. Book 2 concludes with discussion of real and fallacious enthymemes in chapter 24 and techniques of refutation in chapter 25. At the
end of the book Aristotle refers to everything contained in Books 1 and 2
as dealing with the thought (*dianoia*) of a speech. In the terminology
developed in the rhetorical schools in the centuries that follow, these
books are thus devoted to *heurêsis* or *inventio*, the first of the five "parts"
or "canons" of rhetoric.

The last sentence of Book 2 reads, "It remains to go through the
subject of style (*lexis*) and arrangement (*taxis*)." This comes as a sur-
prise, since nothing in the first two books has prepared the reader for
any such discussion and Aristotle's remarks in the first chapter of Book 1
seemed to deny the relevance of such subjects. Book 3 was probably
originally a separate work; possibly it was added to the *Rhetoric* by an
editor when the treatise was finally published two hundred and fifty
years later. There is, however, no reason to doubt that Aristotle wrote
what is now Book 3, except perhaps for the passages connecting it to
Books 1 and 2, and his interest in style and arrangement is evident in

Poetics and other works. The addition of Book 3 to the original plan for the *Rhetoric* is consistent with the tendency already noted in the work to move from an austere philosophical view of the subject to an account that incorporates many features of rhetoric as understood by others. Although Book 3 takes on some of the quality of a handbook of composition, the theory of style and arrangement it sets out is considerably more thoughtful than what is found elsewhere.

In 3.1 Aristotle makes two important points. The first is the proposal that delivery needs some consideration as a part of rhetoric. Aristotle outlines what would be contained in a discussion of delivery, which no one had yet composed: the use of the voice to express various emotions, which is a matter of *megethos*, or volume, *harmonia*, or pitch, and *rhythmos*, or rhythm. He did not regard delivery as a very dignified subject, since it was associated with acting, but his student Theophrastus took up the suggestion and composed the treatise that is here said to be needed.[25] Aristotle reveals some defensiveness about this further step away from philosophical rhetoric. We cannot do without delivery, he says:

> Since the whole business of rhetoric is with opinion, one should pay attention to delivery, not because it is right but because it is necessary, since true justice seeks nothing more in a speech than neither to offend nor to entertain; for to contend by means of the facts themselves is just, with the result that everything except demonstration is incidental; but nevertheless, delivery has great power, as has been said, because of the corruption of the audience. (3.1.5)

A second important point in 3.1 is the distinction between the language of poetry and that of prose, which includes rejection of "magical" qualities of language of the sort taught by Gorgias. Poetry was developed first, and thus prose took on a strongly poetic quality when attempts were first made to create an artistic prose style, but Aristotle says that even poetic forms in his time were moving away from affected diction. He inserts a cross-reference to *Poetics* for those interested in more detail. In *Poetics* also (e.g., chapter 22) he prefers a simple, clear style of composition.

Chapter 3 begins discussion of style (*lexis*), first in the sense of choice of words, with identification of what Aristotle calls its *aretê*, "virtue, excellence." This he defines as "to be clear and neither flat nor above the dignity of the subject, but appropriate." If it is not clear, it will not accomplish its purpose; if it is not appropriate, it will not be artistic. The concept of a mean between extremes is a characteristic doctrine of Aristotelian ethics that finds application to rhetoric as well. Aristotle clearly wishes, however, that artistic style have a quality of distinction or unfamiliarity, and a key to that is the proper use of metaphor. Metaphor is especially important in prose, in his opinion, because other forms of poetic language—rare words, compounds, coinages, etc.—will seem strained, whereas metaphor is a natural device of speech and can become the basis for clarity, charm, and distinction. In chapter 3 various faults in the use of words are listed and in chapter 4 the simile, which Aristotle regards as a subordinate type of metaphor, is discussed.[26] In chapter 5 he turns to the composition of phrases and sentences, beginning with the requirement of *hellenismos*, or correctness of Greek grammar. Chapter 6 lists ways to achieve *ongkos*, "swelling, impressiveness" in composition, and chapter 8 discusses the virtue of *to prepon*, "the appropriate, propriety," in composition. The qualities of good style discussed separately by Aristotle were rearranged by his student Theophrastus in his treatise *On Style* and eventually became a standard list of four virtues: correctness, clarity, ornamentation, and propriety.[27] These are discussed in some form in all subsequent treatments of style.

In connection with the virtues of style, Aristotle discusses prose rhythm and periodicity in chapters 8 and 9. Interest in rhythm as a feature of good prose had developed in the late fifth century and was a major consideration to masters of fourth-century prose like Demosthenes. Rhythm in classical Greek is a matter of the proportion of long and short syllables, not of the recurrence of stress. Aristotle attempted to formulate a principle of prose rhythm as a mean between the rhythmical regularity of verse and a complete absence of rhythm. He found such a mean in the rhythmic feet called paeons, and he recommends beginning a sentence with a long syllable, followed by three short syllables, and ending with three short syllables followed by one long. Although such rhythms can be found in artistic Greek (and Latin) prose, and although later discussions of rhythm often also recommend these metrical feet, other combinations were more often sought. Aristotle seems to have laid down too narrow a rule, derived from his favorite principle of a mean. The discussion of the period in chapter 9 distinguishes a running style, in which phrases or clauses are joined by coordinating conjunctions, from a periodic style, made up of units with a distinct beginning and ending and having magnitude easily grasped by the hearer or reader. He thinks of a period has having two phrases or clauses, either parallel in sense or antithetical, and cites examples from speeches of Isocrates, but he does not undertake analysis of extended complex sentences like the one from Isocrates quoted in chapter 3 and those common in later writers.

Chapters 10 and 11 continue the discussion of ornamentation with further examination of metaphor and stress what Aristotle calls "setting-before-the eyes," "visualization," as a way to make style vivid. Chapter 12 discusses the difference between oral and written style and between the style appropriate to each of the three species of rhetoric. Written style, which includes epideictic, should be more polished than oral style, and the style and argument of juridical oratory should be worked out in greater detail than that of deliberation, which he compares to scene painting, intended to be seen from a distance. An analogy between rhetoric (or poetry) and the arts is pointed out by many ancient writers on rhetoric.

The second half of Book 3, chapters 13 to 19, discusses *taxis*, "arrange-ment" of the parts of an oration. Aristotle begins with a view consistent with philosophical rhetoric as outlined at the beginning of Book 1, say-ing that there are only two necessary parts, the statement or proposition and the proof. He ridicules the several parts defined by handbook writ-ers, but then, just as elsewhere he has modified his austere pronounce-ments in the direction of contemporary practice, acknowledges that "at most" there might be proemium, statement, proof, and epilogue, and in the following chapters he includes narration as well. His discussion takes account of epideictic, judicial, and deliberative speeches. In discussing the proof as a part of a speech (3.17; see also 3.16.6) he identifies what he calls four *amphisbêtêseis*, "points open to dispute": whether something was actually done, whether it did any harm, whether it was of any importance, and whether it was just. This is the earliest reference to what came to be called the determination of the *stasis*, or "question at issue," of a speech. Aristotle has rather little to say on the subject, but later rhetorical treatises made *stasis* fundamental to argumentation.

Aristotle's students in the Peripatetic School, especially Theophrastus, his successor as head of the school, continued his study of rhetoric and modified some of his views.[28] As mentioned earlier, Theophrastus wrote treatises on delivery and style, developing Aristotle's suggestions in *Rhetoric* 3, and he probably created the concept of the epicheireme, or fully stated rhetorical argument, in contrast to the enthymeme, or truncated argument with one premise assumed.

Since Aristotle did not publish his treatise on rhetoric, his ideas were largely known to philosophers and teachers of the Hellenistic period through an oral tradition from his students. According to the first-century geographer Strabo (13.609), the unpublished treatises in Aristotle's library were removed to Asia Minor after his death, stored and forgotten, and only rediscovered in the early first century B.C., at which time they were brought to Rome, edited, and published. This tradition may be exaggerated—some copies of the *Rhetoric* may have existed—but it is generally confirmed by the absence of direct references to the work earlier than Cicero's *On the Orator*, written in 55 B.C. Subsequently, there are occasional quotations from or references to the *Rhetoric* in Greek and Latin writers,[29] but the *Rhetoric* was overshadowed by the many new treatises and handbooks on the subject published from the second century B.C. to the end of antiquity, especially works that discussed aspects of rhetoric not identified by Aristotle, including *stasis* theory and figures of speech. Two Latin translations were made in the thirteenth century, read primarily for their discussion of politics and ethics, but the treatise was not a major influence on the teaching of rhetoric until it was rediscovered and translated into Latin by George Trebizond in the fifteenth century and first printed early in the sixteenth century.

The Philosophical Tradition after Aristotle

A modified "philosophical" tradition can be traced through later centuries. Plato's *Gorgias* and *Phaedrus* were well-known and contributed to attacks on rhetoric by teachers of philosophy in the second century B.C., motivated in part by the increasing popularity of rhetorical schools not only with Greeks but with upper-class Romans. The Stoic School, founded by Zeno in the generation after Aristotle, provided a small place for rhetoric as a counterpart to dialectic in its curriculum. A summary of Stoic views of rhetoric is given by Diogenes Laertius (7.42–43). The Stoics also made major contributions to logic and to language theory, including distinctions between tropes, like metaphor, and figures of speech, a large number of which had been identified and named by the end of the second century B.C. The Epicurean School scorned rhetoric until Philodemus, an Epicurean philosopher of the first century B.C., turned attention to it, criticized views of others, and expounded a theory of artistic epideictic in a work that has partially survived on papyrus buried in the eruption of Mt. Vesuvius.[30]

The most important expressions of a version of philosophical rhetoric in the Greek-speaking world of later antiquity came from the Neoplatonist philosophers, who regarded the works of Plato and Aristotle as in essential harmony and who created a curriculum in which study of rhetoric was primarily an exercise in training the mind. They accepted as basic texts the rhetorical writings of Hermogenes (second century after Christ) on stasis theory and style rather than Aristotle's *Rhetoric*, and under their influence a series of *prolegomena*, or introductions to the Hermogenic texts, were composed that defined the legitimate place of the subject within the fields of learning. Neoplatonists also studied Plato's *Gorgias* and *Phaedrus* and wrote commentaries on them, reconciling the contents to each other and to their new system of Platonic-Aristotelian thought. The Neoplatonic synthesis of philosophical and handbook rhetoric continued to be influential throughout the Greek Middle Ages.[31]

In the Latin-speaking West, the most influential statement of the relationship of philosophy and rhetoric was the preface that Cicero wrote about 89 B.C. to his handbook *On Invention*. The passage is frequently quoted or imitated from late antiquity to the Renaissance. Cicero was a very young man at the time, and despite his claims to originality what he says in this work was drawn almost entirely from Greek sources:

> Often and long have I debated with myself whether facility at speaking and great zeal for eloquence have contributed more good or bad to mankind and communities. For when I consider the troubles of our republic and survey in my mind the ancient ruin of great cities, I see that no small part of the disasters was brought on by men skilled at speaking. When, however, I begin to search from written records knowledge of events remote from our memory because of their old-

ness, I recognize that many cities were founded, very many wars extinguished, and that the strongest alliances and most sacred friendships have been formed not only by reasoning of the mind but also more easily by eloquence. For my part, after long thought, reason itself has led me to this opinion first and foremost: that wisdom without eloquence does too little benefit to states but that eloquence without wisdom for the most part does too much harm and is never advantageous. Therefore, if anyone, neglecting the most correct and honorable studies of reason and duty, gives all his attention to the practice of speaking, he is nurtured in a way useless to himself and pernicious to his country; but he who arms himself with eloquence in such a way as not to attack the welfare of his country but to be able to defend it, this man, it seems to me, will be a citizen most useful and most devoted both to his own and to public affairs. (*On Invention* 1.1)

Many years later, after acquiring extensive political experience and after intermittent study of philosophy, Cicero composed the dialogue *On the Orator*, which attempts a synthesis of philosophical and handbook rhetoric, drawing on Plato, Aristotle, and technical sources, incorporated within the original sophistic concept of the orator as statesman and leader of society. Crucial to the formation of this ideal figure is knowledge of philosophy and law, moral standards, and commitment to the best traditions of Roman society. This work was an important influence on Quintilian, writing over a century later, though Quintilian is less sympathetic to formal philosophical studies than was Cicero, and it is also one of the sources for the discussion of rhetoric in the fourth book of Saint Augustine's *On Christian Learning*, to be discussed in Chapter 7.

Dialectic and Rhetoric in Antiquity

Aristotle's view of rhetoric as a counterpart to dialectic remained strong among philosophers, and philosophy exercised much of its influence on the teaching and practice of rhetoric through the study of dialectical topics. On eight occasions the reader of the *Rhetoric* is referred to the *Topics*, Aristotle's treatise on dialectic, for further information on matters of argumentation. The reference at *Rhetoric* 2.22.10 says that "[i]t is evident that it is first necessary, as described in the *Topics*, to have selected statements about what is possible and most suited to the subject, and when unexpected problems occur, to try to follow the same method, looking not to the undefined but to what inherently belongs to the subject of the discourse." *Topos* in Greek means "place," and a logical or rhetorical "topic" is thus a finding-place for an argument. Aristotle may have borrowed the concept of a topic from the "places" in a handbook where examples of argument from probability or other rhetorical techniques were to be found,[32] or the meaning may be derived from the mnemonic system in which images of words or ideas to be remembered were imagined against a background of places (see *Topics* 8.14.163b28).

Aristotle's *Topics* is a treatise in eight books, to which his work *On Sophistical Refutations* is an appendage. In Book 1 he distinguishes scientific demonstration from probable reasoning, or dialectic, and, as mentioned earlier, explains that a knowledge of topics is useful in mental training, in debate, and in establishing the premises of the sciences. Propositions are of three sorts, ethical, physical, and logical, and become the basis of inductive or deductive reasoning. Deductive reasoning is the more important and takes the form of the syllogism. Every logical proposition or problem involves four predicables: definition, property, genus, and accident (1.4.101b25). These are found in ten "categories": essence, quantity, quality, relation, place, time, position, state, activity, and passivity (1.9.103b20–24). Aristotle also wrote a treatise called *Categories*, which has a similar but not identical list. Syllogisms can be supplied by four means: the provision of propositions, an ability to distinguish different meanings of words, the discovery of differences, and the investigation of similarities (1.13.105a20–34). Books 2 through 7 then give a collection of topics dealing with accident, genus, property, and definition, in that order. One topic is to see if your opponent has treated a genus as an accident: white, for example, is not an accident of color but a member of the genus color. The categories come into such matters in that, for example, white color is an essence (in Greek "some thing") and also indicates a quality. The eighth book of the *Topics* gives advice about reasoning—how to formulate or refute questions in debate. Thus the *Topics* deals with both the finding or invention of arguments and their evaluation, which comes to be called "judgment."

Dialectic, and the arguing of theses, was an important exercise in Greek philosophical schools in the Hellenistic period. Predicables and categories proved useful in many ways, for example, in the study of grammar, which was a special interest of the Stoics. They also had application to the study of rhetoric. *Stasis* theory as developed by Hermagoras in the second century made use of the concepts of definition and quality, and the categories are used as a kind of checklist in the later rhetorical handbook of Cassius Longinus to suggest things a student might say in developing a narration or an argument. Cicero discusses dialectical topics in *On the Orator* (2.162–73) and composed a short treatise call *Topics*, allegedly a Latin version of Aristotle's work with the same title but largely drawn from the list of topics in *Rhetoric* 2.23 or from Stoic sources. Following the general lead of Aristotle, Cicero divided argumentation into two arts, which he called the art of invention, or topics, and the science of judgment, or dialectic. His overall view was to subsume both invention and judgment under rhetoric.

Dialectic was not a subject that appealed to many Romans; they regarded it as abstruse and given to hairsplitting, something best left to impractical Greeks. An exception in late antiquity was Boethius, who was a Roman consul in A.D. 510 and held other high offices but was accused of treason and put to death in 524. He was one of the last thinkers in the West to have a good knowledge of Greek and had a special interest in Aristotle's logical works, some of which he translated into Latin. He also wrote a work entitled *De Topicis Differentiis*, or *On Topical Differentiae*, the fourth book of which is a discussion of rhetoric as a special form of dialectic applied to political questions. This work will be discussed in more detail in Chapter 9. Although Boethius does not seem to have known Aristotle's *Rhetoric*, his work introduced a form of philosophical rhetoric into the western medieval tradition. It is a highly abstract work, with no attempt at practical application, but appealed greatly to scholastic philosophers, and in the thirteenth century was made the basic text for teaching a theory of rhetoric at the University of Paris. A form of the philosophical tradition of rhetoric in the Middle Ages is also found in the *Didascalion* of Hugh of Saint Victor, written in the twelfth century, and the treatise *On the Reduction of the Arts to Theology* by Bonaventura, written in the thirteenth. Philosophical approaches to rhetoric then emerged in the Renaissance and Neoclassical periods (to be discussed in Chapters 10 and 11).

CHAPTER 5

Rhetoric in the Roman Period

The classical phase of Greek history is usually said to have come to an end with the defeat of the Greek states by Macedon at the Battle of Chaeronea in 338 B.C., followed by the short reign of Alexander the Great, who died in 323. Aristotle and Demosthenes, the greatest orator of the Athenian democracy, both died in 322. The next three centuries are known as the Hellenistic Age; although Athens and other Greek cities retained some local autonomy, power in the eastern Mediterranean, Asia Minor, and North Africa was effectively held by Alexander's Greek generals and their successors, ruling as kings of Macedon, Pergamum, Syria, and Egypt. In the course of the second and first centuries B.C. Rome, already a power in the western Mediterranean, became involved in eastern affairs, defeated the eastern rulers and Greek cities, and by 30 B.C. had incorporated the whole area as provinces in the Roman Empire.

The Hellenistic Age is the time when the Greek language and Greek culture spread throughout the East. Greek schools of grammar, rhetoric, and philosophy appeared in Asia and North Africa, and Greek rhetoric came in contact with Judaism and later with Christianity. It was also in this period that Greek rhetorical theory as expounded in schools and in handbooks developed the structures and contents that permanently characterized it. This includes the canonization of rhetoric into the five parts of invention, arrangement, style, memory, and delivery; the development of stasis theory; and the identification of tropes and figures, the latter divided into figures of thought and figures of speech. In the second century Romans began to study rhetoric and write about it in

Latin, drawing heavily on Greek sources. Unfortunately, no treatises or handbooks of rhetoric survive from the third and second centuries; what we know about developments come from occasional quotations and references in later writers.

Hermagoras

Probably the most important contribution to technical rhetoric in this period was the handbook by the Greek rhetorician Hermagoras of Temnos. Little is known about the author, and his work is lost except for what can be reconstructed on the basis of references in Cicero's *On Invention*, the *Rhetoric for Herennius*, and later discussions of rhetorical invention. Hermagoras defined the task of the orator as "to treat the proposed political question as persuasively as possible" (see Sextus Empiricus 2.62). He treated invention in the greatest detail; arrangement and style were more briefly discussed under the rubric "economy";[1] there was probably also a brief account of memory and delivery.[2] Hermagoras is the earliest known source for treatment of the five parts of rhetoric. He divided political questions into two types: *theses*, which are general (for example, "Is it right to kill a tyrant?"), and *hypotheses*, or specific cases (for example, "Did Harmodius and Aristogeiton justly kill the tyrant Hipparchus?"). In his analysis of hypotheses Hermagoras expounded in great detail the important theory of stasis, or how to determine the question at issue in a case, a subject that Aristotle (*Rhetoric* 3.17.1) and other earlier writers had only touched on briefly.

The stasis (in Latin, *status* or *constitutio*) is the basic proposition that a speaker seeks to demonstrate. For example, a man accused of murder may deny that he killed the victim. This is conjectural stasis, or stasis of fact. Or he may admit the action but claim that it was legal (perhaps it was done in self-defense), which is stasis of definition. Or he may seek to justify the action in another way, arguing, for example, that he intended no harm and the death was accidental (stasis of quality). The theory is much more complex than these examples suggest; some details will be considered below in the discussion of Cicero's *On Invention*, which is the earliest surviving work in which Hermagoras's theory appears. Hermagoras emphasized the focus of technical rhetoric on judicial oratory, though stasis can be applied to other species of public address, and he provided teachers of rhetoric with a carefully organized body of material to present to their students. Later rhetoricians, of whom Hermogenes in the second century after Christ is the most important, invented new ways of organizing the determination of the question at issue. Stasis theory remained the heart of rhetorical invention until the end of the Renaissance and continues to have some applications today.

Rhetoric at Rome

Rome began as a small city-state, ruled by kings. According to tradition, the last king was overthrown in 753 B.C. and a "republic" with elected officials, an advisory senate, and legislative assemblies took its place. The Roman Republic was, however, not a democracy in either the Greek or the modern meaning of that term: for most of its history it was an oligarchy in which members of noble and wealthy families controlled the government. From time to time popular uprisings occurred that gradually increased the rights of the lower classes. Beginning in the late second century popular leaders emerged, factionalism and civil wars erupted, and with the dictatorship of Julius Caesar in the middle of the first century constitutional government collapsed, replaced after 30 B.C. by the rule of a single individual, the emperor Augustus and his successors.

Public address and debate in the senate, the legislative assemblies, and the lawcourts was a major feature of the Roman Republic. As in other traditional societies, skills at speaking were long learned by listening to and imitating effective elder speakers. In the second century B.C., however, some wealthy young Romans began to visit Greece to study rhetoric and philosophy, and by the middle of the century some Greek teachers of rhetoric had come to Rome, but the general attitude of the Roman establishment toward study of rhetoric was negative. Skill in speaking constituted a possible threat to the dominant senatorial oligarchy. In 161 B.C. the senate authorized the expulsion from Rome of philosophers and rhetoricians, and as late as 92 B.C. the censors issued an edict against teaching rhetoric in Latin.[3] None of these efforts seems to have been very successful, and by the middle of the first century rhetorical schools, and practice in declamation, were central features of Roman education.

Cicero's *On Invention*

Cicero (106–43 B.C.) was the greatest Roman orator and the most important Latin writer on rhetoric. Fifty-eight of his speeches and well over nine hundred letters giving intimate details of his career survive, as well as a series of works designed to introduce contemporary Greek philosophy to the rather unphilosophical Romans and seven works on rhetoric. *On Invention* was written about 89 B.C., when Cicero was very young, and though it makes some claims to originality it largely expounds the system of technical rhetoric he had studied in his teens.[4] He perhaps wrote it primarily for himself as a way of reviewing the theories he had studied. Of all Cicero's writings on rhetoric, however, it was the most read for a thousand years from late antiquity to the Renaissance. Numerous commentaries were written on it, and it was the major authority for all later knowledge of rhetorical invention, as will be discussed in Chapter 9. Its popularity derived from the fact that unlike other rhetorical works of Cicero, except for the prefaces it is a school book that sets out the terminology and precepts of rhetoric in a way that could be memorized and applied. Cicero had planned to complete similar surveys of other parts of rhetoric but failed to do so at the time and came to regard his early work as unsatisfactory in comparison to the experience he later gained in speaking or the grander view of the orator that he later espoused.

The first book of *On Invention* begins with the philosophical introduction, a portion of which is quoted in Chapter 4. "Wisdom without eloquence," he says, "does too little to benefit states, but eloquence without wisdom does too much harm and is never advantageous." He then gives a speculative history of the development of human society, probably drawn from Stoic philosophy. There must once have been a great leader with persuasive power who brought mankind out of primitive conditions, but such great men are not interested in the day-to-day details of administration, and a lesser class of those skilled at speech took over petty disputes. In the course of time they became accustomed to stand on the side of falsehood. In the resulting strife, the nobler souls withdrew into philosophical speculation. No specific names are mentioned, but presumably Cicero thought this process described the history of Greek thought from the time of wise men like Solon to the sophists, followed by the criticism of rhetoric by Socrates and his successors. Roman statesmen like Cato, Laelius, and Scipio Africanus, in Cicero's view, have better combined wisdom and eloquence. The introduction ends with a eulogy of eloquence reminiscent of those by Gorgias and Isocrates and thus draws on the sophistic tradition:

> From it the greatest advantages come to the state, if wisdom is present as moderator of all things; from it, to those who have attained it, flow glory, honor, and prestige; from it also is secured the most certain and safe defense of one's friends. To me, it seems that although men are lower and weaker than the animals in many ways, they most excel them in that they are able to speak. Thus the man seems to me to have gained something wonderful who excels other men in that very way in which mankind excels animals. Since it is acquired not only by nature and by practice, but by some art, it is not irrelevant for us to see what they have to say who have left us precepts on the subject. (1.5)

The technical treatment then begins with the statement that rhetoric is *civilis ratio*, a part of politics. Its function is to speak in a manner suited to persuading an audience. At this time Cicero had no direct knowledge of Aristotle's *Rhetoric*, and many of Aristotle's subtle distinctions are lost; he does, however, attribute to Aristotle, "who did much to improve and adorn this art," the view that the function of the orator is concerned with three kinds of subjects: epideictic, deliberative, and judicial (1.7). Its parts, "most authorities" agree (1.9), are invention, arrangement, style, memory, and delivery. *Inventio* is the reasoning out of truth, or that which is like the truth, to make a case probable. Arrangement (*dispositio*) is the orderly distribution of what has been found. Style (*elocutio*) is the fitting of suitable words to what has been found. *Memoria* is a firm grasp in the mind of subjects and words. Delivery (*pronuntiatio*) is the control of voice and body suitable to the subject and the words. The parts of rhetoric as Cicero and others describe them are clearly pedagogical devices to suggest to a student the stages in the preparation of a speech.

The rest of the work is devoted to invention. Cicero begins with stasis theory as developed by Hermagoras and uses the Latin word *constitutio* to describe it. *Constitutio*, he says, is the first conflict of the two sides of a case, resulting from rejection of an accusation—for example, "You did it," and the response, "I did not do it." There are four kinds of *constitutio* in Cicero's system: *conjecturalis*, when the fact is at issue, *definitiva*, when the definition of the action is debated (for example, murder or homicide); *generalis*, when there is a question of the nature, quality, or classification of an action, and *translatio*, when the jurisdiction of the tribunal is questioned. These *constitutiones* are taken up in Book 1 and again in Book 2 in this order. Cases are simple, involving only one question, or complex, involving several questions (1.17). Controversies involve either reasoning (*in ratione*) or written documents (*in scripto*) (1.17).

The system as outlined is intended to help the student find what to say. After considering the nature of the case, the student should turn to the basic question at issue, an explanation of the question, determination of what the judge is to decide, and what argument can be advanced for that decision. To do the latter the student must investigate topics, called *loci* in Latin. Cicero leaves the details aside for the moment and goes on to the next step, which is to arrange the parts of a speech in order. There are six parts in his system: exordium, narration, partition, confirmation, refutation, and conclusion (1.19). The rest of Book 1 takes up these parts in this order, describing the qualities that each should have and some of the topics that can be used. Throughout the work it is interesting to see how the rhetoricians of the Hellenistic period had adopted, modified, omitted, or expanded rhetorical doctrines developed in classical Greece. Arrangement of the discussion by the parts of the oration, as was the case in the early handbooks, has been preserved. Although discussion of topics derives indirectly from Aristotle, and his distinction of three species of rhetoric was accepted, his theory of three modes of persuasion—ethos, pathos, logos—was apparently unknown to Cicero, and thus unknown to his teachers, at this time.

The exordium (1.20–26) prepares the audience to receive the speech and should make each listener *benevolus*, *attentus*, *docilis*; that is, well-disposed to the speaker, attentive, and receptive. There are five kinds of cases: the honorable, the remarkable, the humble, the doubtful, or the obscure, and the exordium must be adapted to each type. In some kinds of cases where there is no special problem the exordium can be a simple introduction, but otherwise there will be need of *insinuatio*, which by dissimulation or in a roundabout way will steal into the mind of each listener. In considering Cicero's suggestions about how to make a judge well-disposed, attentive, or receptive we begin to see how a system of commonplaces, differing from Aristotle's dialectical topics, had been created by the rhetoricians. There are, Cicero says, four *loci*, "places," to look for goodwill: in the character of the speaker, such as a modest description of actions and services of the past, or of the speaker's misfortunes; in the character of the opponents, if they are hated, wicked, or unpopular; in the character of the judges, by paying tribute to their courage, wisdom, or mercy; or in the case itself: can it be praised, or can the opponents' case be belittled. Similarly, Cicero lists topics that will encourage attentiveness and receptivity, along with topics for use in *insinuatio*.

The narration (1.27–30) should set forth the case and the reason for the dispute, but may also include a digression *extra causam*, beyond the narrow limits, to attack someone on the other side or make a comparison or amuse the audience. A narration should have three qualities (what in other writers are sometimes called the "virtues" of the narration): it should be brief, clear, and probable (1.28). For example, it will be clear if events are described in the order in which they occur and if clear words are used. As noted in Chapter 3, these requirements may have originated with Isocrates.

The partition (1.31–33) is of two sorts: the speaker can state the matters on which there is agreement with the opponent and what remains in dispute, or can list the points to be proved. In the latter event it is important to be brief, complete, and concise. Cicero notes that there are additional rules for partition in philosophy that are not relevant here.

The confirmation (1.34–77) is the part of the speech where, by argument, we make "our case" secure credence, authority, and strength. Material for argument here is either of a general sort or is useful only in a particular kind of oratory and is derived from topics concerned with persons or concerned with actions. The attributes of a person are name, nature, manner of life, fortune, disposition, feeling, interests, purposes, deeds, accidents, and speeches. The topics of each are defined and discussed in turn. The last three, for example, involve a person's behavior, experiences, or words in the past, in the present, or in the future. Attributes of action are of four sorts: connected directly with the action, connected with the performance of the action, adjunct to the action, or consequent upon the action. Each has its topics. For example, to find arguments relating to the performance of the action the student should consider place, time, occasion, manner, and facility.

All arguments drawn from these topics, Cicero says (1.44), will be either probable or necessary, that is, irrefutable. Necessary argument usually takes the form of a dilemma, enumeration, or simple inference. Probabilities as used in argumentation are either signs, credibilities, official judgments, or comparisons. The form of argument is either *inductio*, induction, or *ratiocinatio*, deduction (1.51). Examples of each are given, and Cicero considers at length how many parts a *ratiocinatio* has. Although he is here discussing what in Greek were called enthymemes and syllogisms, he does not use those terms; it is his practice to find a suitable Latin word wherever possible. His own view (1.67) is that *ratiocinatio* in full form has five parts (what in Greek is called *epicheirema*): proposition, reason, assumption, reason for the assumption, and conclusion; at a minimum in Cicero's theory (not in his practice, where two-part enthymemes are frequent), it must have at least three parts: major premise, minor premise, and conclusion. At the end of the discussion of proof Cicero again notes (1.77) that other intricacies of argument studied by philosophers are not suitable for an orator.

Refutation (1.78–79) is of four kinds: the premises are not admitted; the conclusion is shown not to follow; the form of the argument is attacked as invalid; or a stronger argument is set against what an opponent has stated. Examples of how to perform each kind of refutation are given. Arguments are defective if they are entirely false, too general, too commonplace, trifling, remote, badly defined, controversial, self-evident, controvertible, shameful, offensive, contradictory, inconsistent, or adverse to the speaker's purpose. Each fault is explained.

Digression, according to Cicero (1.97), had been put by Hermagoras at this place in the speech, between the refutation and the conclusion. It might involve praise or blame of individuals, comparison with other cases, or something that emphasized or amplified the subject at hand. Thus it is not literally a digression. Cicero criticizes the requirement as a formal rule and says such treatment should be interwoven into the argument. Ironically, ethical digressions of the sort here described are very characteristic of his greatest speeches, for example, *For Caelius* and *For Milo*, and regularly and effectively occur at this very spot in the structure of the speech.

The *conclusio* (1.98–109), more often called *peroratio* by Roman writers, has three parts: summoning up, or enumeration; the inciting of indignation against the opponent; and the *conquestio*, or arousing of pity for the speaker. Topics are given for each. Here and elsewhere Cicero treats the speaker, whether prosecutor or defendant, as the principal in the case, not as an advocate for a client. This is because he is relying on Greek theory, which reflects practice in Greek courts. In Rome, in most major trials the speakers were *patroni*, or advocates, similar to barristers in the British legal system, who planned the prosecution or defense and conducted cases in court. In the following years Cicero himself often performed this function, which was a development of the Roman patron-client system of earlier times, where members of the upper social or economic class defended the interests of their dependents. Advocates were not supposed to be paid in Cicero's time, but they often received political support, favors, and even presents from their clients.

In the introduction to the second book of *On Invention* (2.4) Cicero claims that he has utilized a variety of sources in the work. He may have read some of these, but probably knew about them mainly from a teacher whose identity we do not know. He then gives a brief survey of the history of rhetoric, including the development of an Aristotelian and an Isocratean tradition, which he says (2.8) have now been fused into a single body of knowledge by later teachers. The purpose of the second book is to describe "specific topics of confirmation and refutation for use in each kind of speech" (2.11).

Every inference, Cicero says (2.16), is derived from the cause, from the person involved, or from the act itself. The four kinds of *constitutio* and their topics for judicial oratory are then discussed. Stasis of quality, which he regards as most important and most complicated is put last (2.62–115). It is divided into two parts: legal topics (2.62–68) and juridical topics, or topics of equity, that have a complicated set of subdivisions (69–115). A juridical question involves either absolutes of right and wrong or assumptive arguments that involve partially extraneous circumstances. Assumptive arguments are used when the action is attacked or defended on the basis of the circumstances under which it was committed rather than as legal or right in itself. There are four subdivisions: an act may be defended by comparison to other possible actions; by putting the blame for the action on the accuser; by shifting blame to someone else; or by confession. Shifting responsibility may involve either the cause of the action or the action itself. Confession may take the form of purgation, in which the speaker claims to have acted in ignorance, by accident, or under constraint, and in any event denies the intent of harm; or it may take the form of deprecation, or pleas for pardon. Each of the categories has appropriate topics to use in both accusation and defense.

Controversies involving written documents are then discussed (2.116–54). The distinction between reasoning and written evidence had been made in 1.17 and is Cicero's version of Aristotle's distinction of artistic and nonartistic proof. Cicero discusses topics under the headings of ambiguity, conflict of letter and intent of the law, conflict of two or more laws, reasoning by analogy where no law specifically applies, and definition.

Up to this point the discussion has concerned only judicial oratory. Deliberative oratory is then given brief consideration (2.155–76). Cicero (2.156) notes that in judicial oratory the "end" or purpose is equity, which he says is a subdivision of the larger topic of honor. He is aware that Aristotle had regarded the advantage or utility of a policy as the objective in deliberative oratory, but he himself prefers to say it is honor and utility. In epideictic it is honor alone. What is honorable is found in the four cardinal virtues as defined by Hellenistic philosophers: wisdom, justice, courage, and temperance, each of which becomes a topic. The honorable when coupled with utility consists of such things as glory, rank, influence, and friendship (2.166). How these might be worked out in an actual speech can be seen in Cicero's oration *On the Manilian Law*, of 69 B.C. *On Invention* then ends with a very brief discussion of praise and blame in epideictic oratory (2.177–78). There was no tradition of epideictic oratory in the Roman Republic, and the genre was thus of little interest to Cicero or his contemporaries.

Cicero's survey of invention ends here. His emphasis is on the actual devices of a speech, primarily a speech in a lawcourt, generally in the order a student might use them in composition. The forms of argument and topics of dialectic are present but are arranged into a system for teaching legal oratory to students. That system, however, is based on the conditions of Greek, not Roman, law and procedure. The litigants are envisioned speaking in their own behalf, which generally would not have been the case in Rome; and even stasis theory, to which so much attention is given, was not entirely applicable to Roman procedures. In civil cases at Rome there was a preliminary hearing of an allegation before the praetor, who determined if the case was actionable and issued a statement of what issues were to be determined by a jury. Stasis theory did, however, have applicability to some criminal trials, and Cicero's use of it can be seen in some of his cases, especially in *For Milo*. His practice, and that of other mature orators, of course, was far more inventive and flexible than anything suggested in *On Invention*, which is a dry hand-book for a novice, and especially for one beginning to practice declamation in a rhetorical school. In declaiming imaginary cases in schools the students were expected to follow the rules for invention, including determination of the question at issue, arrangement, style, memory, and delivery as found in handbooks or expounded by their teachers.

Rhetoric for Herennius

Since Cicero did not write up his early studies of arrangement, style, memory, and delivery, we may turn, as did students of rhetoric in the Middle Ages and Renaissance, to another early Latin handbook that does address those subjects. This is *Rhetoric for Herennius*, a treatise perhaps written by an otherwise unknown Cornificius and dedicated to an unidentified Herennius. Its discussion of invention has many similarities to Cicero's *On Invention*, and it thus probably represents the teachings of the same teacher or school and suggests some of what Cicero might have had to say on other parts of rhetoric. It was composed a few years later than *On Invention*, perhaps around 84 B.C. Through the Middle Ages and until the late fifteenth century the treatise was regarded as a work by Cicero and often known as the *Rhetorica Secunda*. Although, like Cicero, the author has not adapted rhetorical theory to Roman legal process and provides no discussion of ethos, Roman values appear to a greater extent in his work than in *On Invention*. This is especially true of his extended discussion of *dignitas*, which is his term for ornamentation (4.19–68).[5] An attraction of *Rhetoric for Herennius* for the student of the history of rhetoric, in addition to its full description of its subject, is the availability of an excellent edition, with Latin text, translation, and notes, by Harry Caplan in the Loeb Classical Library series.

Rhetoric for Herennius is in four books. The first two cover judicial invention but integrate the material in Cicero's second book into a single account of proof. Book 3 takes up deliberative and judicial rhetoric and then turns to the remaining parts of the subject that had achieved canonical status by this time.

The discussion of *dispositio*, or arrangement, is very short (3.16–18). The author says there are two kinds, one arising from the rules of rhetoric, the other accommodated to the circumstances. The rules of rhetoric, of course, have provided for the exordium, narration, and the like, and the primary reason the discussion is so short is that these parts of the oration have already been discussed in detail. We are now told, however, that it is possible to vary this order if, in the speaker's judgment, something else is more effective. One might, for example, want to start with consideration of a very strong argument made by the opponent, or with the narration. Both Greek and Roman orators indeed do this. In the course of the first century B.C. the need for all parts of an oration in the prescribed order became an important issue between the schools of Apollodorus of Pergamum, who taught that the prescribed order should always be followed, and Theodorus of Gadara, who was more flexible (The dispute is a good example of the pedantic quarrels that often erupted between rival teachers of rhetoric.)[6] The discussion of arrangement in the *Rhetoric for Herennius* ends with a paragraph on the order of arguments within the proof and refutation. The strongest ones should go first and last, with weak arguments in the middle.

Instead of turning next to style, the author reserves that subject for treatment in a separate book and fills out Book 3 with his account of delivery and memory. This arrangement, which is imitated by George Trebizond in the most important new rhetoric of the fifteenth century, results primarily from the author's desire to treat style at greater length and in particular to include numerous examples of his own composition. He was perhaps also influenced by the fact that style was the subject of monographic treatment by others; some readers might only be interested in that subject and would find it convenient if it was written in a separate papyrus scroll.

Having decided to treat style last, the author also reverses the order of memory and delivery. His discussion of delivery (3.19–27) is the earliest we have, except for Aristotle's brief remarks at the beginning of *Rhetoric*, Book 3. Delivery is divided into *vocis figura* and *corporis motus*, a distinction that probably originated in Theophrastus's now lost study of the subject. Voice quality consists of *magnitudo*, or volume, *firmitudo*, or stability, and *mollitudo*, or flexibility. Volume is largely dependent on natural endowment but can be improved by practice. Stability—ability to speak at length without becoming hoarse—is preserved by cultivation. Flexibility also requires exercise and involves three tones or styles: *sermo*, or conversation, *contentio*, or debate, and *amplificatio*, or amplification. Each of the tones is further divided and rules are given for achieving it. An analogy to styles of oratory, which is discussed in the next book, is apparent here and is further developed in Quintilian's account of delivery. Physical movement or gesture is coordinated with the three tones, and advice is given on the use of the face, arms, hands, body, and feet. In moments of pathetic amplification it is even appropriate to slap the thigh and beat the head.

The discussion of memory (3.28–40) is the best account of the subject in any ancient treatise. Mnemonics has a history that apparently began in the fifth century B.C. Throughout the centuries the subject was explored in a series of separate treatises, as well as being given some treatment in rhetorical handbooks.[7] Most of the account here is given over to the "artificial" system of backgrounds and images that a student can use to memorize any kind of discourse. A background is a physical setting, familiar to the student, and can be thought of as a tablet in the mind. Against this background the student imagines pictures that symbolize the ideas or the words of a speech in the order in which they should occur. When the student is speaking, this picture is then passed in review in the mind to suggest the thoughts or words. The system works, and still has some use today, but is cumbersome in memorizing a long text, and is probably most useful in exercising the memory to a point where it can gain unaided an ability to remember a composition, or as a way of remembering some particularly difficult passage verbatim.

Ancient orators sometimes used notes, but the reading of a speech from a written text was considered ineffective in political or legal contexts and usually avoided. There are many ancient testimonies to the great potential of the human mind to remember material verbatim in a society that was far more oral than ours and put high value on such an ability.

Book 4 of *Rhetoric for Herennius* consists of an introduction defending the author's decision to write his own illustrative examples of style (*elocutio*), followed by an account of kinds of style, virtues of style, and ornaments of style. Since there was probably more written on these subjects than on anything else relating to rhetoric in the following centuries, and since the Latin terms employed by the author often did not become the standard terminology, his account of style is less authoritative than his remarks on other parts of rhetoric, but it is a good picture of the subject as understood in the first century B.C. and has been probably the most read part of his work since late antiquity.

Three kinds of style are recognized (4.11–16): the *gravis*, or grand, *mediocris*, or middle, and *adtenuata*, or simple. This is the earliest extant statement of what became a permanent feature of traditional discussions of style. It perhaps originated in Theophrastus's lost treatise on style and had been codified by Greek rhetoricians of the third and second centuries B.C. Each style is illustrated by a passage (on a Roman theme) composed by the author. Furthermore, the three kinds of style have their defective counterparts, which may be called the swollen, the slack, and the meagre, and each of these is illustrated. The reader is not told when to use each style or how to combine them.

The author then discusses qualities that good style should exhibit (4.17–18). These are what Aristotle and Theophrastus had called "virtues." That term is not used—indeed the only general word applied to them is *res*, which means "things"—but the author does speak of *vitia*, or "vices" of style. The qualities he approves are a revision of Theophrastus's system, better known to us from Cicero's *On the Orator* and *Orator* and Quintilian's *Institutio*. Style, he says, should have *elegantia*, *compositio*, and *dignitas*. *Elegantia* may be translated "taste." It consists of two things, correct Latinity and clarity of expression. It may be remembered that Aristotle had identified clarity (with propriety) as the virtue of style and had discussed correctness a little later in his work. Correctness and clarity were the first two virtues in Theophrastus's scheme. *Compositio*, however, does not directly correspond to any of Theophrastus's virtues. It is a polished arrangement of words and is defined as avoiding a series of faults, such as excessive hiatus or alliteration. *Dignitas*, or distinction of style, is ornamentation and consists of the use of figures of speech, divided into those of words and those of thoughts, but neither the Greek word *schêma* nor the Latin word *figura* is used; the devices are called *exornationes*. What follows is the earliest surviving description of figures of speech. Forty-five verbal figures are given Latin names, defined, and illustrated, some being broken down into subdivisions. Sometimes comments are made about the effect of a figure: *repetitio*, the first figure mentioned, is said (4.19) to have charm, gravity, and vigor, but no effort is made to go beyond this to explain the psychology of the figure. The last ten verbal figures consist of those in which language departs from the usual meaning of a word (4.42). These are what the Greeks and later the Romans called "tropes," or "turnings," the most important of which is metaphor. Then nineteen figures of thought are similarly described.

The concepts of tropes and figures were unknown to Aristotle, though he did, of course, describe metaphor and other devices of style that came to be included among them. We do not have adequate sources to trace the early history of the listing and naming of tropes and figures. It was probably largely the work of Hellenistic grammarians and of Stoic philosophers interested in language. Once begun, however, the process became a major interest of Greek and Latin rhetoricians; rhetorical treatises discussed figures at length, and handbooks devoted exclusively to figures were published. Often, "style" was taken to mean the use of tropes and figures, a view that is found throughout the history of rhetoric.

Rhetoric for Herennius sets out the technical system of classical rhetoric in its five traditional parts, with its characteristic emphasis on judicial oratory, explication of stasis theory, and textbook approach. Many other handbooks followed. Most, like the early Greek handbooks, were ephemeral, soon replaced by the work of another teacher. Some of those written in the time of the Roman Empire did survive, however, and were studied by some medieval and Renaissance readers. Among these are the treatises of Apsines and Cassius Longinus in Greek and the works collectively known as the *Rhetores Latini Minores*, discussed later in this chapter. If the later history of classical rhetoric were represented only by these works, it would be a rather dry study. Fortunately, some works of greater intellectual merit have survived to give us a deeper understanding of the role of rhetorical theory and practice in classical culture. Here we shall briefly consider the most important.

Cicero's Dialogue *On the Orator*

Cicero pursued a successful career in politics and the lawcourts, culminating in his election as consul for 63 B.C. His political policy was conservative, aimed at defending the traditions of Rome and the constitution of the Roman Republic, but open to cooperation and compromise with the various socio-economic classes of the time, what Cicero calls a *concordia ordinum*. As consul he successfully put down the conspiracy of Catiline, but four years later Julius Caesar, Pompey, and Marcus Crassus joined power in a "triumvirate" that overrode many constitutional guarantees. Cicero was forced into exile for a year; after his return he was able to plead in the lawcourts but debarred from much political activity. To occupy his mind, he resumed some of his early studies. In 55 B.C. he wrote one of his most admired works, the dialogue *On the Orator*, in which he sought to create a synthesis of the philosophical, sophistic, and technical traditions of rhetoric as he understood them, and to project a vision of the ideal orator as the leader and protector of a just and orderly society.[8] In a letter dating from this period (*To His Friends* 1.9.23) he says he has written in the manner of Aristotle's early dialogues and sought to embrace the oratorical theory of all the ancients, both the Aristotelians and Isocrateans. By this time, Aristotle's *Rhetoric* had been published. Cicero had read it, and he adapts some Aristotelian concepts, including the three modes of persuasion, which are lacking in his earlier work. In addition, *On the Orator* has dramatic reminiscences of Plato in the setting of the dialogue and provides a response to some of Plato's criticisms of rhetoric.

The dramatic date of the dialogue is 91 B.C. The leading characters are the major orators of that time, whom Cicero had known when he was young, and especially Lucius Licinius Crassus, who is the spokesman for Cicero's own views. In Book 1 the question under discussion is the knowledge required of an orator. Crassus claims that an orator should be able to speak on any subject and thus should have studied philosophy, politics, history, and law. Scaevola thinks this ideal unattainable and stresses the need for a technical knowledge of law. Antonius limits the skills of an orator to an ability to use language and argument effectively in the lawcourts and in public meetings.

Antonius is the principal speaker in Book 2. Among other things, he gives an account of rhetorical invention, arrangement, and memory in nontechnical terms. Most important is his discussion of the sources of persuasion: "The whole theory of speaking is dependent on three sources of persuasion: that we prove (*probemus*) our case to be true; that we win over (*conciliemus*) those who are listening; that we call their minds (*animos . . . vocemus*) to what emotion the case demands" (2.115). This is Cicero's version of Aristotle's three modes of persuasion, though with a subtle difference: Aristotle's conception of ethos was essentially "rational," aimed at an impression of reliability; Cicero's *conciliare* is directed more to creating sympathy on the part of the audience.[9] Cicero also adjusts his conception of ethos to Roman procedure by making it apply both to the character of the speaker and to the character of the client (2.182). In a later work entitled *The Orator* (69) a version of the concept reappears and is given the name *officia oratoris*, "duties of the orator," which include *probare*, *delectare*, and *flectere*; that is, to prove, to delight, and to stir. These duties are then identified with the three styles: plain for proof, middle for pleasure, and grand for emotion. The duties of the orator are also discussed by Quintilian (12.10.58–59) and became an important concept in Saint Augustine's discussion of Christian eloquence in the fourth book of *On Christian Learning*.

Crassus is again the main speaker in Book 3, and he gives a long, nontechnical account of style, structured around the four Theophrastan virtues of correctness, clarity, ornamentation, and propriety. These subjects are taken up in greater detail in the later treatise *The Orator*, which is especially important for its account of prose composition and rhythm.

Cicero, like Greek sophists, was convinced from personal experience of the power and richness of oratory. It was, in his view, a true art form, not in the sense of a collection of rules but as a product of the creative imagination. He did much to clarify the study of rhetorical style, and in his speeches he is considered to be the greatest Latin prose stylist. He also had great personal interest in philosophical studies and was convinced that a statesman, to be effective, needed a deep understanding of logic, ethics, and philosophy. *On the Orator* is an eloquent statement of the ideal of the citizen-orator that dominated the culture of the Greco-Roman world in those periods when there was relatively orderly government and freedom of speech. The work influenced Roman views of rhetoric until late antiquity, but was known in the Middle Ages only in an incomplete version. The importance of the rediscovery of the complete text in the fifteenth century is seen in the fact that *On the Orator* was the first book printed in Italy (1465). Its subsequent influence was considerable, and it remains a major work in the history of rhetoric.

Quintilian's *Education of the Orator*

Marcus Fabius Quintilianus (ca. A.D. 39–96) was the author of the most extensive rhetorical treatise that survives from antiquity, the twelve books of *Institutio Oratoria*, or *Education of the Orator*. Quintilian was born in Spain but educated in Rome and practiced as an orator in the Roman lawcourts. About A.D. 71 the emperor Vespasian appointed him to an official chair of rhetoric paid for by the emperor, the first such appointment in history. Quintilian gave lectures to large groups of students and directed their exercises in declamation. On retirement from teaching, about A.D. 92, he spent two years on research and revision of his lectures, and he published his only surviving work—a few others have been lost—around A.D. 95.

Quintilian's *Institutio* is primarily a treatise on technical rhetoric, a vast handbook setting forth the standard theory of invention, arrangement, style, memory, and delivery, in that order and in great detail, with his own sensible comments and revisions.[10] He often begins a new section with a historical survey of the differences of opinion he finds in earlier authorities and then tries to reach a reasoned judgment about what is best. His discussion of the various views of *stasis* (3.6) is a good example of his method. Quintilian was a patient, moderate, reasonable man, dedicated to good teaching, clear thinking, natural expression, and loyalty to the empire. He defines rhetoric (2.15.34) as *bene dicendi scientia*, "the knowledge of speaking well." Use of the term *scientia* does not imply that rhetoric is an exact science; use of *bene*, on the other hand, does imply both artistic excellence and moral goodness, for it is a major theme of Quintilian throughout his work that the perfect orator must, above all, be a good man (see especially the preface to Book 1 and 12.1).

Quintilian incorporates rhetoric into a total educational system. This is perhaps the greatest significance of his work. Rhetoric is to him, following Cicero, the centerpiece in the training of the leaders of society and the responsible citizen. In Book 1 he inquires into the earliest lessons in speech, beginning with the newborn child. He follows the child through the school of the grammarian and in Book 2 arrives at the school of the rhetorician. Training there is considered at length in terms of both theory and practical exercises in declamation, which Quintilian regards only as means to train speakers for public life. He often criticizes the artificiality and excesses of declamation in his own time (e.g., 2.10). Quintilian was a humane educator, with a sincere concern for his students; he believed that they should be treated as individuals, encouraged to do their best, and treated with respect. In the earlier books Quintilian is chiefly addressing parents and teachers; in the later books he increasingly addresses the student directly. The twelfth and final book considers the adult orator. What knowledge does he need of law and history? What cases should be accepted? How should he round out his career? When should he retire?

The system of rhetoric that Quintilian expounds from Book 3 through Book 11 contains many details we would not otherwise know, but in most instances they do not represent innovations of his own. At several points in his work he adjusts Greek theory (as seen, for example, in Cicero's *On Invention*) to the actual conditions of Roman oratory. Changes in theory from the time of *Rhetoric for Herennius* are most evident in the account of style, though heavily indebted to Cicero. He adds a chapter on *sententiae* (8.5), the pointed or epigrammatic statements that had become very popular in the schools of rhetoric in the early empire, a long chapter on composition (9.4), drawn partly from Cicero's later work, *The Orator*; and a chapter on *copia*, or how to secure "abundance" of ideas and words (10.1). Quintilian's discussion of what the student should read to acquire *copia* leads him into literary criticism. By his time, lists of the most approved writers in each literary genre, including oratory, had been established by librarians and teachers, and he reviews these with memorable judgments, but the paramount question throughout this chapter is what literature can most help perfect an orator's skills.

The goal of education to Quintilian is training of a great orator. This orator must be morally good, and ethics is never far from Quintilian's mind; but the orator he envisions is more a part of the sophistic tradition as envisioned by Isocrates than the philosophical tradition from Plato and Aristotle. What Quintilian stresses (12.1) is the orator's ability to lead, to influence, even to dominate a situation. This orator is expected to know something about philosophy and to be good at reasoning, but Quintilian has little sympathy with philosophy as understood in his time. He identifies professional philosophy with trivial disputation or, worse, with social and political opposition to the state as seen among Cynic philosophers (the hippies of antiquity).

Quintilian's eloquent statement of the ideal orator was hardly affected at all by the fact that the Roman principate, or imperial government, had replaced the republic two generations before his birth, bringing with it autocratic government and censorship of publication, though preserving the structure of republican government in the senate and the lawcourts. Quintilian was personally indebted to the emperors and served as the tutor to the heirs to Domitian (4.1), whom he flatters in a conventional way (10.1.92). His contemporary, the historian Tacitus, in his *Dialogue on Orators*, lamented the loss of opportunity for political oratory in this period. Quintilian, in contrast, saw great hopes for oratory, even for an orator greater than Cicero (12.11). That would be very great indeed, since Cicero is very close to Quintilian's ideal. Quintilian sweeps away reactions against Cicero's ideas and style in the early empire—for example, in writings of Seneca the Younger—and reasserts imitation of his works as the basis of great rhetoric. "Cicero," he says in a striking *sententia*, "is the name not of a man, but of eloquence" (10.1.112).

Quintilian's endorsement of the Ciceronian style proved a powerful witness in the Renaissance, when the humanists sought to recover classical standards of style. Similarly, his endorsement of the oratorical ideal helped to ensure the survival of training in public speaking as the major consideration in the schools in later antiquity and into the Middle Ages, when practical opportunities for public speaking were eroded. To be sure, his influence varies over the centuries and is a less constant factor than the influence of *On Invention* and *Rhetoric for Herennius*. *Education of the Orator* was too vast to be used as a handbook by students, but parts were always read by leading scholars and teachers. In late antiquity it was quarried by rhetoricians writing abstracts, of whom Julius Victor is probably the best example. After the Carolingian period the text of Quintilian's work was known chiefly in a mutilated form, but even so, it exerted powerful influence on John of Salisbury, primarily as a work on education. In the fifteenth century, as we shall see, the full text was recovered, and thereafter its influence was great, at times exceeding that of Cicero. To Hugh Blair in the second half of the eighteenth century, the authoritative statement of classical rhetoric was still that by Quintilian.

Tacitus's *Dialogue on Orators*

A few years after the publication of Quintilian's *Institutio*, the historian Cornelius Tacitus (ca. A.D. 56–115), one of the most admired orators of the time, published a short dialogue that provides a vivid picture of the conditions of the time and deserves consideration by students of the history of rhetoric. It may be, at least partly, a negative reaction to Quintilian's optimism. The *Dialogue on Orators* purports to describe a meeting of important Roman orators in A.D. 75, during the reign of Vespasian.[11] Curiatus Maternus, apparently the spokesman for Tacitus, has abandoned public life, weary with the corruption of the times, and is writing tragedies on historical themes that allow him to express criticism of the ruler in a way he could not do openly as an orator. He feels that there has been a general "decline of eloquence." This is denied by Aper, an ambitious younger orator who has been able to exploit contemporary circumstances. A third speaker, Messala, replies to Aper, praising the eloquence of the past and criticizing that of the present as more the art of an actor than of an orator. Maternus urges Messala to explain the causes of decline, and the latter promptly attributes it to "the laziness of youth, the neglectfulness of parents, the ignorance of teachers, and forgetfulness of ancient discipline" (28.2). Somewhat similar complaints can be found in earlier works: for example, in the preface to the book on declamation by Seneca the Elder and in the opening chapter of Petronius's *Satyricon*. Messala then goes on to contrast the education of older times and contemporary schools of declamation with their subjects remote from reality. Part of the text is lost here; when it resumes (36.1), Maternus is speaking. He puts the blame for the decline of eloquence on the lack of subjects for great oratory that existed in the time of the republic. Disorders and dissensions fan the flames of great oratory but are no longer necessary under the government of the empire. An additional factor is that the lawcourts are now more practical and just but allow less scope to an orator. There is in the *Dialogue on Orators* no direct attack on the principate and no explicit complaint of loss of freedom of speech, but it is possible to read between the lines to see that this is felt by Maternus, at least, and all the speakers except Aper clearly feel nostalgia for the time of the republic.

Women in Roman Public Life

Roman women had somewhat great independence than had been true for women in Athens. They could not vote or hold office, but they participated freely in social life throughout Roman history, and some were well educated. The only extant writings by a Roman woman are forty lines of elegiac poetry by Sulpicia, written in the late first century B.C. and preserved with the works of Tibullus. They deal with her love for a young man and are admired for their warmth and lack of artificiality. Some upper-class Roman women exercised considerable influence on public affairs through husbands, brothers, and sons; the most famous examples are Cornelia, mother of the tribunes Tiberius and Gaius Gracchi; Livia, the proud and domineering wife of the emperor Augustus and mother of the emperor Tiberius; and Agrippina, wife of the emperor Claudius and mother of Nero.[12]

Valerius Maximus (8.3) mentions three Roman women who delivered public speeches in the first century B.C.: Amasia Sentia, Gaia Afrania, and Hortensia, daughter of the famous orator Hortensius. Among Quintilian's enlightened views was a recommendation that women should be educated as much as possible, but primarily so that they could contribute to the education of their sons (1.1.6–7). He praises the style of letters by Cornelia and says of Hortensia that the oration she delivered before Octavian, Antony, and Lepidus "is still read and not merely as a compliment to her sex." The speech sought remission of the tax imposed on the 1,400 richest women in Rome in 43 B.C. A version of it, in Greek, is found in the *Civil Wars* by Appian, written in the second century after Christ. Since we know from Quintilian that the speech still could be read around A.D. 95 when he published his *Education of the Orator*, it is possible that Appian's version is a translation of the Latin original, though perhaps abridged. If so, it is the only surviving example of public speaking by a woman from the classical period. According to Appian (4.32–34), Hortensia spoke as follows:

> As befitted women of our rank addressing a petition to you, we first had recourse to your own wives. Experiencing a hostile reception from Fulvia [wife of Antony], we have been driven here to the forum. You have already put to death our fathers and sons and husbands and brothers, complaining that you were wronged by them. If you also take our property from us, you reduce us to a condition unworthy of our birth and manner of life and womanly nature. Now if we women have not voted that any of you should be regarded as a public enemy, and have not destroyed your house or army or led another against you or hindered you from obtaining office or honor, why do we share the penalties when we have no share in the guilt?
>
> Why should we pay this tax when we have no share in public office or honor or military command or political power? Because you say there is a war? When have there not been wars? When have taxes ever been levied on women? Their sex has exempted them in all countries. Our mothers once rose superior to their sex and made contributions when you were in danger of losing the whole empire and Rome itself, at the time the Carthaginians were troubling you. Then they contributed voluntarily, and not from their landed property or fields or dowry or houses, without which life is not livable for free women, but only from their personal jewelry, and not with any fixed valuation nor in fear of informers or accusers nor by constraint or force, but what they were willing to give. What fear is there now among you for the empire or the country? Let war come with the Celts or Parthians and we shall not be inferior to our mothers in regard to the common safety. But we would never contribute to support civil wars nor aid you against each other. We paid no contribution to Caesar or Pompey, nor did Marius or Cinna force us to pay nor did Sulla when he tyrannized over the state. And you claim to be re-establishing the constitution!

Under autocratic governments there is no clear separation of legislative, judicial, and administrative powers as there is in republican or democratic government. The triumvirs were dictators, making and administering the laws, and they sat as a court to hear petitions. Roman emperors did the same, though they frequently referred matters to a council of advisers, and that continued to be the practice of medieval and Renaissance kings. Hortensia's speech is judicial and appeals for justice. She begins with a procedural question, pointing out that the women she represents have sought to resolve the question through the agency of women, and she supports her call for justice by citing the traditional understanding of the position of women. She attests to women's patriotism, anticipating a possible objection from the triumvirs, by a famous incident from the time of the Punic Wars, and she insists that whatever wrongs may have been done the triumvirs (she admits to none), women were guiltless and the alleged wrongs have been fully redressed by the proscriptions (death or exile) of men. The triumvirs were angry at the women and ordered them driven away, but there was a popular uprising on their behalf, and the next day the number of women to be taxed was reduced to four hundred and a general tax on male citizens, foreign residents, and priests was imposed instead.

The Hermogenic Corpus

The single most influential Greek rhetorician of Roman imperial times was Hermogenes of Tarsus, who began life as a sophistic prodigy in the mid-second century after Christ and to whom five handbooks of rhetoric are attributed. Largely unknown in the West until the Renaissance, they achieved an authoritative status among later Greeks, comparable to that of Cicero's *On Invention* in western Europe, and introductions to and commentaries on them were written through the Byzantine period. The five works make up a comprehensive rhetorical corpus, but three of them are of doubtful authenticity and were probably written at a later period. The two indubitably genuine works and the most original are *On Stases* (or *On Issues*) and *On Ideas* (or *On Types of Style*).[13]

Hermogenes' stasis theory resembles what is found in *On Invention*, but with many differences in detail. Instead of four coordinated categories (fact, definition, quality, and transference), he subordinates each kind to the one before it. An allegation is either uncertain or certain. If uncertain, the stasis is one of fact. If certain, the matter is either un-defined, which requires stasis of definition, or defined. If defined, it is either qualified in some way by the circumstances, requiring stasis of quality, or it is not. If it is not, the speaker may hope to deny the court's jurisdiction (transference). The student of declamation—the reader ad-dressed by Hermogenes—is to proceed down the sequence, conceivably ending up with the conclusion that the case cannot be undertaken. We know that sophists of the empire engaged in acrimonious discussion about the proper stasis to use in fictitious cases.

The other part of rhetoric to which Hermogenes made an original contribution was the theory of style. There were two schools of thought about style in the Roman period. One tradition was that there were three kinds of style: the grand, the middle, and the plain, sometimes expanded to four kinds, as in *On Style* by Demetrius. In Greek these were usually called "characters" of style (meaning "stamps, forms," not moral charac-ter). This is the tradition as found in *Rhetoric for Herennius* and in writings of Cicero and Quintilian; it remained authoritative in the West, as seen, for example, in Book 4 of Saint Augustine's *On Christian Learn-ing*. The other view of style, primarily found in Greek writers, is that there is an ideal form of style, made up of various qualities or virtues combined in different ways. This theory was developed by Dionysius of Halicarnassus, as seen in his work *On Composition*. A treatise of the second century after Christ, wrongly attributed to the great sophist Aristides, continued the attempt to define a variety of qualities of style. Hermogenes' *On Ideas* is a complex response to this tradition. The "ideas" or "types" of style that he describes are clarity, grandeur, beauty, rapidity, character, sincerity, and force, but some of these are broken down into subdivisions for a grand total of twenty ideas. Examples are sought in classical Greek writers, especially in Demosthenes, who oc-cupies in Hermogenes' thinking the place of the ideal orator. The con-cept of an "idea" of style perhaps comes from Isocrates' use of that word, but it was easily related to Platonic ideas. Hermogenes' writings on stasis and on ideas appealed to the categorizing instincts of Neoplatonists, the major intellectual leaders of the third, fourth, and fifth centuries in the Greek-speaking world.

Hermogenes' works were little known in the Latin-speaking part of the empire, and Latin writings, even those of Cicero, were little known in the Greek-speaking world. The two cultures gradually drew apart as the centuries passed, until by the early Middle Ages very, very few people in western Europe had any knowledge of Greek, and only a few in Byzantium had any knowledge of Latin. Finally, a Greek emigrant to Italy, George Trebizond, introduced Hermogenes' ideas of style to western Europe in 1426, and they soon became widely known in literary circles. Hermogenes' works again became school texts, and the "ideas" themselves exercised considerable influence on Renaissance literature.[14]

A large number of rhetorical works, including handbooks and commentaries, has survived in Greek from later antiquity. Many of the texts were collected by Christian Walz in the ten volumes of his *Rhetores Graeci*. Some works are available in English translation: among them are translations of the Hermogenic works cited above, handbooks by the Anonymous Seguerianus and Apsines in Dilts and Kennedy, *Two Greek Rhetorical Treatises*, and treatises on epideictic in Russell and Wilson, *Menander Rhetor*.

Rhetores Latini Minores

From later Roman times there are a number of Latin rhetorical handbooks that summarize all or part of the system of classical rhetoric. Their authors are known collectively as the Minor Latin Rhetoricians.[15] Julius Victor, mentioned in the discussion of Quintilian above, is one. Another is Aquila Romanus, who wrote a treatise on forty-eight figures of speech, probably in the third century. At some later time Julius Rufianus added thirty-eight more figures. Sulpitius Victor borrowed his title from Quintilian but went back to now lost Greek sources to restructure theory under the three duties of understanding, invention, and disposition. Fortunatianus composed his *Art of Rhetoric* in the form of questions and answers. Its most unusual feature is the theory of *ductus*, or treatment of the orator's intent, which George Trebizond took up in the fifteenth century. Cicero's *On Invention* was given a running commentary by Victorinus, who shows the influence of Neoplatonist philosophy, and by Grillius; both commentaries had some use in the Middle

Ages. The Minor Latin Rhetoricans were studied in the Middle Ages primarily because their works were briefer and easier to understand than the earlier sources, but also because they limited rhetoric to a more restricted field than had Cicero and Quintilian and thus to something closer to practical concerns of later times. Their contents suggest something of the function of rhetorical studies in the western empire in the fourth and fifth centuries. Although all these handbooks belong more or less in the Ciceronian tradition, there are also signs of a separate, more Greek influence. Their contents are largely confined to discussion of judicial rhetoric, with a strong emphasis on stasis theory. Attention to memory and delivery has almost vanished, and even interest in style has declined, except for figures of speech. These characteristics probably reflect, at least in part, changed conditions in society: training in written argumentation was becoming more important than in speech. Stasis theory continued to be useful in planning a defense or accusation, but procedures in court now debarred the kind of full-scale opening or concluding address with which Cicero had won his fame.[16]

Donatus's *Art of Grammar*

The discipline of grammar developed parallel with that of rhetoric during the Hellenistic and Roman periods, and the two often overlapped.[17] Grammar schools provided training necessary for a student before he entered a school of rhetoric, and some individuals taught both subjects. The most famous Roman grammarian was Aelius Donatus, who lived in the fourth century after Christ and whose works were the basic grammatical texts for the Middle Ages. He also wrote commentaries on the Latin poets Terence and Virgil.

The *Ars Minor* of Donatus, his most read work, is limited to discussion of the eight parts of speech (noun, pronoun, verb, etc.), but his fuller *Ars Grammatica* goes beyond strictly grammatical subjects to discuss, in Book 3, barbarism and solecism as faults of style as well as a number of ornaments of style also discussed by rhetoricians. A barbarism is a mistake in the form, spelling, or pronunciation of a word (in English, for example, pronouncing the *t* in "often" or spelling it without the *t*); a solecism is a mistake in the use of a word (for example, misusing "infer" for "imply" or vice versa). Donatus's position was that figures of thought belong to rhetoric; figures of speech, however, are included in grammar. He gives no general definition of a figure, but names, defines, and illustrates with a single example each of seventeen figures of speech, at least some of which may be familiar to modern students: prolepsis, zeugma, hypozeuxis, syllepsis, anadiplosis, anaphora, epanalepsis, epizeuxis, paronomasia, schesis onomaton, parhomoeon, homoeptoton, homoeoteleuton, polyptoton, hirmos, polysyndeton, and dialyton. The Greek names had become standard in Latin, replacing the attempts at translation in *Rhetoric for Herennius* and in Cicero's discussions. After treating these figures, Donatus turns to tropes, which he says are expressions transferred from the "proper" meaning to another for the sake of ornament or necessity. A trope is "necessary" if there is no proper word in good usage. Thirteen tropes are named and defined, each illustrated with one Latin example; many of the terms are still in use today: metaphora, catachresis, metalepsis, metonymia, antonomasia, epitheton, synecdoche, onomatopoeia, periphrasis, hyperbaton, hyperbole, allegoria, and homoeosis. Donatus's treatment of tropes and figures had great authority and was substantially repeated in handbooks by the Venerable Bede and other later writers. Since grammar was always more widely studied than rhetoric, and often out of Donatus's text, his discussion insured that these ornaments of style were known in later centuries even to students who did not study rhetoric as a separate discipline.

Technical rhetoric (and grammar) is technical and thus often dry. In antiquity it had to be learned by rote by teenage students, although their studies were enlivened by practice in declamation, with its bizarre themes of pirates and ravished maidens. The handbooks imposed rules, regularized, and codified—thus did not provide for subtlety or finesse. Of interest in this respect is the way classical rhetoric traditionally viewed style as a set of ornaments "laid on" to the thoughts that invention had provided and disposition arranged, rather than as something integral to the whole speech.

In contrast, one strength of classical instruction in rhetoric should be noted. It had a concept of unity of the material: it dealt with the whole argument, the whole speech, and in the case of Quintilian, the whole of education. As such, it tended to balance the obsessive concern of the other verbal disciplines, grammar, dialectic, and poetics, with words, single lines, short passages, or separate arguments. Plato's demand for a living discourse had filtered through to the rhetoricians as long as they held to their primary duty of teaching public speaking.

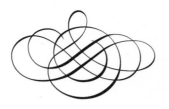

CHAPTER 6

Literary Rhetoric

As explained in Chapter 1, the word "rhetoric" in its primary meaning referred to features of oral discourse. In contrast, "literature," derived from the Latin word for "letters," properly refers to written discourse. The modern concept of "literature" as published works of aesthetic quality developed out of the term "belles lettres" in the seventeenth century in France and the eighteenth century in England.[1] In Greece and Rome there was no exact equivalent of "literature" in this sense. Its place was taken by the tacit assumption that the traditional literary genres—epic, lyric, and tragic poetry, for example—had special prestige. The only prose genres that came to be regarded as inherently "literary" were oratory, historiography, and some philosophical writing, such as the dialogue form. This view prevailed throughout the medieval and Renaissance period, and these are the literary forms discussed by critics until the eighteenth century, when the novel and other genres began to emerge as also deserving critical attention. In recent times, however, the concept of "literature," as well as that of genres and canons, has become somewhat problematic as implicitly elitist and sexist.

Rhetoric can be said to be prior to literature in the sense that oral discourse antedates the use of writing by thousands of years. Writing was invented—in the Near East, China, and elsewhere—to meet commercial and religious needs and was only later used for literary purposes, first for poetry, later for prose. Composition and publication long remained oral; written texts represented an attempt to preserve a particular version of an oral poem. Even when, in the sixth and fifth century

B.C. in Greece, poets began to compose in writing, most texts were being performed or orally recited, and only later circulated in written form; and throughout antiquity most readers, even privately, read aloud. Writers were well aware of the need to take into account the fact that their works would be heard. One sign of this is the concern with rhythm in written prose.

A great deal of Greek literature is in some sense public address, requiring oral performance and performing religious or political functions within the society similar to those of speeches. The Homeric epics and Greek tragedies and comedies were performed at festivals; much of Greek lyric poetry falls into the genres of wedding hymns, odes for the victors in athletic games, exhortations to military or moral virtue, and the like, all of which required oral performance.

Early Greek literature, imitating the society of which it was a part, made much use of the forms of oratory. We have only to think of the "speeches" in the Homeric poems or in Greek drama. Reports of speeches and debates were also a part of Greek historical writing from the beginning in the works of Herodotus and Thucydides. The use of oratorical forms in literary works continued throughout antiquity and was imitated in later centuries, especially in the Renaissance and early modern period. Furthermore, the fiction of orality, reflecting the priority of speech, has been preserved in modern language. Poets "sing," controversialists "speak out," and all writers are quoted as having "said" something.

If literature has been heavily indebted to rhetoric, rhetoric has also had a considerable debt to writing and to literature. It was the literate revolution of the fifth and fourth centuries B.C. in Greece that made possible the composition of the earliest handbooks and the preservation of speeches by great orators to be studied and imitated by later readers. Gorgias's innovative style was derived from imitating devices of poetry. Writers on rhetoric, beginning with Aristotle, constantly drew examples of invention and style from literary sources, and the apt use of quotations from poetry has been an effective rhetorical technique throughout history.

With the increased use of writing for composition and publication in the fourth century before Christ, a "slippage" of the concern of rhetorical studies from an oral to a written art begins to be evident. This process recurs throughout history and affects rhetoric as taught in schools, described in handbooks, and practiced in composition. It has created a "rhetorical literature," and has been given the name of *letteraturizzazione*, the "literaturization" of rhetoric.[2] Most extant Greek and Latin speeches were published after delivery, often in revised form intended to improve their effectiveness. The result was the adaptation of primary, oral rhetoric into a secondary, literary rhetoric for readers. Isocrates lacked the stamina or nerve for speaking in public; he was the first to write and publish speeches that were never publicly delivered and in so doing helped make oratory a literary genre. His speeches show great amplification and a lack of concern for immediate effect on an audience, at the same time that their smoothness of sound and rhythmical patterns indicate an expectation that they will be read aloud by others.

Orality remained a major feature of Greco-Roman society throughout its history; the orator remained the highest type of civic excellence as conceived by sophists, Cicero, and Quintilian; the nominal goal of schools of rhetoric was always training in public address. In this, as in other respects, ancient society was highly traditional. Nevertheless, rhetoricians gradually began to give more attention to reading and to written composition. One reason for this is that public debate on political issues declined in Greece after the fourth century with the loss of independence by the historic city-states, and it declined in Rome with the collapse of republican government in the first century B.C. The application of Roman law throughout the classical world reduced the opportunities for purely rhetorical achievements in the lawcourts, as Tacitus explains in his *Dialogue on the Orators*. Exercises in declamation often lost touch with contemporary realities, a fact lamented by Quintilian, Tacitus, and others. Although declamation provided training in verbal agility, it often came to be regarded as a form of entertainment. The skills students learned in rhetorical schools would be more useful for them now in writing than in speaking, especially if they experimented in later life in literary composition. The influence of rhetoric on literary composition is a striking feature of Greek and Latin literature from the first century B.C. to late antiquity, seen in the use of topics, in the presentation of ethos and pathos, in patterns of arrangement, in application of progymnasmatic exercises and features of declamation, and especially in the use of tropes, figures, and *sententiae*. Only in the case of epideictic, the most artificial and literary of the rhetorical genres, did the field of oratory somewhat expand, to be exploited by the speakers of the Second Sophistic in Greece and Asia Minor. In its most extreme form, found, for example, in the speeches of Himerius in the fourth century, the epideictic oratory of sophists became prose poems, filling a literary vacuum in a period when original composition in verse was in decay.

The clearest manifestation of *letteraturizzazione* is the concern of rhetoricians of the Hellenistic and Roman periods with literary composition, with imitation of literary models, and with the development of rhetorical criticism. This concern is seen particularly in monographs on style that are the commonest extant discussions of rhetoric in Greek from the first century B.C. to the second century of the Christian era. Increased interest in style began with the declining political role of public address and with the expanding role of rhetorical schools in education throughout the Greek- and Latin-speaking world.

Demetrius's *On Style*

The earliest surviving monograph on style is probably the treatise *Peri Hermeneias*, literally "On Expression" but commonly known as *On Style*.[3] It was traditionally attributed to Demetrius of Phaleron, a Peripatetic philosopher and Athenian statesman of the late fourth century B.C., but references in the work as well as some of the contents make this impossible. It was probably written in the mid-first century B.C., after the publication of Aristotle's *Rhetoric*, which is cited three times, and before emergence of the Atticism movement, which is not mentioned. Attribution to Demetrius of Phaleron may result from the fact that this author's name was also Demetrius.

The original opening of the treatise may be lost; where the text begins the author is discussing periodic sentences, based on Aristotle's description but introducing a distinction of three kinds: conversational, historical, and rhetorical. The historical period is regarded as a mean between the other two. The rest of the treatise consists of a discussion of four styles: plain, grand, elegant, and forceful, in terms of diction, composition, and subject matter, each with a corresponding faulty style and each illustrated with examples from classical Greek poetry and prose. The author criticizes earlier writers, probably Theophrastus and his followers, who recognized only two styles, plain and grand, and regarded the others as intermediate. Demetrius offers precepts for good written composition, but his work is also a sensitive piece of literary criticism, based on an implicit concept of taste (see, e.g., §§ 67, 137, and 287). His is the earliest extant Greek work that distinguishes between figures of thought and figures of speech and the earliest to use many technical terms that have become standard names of figures.[4]

An unusual feature of Demetrius's work is a discussion of letter writing (§§ 223–35). Letters, we are told, should be written in a mixture of the plain and elegant styles and are like one side of a dialogue. There is a short passage on letters in the late Latin rhetorical handbook of Julius Victor,[5] but otherwise the subject was neglected in ancient texts on grammar or rhetoric, surprisingly so, considering the great importance of correspondence in antiquity, the development of bureaucracies, and the publication of collections of letters by or attributed to major authors, including Plato, Isocrates, Demosthenes, Aristotle, Cicero, Pliny, and many later writers. Collections of model letters were made, fragments of which survive on papyrus, and there are a few short handbooks of Greek epistolography, identifying types of letters with examples,[6] but the rhetoric of letter writing was not a major concern until medieval times.

Dionysius of Halicarnassus

Dionysius was a Greek rhetorician who came to Rome about 30 B.C., where he taught composition and wrote a history of Rome and a series of works on style that, like the monograph of Demetrius, can be read as both instruction in prose composition for teachers and students and literary criticism of classical texts for readers. The most important of these works are a series of essays entitled *On the Attic Orators*—discussing Lysias, Isocrates, Isaeus, Demosthenes, Hyperides, and Aeschines—and a treatise entitled *On Composition*.[7] The introduction to the former work is the earliest statement in Greek regarding the Atticism movement, the attempt to restore style to the standards of the classical period that became a major objective of sophists in the following centuries. Dionysius also outlines stages in the historical development of Greek prose from the fifth to the fourth century, culminating in the artistry of Demosthenes. He distinguishes several types (*charactêres*) of style and discusses necessary and supplementary virtues of style, but he also considers the authenticity of speeches, the treatment of subject matter, the topics employed in different parts of a speech, and the use of ethos and pathos.

On Composition is the most detailed account we have of how educated Greeks reacted to the beauties of their native language. This subject, Dionysius thought, should fascinate the young and would be, more than argumentation, the most suitable object of their study. In none of his works does Dionysius show much interest in rhetoric as an art of persuasion; to him it is an aesthetic, literary subject. He considers the grouping, shaping, and tailoring of clauses; the four sources of "charm" and "beauty": melody, rhythm, variety, and propriety; and the three kinds of "harmony": the austere, of which Pindar and Thucydides furnish examples, the "polished," illustrated by Sappho and Isocrates, and the "well-blended," as found in Homer and Demosthenes.

Dionysius's studies of style marked an advance over the simplistic theory of three kinds of style as found, for example, in *Rhetoric for Herennius*. The approach was continued by later Greek rhetoricians, especially by Hermogenes in his work *On Ideas of Style*, discussed in Chapter 5.

Canons and Imitation

The Greek word *kanôn* means "a straight-edge ruler," and thus "a standard of measure" or a "model." Dionysius (*Letter to Pompeius* 3) says Herodotus is the best "canon" of historical writing in Ionic Greek, and Thucydides in Attic Greek; otherwise, the word is not much applied in Greek or Latin to authors or to books until it was taken up by Christians in the fourth century to refer to the canon of the books of the Bible, those regarded as divinely inspired. Nevertheless, a process of canonization of texts is evident in Greece, first informally in the acceptance of the Homeric and Hesiodic poems as the classics of the culture, and later more formally when the librarians at Alexandria drew up lists of literary classics, arranged by genres. We know these lists best from the survey of them given by Quintilian (10.1.46–84 for Greek writers, 85–131 for

Latin). Among the works of Plutarch is a spurious treatise *On the Ten Attic Orators*, and a canon of ten—Antiphon, Andocides, Lysias, Isocrates, Isaeus, Demosthenes, Aeschines, Hyperides, Lycurgus, and Dinarchus—has become traditional, but its origin is uncertain. Cicero, Dionysius, and Quintilian seem unaware of it; they omit reference to some orators in the canon and discuss others who are not in the canon of ten, for example, Gorgias and Demetrius of Phaleron.

More important than the existence of a formal canon of orators was the view, adopted by supporters of Atticism, that the great achievements of Greek literature, including oratory, were to be found in the past in the works of Homer, Aeschylus, Sophocles, Euripides, Herodotus and Thucydides, Plato and Xenophon, and the major orators, especially Lysias, Isocrates, Aeschines, and Demosthenes. These were the classic writers who brought the Greek language and the genres of literature to their highest development. Since then, quality was thought to have decayed. The way to recover standards was by "imitation" of these classics.

The word for "imitation" in Greek is *mimêsis*, which is used in several senses. To Plato, the visible world around us was a *mimêsis* of a non-material, eternal reality of "ideas." In Aristotle's *Poetics*, *mimêsis* is used to mean the imitation of action in the plot of a tragedy; and more generally the arts are said in Greek to "imitate" reality. To Dionysius of Halicarnassus, however, and to rhetoricians of the time of the Roman Empire generally, *mimêsis* in Greek and *imitatio* in Latin is the pedagogical method of learning to write by careful imitation of the style of approved models. The subject is discussed in a work called *On Imitation*, by Dionysius, only partially preserved, and more fully by Quintilian (10.2), who recognizes possible pitfalls if imitation is practiced too rigidly. Cicero is to him the finest model, but one should imitate the best qualities of a variety of models, depending on the subject matter, and weakness in some forms of style can be corrected by imitating passages strong in those characteristics. A student whose style is arid and dry should, for example, practice imitating florid passages, while one who tends to excessive ornamentation should seek models in the plain style. Quintilian's survey of Greek and Latin literature is not intended as an excursus on literary criticism; it is a series of suggested authors that students seeking to develop their *copia*, or "supply," of subjects and words, might imitate.

Longinus's *On Sublimity*

The most admired discussion of style in Greek is the treatise *Peri Hypsous*, or *On Sublimity*, attributed in the best manuscript to "Dionysius or Longinus" and "Dionysius Longinus."[8] In the Renaissance and early modern period the author was assumed to be Cassius Longinus, a rhetorician of the third century after Christ, famous in his own time and author of *Art of Rhetoric*, partially preserved. For convenience, modern scholars continue to refer to the author as Longinus, but they reject the attribution to Cassius Longinus and regard the treatise as written by an otherwise unknown writer in the first, or more probably in the second century after Christ. *On Sublimity* was rather little known until the late seventeenth century, when Nicolas Boileau-Despréaux, a leading neoclassical poet and critic, published a French translation and commentary. This began the cult of "The Sublime," which continued through the eighteenth century and will be noted in Chapter 11.

On Sublimity is explicitly intended to help a young student understand elevation in style by study and imitation of great literary models. "Sublimity," Longinus says in the preface,

> is a kind of summit or excellence of discourse and is the source of the distinction of the greatest poets and prose writers and the means by which they have given immortality to their fame. Whatever is beyond nature does not lead the hearers to persuasion but to ecstasy; and the marvelous combined with astonishment always prevails over the persuasive and pleasant because persuasion for the most part is in our own power, while the marvelous and astonishing exert invincible power and force and overwhelm every hearer. Experience in invention and in ordering and arranging material is not something seen in one or two passages but something we gradually see emerging in the web of the whole work. Sublimity, on the other hand, produced at the right moment, tears everything up like a whirlwind, and exhibits the orator's collected power. (1.3–4)

Although here Longinus draws a distinction between sublimity and rhetorical persuasion, he makes many uses of rhetorical concepts throughout the work. In chapter 8, he identifies five sources of sublimity: the power to conceive great thoughts and the use of strong and inspired emotion (*pathos*), which are aspects of rhetoric invention; and figures, word choice, and composition or word arrangement, which are three features of rhetorical style. He gives special emphasis to Plato and Demosthenes as stylistic models and compares Demosthenes with Cicero (12.4), one of very few references to Cicero by a Greek rhetorician.

Admiration for Longinus's treatise derives from his description of genius, in which he both uses and surmounts ordinary rhetorical concepts, and from the sensitive literary criticism found in his discussion of passages from Greek literature, including an appreciation of a poem by Sappho (10.2), which would otherwise have perished, and citation (9.9) of the opening of the Book of Genesis as an example of sublimity, something unparalleled on the part of a pagan Greek. The work ends (44) with discussion of the "decline" of eloquence, somewhat resembling what we found in Tacitus's *Dialogue on the Orators*. Here Longinus rejects what he calls "the explanation generally mentioned," that is, the loss of political freedom and loss of political reward. The fundamental cause, he concludes, is greed, pride, love of luxury, and idleness, which could be said to have dulled perception, turned ambition from civic duty to personal gain, and eroded cultural values.

Rhetoric and Poetics

A few words can be added here about the relationship between rhetoric and poetics as perceived in antiquity. Literary criticism is found in a variety of contents in Greek and Latin literature. Early examples include Aristophanes' comedy *Frogs*, which compares the styles of Aeschylus and Euripides, and Plato's dialogue *Ion*, which deals with poetic inspiration. Aristotle, who first defined many of the disciplines of learning, was the author of the first systematic treatise on poetics. In chapter 19 of that work he notes that what has been said about reasoning, i.e., demonstration and refutation, the use of emotions, and arguments about what is important or not important, in his work on rhetoric equally applies to the composition of speeches in tragedy. Conversely, a passage in the *Rhetoric* (3.2) refers the reader to the *Poetics* for more information on kinds of words.

Reading and analysis of poetry was an important activity in Greek and Roman grammar schools, and the technical features of poetry—

principles of versification and identification of tropes and figures—were discussed in works on grammar. This tradition continued into the Middle Ages and, together with some other parts of rhetoric, contributed to the *Artes Poetriae*, to be discussed in Chapter 9. Several Hellenistic philosophers, however, followed Aristotle's lead in writing treatises on poetics; the only such work to survive is that by Philodemus, part of which was rescued among papyri buried in the eruption of Mount Vesuvius in A.D. 79. Hellenistic speculations about poetry, and especially the lost work of Neoptolemus of Paros, are major sources for the versified *Art of Poetry* by Horace, written near the end of the first century B.C. It too was an important source for medieval discussions of poetry.[9]

Study of rhetoric was a central feature of ancient education, and rhetorical theory was both more fully developed and more widely understood than poetic theory. It is not surprising, therefore, that commentaries on classical texts from Roman and Byzantine times make great use of rhetorical concepts. Examples include the large commentaries on the Homeric poems by Eustathius and on Virgil's *Aeneid* by Servius. Commentaries were also written on the orators, surviving chiefly in the form of marginal notes in manuscripts. Those in Greek often apply the rhetorical theory of Hermogenes to explication of the text.

Overall, poetics can be regarded as parallel to and overlapping with rhetoric. Both share a concern with style, including word choice, tropes, figures, sentence structure, and rhythm. Ancient discussions of poetry are largely devoted to epic and drama, where speeches are attributed to characters, and both rhetoric and poetics are thus concerned with ethos and pathos and with the suitability of what is attributed to the character. "Decorum," corresponding to propriety as a virtue of rhetorical style, is a major theme in Horace's poem and in the literary criticism of later times that derives from his work. Rhetoric has its genres of deliberative, epideictic, and judicial oratory; poetics considers the conventions of epic, elegiac, lyric, tragic, comic, and pastoral poetry. Finally, exercises in *progymnasmata*—especially fables, narratives, descriptions, and comparison—were preparations for the study of rhetoric but were also preparatory for poetic composition.

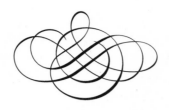

CHAPTER 7

Judeo-Christian Rhetoric

Judaism, Christianity, and, outside the western tradition, Buddhism and Islam, are religions of the word. They are based on sacred writings, and they developed preaching as a feature of their rituals. This was not the case with paganism; pagan priests performed rituals and sometimes delivered prophecies, but they did not preach. Christianity, in particular, had a commandment to preach the gospel. It sought to convert the world through the grace of God and by claims of miracles, testimony, sermons, biographies of saints, epistles, and other appeals or demonstrations; by example or a way of life, including martyrdom in the final necessity; and later in its history by the use of the rhetoric of architecture, sculpture, painting, music, and pageantry. This chapter will examine some rhetorical features of the Old and New Testaments, and the relationship between Christianity and classical rhetoric during the first four centuries of the Christian era, culminating in Saint Augustine's influential treatise, *On Christian Learning*.[1]

Old Testament Rhetoric

The books of the Old Testament were written at different times (some material perhaps as early as 900 B.C., other parts as late as the third century), not in the sequence in which they now appear, and are often the product of redaction, or composition by editors out of earlier material that was sometimes different in form and purpose. What is known as "form criticism" has brought about the recognition of types of biblical narrative, prophecy, poetry, and wisdom literature and of their *Sitz im Leben*, or setting in society, which includes the purpose for which they were written and the often different purposes for which they were used.[2] In antiquity the Jewish philosopher Philo (c. 30 B.C.–A.D. 45), the Christian bishop Augustine (A.D. 354–430), and other learned Jews and Christians made use of their training in rhetoric to interpret the Old Testament. Jewish and Christian interpreters in the Renaissance, including Martin Luther, did so as well, but rhetorical criticism of the Bible faded in the modern period with the decline of rhetoric as a discipline, only to be revived with the rebirth of rhetorical studies in the last third of the twentieth century. There is now a substantial body of scholarship applying the concepts of classical rhetoric and the techniques of modern literary criticism to both the Old and the New Testament.[3]

Taking the Old Testament as we have it, the evidence for rhetoric begins with the first chapter of Genesis, where creation is initially described not in terms of God's action, but of speech: "And God *said*, 'Let there be light'; and there was light." One of the very few references to the Jewish Scriptures by a pagan writer is the quotation of this passage in the rhetorical treatise of Longinus, *On Sublimity* (9.9). In contrast to creation by enunciation, the second chapter of Genesis records a different tradition in which God, like gods of pagan myth, *acts*, forming man, for example, out of the dust of the ground. Whoever put the first chapter first had a strong sense of the power of speech and in particular of the authoritative speech of God.

The fundamental rhetorical technique of the Old Testament is assertion of authority. God has given his law to his people. They are convinced because of who he is, what he has done for them, how he will punish them if they transgress, and how his word is revealed to them. In the New Testament the message of God is extended from a national group to all individuals in the world. Authority is a nonartistic analogy to ethos in classical rhetoric. It is confirmed by miracles and bolstered by pathos in the remembrance of the past suffering of people and by their fears of future punishment or hopes of future reward. In its purest form, Judeo-Christian rhetoric shows some similarity to philosophical rhetoric: it claims to be the simple enunciation of truth, uncontaminated by adornment, flattery, or sophistic argumentation; it differs from philosophical rhetoric in that this truth is known from revelation or established by signs sent from God, not discovered by dialectic through human effort. However, like Greek philosophical rhetoric, Judeo-Christian rhetoric gradually came to use features of classical rhetoric to address audiences educated in rhetorical schools, which appeared in Palestine following Alexander's conquest of the East. Judaism in the Hellenistic period already shows some influence of classical rhetoric, and early Christians gradually adapted features of classical rhetoric to their needs.

The fourth chapter of Exodus gives a valuable picture of rhetoric as found in the Old Testament. God has commissioned Moses to bring the children of Israel out of Egypt, but Moses distrusts his ability to persuade them. "But behold," he says, "they will not believe me or listen to my voice, for they will say, 'The Lord did not appear to you'" (Exod. 4:1). He feels the lack of personal authority. The Lord's reply is typical of the subsequent tradition; it is a series of signs or miracles demonstrating the authority of the commission; a rod is cast down and becomes a serpent, but Moses picks it up and it becomes again a rod; a hand becomes leprous and is restored; the Nile water will become blood. Authority is confirmed by miracles, and this, rather than logical argument, will be the primary mode of persuasion.

Moses, however, is not content. "Oh, my Lord," he says (Exod. 4:10), "I am not eloquent, either heretofore or since thou hast spoken to thy servant; but I am slow of speech and of tongue." The Lord replies (Exod. 4:11–12), "Who has made man's mouth? Who makes him dumb, or deaf, or seeing, or blind? Is it not I, the Lord? Now therefore go, and I will be with your mouth and teach you what you shall speak." The preacher is thus to be a vehicle through which an authoritative message will be expressed. If not Moses, it can be Aaron if Moses instructs him, and in fact it is Aaron who becomes the "orator" of the Jews. Some practical recognition is given to natural ability, but the Judeo-Christian orator, at least in theory, has little need of practice or knowledge of art as is required of the orator in the classical tradition. He needs only the inspiration of the Spirit.

Moses is to go back to Egypt and try to persuade Pharaoh to let Israel leave. In this effort another feature of Judeo-Christian rhetoric appears. Moses' success will depend entirely on the extent to which God allows Pharaoh to listen. "When you go back to Egypt," the Lord tells him (Exod. 4:21), "see that you do before Pharaoh all the miracles which I have put in your power; but I will harden his heart, so that he will not let the people go." And so it is. Moses does not persuade Pharaoh until the Egyptians are utterly despoiled and eager that the Jews depart. Persuasion takes place when God is ready, and not through the verbal activities or even the authority of Moses. Similarly, in the view of many Christians, God must act, through grace, to move the hearts of an audience before individuals can receive the Word, and if he does pour out his grace, the truth of the message will be recognized because of its authority and not through its logical argumentation. In its purest and most fundamental form, therefore, the basic modes of proof of Judeo-Christian rhetoric are grace, authority, and logos, the divine message that can be understood by human beings. These partially correspond, respectively, to the pathos, ethos, and logos of Aristotelian rhetoric.

Reason, or something taking the form of a reason, for belief or action, however, are needed by the human mind, and enthymemes are common in the Bible. The Ten Commandments of Exodus 20:2–17 provide examples, in that five of them are supported with some reasoning. When the Lord proclaims, "I am the Lord your God who brought you out of the land of Egypt, out of the house of bondage," he adds a witness of his authority. The commandment not to make a graven image is followed with an explanation and a threat and a promise, "For I the Lord your God am a jealous God, visiting the iniquity of the fathers upon the children to the third and the fourth generation of those who hate me, but showing steadfast love to thousands of those who love me and keep my commandments." Similarly, the commandment against taking the name of God in vain becomes an enthymeme with the addition, "For the Lord will not hold him guiltless who takes his name in vain." The commandment to keep the Sabbath is followed by an explanatory minor premise and conclusion, "For in six days the Lord made heaven and earth, the sea, and all that is in them, and rested the seventh day; therefore the Lord blessed the Sabbath day and hallowed it." Finally, "Honor your father and your mother," with the reason "that your days may be long in the land which the Lord your God gives you."

Speeches in the Old Testament often contain calls for judgment of the past, narrative of action in the future, and praise or blame, so, with a few exceptions, they are often not easily classifiable in the classical genres of judicial, deliberative, and epideictic oratory. The most characteristic form of extended speech in the Old Testament is the "covenant speech," an address built on the assumption of a covenant between God and the people of Israel. The general pattern of a covenant speech is, first, to strengthen the authority of the Lord by reminding the audience of what he has done; second, to add new commandments; and third, to conclude with a warning of what will happen if the commandments are disregarded. In a sense, the Old Testament as a whole could be thought of a vast covenant speech, consisting of the narrative of God's actions toward the people, his commandments to them, and the warnings of the prophets when the people fall away from their duty. Within the Old Testament there are, however, many specific examples of covenant speeches. Deuteronomy is made up in large part of three (chs. 1–4, 5–28, and 29–30), each containing a narrative of what has happened in the past, commandments, and warnings about the consequences of disobedience or promises of the blessings of obedience.

The pattern can also be seen in examples closer to the situation of classical public address. An example is the speech in the twenty-fourth chapter of Joshua. This consists of a narration of what God has done in Jewish history, put in the mouth of God himself and therefore given heightened authority (24:2–13). Joshua then adds his own injunction: "Now therefore fear the Lord and serve him in sincerity and faithfulness. . . . Choose this day whom you will serve . . . but as for me and my house, we will serve the Lord" (24:14–15). The people accept Joshua's examples as authoritative and agree that they will serve a lord who had done what the Lord has done. Joshua then reminds the people that the Lord is a jealous God, and gets them to commit themselves completely to the covenant, of which he sets up a stone as witness. The covenant speech of 1 Samuel 12 follows the same general pattern but prefaces it with a personal introduction. A characteristic of the covenant speech is that whatever the specific occasion, the basic message of Judaism—the covenant with God—is incorporated in the speech. This survives as a feature of some Christian preaching, in which whatever the text or starting point of the orator, the message tends to come down to a single theme of overriding importance, the kernel of the gospel, that "God sent into the world his only begotten son that through him we may have eternal life."

A second form of address in the Old Testament is that of prophecy.[4] The twenty-fourth chapter of Ezekiel shows how a covenant speech can be adapted to the circumstances of prophecy. Old Testament prophecy was to be very important for Christian rhetoric. Prophecy of the coming Messiah in Isaiah, for example, was converted into a basis of authority for Christianity as early as the preaching of the apostles and the composition of the gospels. Students of form criticism distinguish several different kinds of prophecy in the Old Testament. One is the "prophecy of disaster," which usually consists of an introductory word, an indication of the situation, a prediction of disaster, and a concluding characterization. Thus there is an analogy to the proemium, narration, proof, and epilogue of classical oratory based on the natural logic of development of ideas. Another kind of prophecy is "prophecy of salvation," and there are also some secondary forms, including one based on a trial situation, seen, for example, in Isaiah 41:21–19.[5]

Pure epideictic rhetoric in the Old Testament is represented by speeches in praise of God. In Exodus 15 is the song of praise sung by Moses and the people after the crossing of the Red Sea, and many of the Psalms are songs of praise. The Psalms also illustrate features of style that are characteristic of biblical epideictic. One is parallelism, a basic device of Hebrew poetry and of elevated language in many other cultures around the world. For an example, consider Psalm 80:8–11:

> Thou didst bring a vine out of Egypt;
>> thou didst drive out the nations and plant it.
> Thou didst clear the ground for it;
>> it took deep root and filled the land.
> The mountains were covered with its shade;
>> and the mighty cedars with its branches;
> it sent out its branches to the sea,
>> and its shoots to the River.

The second line of each couplet parallels the first, explaining or expanding it. It thus is a poetic analogy to the use of enthymemes in discursive language. Note too the use of allegory, in this case the "vine" brought out of Egypt. The imagery of the Psalms and of Isaiah, drawn either from nature or the agricultural life, is the source of much of the poetic language of Christian hymns and preaching. There are many examples, the most famous of which is perhaps Psalm 23, "The Lord is my shepherd." Imagery of this sort at first seemed very exotic and obscure to Greek and Roman readers, but it became a characteristic device of Christian style, and allegorical interpretation was accepted at an early time as a necessary tool of biblical exegesis.[6]

The Book of Proverbs, in its present form probably one of the latest parts of the Old Testament, has a special rhetorical interest in that it includes a number of precepts about fine speech. These resemble and are perhaps partly derived from Egyptian wisdom literature, such as the *Instruction of Ptahhotep.*[7] Rhetorical precepts in Proverbs, though not systematically organized, provide rules similar to those of Ptahhotep: for example, initial silence when confronted with verbal attack: "A man of understanding remains silent" (Proverbs 11:12), and, as Ecclesiastes says (3:7), there is "a time to keep silence and a time to speak"; restraint: "A soft answer turns away wrath, but a harsh word stirs up anger" (15:1); fluency: "The words of a man's mouth are deep waters; the fountain of wisdom is a gushing stream" (18:4); and especially truth: "He who speaks the truth gives honest evidence, but a false witness utters deceit" (12:17); and finally, the need for a pleasing style: "Pleasant speech increases persuasiveness" (16:21), and "pleasant words are like a honeycomb, sweetness to the soul and health to the body" (16:24). When in the fifteenth century Judah Messer Leon wrote, in Hebrew, a description of the rhetoric of the Old Testament using classical Greek and Latin concepts, he entitled his work *The Book of the Honeycomb's Flow.*[8]

New Testament Rhetoric

The books of the New Testament were written in Greek by and for speakers of Greek, many of whom were familiar with public address in Greek or had been educated in Greek schools. They thus employ some features of classical rhetoric combined with Jewish traditions and are modified by beliefs and values of Christianity.

Jewish Sabbath services in the Hellenistic period (that is, the last three centuries before Christ) and in later times included the reading of lessons from the Scriptures, followed by interpretation of the passages read and exhortations to the congregation to follow the law or to strive for moral excellence. This form of preaching, rather informal and spontaneous, shared among different members of the congregation, is the ancestor of the homily, the informal sermon of the early Christian churches. The homily was also influenced by Greek forms, in particular the diatribe, or moral exhortation, of the Stoic and Cynic philosophers, and later by methods of Neoplatonic philosophy.[9]

In the fourth chapter of Luke, Jesus is described as coming into Galilee and teaching in the synagogues in the way just described. In Nazareth he reads the lesson for the day, which is Isaiah's prophecy of the Messiah. Then he interprets what he has read: "Today this Scripture has been fulfilled in your hearing" (Luke 4:21). There is murmuring against him, but he refuses to perform miracles here to demonstrate his authority in his own country and with some difficulty escapes from the town. Later, at Capernaum he again teaches on the Sabbath, and "they were astonished at his teaching, for his word was with authority" (Luke 4:32). This time, according to the evangelist, he confirms his authority by expelling an unclean demon from a man, and the reaction in the congregation is: "What is this word? For with authority and power he commands the unclean spirits, and they come out" (Luke 4:36). Similar accounts can be found in Matthew, chapter 4, and Mark, chapter 1.

As a result of Jesus' preaching in the synagogues he attracted crowds from all parts of the country and, according to Matthew (5:1), preached to them the Sermon on the Mount. The sermon may be a composite document put together later by one of Jesus' followers on the basis of a variety of sermons and sayings; in Luke, verbally similar material appears in different contexts. The Sermon on the Mount is, however, the most extensive example of Jesus' preaching as envisioned in the early Church. It consists of five parts, the first being a poetic introduction, the Beatitudes, with their marked anaphora, or repetition of the same initial word in each clause. Second comes an expression of assurance not unlike a classical proemium (5:13–17). Then there is a statement of the relation of Jesus' teaching to Jewish law (5:17–48), followed by a series of injunctions about almsgiving, praying, fasting, and the like (6:1–7:20). Finally, there is an epilogue with a strong warning, and a parable comparing those who build on the rock of authoritative knowledge and those who build on the sand of foolishness (7:21–27). Although some elements are reminiscent of classical rhetoric, the techniques employed, including the parable, are largely drawn from Jewish traditions of speech. The persuasive quality of the sermon comes primarily from the authority projected by the speaker, seen especially in his relation to the law, but supporting statements are added to the Beatitudes and to the injunctions in the second half of the speech, thus creating enthymemes; for example, "Do not lay up for yourselves treasure on earth, . . . for where your treasure is, there will your heart be also" (6:19–21). Jesus is described in the gospels as adept at argumentation. His encounters with the Pharisees show an ability even at dialectic (for example, Matthew 15.1–9 and 22:15–22).

The basis of persuasion attributed to Jesus by the writers of the gospels, writing a generation or more after his death, is much like that found in the Old Testament. In Mark, for example, Jesus envisions Christians brought into court and says:

> But take heed to yourselves; for they will deliver you up to councils; and you will be beaten in synagogues; and you will stand before governors and kings for my sake, to bear testimony before them. And the gospel must first be preached to all nations. And when they bring you to trial and deliver you up, do not be anxious beforehand what you are to say; but say whatever is given you in that hour, for it is not you who speak, but the Holy Spirit. And brother will deliver up brother to death, and the father his child, and children will rise against parents and have them put to death; and you will be hated by all for my name's sake. But he who endures to the end will be saved. (Mark 13:9–13)

Mark may have projected back to Jesus a prophecy for things that happened between Jesus' death and the time Mark was writing. Among the points to be noted in this passage are the importance of testimony up to and including the example of martyrdom; the fact that no special eloquence is required, for as in Exodus God will provide the words; and an apparent assumption that the disciples cannot expect to persuade their judges of the righteousness of their cause: that is God's work, and as with Pharaoh, he seems to intend to harden their hearts. All of this is contrary to the assumptions of the classical orator, who expected to use his eloquence to overcome opposition to his ideas.

The word for "preach" in Mark 13:10 and commonly in the New Testament is *kêrusso*, which literally means "proclaim." It is what a herald (*kêryx*) does with a message, a law, or a commandment. The message is a *kêrygma*, or proclamation, and constitutes the gospel (*euan-*

gelion, or "good news"). Christian preaching in this tradition, which still exists, is thus not persuasion but proclamation, and is based on authority and grace, not on proof. Augustine says (*On Christian Learning* 4:21) that a good listener warms to the Scriptures not so much by diligently analyzing them as by pronouncing them energetically. Scriptural truth must be apprehended by the listener, not proved by the speaker. Somewhat surprisingly, and in contrast to the use of *kêrygma*, the early Church adopted the Greek word *pistis* to mean "Christian faith." In classical Greek, the meanings of *pistis* range over the spectrum of "trust, belief, persuasion"; it was, however, the word used by Aristotle for proof in rhetoric, and this usage became standard among teachers of rhetoric. The acceptance of *pistis* to mean "Christian faith" by the early Church implied at the very least that faith came from hearing speech, and provided a future opening for the acceptance of classical rhetoric within Christian discourse.[10]

A repeated message of the gospels is that not all will comprehend: some lack the strength for the gospel. In the parable of the sower (Mark 4) some seed falls along the path, some on rocky ground, some among thorns, and some in good soil. The parable ends with: "He who has ears to hear, let him hear"; but even the disciples do not understand and have to have the parable explained to them. To the generation after Jesus there was irony in the failure of those who heard or saw him to believe, and this irony is further developed in other ways as well, particularly in Matthew's gospel. The first will be last, the last first; the humble great, the great humble; the one who loves life shall lose it, the one who gives up life shall save it; and so on (cf. 16:25, 183, 20:26–28, 23:11). In these statements, and in the Beatitudes as well, there is a subtle but radical appeal, especially addressed to those in a lowly socio-economic station, to become Christians and identify themselves with the select. Such paradoxes become a permanent part of the Christian style of preaching, as do the vivid metaphors contained in the first-person proclamations so characteristic of John's gospel: "I am the living bread" (6:51); "I am the door to the sheep" (10:7); "I am the true vine" (15:1); and others.

Rhetorical criticism of the gospels and of the other parts of the New Testament, often employing some techniques of form criticism, literary criticism, and social history, has made great progress in the late twentieth century; a substantial body of scholarship is now available.[11] An important goal of rhetorical criticism is to try to hear the biblical texts as an ancient audience would hear them, and that means an audience familiar with classical rhetorical practice whether from study in school or from experience of the secular world. Among the early Christians there were many simple people with little formal education, but there were many others who had had some formal training in Greek language and rhetoric, and in the sophisticated Greek-speaking communities of Antioch, Miletus, Ephesus, Corinth, Alexandria, Athens, and Rome most hearers would have had some expectations of how a speech should be arranged and delivered. The gospels and the epistles were read aloud in Christian churches, and necessarily received by the congregation as speech.

In the case of the gospels, their four authors employ somewhat different rhetorical techniques, resulting from their own education and the audiences they addressed.[12] The gospel of Mark is probably the earliest and is an example of "radical Christian rhetoric," relying on authority with little appeal to logical argument. Matthew seems to have used Mark's gospel as one of his sources, but he is much more inclined to support proclamation with reason. It is notable that statements with no supporting reason in Mark often become enthymemes in Matthew's text. Matthew seems to be addressing a Greek-speaking Jewish audience with some education. Luke was a physician and well educated, probably including some study of rhetoric. He wrote for an audience that included Greeks and used the most polished Greek of the evangelists. His gospel resembles Greek historiography or biography to a greater extent than do the others. John's gospel, written later than the others and making some use of them, was apparently originally addressed to members of a Christian sect in Asia Minor, and has a distinctive eloquence, derived often from metaphor and evident from its opening words: "In the beginning was the Word, and the Word was with God, and the Word was God." The concept of "the Word" as the meaning and reason inherent in existence is found in Greek philosophy, of which John probably had some knowledge. He then identified the Word with Christ. John's gospel carries within it three factors of Christian rhetoric identified earlier—grace, authority, and the message "proclaimed" to mankind—and has provided an image elaborated by Christian preachers through the centuries.

The Apostles

Examples of preaching in the early Church can be found in the Book of Acts, traditionally attributed to Luke. Unfortunately, the picture may not be entirely historical. Many New Testament scholars believe that Acts was influenced by the conventions of Greek historical writing and that the speeches in Acts, like those in Greek historiography, are reconstructions of what might have been said, not evidence for what was actually said. That may be the case, but the speeches are not classical orations; they are generally consistent with Jewish rhetorical traditions and those developing in early Christianity as seen elsewhere. The speech of Stephen (7:2–53), which enrages the high priest and precipitates the first martyrdom, is similar in structure to Old Testament rhetoric as we saw it in the speech of Joshua and may be derived from a Jewish homily. It furnished an example for the rhetoric of later martyrs and is a Christian analogue to Socrates' apology. There are also seven speeches in Acts attributed to Peter and six attributed to Paul. Paul's speech of farewell at Miletus (Acts 20:18–35), his speeches while he was on trial at the end of the book, and Peter's first speech proposing a replacement for Judas (1:16–33) have special features, but the rest fall into the category of what is known as the "missionary sermon," the Christian counterpart of the Jewish covenant speech. A few examples may be considered briefly.

In the third chapter of Acts, Peter, after healing a cripple, stands on Solomon's porch in Jerusalem and addresses the people. He begins with the miracle just performed: "The faith which is through Jesus has given the man this perfect health in the presence of you all" (3:16). In explaining how this can be, Peter recapitulates the prophecy of the Messiah and the life and death of Jesus. He warns the people to repent and supports his warning with the authority of Moses, and at the end he returns to the miracle God has performed. The rhetorical elements are thus the familiar ones of authority or the law, prophecy and fulfillment, and warnings of the future.

Simpler in structure is the sermon delivered by Paul on a Sabbath day in the synagogue at Antioch in Pisidia (13:16–41). The law has been read, an invitation to speak is extended, and Paul rises. He rehearses Jewish history and the prophecy of the coming of the savior. He proclaims Jesus to be that savior and supports his claim with the prophecy of two Psalms. And he ends with a warning to those who do not believe. The only miracle cited is God's raising Jesus from the dead.

The most famous of all missionary sermons is that of Paul on "Mars' Hill," the Athenian Areopagus (Acts 17:22–31).[13] Here the message is adapted to Greek ears: it is not the prophecy of the Old Testament that is fulfilled, but the Greeks' own search for the unknown god, who is the God of all mankind. Paul does not attempt the dialectical reasoning of a Greek orator or philosopher: he proclaims the gospel, but the proclamation is supported by a Greek quotation: "As even some of your poets have said" (17:28). Then comes the usual call to repentance and warning of judgment. Up to this point, God has repeatedly been mentioned, but not Jesus, who is only referred to at the very end as the man through whom judgment will come. God has given assurance of this by raising his son from the dead, so that we have the miracle as a sign, but its truth is dependent, as is the proclamation as a whole, on the willingness of those present to accept Paul's authority. The claim that Jesus rose from the dead would not have seemed totally impossible to Greeks familiar with the stories of the descent into the underworld and return by Odysseus, Theseus, Heracles, and Orpheus; and Stoicism, the leading philosophical movement of this period, entertained monotheistic views not entirely inconsistent with Christianity.

Rhetorical schools were common in the Hellenized cities of the East when Paul was a boy, and he could have attended one, as did some other Jews. One of the most famous rhetoricians of the previous century, Caecilius of Calacte, was a Jew. Paul quotes Greek poets and was certainly familiar with the rhetorical conventions of speeches in Roman lawcourts, the oral teachings of Greek philosophers, and the conventions of Greek letter writing. Some biblical scholars see in his epistles an influence of the arrangement of contents, argumentations, and figures of speech of classical rhetoric that also appear in the diatribes of Stoic and Cynic philosophers.[14] The Epistle to the Galatians, for example, can be analyzed in terms of an exordium, narration, proposition, proof, and epilogue; and conventional rhetorical structures and devices of invention and style have been found in many of his other letters as well. What Paul has to say about rhetoric in his epistles, however, anticipates historically what is found in the gospels and in Acts. Probably the most important passage is the opening of First Corinthians. There were factions in the church at Corinth, and Paul's preaching had apparently been criticized as philosophically simplistic (3:1–4). In reply he says:

> For Jews demand signs and Greeks seek wisdom, but we preach [*kêrussomen*, "proclaim"] Christ crucified, a stumbling block to the Jews and folly to Gentiles, but to those who are called, both Jews and Greeks, Christ the power of God and the wisdom of God. For the foolishness of God is wiser than men, and the weakness of God is stronger than men. (1 Cor. 1:22–25)

The message is proclaimed, not proved; it is persuasive to those who are called or chosen by God. Paul employs an oxymoron, "wise foolishness," which ironically reverses the expectations of those who seek rational wisdom. He continues with an appeal to the less fortunate of the congregation:

> For consider your call, brethren; not many of you were wise according to worldly standards, not many were powerful, not many were of noble birth; but God chose what is foolish in the world to shame the wise, God chose what is weak in the world to shame the strong, God chose what is low and despised in the world, even things that are not, to bring to nothing things that are, so that no human being might boast in the presence of God. He is the source of your life in Christ Jesus, whom God made our wisdom, our righteousness and sanctification and redemption; therefore, as it is written, "Let him who boasts, boast of the Lord." (1.26–31)

This extended sentence has the structure of a syllogism. Its emotional intensity is built up by its constant repetition and by the way it plays on the paradox of the wise and the foolish, the weak and strong. Paul claims that this is all part of God's plan, and it is all summed up in one figure, Christ. Nothing else matters. Paul continues his apology:

> When I came to you, brethren, I did not come proclaiming to you the testimony of God in lofty words of wisdom. For I decided to know nothing among you except Jesus Christ and him crucified. And I was with you in weakness and in much fear and trembling; and my speech

and my message were not in plausible [*peithois*] words of wisdom, but in demonstration of the Spirit and power, that your faith [*pistis*] might not rest in the wisdom of men, but in the power of God. (2.1–5)

Paul is here probably comparing himself to his rival, the more conventionally eloquent Apollos (see Acts 18:24–28). Paul claims that as an orator he himself is nothing; his words are not persuasive as words; all lies with God. He continues:

Yet among the mature we do impart wisdom, although it is not a wisdom of this age or of the rulers of this age, who are doomed to pass away. But we impart a secret and hidden wisdom of God, which God decreed before the ages for our glorification. None of the rulers of this age understood this; for if they had, they would not have crucified the Lord of glory. But as it is written [Isaiah 64:4], "What no eye has seen, nor ear heard, nor the heart of man conceived, what God has prepared for those who love him," God has revealed to us through the Spirit. For the Spirit searches everything, even the depths of God. For what person knows a man's thoughts except the spirit of the man which is in him? So also no one comprehends the thoughts of God except the Spirit of God. Now we have received not the spirit of the world, but the Spirit which is from God, that we might understand the gifts bestowed on us by God. And we impart this in words not taught by human wisdom but taught by the Spirit, interpreting spiritual truths to those who possess the Spirit. (2:6–13)

This dialectical passage, with its succession of enthymemes, seems to reject the whole of classical philosophy and rhetoric. For rhetoric, the Pauline Christian can rely on God, both to supply words and to accomplish persuasion if it is God's will. In place of worldly philosophy there exists a higher philosophy, only dimly apprehended by human beings. Much of the work of Christian exegesis in the following centuries is built on the assumption that there is a wisdom in the Scriptures, deliberately obscure, which human beings can, in part, come to understand with God's help. The view of Saint Augustine and many other Christian exegetes was that God had deliberately concealed that wisdom to keep it from those who were indifferent to it, but would allow those who sought the truth to find a road to understanding.

Apologists and Polemicists

The Roman government was generally tolerant of the many religious cults found throughout the empire so long as these were themselves tolerant of others and did not seem to offer any threat to civil authority or public order. Christians, however, became suspect in the mid-first century and were intermittently persecuted for two hundred and fifty years because of their prophecies of the coming end of the Roman Empire, Romans' misunderstanding of what went on at Christian services, and Christians' refusal to sacrifice to the cult of the deified emperors. There was, however, widespread malaise in the Roman public, brought on by wars, economic depression, political oppression, natural disasters, and epidemics that created a cultural exhaustion and search for meaning outside the present life. Christianity seemed to offer hope to the hopeless and disaffected, and the number of Christians grew. After a final attempt to put down Christianity at the beginning of the fourth century, the Roman government gave in. In A.D. 313 the emperor Constantine issued the Edict of Milan, on toleration of the Christians. Subsequently the Church became more worldly and the phenomenon of the nominal Christian with a good education (the Latin poet Ausonius, for example) made its appearance. During the course of the fourth century the legal standing of the Church changed from an object of persecution, to toleration, to official status, and finally to a position of exclusive religious authority when Theodosius prohibited pagan worship in A.D. 392. Many pagan temples were converted into Christian churches. Worship of the old gods survived privately or among country folk (*pagani*) for two or three centuries, but with little influence. With its political victory, the Church began to exert strong influence on the rulers of the state, and they in turn began to use aspects of Christianity to secure and extend their power in society.[15]

In the second century, when Christianity was growing in many parts of the empire and hostile notice of it was being taken by Roman officials,[16] some educated Christians sought to defend the new religion in written works addressed to influential and educated Greeks and Romans, making use of ideas from Greek philosophy, employing techniques of classical rhetoric, and seeking to refute charges and rumors directed against the new religion. These "apologists" probably did not expect their arguments to convert the addressees or readers to Christianity—that could happen only through the grace of God—but they could hope to improve the public image of Christianity. Charges made against Christians were often outrageous slanders, derived from rumors about what went on in Christian ritual, such as the allegation that Christians met at dawn to kill small children, drink their blood, and eat their flesh. About A.D. 125 a Greek named Quadratus composed a defense of Christianity and presented it to the emperor Hadrian on one of his visits to Athens, a center of schools of rhetoric and philosophy. The single fragment of this work that is preserved (in Eusebius, *Church History* 4.3.2) emphasizes that the miracles of Jesus were genuine and well attested by many people. More philosophical in tone are the extant works of Justin Martyr, who addressed his *Apology* to the emperor Antoninus Pius and also wrote a philosophical dialogue with the Jew Trypho, arguing for the fulfillment of prophecies of Christ. Athanagoras composed his *Apology*, or *Appeal for the Christians*, about A.D. 180 in Alexandria, using references to Greek philosophers and poets to support his claims that Christian worship and teaching were innocent, reasonable, and moral.[17]

The Greek apologist who made the greatest use of the techniques of classical rhetoric is probably Tatian. He composed his *Oration to the Greeks* around A.D. 167. This is largely an invective against Greek claims of intellectual and moral superiority and is an odd mixture of sophistic cleverness and Christian piety. He seeks to show that Moses was older and greater than Homer and that the Greeks learned most of what they claimed to know from non-Greeks, but he says it with figures of speech, a care for composition, and quotations from the Greek poets. Even the Greek language does not escape his criticism, and there are a few nasty words about Greek rhetoric: "You have contrived rhetoric for injustice and slander, for a price selling the free power of speech, and often representing something as now just, and again as not good, and [you have contrived] the art of poetry to describe battles and the loves of the gods and the soul's corruption" (1.2c). The use of rhetoric to denounce rhetoric is not rare in Christian writing, but of course it is also often found in some philosophical writing beginning with Plato's dialogues.

Tatian's rhetorical apology is not unique. Another example from about the same time is the *Letter to Diognetus* by an unknown author who attacks paganism and Jewish sacrifices in an artificial, antithetical style.

The age of the apologists was the age of the Second Sophistic. The great sophists of the time took little notice of the new religion, but in their celebrations of Greek religion and culture it is possible to see a defensive note against new ideas creeping into society. Around A.D. 178 a Greek Platonist named Celsus became alarmed at what he viewed as the threat of Christianity to Roman society and security, and he sought to check the growth of the new religion and persuade Christians to become more responsible citizens in a work called *The True Teaching*. The original text is lost, suppressed later by the Church, but it inspired Origen's reply, *Against Celsus*, which was published in 248 and is often regarded as the greatest of Christian apologetic treatises. We shall return to Origen below.

Apologists also appeared in Latin, where they gave a new vigor to literary composition from the intensity of their feeling against paganism. The first great Latin representative of Christian invective is Tertullian (ca. A.D. 160–225), a native of Carthage who practiced as an advocate in Rome, was converted to Christianity, and returned to Africa to devote himself to the Christian cause. His apologetic works include the fiery appeal *To the Heathen*, which pleads against repression of Christianity, and the *Apologeticus*, written in A.D. 197, which is addressed to the governors of Roman provinces and seeks to refute the arguments against Christians in judicial terms. Tertullian also wrote on moral and doctrinal subjects and attacked heretical groups. When Tertullian became a Christian he did not cease to be a rhetorician. Not only does he fully exercise the stylistic techniques of rhetoric, such as figures of speech, but he follows the rules for judicial oratory as a basis of the structure of his works, he makes use of stasis theory in defining issues, and he draws on traditional topics or finds their counterparts in the Scriptures.[18]

Almost from the beginning, Christianity was divided into sects with differing beliefs about theology and the sacraments. Each group regarded itself as orthodox and others as heretical, and they quarreled bitterly about even trivial matters, promising that their opponents would burn in Hell. Some major Christian thinkers, including Tertullian and

Origen, were accused of heresy by opponents within the Church. Very little of the writing of groups eventually judged heretical survives, since it was suppressed by the victorious orthodox, but there is a considerable body of extant works attacking heresies in which their teaching can be found. The earliest major polemicist whose writing survives was Irenaenus, a Greek from Smyrna who became bishop of Lyons in Gaul in the second half of the second century. His treatise *Against Heresies* not only attacks splinter groups but includes an early systematic presentation of orthodox Christian doctrine. A later and larger work of the same sort is the *Refutation of All Heresies*, written about A.D. 200 by Hippolytus, bishop of Rome, but almost all major Christian writers, including Augustine, engaged in attacks on heresy.

Preaching

There were four major forms of preaching in the early Church: the missionary sermon, prophetic preaching, the homily, and the panegyrical sermon. The first three will be discussed here, the fourth later in this chapter. A missionary sermon aimed at conversion of non-Christians to the new faith. The best early examples are those found in the Book of Acts, discussed above. Prophecy, a continuation of the Jewish tradition, is occasionally mentioned (e.g., Acts 11:27). It was characterized by inspiration, including "speaking in tongues," and might be practiced by anyone and in any kind of setting. No very good example of it survives unless we use the term to describe the so-called *Second Epistle of Clement to the Corinthians*. This is not an epistle and not the work of any known author; the imagery in its seventh chapter suggests that it may be a sermon delivered at Corinth in the second quarter of the second century on a day when the city was thronged with visitors to the games. Passages of Scripture from the Old and New Testaments are taken up and exegesis offered. There is some allegorical interpretation. The language, even when the Bible is not being quoted, is often biblical. There is no clear outline or structure, but the various quotations and themes are strung together to make an exhortation to the Christian life, more moral than theological in emphasis. The greatness of salvation imposes duties on human beings, in the author's view, which they dare not refuse for fear of punishment. Unity is given chiefly by the repeated call to repentance, which becomes more insistent as the end of the work approaches. It is this tone that justifies calling the work an example of the prophecy sermon.

The third, and most important, form of Christian preaching was the homily. *Homilia* is a Greek word meaning "coming together, conversation," or informal address, which came to be used to describe an oral interpretation of a text of Scripture. The word is also used in Latin, though the Latin word *sermo* also meant "conversation" and not a formal sermon (*oratio*). The structure of a homily was determined by the order of words in the text being elucidated, to which material from other texts might be added. In its most natural form, homily is lacking in artifice and does not aspire to systematic exposition of theology. The speaker simply tells the congregation what they need to know to understand the text and apply it to their lives. In an early Christian context the speaker would ordinarily be a bishop, whose chair, like that of a sophist, gave him the right to speak, and the congregation would be made up of catechumens (people preparing for admission to the Church) or fully baptized members.

As the Church gradually began to employ more artificial rhetoric addressed to cultured audiences, some homilies ceased to be simple words, in style, structure, or content, addressed to simple hearts. Around A.D. 165, when the Second Sophistic was in full flower, Melito, bishop of Sardis, composed a sermon on Easter that is a homily, since it is based on a text, but is characterized by a flamboyant literary style reminiscent of the sophist Gorgias.[19] This is how Melito begins:

This account of the Hebrew exodus has been read,
and the words of the mystery have been made clear,
how the Lamb has been sacrificed
and how the people have been saved.
Learn then, beloved,
how the paschal mystery is new and old,
eternal and transitory,
corruptible and incorruptible,
mortal and eternal:
but new according to the Word,
ancient according to the Law,
transitory in prefiguration,

eternal in grace,
corruptible through slaughter of the Lamb,
incorruptible through the life of the Lord,
mortal through his burial in the tomb,
immortal through his resurrection from the dead.

The text is prose, but setting the words as poetry illustrates the affinity of the style to Hebrew poetry.

Less flamboyant in style but more sophistic in content is the homily *What Rich Man Is Saved?* by Clement of Alexandria, dating from around A.D. 200. Clement was a learned Greek, a student of Platonism who became a teacher in the Christian catechetical school in Alexandria. In his numerous and often elegant writings Clement began to make serious use of Greek philosophy and to take a step toward the Christian Platonism of the following century. Clement's sermon is a homily on Mark 10:17–31 and was addressed to a prosperous congregation that found biblical injunctions against wealth rather inconvenient. After a proemium comparing rich men to athletes, a prayer, and a reading of the text, Clement enters on exegesis. Ostensibly simple passages, he says, often require more careful attention than obscure ones. In telling the rich man to sell all that he has and give to the poor, Clement says, Jesus is not literally talking about wealth, but enjoining man to strip his soul of its passions! The style of this homily is antithetical, and the thought is often complex. Most quotations are from the Bible, but there are references to pagan philosophy (for example, in chapter 11).

Origen

The history of homiletics, and preaching in general, is closely related to the history of hermeneutics, the science and method of exegesis or interpretation of texts. What dialectic is to rhetoric in Aristotelian rhetoric, hermeneutics is to homiletics in Christian rhetoric. The most important figure in the development of Christian hermeneutics and the greatest Christian thinker between Paul and Augustine was Origen (ca. 184–254), who passed his life in times of trouble and persecution in Egypt and Palestine. It is largely because of Origen's scholarship that the homily abandoned casual structure, even when keeping a simple style of expression, and took on the complexity of analysis of a text at several layers of meaning.[20] Allegorical interpretation was fundamental to Origen's method, and here he had the model of interpretations of Greek poetry by Stoic and Neoplatonic philosophers and of the Old Testament by the Jewish philosopher Philo.

In the fourth book of his treatise *De Principiis*, or *On First Principles*, Origen discussed the interpretation of the Scriptures. His discussion was widely known both in Greek in the East and in the West in the Latin translation of Rufinus. Origen regarded the Bible as divinely inspired in every respect. Just as man consists of body, soul, and spirit, so does Scripture have three similar levels, arranged intentionally by God for man's salvation (4.1.11). The corporeal level is that of the letter, the literal meaning, and is addressed to those who are still children in soul and do not yet recognize God as their father. This level of meaning, however, imparts edification (knowledge of religious law and history, for example). The interpretation is one of the soul when a passage is interpreted to have a specific but nonliteral application to the audience addressed. This might often be regarded as the moral level. Origen has the least to say about this level, but he cites 1 Corinthians 9:9, where Paul applies to his own ministry an injunction from Deuteronomy against muzzling the mouth of an ox: "Is it for oxen that God is concerned? Does he not speak entirely for our sake?" Finally, the interpretation is spiritual when we recognize in it essential truths of Christianity. This might be called the theological level.

Since all of the Bible was regarded as inspired, all of it contains the spiritual level. Origen thought, however, that there were many things in the Scriptures that could not possibly be interpreted literally. Such otherwise incomprehensible passages include metaphors or figures to be interpreted allegorically. Origen calls these figures *typoi*, or types (4.1.9), and explains their function: "God has arranged that certain stumbling-blocks, as it were, and offences and impossibilities should be introduced into the midst of the law and the history in order that we may not, through being drawn away in all directions by the merely attractive nature of the language, either altogether fall away from the true doctrine, as learning nothing worthy of God, or by departing from the letter come to the knowledge of nothing more divine" (4.1.15). Obscurity thus alerts the attention of the reader and encourages meditation. Origen was not troubled by the possibility that many different meanings can be found in a single text when interpreted allegorically, for we may be sure that the inspiration of Scripture contains far more meaning than we can ever succeed in fathoming (4.1.26). Nor was he disturbed by the possibility of misinterpretation, since by definition the spiritual meaning is a portion of the universal message of Christianity, which provides a test of validity. Origen concludes the discussion (4.1.27) by saying that we must not be concerned about words and language, for every nation has its own, but look to the meaning of the words, remembering at the same time that there are things that cannot be conveyed by the words of human language and are made known directly through apprehension. The truth of the Christian message is seized by the soul without reasoning about it. This apprehension is then strengthened and explored by study of Scripture, where meaning exists at an immediate logical level, but where there are one or more parallel and higher levels of meaning that the Christian can hope to perceive. Such a view opens the floodgates of mysticism and allegory but is inconsistent neither with Christian rhetoric as it had earlier been defined nor with the use of myth in the works of Plato, which Origen knew well. Origen's three levels of interpretation might be renamed the logical, the ethical, and the emotional. In that case, they can be thought of as hermeneutic counterparts of Aristotle's logos, ethos, and pathos, the modes of rhetorical persuasion. Origen's emphasis on seeking God's intent in a text rather than in the literal meaning can be compared to that part of stasis theory in rhetoric that explored the issue of the intent versus the letter of a law.

Origen applied his hermeneutic theory in homilies and commentaries on books of the Bible. We have 21 homilies in Greek and another 186 in Latin translations made by Saint Jerome (ca. 348–420) and by Rufinus of Aquileia (345–411). Like the homilies of other famous Fathers of the Church, these were read in churches in later times in place of original sermons. Some seem addressed to a general congregation, some to catechumens, some to a small group of disciples. According to Eusebius (*Church History* 6.36), Origen allowed shorthand writers to take down his *dialexeis*, or disquisitions, which he delivered in public later in life at Caesarea in Palestine. (A system of shorthand had been developed in the first century B.C. and was widely used during the Roman Empire in both Greek and Latin.) It is occasionally possible to compare Origen's treatment of a biblical text in a homily with his treatment in a commentary. The content is generally similar, but the style is different. In the homily the speaker is mindful to persuade his audience not only to understand and believe the text but to live in accordance with it, whereas the commentaries are generally limited to exposition of the meanings. The three levels of meaning discussed in *On First Principles* can all be illustrated in the homilies, but the emphasis is on the moral and spiritual levels. The homilies are in a simple, generally classical style, filled with direct address, imperatives, and rhetorical questions to maintain audience contact. The structure is essentially that of the text, but considerable intensity of emotion is sometimes achieved. This is chiefly because of the spiritual nature of the material and the fact that since all the text is inspired, the great features of the Christian message are inherent in every verse.

Gregory Thaumaturgus

From A.D. 230 until his death in 254 Origen was head of a school of Christian studies at Caesarea in Palestine. One of his students was Gregory of Pontus, usually distinguished from the many other Gregorys by the name Gregory Thaumaturgus, "The Wonderworker." Gregory was born around A.D. 215, studied rhetoric and Latin in Pontus, and at the age of around fourteen was sent to the famous school of Roman law that had developed at Beirut. Because of family connections he ended up in Caesarea instead, and entered Origen's school. He remained there eight years before returning to play an important role in the Christianization of his native province. On departing from Origen's school, about A.D. 238, Gregory delivered a speech of which a text survives. It is the first true example of Christian epideictic oratory, one of the very few surviving speeches of the third century, and the only extant example of a Greek farewell speech.

Despite a general movement away from rhetorical conventions as the speech unfolds, there can be no doubt that Gregory set out to create an epideictic speech in the manner of the sophists. The style, for which he apologizes on the grounds that for some years he has been studying Latin and law and not Greek oratory, is the affected Greek of a rather inept sophist, filled with elaborate sentences and amplification. The proemium, by far the most sophistic part, utilizes commonplaces from the rhetorical schools, including the inexperience of the orator and the analogy of oratory and painting. There are echoes of Homer, Euripides, Demosthenes, and Plato and a quotation (141) from the Delphic oracle. Although the point of view is certainly Christian, Christianity is treated as philosophy and there is no mention of Christ. It is very much the kind of speech that a student leaving the school of a sophist might give as a tribute to his teacher if the latter were a Christian and if the audience were made up of individuals educated in both Christianity and sophistic rhetoric.

It is clear that some tension existed between rhetoric and religion in Gregory's society. He attempts to meet this problem by careful definition. He says (4–5) that it is not the case that Christian philosophers do not desire beauty and accuracy of expression for their thoughts, but rather that they give a second order of priority to words, and faced with the choice between cultivating holy and divine power of thought or practicing speech, they choose the former. Origen, says Gregory (74), had used every resource of speech to persuade him to join the school, although he regarded the teaching of rhetoricians as a small and unnecessary thing (107). In fact, Gregory found Origen's love and moral influence the most persuasive thing about him (84). He treats Origen as almost divine (10, 13) and describes the relationship between them in terms of David and Jonathan in the Old Testament (85). Gregory criticizes pagan philosophers at length (160–69). They are irrational, choose doctrines at random, and stick to them unreasonably without considering the evidence, as opposed to the more objective and truth-loving Christian philosophers. Origen in particular has, he says, encouraged his students to study widely in all but the atheistic writers and to draw conclusions on the basis of the evidence. It would be interesting to know what Origen thought of this performance. His reaction may have been negative. A letter from Origen to Gregory survives, probably written after the oration. It is time, Origen says, for Gregory to move beyond philosophy to Christianity and to become a partaker of Christ and of God.[21]

Eusebius

Gregory's speech is not a sermon and thus not an example of Christian preaching, but it serves as an introduction to the fourth form of preaching, which is Christian epideictic, sometimes also called the panegyrical sermon. This is chiefly known from the fourth century, when Christianity and public life came together. Unlike other forms of preaching it has no Jewish antecedents. An early figure in Christian epideictic was Eusebius (A.D. 260–340), who had been trained in the same Christian school in Caesarea that Origen had once headed and is a leading authority for our knowledge of Origen. After escaping the persecutions of the opening years of the fourth century, Eusebius became bishop of Caesarea and later a friend and adviser of Constantine, the first Christian emperor. His most famous work is his *Church History* in ten books, which includes a panegyrical sermon he delivered at Tyre, probably in 326 or 327.[22] It ostensibly honors Paulinus, bishop of Tyre, for his reconstruction of the church there, which had been destroyed in the persecutions. Eusebius says that all of the rulers of the Church delivered panegyrics to the assembly in the rededicated church. "One of moderate talent," that is, himself, then came forward, having prepared an arrangement of a speech. This probably means that he had premeditated his topics and their order, but perhaps not his expression, for which he relied on extempore inspiration and experience. Possibly a shorthand transcription was made at the time of delivery; in any event, the speech was written up, polished, and published in the *Church History* (10.4).

Although Eusebius calls this speech a panegyric, it has few of the elements of sophistic encomium. We are told nothing at all about Paulinus except that he directed the rebuilding of the church. The church itself, however, is described in detail (10.4.37–46), in which we may see an example of rhetorical ecphrasis. The visible and material church is made a counterpart of a greater and invisible spiritual Church; God has chosen the emperor to cleanse and reconstruct the spiritual world. The speech has a strong religious movement, and the issues involved were life-and-death matters to the speaker, who had witnessed the persecutions and the victory of his faith. On this occasion he symbolically recapitulates the whole history of Christianity and sees it justified. There are often great advantages to a speaker in being against something as well as for something; Eusebius exploits this in saying that the devil's frustrations at Christ's power led him to attack the rebuilding of the church. This leads to a comparison (*syncrisis* in rhetoric) of Christ and Satan (10.4.14); but Christ is the cornerstone, and the devil is foiled again.

A second panegyrical sermon by Eusebius is the speech he delivered in A.D. 336 in honor of Constantine's thirtieth jubilee.[23] The first ten chapters seem to be addressed to the court and celebrate the emperor's rule and his theological, political, and moral virtues. That the emperor had come to power by deceit and violence, including murder, is overlooked; Christian panegyrists were no less given to flattery than were pagans. There is very little use of Scripture here, but neither does the speech observe the specific topics of classical encomium. The second half (chs. 11–17) is addressed to Constantine and is a sermon on the glory of God, intended to lead the uninitiated to the truth and to show the religious basis of Constantine's deeds. This part of the speech draws more heavily on scriptural sources and makes a spirited attack on pagan cults.

The great masters of the panegyrical sermon are the three Cappadocian Fathers, Gregory of Nazianzus (ca. 329–89), his friend Basil the Great (ca. 330–79), and Basil's younger brother, Gregory of Nyssa (ca. 331–95). Gregory of Nazianzus and Basil studied rhetoric and philosophy together at Athens in the 350s. One of their teachers was the pagan Himerius, whose highly artificial declamations and orations survive; another was Prohaeresius, who was a Christian, although his school seems to have differed very little from those of his pagan counterparts.[24] All three of the Cappadocians were intimately familiar with classical Greek literature, especially with the works of Plato. All three were masters of Greek prose, Gregory of Nazianzus being the most ornate, Basil the most restrained. Virtually every figure of speech and rhetorical device of composition can be illustrated from their sermons, treatises, and numerous letters; they were also influenced by rhetorical theories of argumentation and arrangement, and probably by theories of memory and delivery as well, though direct evidence is lacking. Yet all three are repeatedly critical of classical rhetoric as something of little importance for the Christian, and none of them made, or even seriously attempted, a synthesis of classical and Christian rhetorical theory to describe their own practice. They were more successful in uniting Greek philosophy with Christian theology.

Gregory of Nazianzus

Forty-four orations by Gregory of Nazianzus are extant.[25] A number of these deal with specific occasions in his life or events involving members of his family. Others are doctrinal, such as the sermon on baptism (40) or the five "theological" sermons preached in Constantinople in 380. Two (4 and 5) are invectives against the emperor Julian, who attempted to reestablish paganism, and are interesting for Gregory's outrage at Julian's prohibition against Christians teaching classical literature and rhetoric. Eight speeches are encomia showing strong influence of the structure and topics of such works as delivered by sophists of the period or as described in the handbook on epideictic by the rhetorician Menander. Funeral orations for Gregory's father, his sister Gorgonia, and his brother Caesarius, as well as his encomium for Basil, are especially close to sophistic models. The latter is probably the masterpiece of sophistic Christian oratory, an extraordinary tour de force, replete with subtle variations on familiar topics, figures of speech, rhetorical comparisons, reminiscences of Plato and Greek history and mythology, and an emotional peroration. The following passage shows some of the equivocation, or at least complexity, of Gregory's feelings about the place of eloquence and pagan learning in Basil's life:

> When he was sufficiently instructed at home, as he was to neglect no form of excellence nor to be surpassed in diligence by the bee that collects what is most useful from every flower, he hastened to the city of Caesarea [in Cappadocia] to attend its schools. I mean this illustrious city of ours, since she was also the guide and mistress of my studies, and not less the metropolis of letters than of the cities which she rules and which have submitted to her power [as provincial capital]. To rob her of her supremacy in letters would be to despoil her of her fairest and most singular distinction. Other cities take pride in other embellishments, either old or new, depending, I think, on their annals or their monuments. This city's characteristic mark, like the identification marks on arms or on plays, is letters.
>
> What followed, let those tell the story who instructed him and profited by his instruction. Let them tell of his standing in the eyes of his masters and his companions, as he equaled the former and surpassed the latter in every form of learning. Let them tell what glory he attained in a short time in the sight of all, both of the common people and the leaders of the city, exhibiting a learning beyond his years and constancy of character beyond his learning. He was an orator among

orators even before the sophist's chair, a philosopher among philosophers even on questions of philosophical theory. And, what constitutes the highest tribute in the eyes of Christians, he was a priest even before attaining the priesthood. In such wise did all defer to him in everything. With him, eloquence was only an accessory, and he culled from it only what would be helpful for our philosophy, since its power is necessary for the exposition of thought. For a mind incapable of expressions is like the movement of a paralytic. But philosophy was his pursuit, as he strove to break from the world, to unite with God, to gain the things above by means of the things below, and to acquire, through goods which are unstable and pass away, those that are stable and abide.[26] (§ 13)

Gregory goes on to describe their years together in Athens, "the home of eloquence, Athens, a city to me, if to anyone, truly golden, patroness of all that is excellent."

Basil himself is not so outspoken about the glories of eloquence. He delivered several panegyrical sermons, but even in one of these (*On Gordius the Martyr* 142d–143a) he belittles the rules of encomium that he sometimes employs. As a preacher he is best known for his homilies, especially the *Hexahemeron*, a series on the six days of creation. A work of considerable interest is a short address, *To the Young On How They Should Benefit from Greek Literature*.[27] This is in the general tradition of Plato's exclusion of the poets from his ideal state, but it takes a moderate point of view: pagan literature can be usefully read by Christians, but careful choice should be exercised to avoid mythological stories contrary to truth and morality. Portions of the poems of Homer, Hesiod, and Theognis, and Prodicus's *Choice of Heracles* are approved. Nothing is said about the study of oratory or prose style.

John Chrysostom

The most admired Christian orator in Greek is John Chrysostom ("John the Golden-Tongued," A.D. 347–407), a student of the pagan sophist Libanius and later patriarch of Constantinople. A number of his panegyrics survive, of which seven on Saint Paul are the most famous, but he was most at home in the homily. Even so, the style and mannerisms of classical rhetoric were a part of his nature, and he could not resist flamboyant comparisons, jingles, and parallelisms.[28] His most striking homilies are probably the twenty-one entitled *On the Statues*, delivered in 377, which illustrate his compassion as well as his social responsibility in a time of political crisis. He acknowledges that style can be helpful in relieving the tedium of an audience and in securing variety, and says, "When we have the care of the sick, we must not set before them a meal prepared at haphazard, but a variety of dishes, so that the patient may choose what suits his taste. Thus we should proceed in the spiritual repasts. Since we are weak, the sermon must be varied and embellished; it must contain comparison, proofs, paraphrases, and the like, so that we may select what will profit our soul."[29]

The rhetorical practice of Gregory of Nazianzus and John Chrysostom, and to a lesser extent Basil and Gregory of Nyssa, goes considerably beyond what they seem to tolerate in theory. The reason for this is partly their education; they were so thoroughly imbued in school exercises with the use of figures of speech and devices of comparison that these had become second nature to them. Partly their audiences are responsible. Chrysostom tried in vain to prevent congregations from applauding in church (see *Homilies* 30.4 = 60, p. 225 Migne). We need not charge such thoughtful Christians as Gregory or John with pandering to the mob, but they were concerned with moving the hearts of their audience and inspiring their lives; their sermons were usually addressed to sophisticated urban congregations, and the devices of sophistic rhetoric had become the cues to which their audiences responded and by which their purposes could be best accomplished. This trend was a victory for classical rhetoric. Ambitious young Christians now did not hesitate to study in the schools of rhetoric, and as the fourth century advanced, the Christian communities included more and more educated people.

A case in point, and the most classical of fourth-century Christian preachers, was Synesius of Cyrene (ca. 370–413), who became a Christian bishop on the stipulation that he be allowed to keep his wife and to retain his Neoplatonic philosophical belief that human souls existed before birth. Among his works is a striking epideictic speech, *On Royalty*, delivered to the young emperor Arcadius in 400, urging him to be a ruler in the image of God. Such "royal discourses" were a tradition among sophists. His playful encomium of baldness is also preserved. His treatise called *Dion* is named for the sophist Dio Chrysostom and starts with him, but becomes an apology for Synesius's Greek way of life and his interest in philosophy and rhetoric. Intellectually and morally, Synesius was superior to many sophists, but he retained a sense of the traditional culture and kept his independence.[30]

The Latin Fathers

By the end of the fourth century, leaders in the Greek Church had reached an accord with classical culture that made it possible for some Christians to draw on the rich tradition of Greek philosophical thought and to utilize the forms of classical rhetoric, but no theoretical restatement of a Christian Greek rhetoric was made. Consideration of this subject will be resumed in Chapter 8. In the Latin-speaking West the situation was somewhat different. There was, long before Christianity, some Roman hostility to Greek culture, which never entirely faded away. For example, Gn. Julius Agricola, governor of Britain in the late first century after Christ and the subject of a biography by his son-in-law, Tacitus, always remained grateful to his mother "for preventing him from going more deeply into the study of philosophy than was suitable for a Roman senator" (Tacitus, *Agricola* 4.4). The teaching of rhetoric had met with initial hostility at Rome in the second and early first centuries B.C., but by the Augustan period rhetoric was entirely acclimatized throughout the Roman Empire. Unlike philosophy, it seemed to be useful, concrete, and manly. This distrust of philosophy and acceptance of rhetoric is often reflected in the Christian Latin writers. In addition, it is a remarkable fact that of the eight greatest Latin Fathers of the Church, five (Tertullian, Cyprian, Arnobius, Lactantius, and Augustine) were professional teachers of rhetoric before they became Christians, while the other three (Ambrose, Hilary, and Jerome) had been thoroughly trained in the rhetorical schools.

Tertullian (ca. A.D. 160–225) had deep distrust of Greek philosophy; it was he who phrased the famous questions "What has Athens to do with Jerusalem? What concord is there between the Academy and the Church?" (*On Prescription of Heretics* 7), but the sentence following these questions, and the context as a whole, shows that what really concerned him was the way philosophical arguments became the basis of heresies or agnosticism. Tertullian wrote with respect of Demosthenes and Cicero (*Apologeticus* 11 and 15–16), and he never directly attacked rhetoric as such.[31] Christians should not teach it; they can and must study it (*On Idolotry* 10). We have already seen how deeply colored by rhetoric was Tertullian's own writing.

Cyprian (*To Donatus* 2), writing in the mid-third century, and Arnobius (*Against the Nations* 1.58–59), writing late in the third century, both distinguished secular from Christian rhetoric, claiming that in the latter the subject and not the style mattered, although Arnobius regarded syllogisms, enthymemes, and the like as useful to a Christian controversialist. Ambrose (ca. 337–97) anticipated Augustine in finding eloquence in the Scriptures, especially in what he called the "historical" style of Luke's gospel (*On Luke*, prologue 1). He was himself an orator of great power, both in the homily form, where he follows the exegetical method of Origen and shows the influence of Basil, and in the panegyrical sermon, such as his funeral orations for the emperors Valentinian II and Theodosius. These are the earliest extant Christian panegyrics in Latin.[32]

Of all the Fathers, Saint Jerome (ca. 348–420) was the one most torn between a feeling for style or love of eloquence and a belief that the art of rhetoric is a worldly product, at best of no true importance for a Christian and possibly inimical to the Christian life. His greatest achievement was his Latin translation of the Bible, and he says that translations of Scripture should avoid deliberate literary qualities in order to speak more directly to the human race in general than to rhetoricians or philosophers (*Epistles* 48). Characteristic of Jerome is the story he tells in the long epistle to Eustochium[33] in which, imitating Tertullian, he asks, "What has Horace to do with the Psalms, Virgil with the gospels, Cicero with the apostle?" (*Epistles* 22.29); we ought not to drink both the cup of Christ and that of the devils. Jerome describes how he had tried to cut himself off from pagan learning but could not forego his library. He would fast, but he would then read Cicero. When he read the Old Testament prophets, their style revolted him. He became distraught and ill; preparations were made for his funeral. Suddenly, in a dying condition, he had a vision (22.30) in which he seemed to be caught up to heaven and the judgment seat. He threw himself on the ground and averted his eyes before the heavenly judge, who asked him to state his "condition." Jerome replied that he was a Christian. "You lie," came the answer. "You are a Ciceronian, not a Christian; 'For where your treasure is, there will your heart be also' [Matthew 6:21]." The bystanders prayed for his forgiveness, and Jerome himself promised to mend his ways: "Lord, if I ever have secular books, if I ever read them, I have denied thee." Like Saint Peter, it is doubtful that he could keep his promise.

Lactantius

Two Latin writers attempted statements of rhetoric in terms that could, perhaps, resolve some of the tensions felt by Christians like Jerome. The earliest of these is Lactantius (ca. 250–320), whose major work was written forty years before Jerome's birth. Although Lactantius's literary abilities were appreciated in antiquity, the synthesis he attempted was not widely understood until the Renaissance, when he emerged as a founder of Christian humanism: "the Christian Cicero."

Lactantius was a North African teacher of rhetoric who acquired fame and was appointed by the emperor Diocletian to teach Latin rhetoric in the Greek-speaking city of Nicomedia in Bithynia, the eastern capital of the empire before the foundation of Constantinople. There he was converted to Christianity and lost his chair under the oppressive Galerius, but later Constantine named him the tutor of his son Crispus. Lactantius is the master of a beautiful Ciceronian prose style and was very familiar with Latin literature and classical philosophy. As a Christian, he saw in philosophy numerous superstitions and errors that needed refutation, but he also saw a reflection of the same divine truth that was more authoritatively revealed in the Bible. It troubled Lactantius that educated pagans would not give serious attention to Christianity because of the illiterate style in which the Scriptures were written and because Christian apologists defended their faith with prophecies and revelations that seemed absurd to many intellectuals. He thus took upon himself the mission of setting forth the teachings of Christianity in a style that would win the respect of the most discriminating readers, with arguments based on evidence in Greek and Latin writers, not solely on that in the Bible. The most important result of this effort was the treatise in seven books entitled *Divine Institutes*, completed around A.D. 313.[34] The time was a crucial one. Constantine had decreed the toleration of Christianity and many people were beginning to give serious attention to the new faith for the first time.

The introductory chapters to the separate books of *Divine Institutes* contain discussion of Lactantius's objective and methods, and from these and a few other passages (e.g., 3.13) a philosophical Christian rhetoric emerges. Although Lactantius had probably read Plato, his main sources are the writings of Cicero and the Neoplatonists of his own time, and secondary Latin sources. Lactantius's basic position is not unlike Aristotle's: if the truth is defeated, we have only ourselves to blame; if the attention of the audience is once secured, the truth can be demonstrated, and good will prevail. To Lactantius, of course, the truth is divine truth, the Word. He does not reject inspiration, revelation, and miraculous conversion, and he claims (e.g., 6.1.1) the tutelage of the Holy Spirit, but he associates divine intervention in the rhetorical act with the mind's recognition of truth when effectively presented. The Christian orator thus has much he can do. The passage in which this view is best summed up is the introductory chapter to the third book.

Though a learned, reasonable, and eloquent man, Lactantius was not a powerful thinker. His work probably had the greatest appeal to an audience already favorably disposed to a religion being adopted by the court, but unwilling to put aside everything education and tradition had taught it to admire. Lactantius's synthesis did not satisfy a Christian like Jerome, who was still troubled by the conflicting claims of Christian and classical learning. A more successful and more widely accepted answer was to be that of Augustine.

Saint Augustine

Aurelius Augustinus was born 13 November 354 at Thagaste, about two hundred miles southwest of Carthage on the edge of the Numidian desert.[35] In the *Confessions*, completed about 400, he has left a remarkable portrait of his psychological, religious, and intellectual development from birth to middle age. Although Monica, his mother, was a devout Christian and a strong influence upon him, Augustine was thirty years old before he fully accepted Christianity. After elementary studies at Thagaste he was sent to the larger town of Madaura to begin rhetoric. His father, however, wanted more for him and decided to keep him home for a year while money was saved to pay for rhetorical studies in Carthage. These he began in 370 and continued for three years, planning a career as a pleader in the lawcourts (*Confessions* 3.4.6), but at this point there occurred the first step in what proved eventually to be his conversion to Christianity: "In the usual order of study I came to a book of a certain Cicero, whose tongue almost all admire, but not his heart to the same extent. But there is a book of his containing an exhortation to philosophy and called *Hortensius*. That book changed my perception and changed my prayers, O Lord, to you" (*Confessions* 3.4.7). Strangely, given Augustine's praise of it, the dialogue *Hortensius* is one of the few works of Cicero that medieval scribes neglected, so it has not survived.

As Augustine goes on to explain, what pleased him in Cicero was the advice to love and search for wisdom, though what gave him pause was the absence of the name of Christ. Under his mother's influence, it was to Christianity to which he tended to look for "philosophy"; thus he turned, apparently for the first time, to the serious reading of the Scriptures. And he was totally put off. This may be partly the result of the version he read: Augustine's knowledge of Greek was not very good; Jerome's translation of the Bible had not yet been made, and Augustine read the Scriptures in an inferior earlier Latin version. But even with a better version of the Bible he probably would have been dissatisfied. The whole object of his education up to this point had been the cultivation of literary taste. What he found in the Bible seemed quite "unworthy to be compared to the dignity of Cicero" (3.5.9). Dissatisfied with Christianity, he turned to Manichaeism, which combined some features of Christianity with a dualism of good and evil, derived from Zoroastrianism. He says (4.1.1) that from his nineteenth to his twenty-eighth year he was led astray and led others astray. What he means is that he continued his association with the Manichaeans and that he supported himself as a teacher of rhetoric, teaching declamation first in Thagaste (4.4.1–7), after 376 in Carthage (4.7.12). He tells only a little about his school (4.2.2–3) but claims he was motivated by a desire to make money and that though he taught how to save the guilty, he did not teach how to condemn the innocent. Cicero had recommended the same principle (*De Officiis* 2.51).

In 383 Augustine decided to go to Rome and teach rhetoric there. Friends urged him to do so, and he claims he was persuaded, not because of the higher fees and great glory he could earn there, but because student discipline was so much better than in Carthage (5.8.14). About this time he became dissatisfied with Manichaeism and interested in Academic philosophy, by which he means the skeptical tradition found in Cicero's philosophical works. He spent less than a year in Rome (5.12.22–13.23). Although his school seems to have been successful, and discipline was indeed better than at Carthage, he was not really satisfied with the situation. When the great pagan orator Symmachus was asked to nominate a candidate for the chair of rhetoric at Milan, Augustine applied. Symmachus listened to him declaim and gave him the nomination. Thus Augustine arrived in the city that was the administrative capital of the western empire and far more thoroughly Christianized than either Carthage or Rome at the time. In Milan he taught rhetoric for two academic years (384–86), but he also heard the sermons and enjoyed the friendship of Ambrose, bishop of Milan, and from him learned the method of explaining the Old Testament figuratively, which made it possible for him to accept the Scriptures with full faith.

Augustine's spiritual and intellectual quest culminated in the summer of 386 with the events in the garden that he describes in the eighth book of the *Confessions* and that involved the act of will that made him in his own eyes a Christian. One consequence of that conversion was the resignation of his chair of rhetoric, but he resigned quietly, waiting until the fall vacation and alleging poor health as a reason (9.2.2–4 and 9.5.13). With a group of relatives and friends he then withdrew into the country to engage in meditation, study, and conversation, which resulted in a series of philosophical dialogues including *Against the Academics*, *On the Happy Life*, and *On Order*. In the spring of 387 he returned to Milan and was baptized by Ambrose on Easter Sunday. In the following years he went to Ostia, to Rome, to Carthage, and home to Thagaste. In 391 he was ordained a priest at Hippo and in 395 was consecrated bishop there, a position he held until his death in 430.

Augustine's output of sermons, commentaries, treatises, and letters was enormous and is in large part preserved. Those that are most directly related to rhetoric are reviewed in the following paragraphs.

In the spring of 384, perhaps as preparation for beginning to teach in Milan, Augustine planned a series of handbooks on the liberal arts. He apparently completed the one on grammar, though it does not survive.

In the case of the other arts, including rhetoric, he wrote some notes, but only those on dialectic survive. There is a small Latin treatise on rhetoric that is attributed in one manuscript to Augustine; it is of some importance for information about Hermagoras's stasis theory but is probably not by Augustine.[36]

The early dialogue *On Order* is a discussion of divine providence in terms that reminded Augustine of his earlier composition of a panegyric (1.9.27). It culminates in a description of the introductory studies appropriate for those who wish to understand the order of the universe and to live in accordance with God's law. Knowledge, Augustine says (2.9.26), comes by authority or by reason, and reason embraces an exposition of the seven liberal arts of grammar, dialectic, rhetoric, arithmetic, music, geometry, and astronomy, all somewhat purified of pagan elements. Dialectic, to be studied before rhetoric, deals with how to teach and how to learn, in which reason reveals its nature, desires, and powers. But ordinary people follow their feelings and habits, and for them to be taught the truth it is necessary not only to make use of logical reasoning, but to arouse emotion. Here is the realm of rhetoric, which is described as a seated allegorical figure with a lap full of charms to scatter to the crowd in order to influence it for its own good (2.13.38). We shall meet a similar allegory in Martianus Capella's slightly later treatment of the liberal arts. What is said in *On Order* can be taken as Augustine's preliminary thoughts in the winter between his conversion and his baptism. It was to be followed by more profound considerations of the role of rhetoric in Christian knowledge.

The dialogue *On the Teacher* (*De Magistro*) was finished around 389. From the outset the tone is more religious and Christian than in *On Order*, but references to Cicero and Virgil still came naturally to Augustine. The basic argument is to deny the possibility of human communication through rational signs (words) without a knowledge of reality (God). Persuasion cannot be accomplished by rhetorical means unless the truth is first known or simultaneously revealed by divine grace.

Augustine wrote many controversial or polemical works intended to refute heresies. His antagonists were at first Manichaeans, later, Donatists, and toward the end of his life, Pelagians. About A.D. 400 he composed a treatise attacking a Donatist bishop named Petilian. (Donatism was an austere Christian sect that required rebaptism of anyone who joined it.) In reply, the grammarian Cresconius took up Petilian's cause and attacked Augustine. The latter then composed the four books *Against Cresconius* around 406. Cresconius had not only attacked Augustine's arguments but had criticized his eloquence and dialectic as unchristian, and it is to this point that Augustine devotes three-fourths of the first book. His position is that neither eloquence nor skill at disputation is un-Christian, which he seeks to prove by numerous scriptural examples, especially those of Jesus and Paul. Eloquence, he says (1.2), is the faculty of speaking or explaining appropriately what we feel. It is to be used when we have perceived truth. The utility of eloquence is a function of the utility of what is being said, and the speaker is comparable to the soldier. We cannot fail to take up arms for the state just because arms are sometimes used against the state. The true disputator seeks first to be sure he is not himself being deceived (1.19), then he tries to use his audience's knowledge of some of the truth. Although Augustine does not explain here how knowledge of the truth is to be discovered, it is clear from his method that consistency with Scripture is an important test. A Christian may use dialectic and rhetoric, but a Christian bishop must do so. He cannot allow error to continue, and his responsibility is not limited to his own church, but extends to the world around him. As is often the case, Augustine advances his views vigorously and pushes Cresconius hard, but without personal abuse; he is chiefly concerned to show the inconsistency of his opponent's view and to confront him with dilemmas. For example, if Cresconius is not himself a dialectician, why does he engage in dialectic? If he is, why does he object to dialectic (1.16)? Some of the contents foreshadow the fourth book of *On Christian Learning*, and in one passage (1.20) there is even allusion to the existence of different kinds of style, a major theme in the later work.

On Christian Learning (*De Doctrina Christiana*) is Augustine's major contribution to the history and theory of rhetoric.[37] From reference to it in his *Retractations* (2.4.1) and elsewhere it seems likely that the first two-thirds of the work (through 3.25.35) was written in the early months of 397, not long after he became bishop of Hippo. Before that, he had taught catechumens; as bishop he was expected to preach regularly to a Christian congregation. The rest of the work was completed in 426 or

427. It is thus a fully mature work, and the discussion of rhetoric in it represents Augustine's views near the end of a lifetime of Christian study and preaching. What he says about Christian rhetoric here is generally in accord with his own practice in homiletic preaching. He does not discuss panegyrical sermons and did not practice Christian epideictic.

In a short prologue, Augustine states that he is writing precepts for treating the Scriptures that will be useful to teachers, and proceeds to a *praemunitio*, or anticipation of the objections that some may make. One category of objections is that everything that should be known about the obscurities of Scripture will be revealed by divine assistance to the preacher or teacher. Augustine's answer is that this claim is a form of pride and leads to the extreme position in which one would not go to church nor read the Scriptures at all: "The condition of man would be lowered if God had not wished to have men supply his word to men" (Prologue 6).

Book 1 then begins with the statement that there are two things necessary in the treatment of the Scriptures: discovery of what is to be understood there, and teaching of what has been learned there. The first subject is discussed in Books 1 through 3, the second in Book 4. The subjects correspond respectively to dialectic and rhetoric. In Augustine's view, all doctrine concerns "things" or "signs" (1.2). A natural object like a stone is a "thing," but it may also be a "sign" of something else, as when in Genesis 28:11 Jacob places a stone on his head. This distinction becomes the basis of finding separate levels of meaning in the sacred text. Book 1 is devoted to things. Some are to be enjoyed, some to be used, some to be enjoyed and used (1.3). Things to be enjoyed are the Father, Son, and Holy Spirit, discussed in sections 5 through 21 (as numbered in Robertson's translation). Things to be used include four kinds of things to be loved: those above us, ourselves, those like us, and those below us. These are discussed in sections 22 to 38. The direction of Augustine's thought emerges clearly at the end of Book 1 (1.39–40), where he says that the sum and end of the Scriptures is the love of God. The whole temporal dispensation was made that we might know and implement this love, and the basis of all interpretation of Scripture is love: "Whoever, therefore, thinks that he understands the divine Scriptures or any part of them so that it does not build the double love of God and of our neighbor does not understand it at all. Whoever finds a lesson there useful to the building of love, even though he has not said what the author may be shown to have intended in that place, has not been deceived, nor is he lying in any way" (1.40).

Books 2 and 3 are devoted to signs. Signs are natural or conventional; known, unknown, or ambiguous; literal or figurative. God has provided unknown and ambiguous signs "to conquer pride by work and to combat disdain in our minds, to which those things that are easily discovered seem frequently to become worthless" (2.7). That which is sought with difficulty is discovered with more pleasure (2.8). Knowledge is the third of the seven steps to wisdom (2.9–11), and Augustine asks what knowledge is necessary for the Christian teacher, much as Plato, Aristotle, Cicero, and Quintilian had considered what knowledge was necessary for the civic orator. Augustine's speaker needs, first, a thorough knowledge of the Scriptures. He can thus use those things that are clear to explain those that are not. All teaching involving faith is said openly in the Scriptures, as is that necessary for the Christian life. If we know this, we have a basis for explaining what is obscure (2.14). In subsequent chapters Augustine considers knowledge of languages, numbers, and music.

More delicate is the matter of knowledge of literature and philosophy. Should the Christian study pagan writings? Yes. "We should not think that we ought not to learn literature because Mercury is said to be its inventor" (2.28). Doctrines current among the pagans are said to involve either institutions (2.36–40) or things we perceive (2.41–58), the latter through the body or through reason. Augustine dislikes sophistry and criticizes argument for the sake of argument (2.48), but he thinks that valid inference was instituted by God and then observed by humans (2.50). Definition, division, and partition are part of the order of things (2.50). The Christian has every right to take true ideas from the Platonists and transform them as "Egyptian gold" (2.60). Augustine suggests that it would be useful to have an index of the various signs used in the Scriptures, a suggestion that was taken up by later students and led to the collections of *distinctiones* current in the Middle Ages.[38]

Book 3 deals with ambiguous signs. When literal interpretation causes ambiguity, the rule of faith as found "in the more open places of the Scriptures and in the authority of the Church" (3.2) should be consulted. There is considerable danger in too literal interpretations (3.9):

"The letter killeth, but the spirit quickened," as Paul said (2 Corinthians 3:6). If an admonition in Scripture is to something useful or good, it is not figurative; if it is to something criminal or vicious it must be figurative (3.24). Figurative signs do not have the same meaning in all passages (3.35); the context must be judged. Augustine is not concerned that something may be read into a passage that the author did not intend (3.39). What is important is the intent of God, who foresaw whatever is found in the passage and more. The rule of faith and the context are the best guides to the interpretations of Scripture. In the last resort, reason can also be used, but it is dangerous (3.39). Book 3 ends (42–56) with a critique of the "Rules" of Tyconius. These are categories of figurative language that resemble topics, some more than others. For example, the third rule, "of promises and the law," deals with matters of the spirit and the letter, and the fourth rule with matters of species and genus.

Having completed his discussion of the discovery of the meaning of Scripture, Augustine turns in Book 4 to the teaching of what has been discovered.[39] This fourth book falls into six parts: a brief introduction (§§ 1–5), a description of Christian eloquence (§§ 6–26), an examination of the duties of the orator applied to Scripture and preaching (§§ 27–33), a similar examination of the three kinds of style (§§ 33–58), a discussion of ethos (§§ 59–63), and a conclusion (§ 64).

Augustine does not set out all the rules of rhetoric. They are useful, he says (4.2), but should be learned elsewhere. Yet he summarizes many of them in one characteristic passage:

Who would dare to say that truth should stand in the person of its defenders unarmed against lying, so that they who wish to urge falsehoods may know how to make their listeners benevolent or attentive or docile in their presentation [i.e., in the exordium], while the defenders of truth are ignorant of that art? Should they speak briefly, clearly, and plausibly [in the narration], while the defenders of truth speak so that they tire their listeners, make themselves difficult to understand and what they say dubious? Should they oppose the truth with fallacious arguments and assert falsehoods [in the proof], while the defenders of truth have no ability either to defend the truth or to oppose the false? Should they, urging the minds of their listeners into error, ardently exhort them, moving them by speech so that they terrify, sadden, and exhilarate them [in the peroration], while the defenders of truth are sluggish, cold, and somnolent? Who is so foolish as to think this to be wisdom? While the faculty of eloquence, which is of great value in urging either evil or justice, is in itself indifferent, why should it not be obtained for the uses of the good in the service of truth if the evil usurp it for the winning of perverse and vain causes in defense of iniquity and error? (4.3)

Rhetoric may be studied by the young and by those not engaged in something more important, Augustine continues, but the Christian speaker must beware of forgetting what should be said while considering the artistry of the discourse (4.4). In fact, study of rules is not necessary at all, for eloquence can be learned from imitation of eloquent models (4.5). Imitation had, of course, been a major pedagogical tool of classical rhetoricians, based on a canon of models such as those discussed in Quintilian 10.1. Augustine would replace that canon with a new canon of the Scriptures and the Fathers of the Church.

The description of Christian eloquence (4.6–26) begins with the statement that the expositor and teacher of the Scriptures should teach the good and extirpate the bad. There is thus both a positive and a negative form, as there was in the three species of civic oratory. Augustine anticipates here his later discussion of the duties of the orator, saying that the Christian teacher should "conciliate those who are opposed, arouse those who are remiss, and teach those ignorant of his subject" (4.6). In the subsequent discussion, he finds many examples of classical rhetorical techniques in writings of Paul and the Old Testament book of Amos, including climax, periodic sentences, and tropes. But he concludes of Amos, "A good listener warms to it not so much by diligently analyzing it as by pronouncing it energetically. For these words were not devised by human industry, but were poured forth from the divine mind both wisely and eloquently, not in such a way that wisdom was directed toward eloquence, but in such a way that eloquence did not abandon wisdom" (4.21). As to the virtues of style as seen in the Scriptures or practiced by a Christian, clarity is the only real consideration (4.23), though appropriateness was noted earlier (4.9). Ornamentation and grammatical correctness, the two other traditional virtues of style, are not of great importance to Augustine (4.24).

Next (4.27–33) comes consideration of the three duties of the orator—to teach, to delight, and to move—which Cicero had developed out of the Aristotelian modes of proof. To teach is, of course, the most important, but Augustine holds that it is necessary to delight listeners in order to retain them as listeners and to move them in order to impel them to do what is right. Moving is equated with persuasion (4.27). Moreover, "When that which is taught must be put into practice and is taught for that reason, the truth of what is said is acknowledged in vain and the eloquence of the discourse pleases in vain unless that which is learned is implemented in action" (4.29). Persuasion is thus not left entirely to God. Ultimately, the orator needs both expertise and divine guidance: "He who would both know and teach should learn everything which should be taught and acquire a skill in speaking appropriate to an ecclesiastic, but at the time of the speech itself he should think what the Lord says more suitable to good thought" (4.32). And then Augustine quotes the familiar passage from Matthew (10:19–20): "For it is not you that speak, but the spirit of your father that speaketh in you."

In sections 33 through 58 Augustine ties the three duties of the orator to the three kinds of style, as Cicero had done in *The Orator*: teaching to the plain style, delighting to the middle style, and moving to the grand style. Examples of each are given, both from the Scriptures and from the Fathers (Cyprian and Ambrose). The three styles should be mingled, "but the whole speech is said to be in that style which is used most in it" (4.51). He concludes, "It is the universal office of eloquence in any of these styles to speak in a manner leading to persuasion; and the end of eloquence is to persuade of that which you are speaking. In any of these three styles if an eloquent speaker speaks in a manner suitable to persuasion, but without persuasion the end of eloquence has not been attained" (4.55).

Addressing the fifth topic, character (4.59–63), Augustine points out that the life of the speaker as known to the listeners has greater weight than any grandness of eloquence. He thus revives ethos as a major factor in rhetoric, though not ethos as projected in a speech, which is what Aristotle discussed. That quality had been transmuted by Cicero into the second duty of the orator, to delight. To Augustine, ethos is Christian works, the life of the teacher, and the extent to which it accords with his teaching, as known to the audience. Ethos thus becomes moral authority. Under certain circumstances, however, a bad man can become a good orator. Quintilian would have been surprised. Augustine recognizes that there may be someone who can speak well but cannot think of anything to say. Such a preacher can take eloquent sermons composed by another and deliver them to his congregation, as was often done in the following centuries. Thus, "it may happen that an evil and wicked man may compose a sermon in which truth is preached which is spoken by another not wicked but good. And when this is done, the wicked man hands down to another what is not his own, and the good man accepts what is his from another" (4.62). This doctrine, original with Augustine, has reappeared in modern criticism in the view that the value of a work of art is not dependent on the morality of the author.

Several observations may be made about *On Christian Teaching* as a whole. First, it is not concerned with either missionary preaching or panegyrical preaching. What Augustine discusses is teaching those already drawn to Christianity who are undertaking instruction preparatory to baptism (i.e., catechumens) and homiletic preaching to a Christian congregation in church. The function of Christian eloquence in these contexts is to deepen understanding and to convert belief into works. Now that persecution was over and Christianity was the established religion of the state, there were many Christians who lacked the intensity and dedication of those in earlier times. There was in Augustine's view also the ever-present danger that some Christians might be attracted by the false doctrines of heretical sects.

Second, Christian rhetoric as viewed by Augustine is popular rhetoric. Christianity is addressed to all sorts and conditions of life, and the Christian teacher or preacher should be able to instruct and move the illiterate and unlearned as well as the sophisticated and erudite. The importance of rhetoric was surely especially evident to Augustine because of his background as a rhetorician.[40]

Third, Augustine deals with two related matters: in Books 1, 2, and 3 with discovery of the meaning of the Scriptures, in Book 4 with exposition of that meaning. As suggested earlier, these correspond to dialectic and rhetoric in classical education. In religious studies they are regularly given the names of hermeneutics and homiletics, respectively, and are the arts of exegesis and of preaching.

Fourth, rhetorical invention in Christian rhetoric as described by

Augustine is limited to the exposition of the Scriptures and their meaning for the Christian life, especially for the cultivation of the love of God and of one's neighbor. Proof in Christian rhetoric derives from the authoritative utterances in the sacred texts and from the moral authority of the speaker, not from argumentation. In practice, the testimony of witnesses and examples of the saints were also often important means of persuasion, but these are not discussed here. Augustine engaged in argumentation with other Christians on matters of doctrine, but his views of rhetoric and preaching left open to dialectic the whole area of religious disputation, which was much cultivated in later centuries.

Fifth, matters of style play a greater role than does invention in Augustine's account of Christian rhetoric. The fourth book of *On Christian Learning* helped to canonize the view that rhetoric is largely a matter of style. Even Christian exegesis is more strongly influenced by the factor of style than by reasoning, since much exegesis involves the interpretation of figurative signs. Peter Brown has pointed out how characteristic this was of a writer of late antiquity: "No one else would have made such a cult of veiling his meaning. Such a man lived among fellow-connoisseurs, who had been steeped too long in too few books. He no longer needed to be explicit; only hidden meanings, rare and difficult words and elaborate circumlocutions, could save his readers from boredom, from fastidium, from the loss of interest in the obvious that afflicts the overcultured man. He would believe . . . that the sheer difficulty of a work of literature made it more valuable."[41]

Sixth, although Christian rhetoric as described by Augustine has a distinct subject matter, he does not distinguish it as an art from secular rhetoric. It is characteristic of him to strip secular institutions and arts of their pagan associations. In *The City of God*, even the Roman Empire is so treated, and Augustine's writings on grammar, dialectic, music, rhetoric, and other subjects equally show his effort to make them religiously neutral, capable of utilization by a Christian for Christian purposes.[42]

Seventh, *On Christian Learning* has sometimes been viewed as a repudiation of the sophistic tradition.[43] This is only partially true. In common with most other Christians and with philosophically minded pagans, Augustine rejected empty bombast and trivial forms of declamation practiced in rhetorical schools in the late empire. On the other hand, certain features of sophistic are retained, including emphasis on the function of the orator as well as on imitation and style. Augustine's account of rhetoric belongs largely in what we have called the technical tradition of the handbooks, with some features of the sophistic tradition, and a demand for truth characteristic of the philosophical tradition.

Finally, *On Christian Learning* exemplifies two sound critical principles that had been more appreciated by the rhetoricians than by grammarians and dialecticians: interpretation should be based not only on an understanding of the context in which a word or passage occurs but also on the overall meaning or structure of the work in which it occurs. Christianity, with its consciousness of its message, would have everything consistent with one theme.

On Christian Learning proved to be an authoritative statement of Christian rhetoric for many medieval writers. Among others, Hrabanus Maurus, Thomas Aquinas, Alan of Lille, Humbert of Romans, Robert of Basevorn, Hugh of Saint Victor, and Peter Lombard drew on it, and it continued to be influential later, for example, on Fénelon. Augustine's defense of scriptural obscurity became a part of poetic theory from Petrarch to the sixteenth century. Augustine had made it possible for Christians to appreciate and teach eloquence without associating it with paganism, and in so doing permanently enriched Christian literature and criticism.

CHAPTER 8

Greek Rhetoric in the Middle Ages

Knowledge of classical rhetoric survived through the Middle Ages, precariously at times, both in the East in the Greek-speaking Byzantine Empire and in western Europe, where Latin remained the language of religion and scholarship. Until the Renaissance, Greek scholars very rarely had any knowledge of Latin and western scholars were equally ignorant of Greek. The two traditions are somewhat different: in the East it is largely the sophistic strand that was strongest, with some philosophical influence from Neoplatonism. Public address was an important factor in the cohesion of the state, and orators were held in honor. Many speeches were published for the reading public. Writing *about* rhetoric largely took the form of commentaries on earlier treatments. In the West, the handbook tradition of Latin rhetoric was continued in new works and handbooks of letter writing, poetry, and preaching were eventually produced, a development less evident in the East. Western writers composed prose panegyrics and encomiastic poetry, but no leading role in society was granted the orator as it was in the East.

Some reasons for the difference between East and West are clear. Sophistry and philosophy were much more strongly established in the Greek portion of the Roman Empire than in the West. The serious application of epideictic to Christianity began in the East, as seen in orations of Gregory of Nazianzus and John Chrysostom, and continued throughout Byzantine history. In contrast, epideictic was somewhat less practiced in the West, where interest in rhetoric was traditionally connected with the study and practice of law and civil procedure. In the East, Roman government was a continuity, with the result of greater cultural continuity than in the West: educational and cultural functions performed by Greek sophists of later antiquity continued to be performed throughout Byzantine history once they had been adapted to Christianity. Although there were serious threats to the survival of the eastern empire (for example, from the Arabs in the eighth century and from the Crusaders in the thirteenth), survive it did until the Turkish conquest in 1453. The western Roman Empire did not survive as such after the fifth century. In the East, Greek was continuously spoken, although the popular dialect significantly deviated from the formal, official language. In the West, the new rulers brought new languages with them, even though Latin continued to be important throughout the region.[1]

Because of the threats to the survival of Greek culture and the Greek Church, Byzantine civilization was often nervous, defensive, and in awe of its classical past. In the case of rhetoric, Byzantine conservatism is seen in the continued imitation of classical models and in adherence to late classical textbooks, especially those of Hermogenes, and in preservation of sophistic forms of oratory. The greatest importance of Byzantium in the history of rhetoric, and in the history of literature, is as the preserver and transmitter of classical Greek texts. The period of greatest danger for the survival of texts was the eighth century, when the Iconoclasm movement in the Church destroyed works of art and turned against classical culture generally. Greek works that scribes did not copy and preserve in this period were permanently lost except for some fragmentary discoveries in papyri buried in the sands of Egypt or under the eruption of Mount Vesuvius.

Byzantium (modern Istanbul) had been made the eastern capital of the Roman Empire by Constantine in A.D. 324 and was refounded as Constantinople in 330. After the death of Theodosius in 395, the Roman Empire was permanently split into eastern and western halves, and as the western parts slipped into the control of Germanic rulers in the course of the next century, the eastern empire emerged as the sole remnant of Roman power. Subsequent Byzantine history is usually divided into three periods. The first had no sharp break with antiquity. It includes the vigorous age of Justinian (527–65) and ends with the siege of Constantinople by the Arabs in 717. The second period gradually emerges into a renaissance of learning in the ninth century, contemporary with the Carolingian renaissance in the West. This development continued in the tenth century during the reign of the scholar-emperor Constantine VII Porphyrogenitus and reached a climax in the eleventh century, the time of the greatest Byzantine writer, Michael Psellus. Some decline is noticeable in the twelfth century, which nevertheless produced the classicizing historian Anna Comnena and Eustathius, author of an enormous commentary on the Homeric epics. This second period may be said to have ended with the fall of Constantinople to the Latin Crusaders in 1204. The final period includes the Greek recovery of Constantinople in 1261 and the succeeding cultural renaissance under the dynasty of the Palaeologi, which facilitated the transmission of Greek learning to the West. The fall of Constantinople to the Turks in 1453 marked the end of Byzantine, and thus of Roman, history. Throughout its history the Byzantine state, like the later Roman Empire, was an autocracy, with parallel and overlapping hierarchies in civil, military, and ecclesiastical government. Administration was carried on by a highly developed scribal bureaucracy—hence the use of "byzantine" in English to describe bureaucratic methods. An important function of formal education was training future bureaucrats and leaders of Church and State.

Grammar Schools

As heir to the language, the literature, and the religion of classical Greece, Byzantine scholars sought to transmit them to future generations as unchanged as possible. The truth had been revealed and methods of study had been canonized, but standards were difficult to maintain. Grammar schools taught the rudiments of the Greek language, reading of Greek texts, and progymnasmatic exercises in composition. Secondary education, where it existed, continued to be based on schools of rhetoric. A few students might then continue to study dialectic as an introduction to philosophy, thus completing a program analogous to the trivium in the West.[2] A counterpart of the quadrivium is also attested at times.[3] The most significant addition to the subject matter of classical education was study of the Bible and Fathers of the Church. The Old Testament book of Psalms, in Greek translation, became a basic school reader, but Homer and other poets, Plato, and the orators continued to be studied by more advanced students.

Greek grammar was usually taught from the textbook of Dionysius Thrax, written about 100 B.C. It remained authoritative for knowledge of the classical language for fifteen hundred years and received many commentaries. *Progymnasmata*, the exercises in composition discussed in Chapter 5, were most often studied in the textbook of Aphthonius,[4] which also received commentaries. Early examples of these are one by John of Sardis dating from the ninth century and one by John Geometres dating from the tenth. The former work contains no reference to Christianity, but the latter draws on examples from Gregory of Nazianzus. The incorporation of Christian writers into the literary canon was a process that continued throughout the Byzantine period. The best late classical examples of *progymnasmata* were those by the fourth-century sophist Libanius. Though he was a pagan, his writings were studied for their style in the Byzantine period. Many examples of Byzantine *progymnasmata* survive and are often interesting. Those by Nicephorus Basilaces, for example, written in the mid-twelfth century, combine compositions about Zeus and Ajax with those about Samson and the Virgin, and an *ethopoeia* on what the Greek god of the Underworld, Hades, said when Lazarus was raised from the dead. (Christian theologians did not, in general, deny the existence of the pagan gods, which they regarded as devils.) The various forms of *progymnasmata*—narratives, chrias, encomia, comparisons, etc.—exercised direct influence on literary composition and were incorporated into homilies or histories or saints' lives as a form of amplification. A good example of a syncrisis, or comparison, in literary form is the essay by Theodorus Metochites (ca. 1260–1332), *On Demosthenes and Aristides*.[5] The *ethopoeia*, or personification, influenced the writing of epistles, often revised and published as literary creations.[6] Another favorite was the ecphrasis, or description, which was given a Christian treatment as a description of a church or work of art. Probably the most famous example, and certainly one of the most ambitious, was the work *On Buildings* by Procopius of Caesarea (d. 565), with a celebrated description of the church of Hagia Sophia in Constantinople.[7] Procopius seems to have intended the work as an encomium of the church's builder, Justinian, whom he did not admire but thought it prudent to praise.

Rhetorical Schools

In the fourth century of the Christian era teachers of rhetoric could be found in every city of the Roman Empire and students traveled many miles for more advanced study with the great sophists of Athens, Antioch, Constantinople, and elsewhere. In the fifth and sixth centuries Gaza in Palestine was a leading center of rhetorical studies under Zosimus, Procopius, and Choricius, some of whose works have survived.[8] Their compositions included panegyrics, ecphrases, prose monodies, and commentaries on the Attic orators. The rhetors of Gaza were Christians and contributed to the integration of Christian and pagan models of style and drew illustrative examples from both Christian and pagan classics.

The philosophical schools of Athens were closed by Justinian in 529, but the effect of that action has probably been exaggerated by modern historians who like to couple it with the establishment of the monastery at Monte Cassino in Italy in the same year to designate the end of the classical and beginning of medieval institutions of learning. More significant at the time was Justinian's termination of the requirement that municipalities throughout the empire pay the salaries of teachers (see Procopius *Secret History* 26.5); many cities probably could not afford the cost in this period of general economic decline. Thereafter, private teachers of grammar and rhetoric could be found in some major cities, but formal education languished for the next three centuries.

What Dionysius Thrax and Aphthonius were to the grammar schools, Hermogenes was to the study of rhetoric throughout the Byzantine period. The popularity of his works resulted from several qualities. First, his major (and genuine) treatises *On Stases* and *On Ideas* had potential utility in teaching argument and style, useful in any form of writing or speaking. Second, Hermogenes was strongly classicizing. His great rhetorical model was Demosthenes, who more than any other seemed to combine all "ideas" of style. This classicism constituted an initial appeal to early Byzantine scholars, but the acceptance of Hermogenes' authority, especially in the middle Byzantine period, helped to perpetuate classicism, including admiration of Demosthenes at a time when political and social conditions were radically different from what Demosthenes had known. Third, Hermogenes was systematic, specific, and generally clear. He defined his terms, gave examples, and above all was given to categorization and subdivisions of concepts in a form that students could be expected to memorize. This rather pedantic approach appealed to the Byzantine mind, which proceeded along similar hierarchical channels in theology, philosophy, law, bureaucratic government, court ceremonies, and other aspects of life. Hermogenes had combined complex details into a unified system that paralleled Byzantine concepts of human life as a microcosm of eternal life, and his twenty forms of style could be mingled, combined, and varied to produce a kaleidoscope of aesthetic effects congenial to the Byzantine taste for color, symbol, and mystical expression, as seen, for example, in mosaics. A good example of the application of the Hermogenic ideas of style can be found in the homilies of Photius, even though Photius never mentions Hermogenes by name.[9] Photius, Patriarch of Constantinople from 856 to 867 and 878 to 886, was the most important Byzantine scholar of the ninth century, and largely responsible for the renewed study of the classics in this period of cultural renaissance. In particular, his *Lexicon* provided readers with a dictionary of Attic Greek that facilitated the anachronistic use of the high style in all serious communication.

Hermogenes' treatises were the subject of numerous commentaries through Byzantine times. For the work on stasis, for example, commentaries include one from the fifth century by the Neoplatonist philosopher Syrianus[10] and from about the same time commentaries by Sopater and Marcellinus. From the eleventh century come the commentaries of John Doxapatres, and from the thirteenth the commentary of Maximus Planudes, a scholar and poet who also commented on Hermogenes' work on ideas of style and on two other works then attributed to Hermogenes, *On Invention* and *On Method*, drawing chiefly on earlier discussions. For the work on ideas of style there is a commentary by Syrianus again, and an anonymous commentary probably dating from the tenth century that draws on older material but adds references to Christian writers, chiefly Gregory of Nazianzus, as well as a more Christianizing commentary by John Siceliotes from the eleventh century[11] and again the commentary by Planudes.

Most commentaries begin with a *prolegomenon*, or introduction, to the study of rhetoric, similar to the introductions to philosophy composed by Neoplatonists.[12] These discuss the definition and parts of rhetoric and its early history in Greece. There are also a number of Byzantine works on figures of speech that show Hermogenes' influence, as well as synopses of Hermogenes' theories by Michael Psellus, George Pletho, and others.

Although the Hermogenic works were the major authority on rhetoric for the Byzantines, writings of Dionysius of Halicarnassus and Menander Rhetor and other handbooks and treatises were available to scholars in some libraries and were sometimes combined into single large manuscripts. *Parisinus Graecus 1741*, copied in the tenth century and now in the Bibliothèque Nationale in Paris, is a vast compendium of rhetorical texts; it includes Aristotle's *Rhetoric*, Demetrius's *On Style*, the rhetorical works of Dionysius of Halicarnassus and Pseudo-Aristides, Alexander's handbook of figures of speech, Apsines' rhetorical handbook, and other works.

An unusual feature of Byzantine teaching and one of the few innovations in the theory of style inherited from Hermogenes was the belief that obscurity can at times be a virtue. Arethas of Caesarea in the tenth century was the author of a tract entitled *To Those Who Have Accused Us of Obscurity*, in which he claims his detractors do not understand when obscurity should be used. John Geometres in the eleventh century took the further step of saying that not every instance of obscurity is a vice and it may even be a virtue, and this claim is echoed by later writers.[13] The obscurities of the Scriptures and the Fathers of the Church, and of Greek philosophers as well, given allegorical interpretation as discussed in Chapter 7, provided justification for this view. Religious truth was regarded as hidden by a veil of obscure language to protect it from the profane and to give it value from the labor required to understand it, and Byzantine writers imitated the style. In addition, some secular truths might be dangerous to express too clearly but could be said in ways that those in sympathy with the writer could understand.

Rhetorical schools were not so common as grammar schools at any time, and declamation does not seem to have been widely practiced after the sixth century. Some Byzantine writers, however, wrote declamations as a literary exercise, and a few survive, such as those by George Pachymeris, who lived in the thirteenth century and also composed *progym-*

nasmata. In his fifth declamation, faithful to the tradition of the sophists, he imagines himself as Demosthenes advising the Athenians what to do about Philip's capture of Elatea.

Plato's works, including *Gorgias* and *Phaedrus*, were much studied in the early Byzantine period, when Christian and pagan Neoplatonists dominated the schools of philosophy. Neoplatonist critical and aesthetic theory was an important influence on Byzantine art and writing.[14] Hermias of Alexandria wrote a commentary on *Phaedrus* in the mid-fifth century, and Olympiodorus one on *Gorgias* in the late sixth century.[15] In later Byzantine periods Aristotle was more read than Plato, largely because of the place of his logical works in the curriculum, but there were enthusiastic Platonists, of whom Michael Psellus was one. Aristotle's *Rhetoric* was regarded as part of the *Organon*, or collection of his logical treatises, and occasionally read in that connection.[16] Two Byzantine commentaries on the *Rhetoric* have survived, probably dating from the middle Byzantine period, but there is little sign of direct influence of the ideas of Plato and Aristotle about rhetoric.

Advanced Education in Constantinople

In Constantinople a school of advanced studies, called "the University" by modern scholars, had been organized in A.D. 425 by an edict of Theodosius II (*Codex Theodosius* 14.9.2). The faculty consisted of ten teachers of Greek grammar, five of Greek rhetoric, ten of Latin grammar, three of Latin rhetoric, two of law, and one of philosophy. The curriculum was remarkably secular, intended to train young men for positions at all levels in government. How long this institution survived is not known. It is unlikely to have survived the eighth century and may have collapse, or faded away, much earlier. The view to be found in some older books on Byzantium, that "the University" survived with a series of refoundings and reforms until 1453, is without substance. There was no continuous tradition of higher education in Constantinople and no consistent government support.[17] There were private teachers of philosophy and rhetoric and some other subjects, and occasionally one of these achieved official support, as did Leo the Philosopher in the ninth century and Michael Psellus in the eleventh. Psellus and Xiphilinus, an eminent legal scholar, were the heads of competing schools, and Constantine IX Monomachus intervened in the dispute between them and briefly provided some subsidy for a school of law under Xiphilinus and a school of rhetoric and philosophy under Psellus, but the system soon collapsed.[18] Our best source of information is Psellus's *Funeral Eulogy for Xiphilinus.*

Michael Psellus (1018–ca. 1078) was an official at court, an orator, a Platonist whose philosophical views were condemned by the Church, and the author of many works, of which the best known is the *Chronographia*, a rather personal history of his own times. He also wrote on scientific and philosophical subjects and composed a versified summary of Hermogenes' rhetorical theory. Versification of technical writing was common in both East and West as an aid to memorization of the contents. The importance of sophistic rhetoric in Psellus's thinking emerges in a speech he composed on the rhetorical character of Gregory of Nazianzus. The speech employs the theory of ideas of Hermogenes and is modeled on Dionysius of Halicarnassus's essays on the ancient orators. Gregory is found to be the exemplar of all "ideas" of style; each quality is taken up in turn. Psellus's major speeches are three funeral orations on distinguished contemporaries, Kerullarius, Leichudes, and Xiphilinus. In *Chronographia* (6.41) he speaks of learning as divided into two parts, rhetoric and philosophy. He describes as his personal goal to mold his tongue to eloquence by rhetorical discourse and to purify his mind by philosophy (6.107). Statements in his letters are consistent with this goal. Writing to a correspondent about Hermogenes, he says, "Perhaps you know philosophy and rhetoric, but you do not know how to put them together; there is a philosophizing rhetoric as well as a rhetoricizing philosophy"; and elsewhere, "Just as Plato in the *Timaeus* combines theology with physical science, so I write philosophy by means of rhetoric and fit myself to both through the use of both."[19] This reflects the tradition of philosophical rhetoric but is a nobler vision than that held by most in Byzantium.

Probably more continuous than "the University" was the Patriarchal School of Constantinople, which is first heard of in the seventh century and best known from the twelfth, when its three teachers of Scripture were joined by a fourth, the master of the rhetors.[20] The faculty of the Patriarchal School at that time had important public oratorical functions: the delivery of panegyrics, funeral orations, and other official speeches, which were published and preserved. Among the masters of the rhetors were Nicepherus Basilaces and Eustathius, the latter best known for his commentary on the Homeric poems in which he makes use of Hermogenic concepts of style.[21] Constantinople dominated Byzantine culture, but there were some other centers of education, including Antioch, Nicea, and Thessalonica. There were also important monasteries in Asia Minor and Greece and on the islands that copied manuscripts and preserved classical texts throughout the later centuries.

Attic Greek

Although a popular literature, seen, for example, in simple, often anonymous lives of the saints and in folk poetry, was composed during the Byzantine period using the contemporary Greek of the time, the official language of the Byzantine Empire was the literary Greek of late antiquity, artificially preserved by educated persons for over a thousand years.[22] Although generally referred to as "Attic," in contrast to the demotic, or language of daily life or the speech of the uneducated, this formal language had its origins in the Koine Greek of the Hellenistic period, found in the New Testament. It was refined by the Atticizing speakers and writers of the Christian era, continually reinforced by the attention paid to true Attic prose models, including Demosthenes and Plato, as well as to Atticizing prose written by Aristides, Libanius, Gregory of Nazianzus, and others in late antiquity, and expanded somewhat by the inclusion of words and phrases from poetry. Pronunciation was allowed to follow a natural development, but Byzantine writers, Psellus, for example, repeatedly tried to reassert the lexical and grammatical standards of classical Greek in writing in the high style. And Anna Comnena "dislikes to record even the names of barbarians, for fear they may defile the pages of her history."[23] Serious writers were also expected to follow the conventions of classical literary genres and to sprinkle their works with allusions to the Greek classics and the Bible. One result of the lack of change in the formal language is that it is often impossible to date a Byzantine literary work unless one has external sources of reference to it or its writer.

The anachronistic use of Atticizing Greek for all serious communication, including the writing of personal letters, like the use of formal languages in other cultures, sharpened the division between the educated and the uneducated. It was made possible by the continuation of traditional grammatical and rhetorical education, encouraged by the Church, which drew its authority from the Greek Scriptures and the writings of the Fathers and was anxious to preserve knowledge of their language. The extraordinary value put on classical language and style, exceeding the role of Latin in the West, was part of a search for cultural stability and permanence in the face of the destruction of the classical world and the dangers from alien societies, including Slavs to the north, Arabs to the south, Turks to the east, and varied hordes of semibarbaric "Latins" to the west. In addition, the requirement of its use helped to ensure the political and social power of those with access to education.

Functions of Rhetoric in Byzantium

One reason that rhetorical studies did not significantly change throughout the Byzantine period is that there was little significant change in the need for rhetoric, its functions, or its forms, as perceived by the leaders of society. Rhetoric in most cultures has more often been a tool of preservation of the status quo than of change. Knowledge of the right language and right forms was the prerequisite for a career in Church and State in Byzantium, and the attitudes inculcated with that knowledge were extremely conservative.

In such a situation, and considering the Church's greater interest in the language than in the content of the classics, it is easy to see that style would be the most important aspect of rhetoric. Study of stasis theory kept alive the logical side of the subject to some extent, and the Byzantines studied Aristotelian logic but without developing that subject into the scholastic discipline so congenial to western scholars in the Middle Ages. Their willingness to acknowledge deliberate obscurity as a virtue of style, in contrast to Aristotle's insistence on clarity, is one of their unusual themes, parallel to the use of rhetoric to retard rather than to facilitate social and political change. But even this concept developed out of Hermogenes' treatise on ideas and the aesthetics and biblical exegesis of late antiquity rather than being entirely new, and it has some counterpart in views of Augustine and other western writers.

The Byzantine Empire had a senate and a system of lawcourts, descended in both cases from institutions of the Roman Empire, but neither deliberative nor judicial oratory were major forms of discourse in the East. The function of public address in Byzantium was to present decisions to the public and to strengthen loyalty to Church and State through the use of epideictic forms. The church year presented a series of opportunities for panegyrical sermons, especially in Constantinople, and many of these are preserved, as are many funeral orations of famous persons. Both types were consistently modeled on the great works of Gregory of Nazianzus, which were studied as classics. Literally thousands of homilies also survive, often indebted to John Chrysostom, another classic to the Byzantines; some are highly rhetorical and some are in the simpler form of the ancient homily. Collections of homilies were also made. Leo the Wise, emperor from 886 to 912, seems to have been especially influential in the creation of these collections.[24]

Outside the specific functions of the Church, though not outside church influence, are numerous epideictic orations that were given on public occasions. The most important group are the encomia of emperors and members of the imperial family by officially approved orators.[25] Examples of these survive from all periods, including the encomium of Anastasius I by Procopius of Gaza, encomia by Psellus of the empress Theodora, of Constantine IX Monomachus, and of Michael VII Ducas, and encomia by Nicetas Choniates of Isaac II and Alexis III. There are also encomia of patriarchs, including that by Eustathius on Michael III (1170–78). Other epideictic takes the form of funeral orations for the great and monodies, or prose laments, such as Psellus's for Andronicus Ducas, son of Constantine X. The monody was a classical form for which models could be found among the works of Aristides (for Smyrna after an earthquake) and Libanius (on the death of Julian the Apostate). In addition, there are *prosphonetics*, or speeches of official welcome, *propemptics*, or speeches of farewell, and *genethliacs*, or birthday speeches, and many others forms, most of which had been described in the handbooks of Menander Rhetor. In addition to real speeches, there were also written addresses to influential persons in the tradition of Isocrates' *To Nicocles*, and rhetorical autobiographies, for which the first oration of Libanius was a model.[26]

The static quality of formal Byzantine rhetoric does not mean that the period is not important in the history of rhetoric. The schools of grammar and rhetoric of Byzantium and the compositions of Byzantine orators preserved classical rhetoric as a living tradition for a thousand years. It is because of Byzantine scholars and scribes that Greek writings and ideas survived to be carried to Italy for study and imitation and to become a factor in cultural tradition when increased wealth and motivation made high levels of culture possible in the Renaissance and when Byzantine civilization itself was terminated by the Turkish conquest. Byzantium is a time capsule in which the teachers of rhetoric sealed the best of the past as they saw it, including works by Plato and Aristotle. The Church connived at this preservation because of interest in the status quo, but a distaste for worldly knowledge lingered, especially among the monks. The Greek Church did not love the classics but did love the language of the New Testament and the Fathers. Study of rhetoric had become one of the roads to knowledge of the Scriptures and patristic literature.

The last important figure in Byzantine rhetoric was George Trebizond. Born in Crete in 1395 and educated in Greek rhetoric, he arrived in Italy in 1416 and brought with him a knowledge of the Hermogenic tradition, unknown in the West. Combining this knowledge with the Ciceronian tradition of the West, in 1424 he published, in Latin, the first complete rhetorical treatise of the Renaissance, *Rhetoricorum Libri V*, or *Rhetoric in Five Books*. It became widely known later in the century after the new technology of printing was introduced. From this point, the histories of eastern and western European rhetoric begin to converge.

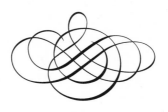

CHAPTER 9

Latin Rhetoric in the Middle Ages

Although study of rhetoric triumphantly survived the victory of Christianity over paganism in the West as well as in the East, it almost succumbed to the collapse of its native environment as the cities of the empire were destroyed or depopulated in the face of barbarian attack beginning in the early fifth century. With the end of orderly civic and economic life not only did public support of education disappear, but the reasons for rhetorical education in its traditional form declined. Fewer councils remained in which an orator could speak, and legal procedures were disrupted; on the other hand, barbarian kings easily acquired a taste for being extolled in Latin prose or verse, even if they did not understand what was being said. Poverty, fear, and poor communications became endemic; libraries were destroyed; books disintegrated and were not recopied; and knowledge of Greek faded throughout the West.

But classical rhetoric did not die. A few private teachers of grammar and rhetoric could probably be found at most times in the cities of Italy and Gaul. In the mid-sixth century Cassiodorus introduced the liberal arts into monastic schools. The prose and poetry of the sixth and seventh centuries show some knowledge of classical rhetoric and occasions for persuasive speech. By the eighth century, the first glimmerings of a new civic life emerged in Italy: Venice in the relative safety of her lagoon had begun to elect her doges and manage her own affairs. In the ninth and tenth centuries Pisa, Pavia, Bologna, and other Italian cities became important commercial centers, and by the eleventh century the commune movement had created assemblies, councils, and courts of law with a jury system in many Italian municipalities. It was in this setting, not totally different from the city-states of antiquity, that rhetoric re-emerged as a practical subject of study in Italian schools and at the University of Bologna in the period between the eleventh and fourteenth centuries.

North of the Alps, in the ninth and tenth centuries the Carolingian Age brought to western Europe the first of several "renaissances" that found a place for rhetoric in the schools on the basis of the need for administrators, teachers, and a literate clergy. Although progress was by no means steady, the restoration of education in the Carolingian Age eventually led to the cathedral schools of the eleventh and twelfth centuries, where rhetoric was a regular discipline within a framework of study of the liberal arts. Rhetoric found application in litigation, in religious disputation, in official letter writing, in preaching, and in poetry. *On Invention* and *Rhetoric for Herennius* received new commentaries in this period, and there was a revived interest in Cicero's other works and that by Quintilian. With the development of universities in the twelfth century, dialectic came to dominate higher education, especially at Paris and Oxford, and rhetoric was chiefly studied as an adjunct to it. Boethius's work on topics replaced Cicero's writings as the favored authority for rhetoric, and new preaching manuals were composed emphasizing thematic development of arguments. The thirteenth century, when scholastic philosophy reached the height of its popularity, was something of a low point for classical rhetoric in many parts of Europe despite the recovery of Aristotle's *Rhetoric* in Latin translation at that time. The fourteenth century, however, saw renewed study of Cicero, not only in the Italian cities, but in France and England, shown again in new commentaries on the traditional authorities, *On Invention* and *Rhetoric for Herennius*.[1]

Martianus Capella

The medieval program of seven liberal arts can be traced back to the *enkyklios paideia*, or comprehensive education of classical Greece, that was included in the broad cultural studies of some Romans like Cicero.[2] In antiquity, however, the seven arts were an ideal in the minds of philosophers or a program of reading and study for leisured (*liberi*) adults, not a series of graded levels of study in school, as they became in the later Middle Ages. Grammar and rhetoric were the two stages of ancient education, both supported during the Roman Empire from public funds in towns of any size; but dialectic, the third art of the trivium (as the verbal studies came to be called), was an introduction to philosophy, which was undertaken by only the few. To learn the quantitative arts that became the medieval quadrivium—arithmetic, geometry, astronomy, and music theory—would have required independent study.

In the second and first centuries before Christ, practical-minded Romans began to put together surveys of Greek research and to create the earliest "encyclopedias." Cato the Elder composed one for his son, with sections on medicine, agriculture, rhetoric, and perhaps other subjects. Varro, Cicero's contemporary, wrote an encyclopedia of nine liberal arts, including not only grammar, dialectic, rhetoric, geometry, arithmetic, astronomy, and music, but also sections on medicine and architecture. In the first century after Christ Celsus composed another encyclopedia. All of these texts have been lost except for the section on medicine from Celsus's work. The earliest surviving encyclopedia is the work of Martianus Capella, written in Carthage between 410 and 439 and thus contemporary with Augustine's *On Christian Learning*. The content is drawn from standard sources. In the case of the discussion of rhetoric, contained in the fifth book, the primary source is Cicero's *On Invention*, to which is added an account of figures of speech based on the handbook of Aquila Romanus and some other material.

Modern readers have usually reacted with distaste to Martianus Capella's work, but the very features that make it least attractive today contributed to its medieval popularity. The title is *On the Marriage of Philology and Mercury*, and the first and second books are a fantastic, cumbersome allegory in which Satire tells Martianus how Mercury desired a wife and at Apollo's suggestion decided to marry Philology.[3] All sorts of divine and allegorical figures are introduced, the most important of whom are seven handmaids who are personifications of the seven liberal arts. In subsequent books each handmaid presents her discipline: grammar, dialectic, rhetoric, geometry, arithmetic, astronomy, and music, in that order. Two traditions existed about the order of studies in the trivium. In ancient schools, rhetoric ordinarily followed grammar and preceded any study of dialectic, and that order is followed by Cassiodorus and some others; Martianus, on the other hand, follows Varro in making dialectic a bridge between grammar and rhetoric. Boethius and his followers also treat rhetoric third, reflecting a philosophical view that knowledge is first discovered dialectically and then expressed rhetorically.

The technical parts of Martianus's work are written in a simple, if pedantic style, but the allegorical portions are presented in the highly artificial and obscure Latin that passed for eloquence in late antiquity. Medieval readers appear to have loved the allegory, excused the paganism because of it, and delighted in trying to penetrate the obscurity. The technical books appealed to them because of their superficiality: the account of the arts was concise, authoritative, and capable of being memorized. In any event, the popularity of the work is undoubted: at least 243 manuscripts exist in European libraries. A significant percentage of these come from the ninth and tenth centuries, the Carolingian Age, when the trivium and quadrivium began to emerge and commentaries were written on Martianus's encyclopedia.

Martianus's influence helped make rhetoric a part of the medieval liberal arts, but a minor part. The goal of classical education was primarily to train effective citizens; Martianus shows little awareness of that. His objective often seems the personal one of demonstrating his learning, but if a product of the studies he describes can be envisioned at all, the product is an amateur philosopher. To judge from references to it, Martianus's book on rhetoric was one of the least popular parts of his work. Fortunately, he made clear where a reader should turn for a more authoritative discussion, namely to Cicero, whom he mentions with the highest praise.

Cassiodorus

Martianus was a pagan, and his authority might not have ensured the survival of the formal study of rhetoric in the Middle Ages if his approach had not been taken up by Cassiodorus a hundred years later. Even the great authority of Augustine would probably not have been enough to ensure a place for rhetoric in religious training if Cassiodorus had not created a system that made minimal intellectual demands and was enforced by the discipline of monastic life.

Born in southern Italy around 480, Cassiodorus was well educated himself and held high office in Ravenna under the Ostrogothic kings at the same time as Boethius. But after the victories of the Greek Belisarius he withdrew to a monastery of his own founding at Vivarium in the toe of Italy. This establishment was remarkable for the emphasis it placed on the preservation of texts, both Christian and secular, and on the education of its monks. In addition to collecting, editing, copying, and commenting on texts, Cassiodorus composed, around 551, a work called *Institutiones Divinarum et Humanarum Lectionum*, or *Introduction to Divine and Human Readings*.[4] It became a basic reference work and educational handbook for centuries and was to be found in almost every medieval library. Cassiodorus addresses his monks about the importance of secular studies as follows:

> We can understand much in sacred literature as well as in the most learned interpreters through figures of speech, much through definitions, much through dialectic, much through the science of arithmetic, much through music, much through the science of geometry, much through astronomy; it is thus not unprofitable in the book which follows to touch briefly upon the elements of instruction laid down by secular teachers, that is, upon the arts and sciences, together with their divisions, in order that those who have acquired knowledge of this sort may have a brief review and those who perhaps have been unable to read widely may learn something from the compendious discussion. Beyond any doubt, knowledge of these matters, as it seemed to our Fathers, is useful and not to be avoided, since one finds this knowledge diffused everywhere in sacred literature, as it were in the origin of universal and perfect wisdom. When these matters have been restored to sacred literature and taught in connection with it, our capacity for understanding will be helped in every way. (*Institutiones* 2.27.1)

Clearly, many of Cassiodorus's monks had little or no education in such things as grammar or rhetoric, while he himself regarded some knowledge of those subjects as essential for the understanding of the Scriptures. The knowledge he expected, however, was of a very limited sort. In the second book, after a short chapter on grammar based on the standard work of Donatus, he turns to rhetoric, which is treated in hardly greater detail (2.2.1–17). Sources cited are Cicero's *On Invention* and

On the Orator, Quintilian, Augustine, Martianus, and two of the Minor Latin Rhetoricians, Fortunatianus and Victorinus. Although Cassiodorus had earlier mentioned figures of speech as a subject common to grammar and rhetoric (2.1.2), his discussion of rhetoric is chiefly devoted to summaries of stasis theory and rhetorical argumentation. Thus its logical side is emphasized, but nothing is done to illustrate how this knowledge can be applied to the study of the Scriptures or the teaching of Christianity. The barren nature of the account of rhetoric in all the early medieval encyclopedias is seen in their failure to adapt rhetorical theory to its commoner uses of their time: preaching, panegyric addresses to rulers, and the writing of poetry. Their interest was in preservation of some memory of rhetoric as it had been earlier taught and used.

Boethius

Boethius was mentioned in Chapter 4 as an important figure in the transmission of philosophical rhetoric to the Middle Ages, but his system of rhetoric deserves more attention here both because of its intrinsic qualities and because it became authoritative among scholastic teachers in the later Middle Ages. Boethius was born in 480, the same year as Cassiodorus, to a noble Roman family, and like Cassiodorus held high office under Theodoric, Ostrogothic king of northern Italy, delivering panegyrics at court and speaking in what passed for a senate. In 522 he was accused of conspiring against the king on behalf of the eastern emperor, was imprisoned, and in 524 was executed. In *The Consolation of Philosophy*, written in a combination of prose and poetry, he eloquently imagines the visit of Philosophy to him in prison and the consolation that she offered. It had been the boast of classical orators that they could bend the most stubborn heart, but Boethius does not address his eloquence to Theodoric or to his friends at court, as Seneca the Younger, for example, had done when exiled five hundred years earlier. Like Socrates in *Phaedo* he prepares himself for death. As did many others in late antiquity, he turns from civic life to the contemplation of eternal life. We have seen that his friend Cassiodorus withdrew from public to monastic life, and Gregory the Great, fifty years later, also laid down office in Rome for the cloister.

Boethius was one of the last Romans to know Greek well and to have access to a library of Greek philosophical literature. His introductions, translations, and commentaries were the source of knowledge of Aristotelian logic, including the topics, throughout the Middle Ages. His most important work on rhetoric is the fourth book of *De Topicis Differentiis*,[5] a title that might be translated *On Topical Differentiae*, *differentiae* being the basis of categorization in logical divisions of a question. The first three books of this work discuss dialectical topics; book four extends consideration to rhetoric. The main sources are Aristotle's *Topics*, Cicero's *On Invention* and *Topics*, and a work on topics by the late Greek philosopher-sophist Themistius. Boethius's objective is to identify the place of rhetoric within a theory of knowledge, to distinguish it from dialectic, and to catalogue rhetorical topics. The result is a theoretical discussion of philosophical interest rather than a practical handbook. He claims (1206c26) that there is no "tradition from the ancient authors on this subject," but that is not entirely true. He apparently had no knowledge of Aristotle's *Rhetoric* and of the *prolegomena* being composed by Greeks as introductions to Hermogenic rhetoric, but he could have found the subject discussed in Quintilian's *Institutio*.

Boethius distinguishes dialectic from rhetoric on several grounds. Dialectic examines only a general thesis; rhetoric investigates hypotheses that involve particular circumstances. Dialectic is restricted to question and answer; rhetoric constructs a continuous discourse. Dialectic uses complete syllogisms; rhetoric is content with enthymemes in which one proposition is omitted. In dialectic, one person states a thesis and another, the questioner, judges the argument; in rhetoric the judge is someone other than an opponent. Boethius's description of an enthymeme as a truncated syllogism helped make that the standard view in later times. His failure to differentiate rhetoric from dialectic, which is limited to logical argument, on the basis of the use of ethos and pathos in rhetorical persuasion is a major weakness, with serious implications for some later discussions of invention. It is another sign of his lack of knowledge of Aristotle's *Rhetoric*, or his neglect of such major Latin works as Cicero's *On the Orator* and Quintilian's treatise. It was perhaps an oversight, since subsequently (1208c6–8) he defines the work of rhetoric as to teach and to move, and one of the few examples of the use of a topic he cites is the argument that Catiline plotted against the state because he was a person marked by the baseness of vices (121b11). There is no recognition, however, of the character and authority of a speaker as important features of rhetoric but not of dialectic, or that the emotions might be moved in any other way than by argument.

Boethius's view of rhetoric is summed up in the following paragraph:

> The *genus* of rhetoric is knowledge. There are three *species* of rhetoric: judicial, epideictic, and deliberative. The *matter* is the political question, which is called a "case." The *parts of this matter* are issues (i.e., forms of stasis). The *parts of rhetoric* are invention, arrangement, style, memory, and delivery. Its *instrument* is discourse. The *parts of the instrument* are exordium, narration, partition, confirmation, refutation, and peroration. Its *work* is to teach and move. The one who does this work (i.e., the *agent*) is the orator. Its *function* (or end) is to speak well, sometimes to persuade. (1211b18–28)

The latter point had been explained earlier (1208c22–33): Boethius distinguishes an internal end, "within the orator," of having spoken well and an external end, "within another," as having persuaded an audience. Much of the rest of the book is devoted to explication of the topics useful in various forms of stasis. Boethius's discussion, brief as it is, is beautifully systematic. It is not surprising that it appealed to the scholastics of Paris in the thirteenth century, when the work became the standard text on rhetoric.

Isidore

A fourth person who contributed to the survival of some knowledge of classical rhetoric in the early Middle Ages was Isidore of Seville (ca. 570–636). He was the author of a vast work entitled *Origines*, or *Etymologiae*, which, like the works of Martianus and Cassiodorus, served as an encyclopedia of ancient learning through the following centuries. It outlines the trivium and quadrivium in the first three books. The brief account of rhetoric (2.1–22)[6] is based on that in Cassiodorus and is really a series of snippets on various subjects with little organization. The longer chapters are on stasis theory, the syllogism, and figures of speech and thought. A chapter on law (2.10) is inserted between the discussion of the syllogism and that of style and implies that Isidore thought rhetorical invention was useful in the courts of his time. Isidore was perhaps writing primarily for the education of the Spanish episcopacy, which was involved in legal and political decision making to a greater extent than elsewhere.[7]

Applications of Rhetoric in the Early Middle Ages

Classical rhetoric as understood in the early Middle Ages found a limited practical application in a number of oral and written forms. Much of the preaching was then of a very simple sort, but in major ecclesiastical or political centers there was need for a preacher to demonstrate knowledge of theology, biblical exegesis, and perhaps some rhetorical skill. The Second Council of Vaison in 529 extended the right to preach from bishops to priests and provided that if no priest were available, a homily by one of the Fathers was to be read by a deacon. Augustine's treatise *On Christian Learning* was an important work in establishing the tradition of homiletic preaching, but its influence was not great before the Carolingian Age. A more widely read work, but one that contributed to *reducing* the role and influence of rhetoric, was the *Cura Pastoralis*, or *Pastoral Care*, by Gregory the Great (pope 590–604). It became a basic handbook of church administration. Although Gregory stresses the importance of preaching and of adapting a sermon to the congregation, he restricts his remarks to the content of sermons and says nothing about their rhetorical qualities.[8] Gregory had held high office in Rome, served as an ambassador to Constantinople, played a political role as pope, and encouraged missionary activity. He himself wrote a highly rhetorical Latin, but his attitude toward classical literature was negative, as seen in a celebrated letter rebuking Bishop Desiderius for teaching grammar and poetry (*Epistles* 11.54).

Before the Carolingian period, rhetoric was studied with a few private teachers and in some monastic schools, which were open to the public but were primarily intended to train those entering the life of the Church. Discussions of stasis theory and forms of argument, like the syllogism, overlapped with dialectic and could serve as an introduction to theological disputation for those who became involved in that activity. The definitions of rhetoric given in the encyclopedias and by Boethius associate it with civic life, and especially with legal procedures, which chiefly took the form of hearings before a civil or ecclesiastical official, and both the judge and the petitioner needed some knowledge of law, of public speaking, and of argumentation. The best picture of the practical uses of judicial rhetoric in the sixth century, as well as the dangers and disruptions on all sides, can be found in *History of the Franks* by Gregory of Tours, completed in 594.[9] To cite one example, Gregory gives (5.18) a full account of the trial of Praetextatus, bishop of Rouen, before an ecclesiastical court. Although no lengthy addresses were permitted, application of stasis theory and rhetorical forms of argument are evident.[10] Another application of rhetoric was in the addresses of ambassadors sent back and forth between warring kings and between officials of the Church. Our knowledge of public address in the early Middle Ages is rather limited; it is likely that there was more occasion for it than can be documented from extant sources. It is, however, significant that from the end of the fifth century to the beginning of the Renaissance no one in western Europe, in contrast to the situation in the East, seems to have acquired fame as a civic orator.

Progymnasmata, the systematic exercises in composition, were known in the West in the early Middle Ages. Some teachers may have known the discussion in the second book of Quintilian's *Education of the Orator*. The handbook of *progymnasmata* attributed to Hermogenes was translated into Latin by the grammarian Priscian around A.D. 500; it is said to be found with other works of Priscian in numerous manuscripts and thus may have been widely used.[11] It describes how to write fables, narratives, chrias, encomia, comparisons, personifications, and other types of composition, and early medieval writers were certainly familiar with these forms. Fables of the sort attributed to Aesop were known from the earlier Latin collections of Babrius and Phaedrus, and the reading and writing of fables in prose and poetry was popular throughout the Middle Ages. Exercises in narrative and personification would have been useful in the training of a historian like Gregory of Tours, and exercise in encomia for praise poetry, which is found in all periods. Latin poetry in late antiquity had required the application of a thorough knowledge of rhetoric and had exploited rhetorical genres in the composition of panegyrical poetry and principles of arrangement and style in all forms of composition. Throughout the Middle Ages poetry remained a major field for rhetoric. Important rhetorical poets whose works have survived include Ausonius and Claudian in the fourth century and Sidonius Apollinaris in the fifth. This tradition continued even in the darker days that followed. The best example from the late sixth and early seventh century is Venantius Fortunatus, who composed panegyrical poetry with considerable competence at the court of the Merovingian kings.[12]

Bede

Glimpses of the role of rhetoric in Britain in the seventh and eighth centuries can be found in the writings of the Venerable Bede (673–735). His homilies show how he applied a knowledge of rhetoric to preaching, but the only one of his works to discuss rhetoric directly is a small book entitled *On Tropes and Figures*.[13] It was intended to help readers of the Bible identify these devices, and the illustrations are entirely biblical. Bede's sources were Donatus and Cassiodorus.

More interesting are references to speech in Bede's great *Ecclesiastical History of the English People*.[14] Missionary preaching is seen in Bede's description of the arrival in Britain in 597 of the monk Augustine, who became the first archbishop of Canterbury. The pagan king Ethelbert gave the missionary a hearing in an open field on an island (1.25), and Bede vividly describes how Augustine and his company advanced to meet the king, singing the litanies and preceded by a cross of silver and a painted image of Christ. All then sat down, and Augustine preached "the word of life" to the king and his household. Bede apparently had no sources about what Augustine said, though he does quote the reply in which the king refuses to abandon the traditions of his people but grants Augustine the necessities of life and freedom to preach. The later missionary activities of Wilfrid in Frisia are also described by Bede (5.19). Some additional information on missionary preaching in the north in this period can be found in saints' lives and letters, such as those of Boniface. It seems clear that the rhetoric resembled that of the early Christians, with reliance on claims of authority and external means of persuasion.

An occasion for debate was provided by the synods of the Church, such as that at Whitby in 664 when Bishop Colman of the Scots contended against the same Wilfrid, advocate for Bishop Agilbert of the West Saxons, on the true date for Easter, with King Osway as judge. Bede gives a version of the speeches on both sides (3.25), and one can see that Wilfrid in particular had considerable skill in argumentation. The king reduces the question to the issue of whether Saint Columba, who had brought Christianity to Scotland, had any special authority in his date for Easter to match that of Saint Peter, which Wilfrid had invoked. Bishop Colman has to admit he has none, and the king declares that Wilfrid has prevailed and orders the Church to observe the orthodox date for Easter.

Bede himself never seems to put a very high value on eloquence. As a Christian, he doubtless trusted in the power of the spirit to work belief in the truth. He did, however, value learning, in which he would have included the liberal arts and some secular literature. For example, he describes how (4.2) Theodorus, in 669 the first archbishop to be accepted by all the English Church, encouraged the liberal arts and how he himself as abbot at Jarrow played a major part in educational efforts in Northumberland. Study of rhetoric declined, however, in Britain during the next two hundred years, perhaps partly because of the austere influence of Benedictine monks.[15]

The Carolingian Age

The political map of Europe was changed in the late eighth century by the military conquests in France, Germany, and Italy of the Frankish king known to history as Charlemagne, "Charles the Great," who was eventually crowned in Rome as the first "Holy Roman Emperor" on Christmas day 800. He could not reverse the decentralization of government, but he did control the power of the nobles, maintained a degree of law, raised the standard of living, and improved education. As a result, the ninth and tenth centuries in France and Germany saw a modest cultural renaissance from the Dark Ages in art, learning, and literature. Many of the best surviving manuscripts of the Latin classics were made in this period, using the new, easily readable minuscule script, and new writings on rhetoric appeared that continued to draw on the classics but began to adapt the tradition to the needs of the times.

Alcuin

In 781, Charlemagne invited Alcuin, called Albinus in Latin (ca. 732–804), to take charge of the Palace School at Aachen in Germany. Alcuin had been trained in Britain by successors of Bede, and brought a tradition of ancient learning that had languished on the continent. He not only taught many individuals at Charlemagne's court but seems to have contributed to *De Litteris Collendis*, the emperor's mandate encouraging verbal education, issued about 795.[16] The objective of the mandate was to encourage churches and monasteries to provide instruction in grammar and rhetoric so that individuals could attain their full capacity to read and understand the holy writ. Even among ecclesiastics the level of literacy was low; a literate clergy for the future was certainly a major goal, but Charlemagne was doubtless concerned also for the education of future officers of the imperial administration. Instruction in grammar was the primary aim, but the mandate mentions "figures, tropes, and other things like them commonly found in the sacred writings." Although no specific provisions were made for enforcement of the mandate, it contributed to improved educational opportunities offered by the Church. Eventually monastic schools including Bec in Normandy and Bobbio in Italy and cathedral schools including Chartres and Rheims in France became major educational institutions. Rhetoric did not recover its old influence, but it had an established place as a link between grammar and dialectic, which the controversial needs of the Church gradually elevated into the most important of the liberal arts in the later medieval period.

Toward the end of his life Alcuin wrote his *Disputation on Rhetoric and on Virtues* in the form of a dialogue between himself and Charlemagne.[17] Though rather little read in succeeding centuries, this work is important as the first attempt to consider the secular uses of rhetoric in the Middle Ages. In the opening pages Charlemagne points out that the strength of the art of rhetoric lies entirely in dealing with civil questions. He himself is involved in such matters on a daily basis and he would therefore like Alcuin to open to him "the gates of the rhetorical art of dialectical subtlety." In what follows Charlemagne asks brief questions and Alcuin replies, with agreement by the king and sometimes further comments. Although the dialogue probably never took place in this form, it is likely that Alcuin had discussed the need for instruction in rhetoric with Charlemagne and knew he would approve. The practical utility of the subject is mentioned again at the end of section 3, and Alcuin has specifically adapted the judicial rhetoric of antiquity to contemporary conditions at some points.[18] It is possible, however, to read the work as an effort by Alcuin to encourage Charlemagne to recreate a system of legal procedure resembling that of Roman times. Although the distinction of three kinds of oratory is made (§ 5), the actual discussion is limited to judicial rhetoric. That rhetoric had application to preaching, letter writing, or poetic composition is not mentioned.

The dialogue gives a brief systematic account of rhetorical invention derived from Cicero's *On Invention*, supplemented with material from the handbook of Julius Victor for subjects not discussed by Cicero. In contrast to Boethius, Alcuin stresses the function of character and authority in persuasion (see, e.g., § 26). One brief passage on sophistic discourse (§ 35) is inserted to show the absurdities to which dialectical controversy could be reduced. Such controversy had apparently become a fashion in the court, foreshadowing the development of scholasticism. On the subject of memory Alcuin quotes Cicero (§ 39) but was unaware of mnemonic systems.[19] He has considerably more to say about delivery (§§ 41–43), which had been neglected by previous medieval writers,[20] revealing that public address had some importance in his time, and he recommends practical exercises in speaking. Charlemagne replies that it seems to him the young should, from an early age, be practiced in the kind of speaking that is important in civil cases and secular business. This may mean that Alcuin had reintroduced declamation into rhetorical studies and is here attributing approval of it to Charlemagne. After surveying the five parts of rhetoric, Alcuin concludes with a brief consideration of the four cardinal virtues of prudence, justice, courage, and temperance, also based on Cicero and here recommended as a good subject for practice in speaking (§ 44). Thus, without expressly noting it, some material for panegyric is provided and Alcuin can be read as commending qualities of the ideal ruler in his patron.

Hrabanus Maurus

A second important writer on rhetoric in the Carolingian period was Hrabanus Maurus (778–856), a student of Alcuin. He was German in origin and became abbot of Fulda, near Frankfurt, where he wrote a handbook of church liturgy and practice for Germans entering the priesthood. The third book of this work, *De Clericorum Institutione*, or *On the Education of Clerics*, is the major treatment of preaching in the early Middle Ages.[21] There are first short chapters on each of the liberal arts. That on rhetoric (3.19) points out that it is useful not only for civil questions but for the ecclesiastical discipline, and stresses that it should be part of the trivium of introductory studies but not allowed to take up the attention of an adult preacher. What follows (3.27–39) consists largely of excerpts from Augustine's *On Christian Learning* in the order of Augustine's text, including the account of the three kinds of style and the duties of the orator, with borrowings from Cassiodorus and Gregory the Great. Most preaching was, of course, homiletic, but an example of a panegyric sermon survives in Hrabanus's *Encomium of the Holy Cross*.

Notker of St. Gall

Adaptation of classical rhetoric to medieval needs was more extensively attempted by a German monk at the monastery of St. Gall named Notiker, probably to be identified as Notker Labeo who lived from around A.D. 950 to 1022. He was the author of a *New Rhetoric*, a short treatise that reorganizes traditional classical doctrine in an original way, illustrates it from Scripture and contemporary life, and provides terminology in German for monks with a weak understanding of Latin.[22] In the preface, Notiker, who had translated Martianus Capella's *Marriage of Philology and Mercury* into German, laments the loss of "Rhetorica" in allegorical terms: "It is difficult to describe her as she was, for much time has passed since she ceased to be." He outlines a cyclical theory of the history of rhetoric, beginning with an original natural eloquence, then (throughout the classical period) the reign of "her artificial daughter," and finally, after that became extinct, the return of natural eloquence in his own age.[23] The time, he thought, was ripe for a new succession as he will present it, which is to take the form of the study of the "material" of rhetoric and of the "art" of controversial speech. Notker envisioned rhetoric as broadly concerned with resolution of any controversy. Its goal is to reconcile differences, to reach consensus on wise policy, and to demonstrate who is worthy of appointment to civil and religious office. Although the latter point is most unusual, envisioning as it does speeches praising candidates for office, these goals are, of course, the judicial, deliberative, and epideictic functions of traditional rhetoric. Notker regarded rhetoric as applicable to monastic activities in writings, studying, and communal relationships, as well as in aiding understanding of the diverse kinds of learning for which a monastery was responsible.[24] For all the intrinsic interest of his work, it seems to be unique in its conceptions and was little known outside St. Gall.

There were a number of other significant figures in the revival of classical rhetoric in the Carolingian period, too many to be discussed in this survey. A better knowledge of Ciceronian rhetoric was a goal of some teachers, who sought out better texts and made new, improved copies. Servatus Lupus of Ferrières is an example in the ninth century.[25] He owned a partial text of Quintilian and wrote to the pope in search of a complete version. In the tenth century Gerbert of Reims, who became Pope Sylvester II in 999, obtained texts of *On the Orator*, *Topics*, and orations of Cicero and revived the practice of declamation in his school.[26]

Rhetoric in Medieval Italy

Latin survived, in what is called "Vulgar Latin," as a spoken language in Italy well into the Middle Ages and with it some study of the verbal arts of the classical period. Adaptation of these to Italian was not difficult. As mentioned earlier, civic life resumed in Italian cities in the ninth and tenth centuries, creating practical needs for secular speech and writing. Conversely, Italian scholars did not develop the consuming interest in dialectic and systematic theology that came to dominate study of the liberal arts in northern Europe.

An Italian of peculiar interest in the history of rhetoric was Anselm of Besate (ca. 1000–1060), who had been trained in secular rhetoric and around 1047 wrote a work entitled *Rhetorimachia*, or *The Battle of Rhetoric*, in three books.[27] Anselm had a personality similar to that of some of the later Italian humanists: he has much to say in praise of his learning, morals, and achievements, and he shows himself to be ambitious, combative, and touchy. *Rhetorimachia* takes the form of an invective against the rhetorical ignorance and moral failings of his cousin Rotiland and a defense of Anselm's own learning and morality. He calls the work a *controversia* (like those in Roman schools) and presents it as a model of judicial rhetoric based on teachings of the late Latin grammarian Servius, Cicero, Quintilian, Victorinus, Grillius, and Boethius. In the first book he attacks the form and style of a letter from Rotiland on the basis of rhetorical principles and the validity of Rotiland's claim to understand rhetoric better than he himself does, and he ends by attacking Rotiland's claims to moral virtue. The second book begins with a dream in which Anselm sees the allegorical figures of Dialectic, Rhetoric, and Grammar in Elysium; they beg him to return to earth since without him their skills will not be known to human beings. The rest of Book 2 is a defense against moral charges imagined to have been made against Anselm by Rotiland. The third book is an attack on Rotiland's character and ends with an epilogue in which Anselm claims that his work has illustrated on a small scale the extensive teaching of the rhetorical authorities of the past. The work seems to have had little or no influence on later rhetorical writing, but it provides a vivid glimpse of how one scholar viewed the uses of speech and writing in eleventh-century Italy.

Classical rhetoric was primarily an oral art that taught how to compose and deliver a speech before a living audience. Although these conditions existed to a limited extent in medieval Italy, the use of the art of persuasion in writing, especially in petitions, letters, and archival documents was somewhat more important. In the eleventh century revival of interest in and knowledge of Roman law began to overshadow rhetoric in the study of civic or ecclesiastical communication. Justinian's *Digest*, unknown in western Europe in the early Middle Ages, became an important influence on jurisprudence. Twelfth-century Bologna produced Irnerius, who first taught rhetoric and the other arts but later became the greatest medieval authority on Roman law. To meet the needs of lawyers, notaries, and ecclesiastical officials, the discipline of rhetoric turned to creation of a rhetorical art of letter writing, known as the *dictamen* or *ars dictaminis*.

Handbooks of Dictamen

Hierarchical, literate societies around the world develop polite conventions for address, used in court ceremonial and in letters. The earliest examples can be found in political and commercial correspondence in the Near East in the second millennium B.C. It was important to use the correct title in addressing a superior, to put the name of the person claiming higher status first, whether addressee or writer, and often to include the hope that the recipient was well and assure him of the goodwill of the writer. Similar conventions can be found in ancient Greek letters, where the salutation was sometimes given further rhetorical development. The most familiar examples are the opening lines of the epistles of Saint Paul; for example, "Paul, an apostle of Christ Jesus, by the will of God, and Timothy our brother, to the church of God which is at Corinth, with all the saints who are in the whole of Achaia: Grace to you and peace from God our Father and the Lord Jesus Christ" (I Cor. 1:1–2).

Greek and Latin rhetorical treatises, concentrating on judicial oratory, usually omit discussion of the rhetoric of letters; the chief exceptions are short passages in Demetrius's Greek work *On Style* (§§ 223–35) and in the late Latin handbook of Julius Victor (ch. 27). There are, however, several short Greek handbooks devoted to classifying kinds of letters and giving examples of how to write them;[28] these were probably used in training scribes in the East. Something like them may once have existed in Latin, but formal letter writing was probably largely learned by imitation of model letters. The Middle Ages put high value on respect for rank and the use of the right words in written or oral formal address. Extensive correspondence was carried on by the papal court, the courts of rulers and nobles, scholars, and individuals seeking privileges or redress of wrongs. To be effective, such letters had to observe the conventions expected at the time and be well written. To help meet this need, medieval teachers developed a new kind of rhetorical instruction, the rhetorical art of letter writing known as *dictamen* (from Latin *dictare*, meaning to dictate a letter to a scribe).[29] Some of the later dictaminal works were written in verse, presumably to encourage memorization.[30]

Formal study of dictamen seems to have begun first in the school of the monastery of Monte Cassino in southern Italy, and its first great teacher was apparently Alberic, who lived around the middle of the eleventh century. Alberic's *Flowers of Rhetoric* deals primarily with ornamentation of the style of letters, his *Breviarium* deals with the content and form, including the use of prose rhythm.[31] In the twelfth century, dictamen, like law, was taught in the University of Bologna. Classical rhetorical precepts about the parts of an oration and figures of speech as found in the classical Latin rhetorical handbooks were adapted into a standard five-part epistolary structure: the *salutatio*, or greeting, with the names and titles of the addressee and writer in the proper sequence; the *captatio benevolentiae*, or exordium, designed to make the reader attentive, receptive, and well-disposed; the *narratio*, explaining the facts and situation; the *petitio*, or specific request, demand, or announcement; and a relatively simple *conclusio*. Alberic gives most attention to the first two parts.

Dictamen was primarily concerned with the conventions of diplomatic and legal correspondence, both civil and ecclesiastical. The papal court in particular sought high standards of accuracy and dignity in letters issued and received there. There was thus considerable demand for persons trained in the proper forms of communication, and the art was taught in schools and universities and described in numerous handbooks. There were also catalogs of titles to be used in addressing recipients as well as "formularies," or collections of commonplaces for use in letters, and like Greek handbooks of *progymnasmata*, works on dictamen often included models for imitation. This is true, for example, of the treatises of Adalbertus Samaritanus and of Hugh of Bologna, two of the most famous writers on dictamen in the early twelfth century. About the middle of the thirteenth century *ars dictaminis*, as a study at the University of Bologna, was replaced by *ars notaria*, concerned with how a notary should draw up legal, commercial, and diplomatic documents; this included dictaminal rules but was legally oriented. In the fourteenth century Peter de Labrancha, captain of the Commune of Bologna, assembled the people and announced that rhetoric was indispensable to states and people, but had ceased to be studied in the university. He was, therefore, appointing a scholar named Bartolinus to a chair in rhetoric at a salary of thirty pounds a year. He was to give two lecture courses a year on *Rhetoric for Herennius* and teach dictamen and public speaking, "so that both commoners and the literate and any person at all might learn the art from him."[32] Meanwhile, the study of dictamen had begun also in France, where a more artificial style was encouraged,[33] and in England, where it was introduced by Peter of Blois to the curriculum at Oxford in the late twelfth century and later studied as an aid to English composition.[34]

Although the handbooks of dictamen were devoted to letter writing, they often defined that art broadly as the art of writing and distinguished several genres, including qualitative poetry, accentual poetry, and rhythmical prose, before concentrating on the latter as appropriate in letter writing. Ever since Aristotle, writers on rhetoric had recognized that good prose should be rhythmical. Beginning in late antiquity, however, feeling for the quantity of long and short syllables, the basis of meter in classical Greek and Latin, waned and was replaced by an increased perception of stress accent in words, as found in modern poetry. Patterns of stress accent then became the basis of a new system of prose rhythm, replacing the quantitative system described by Cicero and Quintilian. This new system of prose rhythm is called the *cursus*; it involves rhythmical flow of stress on certain syllables at the end of a phrase, clause, or sentence, and its three main forms can be illustrated by the English phrases "hélp and defénd us," which is *cursus planus*; "góverned and sánctified," which is *cursus tardus*; and "púnished for our offénses," which is *cursus velox*. First developed in Latin, the cursus was imitated in the formal prose of English and other languages in the late Middle Ages and Renaissance; it is, for example, a feature of the style of the King James Version of the English Bible.[35]

Although the dictamen is the most distinctive development of Italian medieval rhetoric, the circumstances of life in Italian cities required a variety of forms of public address; these included funeral orations, speeches for academic occasions, and other kinds of epideictic, as well as speeches by ambassadors and some judicial oratory. Writings on rhetoric in the thirteenth century included models for such speeches and rules for their composition.[36] Guido Faba (ca. 1190–1244), author of an important handbook of dictamen, also wrote model letters and speeches,[37] and model speeches can be found in other works intended for instruction of city officials.[38] One of the more interesting works is the *Rhetorica Novissima* (1235) by the eccentric and aggressive Boncompagno of Signa, modestly intended as a replacement for Cicero.[39] It consists of thirteen short "books" on the origin of law, the parts of rhetoric, exordia, narratives, arguments, panegyric and invective, and memory. Much of it is in the form of question and definition. Although the work applies to letter writing, the material would be useful to an advocate in a court of law. Boncompagno had earlier compiled a collection of model salutations for letters and also a *Rota Veneris*, or *Wheel of Venus*, which is a manual on how to write love letters. Another sign of thirteenth-century Italian interest in judicial rhetoric is the *Ars Arengandi*, or *Art of Haranguing*, by

Jacques de Dinant, who was apparently a monk and teacher of rhetoric in Bologna in the late thirteenth century.[40] It consists of a short introductory poem and extracts from *Rhetoric for Herennius* on the parts of rhetoric and the form of judicial oratory. Dinant also wrote on dictamen and composed the first full-scale commentary to *Rhetoric for Herennius*. Brunetto Latini (1220–94), teacher of Dante, wrote a treatise in French on the liberal arts, called *Trésor*[41] and translated into Italian portions of Cicero's *On Invention* and three of Cicero's speeches. His works mark the beginning of the study of rhetoric in the vernacular languages.

The teaching of technical rhetoric in Italy in the later Middle Ages is an important antecedent for the flowering of rhetoric in Italy in the Renaissance. The humanists of the fourteenth and fifteenth centuries added their great enthusiasm for classical models and their acquaintance with many more texts to a living art of speaking and writing that had already adapted some features of Ciceronian rhetoric to contemporary needs.

Rhetoric in Medieval France

The eleventh and twelfth centuries in France were in many ways the high point of medieval culture: the period of the greatest achievements in art and architecture, of the foundation of the University of Paris, of the flowering of scholastic philosophy, and of original works of vernacular literature.[42] As a result of the Norman Conquest of Britain in 1066, there were close cultural ties between France and England, and the revival of rhetorical studies in these countries eventually made itself felt also in Spain.[43]

Italian study of rhetoric may have contributed to increased interest in the discipline in French schools in the eleventh century. Lanfranc, for example, born in Pavia around 1005, was educated in rhetoric and law in Italy before going to Bec in Normandy to teach. He became acquainted with William the Conqueror and ended his life as archbishop of Canterbury, from 1070 to 1089. But the schools of northwestern France, and especially the cathedral school of Chartres, already were giving serious attention to the trivium and quadrivium when Lanfranc arrived there.[44] The leading figure in the rise of Chartres to eminence was Fulbert, bishop from 1006 to 1028. He was followed by other distinguished teachers over the next century and a half, among them Bernard, Bernard's brother Thierry, and their student, John of Salisbury.[45] The fullest discussion of the liberal arts as understood in the Middle Ages is probably that found in the enormous, uncompleted encyclopedia by Thierry, the *Heptateuchon*, written about the middle of the twelfth century and as yet unpublished.[46] Quintilian's *Education of the Orator*, though known only in a mutilated text, was unusually popular in Chartres, especially its discussion of elementary education and grammar.[47] Quintilian influenced the teaching of Bernard and John and was frequently cited by John in his major works, *Metalogicon* and *Policraticus*. Orations of Cicero were copied and extensively studied, and ancient collections of declamations were also read; these included the work by Seneca the Elder and declamations wrongly attributed to Quintilian. There is some evidence that practice of declamation on fictitious themes took place in some schools of the twelfth century.[48]

Thierry also authored a commentary to Cicero's *On Invention*, the only example of such a commentary available in a modern edition,[49] and mention of it here provides an opportunity to say something about the commentary tradition in rhetoric.[50] Although commentaries were written on the writings of Martianus Capella, Boethius, and a few other texts, Cicero's *On Invention* was the overwhelming favorite until the middle of the twelfth century, when commentaries to *Rhetoric for Herennius*, which was then believed to be by Cicero, began to replace it. The earliest extant commentaries to *On Invention* are those by Victorinus, dating from the fourth century, and Grillius, written in the early sixth century. These, especially that by Victorinus, were studied throughout the Middle Ages and influenced the content of later commentaries, which began to become common in the early twelfth century. A large number of commentaries composed between the twelfth and the sixteenth centuries survive in manuscript, often only a single manuscript of any one work. They originated in the lectures of teachers in schools throughout western Europe, but they have been revised and edited by their authors into a fuller form for readers, either students or other teachers. Some are quite elaborate, with extended prefaces, quotation of a lemma—words or phrases of the text—and detailed explication of it, often with examples or with digressions on related matters of interest to the writer. In addition to these comprehensive running commentaries there are also manuscripts containing *On Invention* and *Rhetoric for Herennius* with extensive marginal notes.

The commentaries give a glimpse of how rhetoric was taught in the twelfth century and later and how this knowledge seemed relevant to the times. As John Ward has shown,[51] the commentaries provide a kind of general education about the past and the present, including the customs, practices, and literature of the classical past and contemporary times; they discuss canon and civil law, monastic usages, the nature of time, the relationship between the letter of the text and the intent of the author, and how teaching is imparted; they apply rhetorical issues to biblical or religious situations; they provide vocational training for ecclesiastics in memorizing texts, in delivery, in scriptural exegesis, in theological debate, in the writing of letters and documents, in deliberative oratory at councils and synods, in church and state politics, and in the delivery of sermons. Particularly important was their possible application to legal cases involving clerics. Some examples of pleadings in canon law have survived from the twelfth century; they rely on argument from the letter of the law, show the structure of classical judicial oratory, and make some use of figures of speech, but are otherwise of a very simple sort.[52]

The Boethian tradition of subordinating rhetoric to dialectic had adherents throughout the Middle Ages and grew stronger beginning in the eleventh century. Fulbert of Chartres made a digest of the fourth book of Boethius's *On Topical Differentiae*, and Abelard wrote a commentary on it. There were also more pointed critics of rhetoric. In the eleventh century, for example, Onulf of Speyer advised against use of figures of speech and criticized rhetorical debate as inimical to Christian peace and tranquility.[53] In the twelfth century, in his versified allegory of the liberal arts, *Anticlaudianus*, Alan of Lille reduced rhetoric to specious adornment.[54] A statute of 1215 describing the curriculum of the young University of Paris indicates that rhetoric was only a subject of lectures outside the standard course and was to be based on Boethius.[55]

The texts of Aristotle's logical works in Latin translations were fundamental to teaching philosophy in Paris and elsewhere, and efforts were made to acquire Latin translations of other works by Aristotle that had been heard about from Arabic commentators or were thought to exist in Byzantium. About 1240, Hermannus Allemanus (Herman the German) made a Latin translation of an Arabic commentary on Aristotle's *Rhetoric* attributed to Al-Farabi. Soon thereafter the *Rhetoric* itself was translated for the first time. This is known as the "old translation," sometimes attributed to Bartholomew of Messina, though the name of the translator is not known with certainty. Around 1270, William of Moerbeke produced a second translation, which became more widely known and survives in many manuscripts. William, who was born in Flanders, was a member of the Dominican religious order and had spent several years in Greek-speaking areas; he learned the language and was urged by Thomas Aquinas to translate texts of Aristotle. In addition to the *Rhetoric* he produced rather literal versions of Aristotle's *Politics* and *Metaphysics* and of some Greek commentators on Aristotle. About ten years later Aegidius (or Giles of Rome, as he is sometimes known) wrote a Latin commentary on William's version. The emphasis of this commentary, along with the groupings of the *Rhetoric* with other texts in bound manuscript volumes of Aristotle, seems to make it clear that the *Rhetoric* was read in the thirteenth and fourteenth centuries primarily as a moral and political treatise because of the discussion of those subjects in Books 1 and 2 and that it was little used for study of rhetoric.[56]

Thomas Aquinas (1224–74) was the most famous and influential of the scholastic philosophers of Paris. He can hardly be said to have had much interest in rhetoric, but he was familiar with Cicero's *On Invention*, which he quotes in discussing law and justice, natural law, custom, and related subjects.[57] In his *Summa Theologica* 1.9–10 he discusses the use of metaphor in the Scriptures and whether a word in the Bible can have more than one meaning. His conclusion, which was substantially the view Augustine advanced in *On Christian Learning*, is that metaphor is a device of poetry, which he calls the least of all the sciences, but that sacred doctrine required the truth to be veiled as an exercise for thoughtful minds and as a defense against the ridicule of unbelievers. He also concluded that a word in the Scriptures can have a literal, an allegorical, a tropological or moral, and an anagogical sense, the latter relating to eternal glory. He noted, however, that some theologians combined the allegorical and anagogical into one. Elsewhere in the same work (2.2) he discusses memory, drawing on *Rhetoric for Herennius*, but his interest in memory, like that of most medieval thinkers, was ethical, not rhetorical.[58]

The Arts of Poetry

The most characteristic contributions to rhetoric in the Latin Middle Ages are the numerous and extensive commentaries to *On Invention* and *Rhetoric for Herennius*, the handbooks on letter writing (*ars dictaminis*), the handbooks on verse composition (*ars poetriae*), and the handbooks on thematic preaching (*ars praedicandi*). The first two have been discussed above; this chapter will conclude with brief consideration of the last two of these developments.

Medieval poets, whether writing in Latin or in the vulgate languages, were trained in the liberal arts of grammar and rhetoric in which they learned the use of topics and arguments, the principles of arrangement and amplification, the names and uses of tropes, the figures of speech, the concept of the grand, middle, and plain style, the use of topics and forms of argument, and the conventions of literary genres. To a considerable extent, a work's ability to apply and vary this teaching, to employ allegory, and to incorporate allusions to biblical and classical literature was what made it seem "literary" to the ears and eyes of medieval audiences. Erich Auerbach's *Literary Language and Its Public in Late Latin Antiquity and in the Middle Ages* is a standard discussion of many of these features of composition. Young students of grammar and rhetoric, usually about the age of junior high school students in America today, were practiced in Latin prose composition along the lines of the traditional *progymnasmata* and in verse composition. They might, for example, be assigned to compose a poem in praise of a swallow. All instruction and all exercises were in Latin. In the twelfth and thirteenth centuries, handbooks of verse composition began to be composed.[59] The versified *Art of Poetry* by the first century B.C. Roman poet Horace was studied throughout the Middle Ages and provided a model for the later handbooks; they repeat some of its precepts but omit discussion of drama, which takes up a large portion of Horace's work.

The earliest medieval handbook of poetry to survive is the *Ars Versificatoria* by Matthew of Vendome, who taught grammar at Orleans and Paris in the mid-twelfth century.[60] Matthew wrote for elementary students, providing definitions and topics and discussing the forms of words, the use of figures and tropes, the faults in style, and the overall execution of the subject.

The *Poetria Nova* of Geoffrey of Vinsauf, written in the early thirteenth century, was addressed to more advanced students and is written in verse, thus exemplifying some of the principles it lays down.[61] Geoffrey begins with some general remarks: the ideas of a poem should be planned out in detail and the parts arranged before being written down; then the poetic art should be applied to clothe the matter with words. In what follows he discusses arrangement; amplification by use of repetition, periphrasis, comparison, apostrophe, digression, and descriptive passages; and ornaments of style, divided into "difficult" ones, such as metaphor and metonymy, and "easy" ones, which are the figures of thought. Then there is discussion of decorum, of the appropriate treatment of persons and things, and of meter. Finally come sections on memory and delivery. The work thus progresses through the rhetorical canons of arrangement, style, memory, and delivery; discussion of invention is spread throughout, chiefly in the form of illustrations of what to say.

A third work is by John of Garland, who criticizes other grammarians for taking too narrow a view of the subject. His treatise is entitled *On Art Prosaic, Metrical, and Rhythmical* and is divided into the following parts: the doctrine of invention; the method of selecting material; arranging and ornamenting the material; parts of letters and faults in letter writing; amplification and abbreviation; memory; and examples of letters and of metrical and rhythmical composition.[62]

Among other arts of poetry are the works of Gervaise of Melkey and Eberhard the German.[63] Collectively, these works are interesting because they are the creation of an innovative genre of rhetorical teaching; because medieval poets—the authors of the French *romans* and Chaucer, for example—had studied them and used their techniques, even though the accomplishment of great poets goes beyond anything these handbooks envision; and finally because they foreshadow the development of literary criticism in the Renaissance.

The Arts of Preaching

Another medieval activity that recast classical doctrine for its own needs was preaching.[64] As mentioned earlier, Augustine's treatise *On Christian Learning* had been used by Hrabanus Maurus, and it became widely known in the later Middle Ages, but Augustine's lofty stylistic concepts were beyond the reach of most medieval preachers. Gregory the Great's *Cura Pastoralis* had greater influence but did not contain a theory of preaching. Its most important rhetorical feature was Gregory's insistence on the importance of adapting a sermon to the audience. Otherwise, in the early Middle Ages there seems to have been a decline in preaching as in other arts. When they revived in the eleventh century, preaching did too. One of the most effective sermons preached in the Middle Ages was that by Pope Urban II at the Council of Clermont in 1095, which precipitated the First Crusade.[65] Handbooks of preaching began to appear in the twelfth century, and from the thirteenth to the fifteenth centuries they were compiled in large numbers. During this period, preaching became a popular art throughout western Europe. This phenomenon can be associated with the rise of new preaching orders, including the Franciscans and Dominicans, the spread of mysticism, the influence of scholasticism, and a generally improved level of culture.[66]

The early stages of the development are represented by works by Guibert of Nogent (ca. 1084) and Alan of Lille (ca. 1199). Guibert's *Book about the Way a Sermon Ought to be Given*, written as an introduction to his commentary on Genesis, discusses the purpose of preaching and the forms of scriptural interpretation, four of which are distinguished: the historical or literal, the allegorical, the tropological or moral, and the anagogical or mystical.[67] These four levels are developments of the three levels distinguished by Origen. They first appear in Latin in the fourth century, and, with occasional minor variations, became standard principles of exegesis.[68]

Alan of Lille has been mentioned earlier as the author of an allegorical poem on the seven liberal arts entitled *Anticlaudianus*. His treatise *On the Preacher's Art* was strongly influenced by Gregory the Great's *Cura Pastoralis*.[69] Much of it consists of models of how to rebuke sinners, in which Alan seems to follow a systematic method of distinguishing different meanings of a word and supporting each with citation of other scriptural passages. His logical divisions are reminiscent of the topics of rhetoric as found in Cicero or Boethius, but he has nothing to say about the organization of a sermon or about style.

In the early thirteenth century handbooks of "thematic" preaching began to appear, perhaps first in England, with the manuals of Alexander of Ashby and Thomas Chabham of Salisbury.[70] These works adapt the parts of the oration as described in *Rhetoric for Herennius* to the needs of preachers addressing medieval congregations, much as dictaminal works adapted them to the needs of letter writers and recipients. The works reflect an interest in the form and technique of sermons, not just the contents, and foreshadow the "thematic" preaching that became popular at the University of Paris and elsewhere in a few years.[71] What is meant by "thematic" preaching is systematic, logical preaching, as opposed to the informality and lack of structure of the homily. The theme takes the form of a quotation from Scripture. The preacher then divides the theme into a series of questions, which may be as numerous as the number of words in the quotation. He takes up each of these divisions in turn, interpreting them by other quotations from Scripture and applying them to the life of his congregation. Richard of Thetford's *Art of Amplifying Sermons* (ca. 1245) describes eight modes of amplifying divisions of the theme.

Thematic preaching was not directed at converting the audience. The congregation was assumed to believe in Christ, as the vast majority of people in medieval Europe did. The preacher instructs them about the meaning of the Bible, with emphasis on moral action. Just as dictamen combined features of rhetoric, social status, and law to meet a perceived need in writing letters, so the preaching manuals drew on a variety of disciplines to outline their new technique. Biblical exegesis was one; scholastic logic was another—thematic preaching, with its succession of definitions, divisions, and syllogism can be regarded as a more popular form of scholastic disputation; and a third was rhetoric as known from Cicero and Boethius, seen in rules for arrangement and style. There was also some influence from grammar and other liberal arts in the amplification of divisions of the theme.

Handbooks of preaching were very common in the late Middle Ages and Renaissance. No one of them, however, was widely circulated to become the standard work on the subject. An easily available example of a late medieval treatise on preaching, one representative of the genre, is *The Form of Preaching* by Robert of Basevorn, dating from around

1322.[72] Robert's primary interest is the method of constructing thematic sermons. In the prologue he compares the method of preaching on every subject to logic, which is the method of syllogizing on every subject. He defines preaching as "the persuasion of the multitude, within a moderate length of time, to worthy conduct"; it is thus moral and instructional. There follows a brief consideration (chs. 2–5) about who can be a preacher and a description (6–13) of earlier methods of preaching: those of Christ, Saint Paul, Augustine, Gregory the Great, and Bernard of Clairvaux. This section ends with a quotation from Pope Leo: "This is the virtue of eloquence, that there is nothing foreign to it that cannot be extolled. Who will hesitate to say that wisdom and eloquence together move us more than either does by itself? Thus we must insist upon eloquence and yet not depart from wisdom, which is the better of the two." The statement is derived from Cicero's remarks in the preface to *On Invention* and consistent with the teaching of Augustine. Indeed, Robert cites Augustine's formulation of the duties of the preacher, derived from Cicero's duties of the orator: to teach, to please, and to move.

The body of Robert's treatise consists of twenty-two "ornaments employed in the most carefully contrived sermons." These are a strange mixture of devices with antecedents in classical rhetoric relating to invention, arrangement, style, and delivery but all applied to the statement of a theme, its divisions, and the amplification of the divisions. Examples are given, and the treatment of most of the ornaments involves a further process of division. The fourth ornament, for example, is "introduction" (31). It can be formed by authority, by argument, or by both together, and each of these is further divided. Fifteen of the ornaments, Robert says (50), apply to the form or execution of the sermon. The last seven contribute to its beauty. These are coloration, including the rhetorical figures, for which the reader is referred to the fourth book of *Rhetoric for Herennius*; voice moderation as described by Augustine; gesture as described by Hugh of Saint Victor; humor as described by Cicero; allusion to Scripture; a firm impression, which seems to be systematic repetition of allusion to a scriptural passage; and reflection, or consideration of who is speaking to whom, what is being said, and for how long. Robert's treatise seems to have been a practical aid to the composition of the kind of sermon approved in his time. He mentions

Oxford and Paris as two centers of preaching, each characterized by a slightly different style.

Aristotle divided the subject of rhetoric into that which did not demand a judgment from the audience and that which did. The former was epideictic. The latter either involved judgments of the past, which was judicial rhetoric, or of the future, which was deliberative. The adaptations of classical rhetoric in the later Middle Ages seem to call for a different basis of distinction. For that age, it would be truer to say that the art of rhetoric was regarded as either oral or written. If oral, its main forms were those of preaching and oral controversy, though we have seen in Italy the appearance of opportunities for political and legal oratory, and these probably existed elsewhere as well to some extent. If written, rhetoric could be in either verse or prose. If in verse, it inherited some traditions of ancient epideictic and poetics and manifested itself in topics, tropes, and figures. If in prose, it was best found in the epistle. Thus, the three most characteristic forms of rhetoric in the later Middle Ages were preaching, epideictic poetry, and letters. In none of these areas did theory or criticism make a significant advance; in all three forms systems that were regarded as useful for the times were devised.

Of the three elements in the rhetorical act—speaker, speech, and audience—that of the speaker, characteristic of the sophistic strand of rhetoric, lost ground in the western Middle Ages, though the tradition was preserved in the East. The speech itself, the central focus of the technical or handbook tradition, remained central in western thinking, an attitude probably reinforced by medieval study of grammar and dialectic. Some interest in the audience is demonstrated by writers on dictamen and on preaching. Philosophical rhetoric is represented in the Middle Ages primarily by the view of some thinkers, especially the scholastic philosophers, that rhetoric was a part of dialectic.

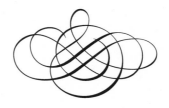

CHAPTER 10

Classical Rhetoric in the Renaissance

Italian civic life served as the environment for a remarkable renaissance of classical rhetoric throughout Europe in the fourteenth, fifteenth, and sixteenth centuries.[1] A knowledge of Greek and of works of Greek literature, including rhetorical treatises and orations, was recovered in the West; important Latin rhetorical works, long thought to have been lost, were discovered in old manuscripts lying in out-of-the-way places in monasteries; translations, commentaries, and new works were written in considerable numbers; and finally, the invention of printing greatly facilitated the dissemination of learning.[2] Cicero's *On the Orator*, *Brutus*, and *Orator* in 1465 and *On Invention*, *Rhetoric for Herennius*, and the complete treatise of Quintilian in 1470 were among the earliest texts printed.

The Italian Humanists

The individuals known as humanists were the agents of these developments, first in Italy, and later in all parts of western Europe. A humanist was not a humanistic philosopher but a teacher or advanced student of the subjects collectively known as *studia humanitatis*, including grammar, rhetoric, history, poetry, and moral philosophy, all studied on the basis of classical models and theories.[3] These subjects came to constitute the basic curriculum that began in schools and extended through the arts course in universities. With the exception of a few remarkable writers like Petrarch (1304–74), the Italian humanists usually earned their living either by teaching rhetoric or some aspect of classical studies or by working as a secretary to a prince, pope, or commune. In this capacity

they put to practical use their knowledge of rhetoric, including dictamen, in the composition of Latin letters and speeches. The most famous
Italian humanists, Coluccio Salutati (1331–1406), Leonardo Bruni (ca.
1370–1444), and Poggio BraccioLini (1380–1459), served as secretaries of
the papal chancery and of the Florentine republic. Lorenzo Valla (1407–
57) was a papal secretary and also lectured on rhetoric in Rome. Poli-
ziano (Politian) (1454–94) was tutor to the children of Lorenzo Medici
and gave public lectures on Greek and Latin literature to large classes in
Florence.

In function, the Italian humanists were thus a continuation of the
teachers of grammar and rhetoric and the notaries of the later Middle Ages. What was new was an extraordinary enthusiasm for classical
literature that spread among these functionaries in the fourteenth and
fifteenth centuries, analogous to an interest in classical architecture,
sculpture, and other arts seen in the same period. This classicism had
not characterized Italian culture earlier and seems to have come from
France, where an admiration for classical models was already found at
the school of Chartres, as discussed in Chapter 9. In any event, the
Italian humanists were intoxicated with the language and literature of
antiquity and sought to recover all possible knowledge of it and to make
that knowledge the basis of the twin ideals of wisdom and eloquence in
the culture of their times, which they regarded as awakening from a long
sleep.[4] The two factors of rhetoric and classicism reinforced each other,
since the more the humanists learned about the classics, the more they
discovered that rhetoric was the discipline that had created the forms,
disposed the contents, and ornamented the pages that they admired and
sought to imitate. Rhetoric proved to be not the arid study of the medieval trivium or the technical teachings of On Invention, but a noble and
creative art, characteristic of human beings at their best. The humanists
can be said to have resembled the leading figures of the Second Sophistic, who were also teachers, admirers of the classics, orators, and letter
writers, and they revived the sophistic tradition that had been kept alive
in the Greek-speaking East.

Latin oratory reemerged as a major form of human communication
in Renaissance Italy. As we have seen, there was political, academic, judicial, and occasional oratory in Italy in the later Middle Ages. With the
Renaissance the quantity of this oratory greatly increased and the qual-

ity greatly improved. Quality included the Latinity, of which classical standards of grammar and vocabulary were again achieved, and the control of style, but also the rhetorical effectiveness of the whole. Eloquence was an ideal of the age: speeches or works in the form of speeches were published, read, and copied. For example, Leonardo Bruni's *Laudation of the City of Florence*, composed in the spirit of the Second Sophistic and delivered about 1403, was widely admired and was imitated by Pier Candido Decembrio for Milan and by Enea Silvio Piccolomini for Basel. The most famous Renaissance work in oratorical form is doubtless Pico della Mirandola's *Oration on the Dignity of Man* of 1487. A great deal of surviving Renaissance oratory is concerned with praise or blame and fits comfortably into the limits of classical epideictic,[5] but in Florence and Venice and other free cities there had developed around 1400 a new sense of civic responsibility and appreciation of liberty. Oratory, as well as the writing of epistles, histories, dialogues, and poetry, took on a practical political purpose, which became primary rhetoric even in the hands of scholars. Within the Church, medieval forms of preaching faded, and classical models were adopted, with attendant discussion of the theoretical problems involved, especially in the period after 1450.[6] Considering the uses of rhetoric by the humanists and their successors and by Renaissance preachers and letter writers, it is not surprising that style, rather than invention, seemed to many the most important part of the discipline.

Petrarch, in many ways the founder of the humanist movement, envisioned a synthesis of wisdom and eloquence in oral expression and in both civic and academic contexts, and this view was taken up by some of his successors, including Coluccio Salutati and Lorenzo Valla.[7] Their efforts ultimately failed; the devastation and disruption caused by French, German, and Spanish invasions in the sixteenth century frustrated the earlier political initiative, and there revived among Italian educators the feeling inherited from the Middle Ages that rhetoric was essentially a discipline to be studied by the very young or to be absorbed into the aesthetics of literary criticism; but for some two centuries rhetoric made a claim to be queen of the arts.

The recovery of texts crucial to the revival of classical rhetoric in the Renaissance can be said to have begun with the Latin translations of Aristotle made in the thirteenth century, even though these were not immediately put to rhetorical use. Petrarch's discovery in 1345 at Verona of a manuscript of Cicero's previously unknown letters to Atticus, Quintus, and Brutus brought to life the career of the greatest Roman orator with an intimacy not then known and contributed to Renaissance interest in the individual's role in the state and the complexity of the problems of the orator. The fourteenth century also saw the beginnings of a recovery of knowledge of Greek in Italy. Petrarch's friend Giovanni Boccaccio (1313–75), whose writings included the *Decameron* and a work on classical mythology, studied Greek with a Calabrian named Leonzio Pilato and secured his teacher's appointment as a public professor of that language in Florence in 1361. More influential was Manuel Chrysoloras, who came to Italy as an ambassador from Constantinople and taught Greek in Florence from 1396 to 1400. Leonardo Bruni combined his active life as chancellor in Florence with a study of the classics, translating Plato's *Gorgias*, *Phaedrus*, and other dialogues, as well as speeches of Demosthenes and Aeschines, into Latin. Even more influential were the Latin translations of all of Plato by Marsilio Ficino, begun in 1463 and completed about 1470.[8]

In terms of immediate effect on Renaissance knowledge of rhetoric and enthusiasm for classical studies, the most important discoveries were those of Poggio. He had already discovered manuscripts of some of Cicero's speeches, when in 1416 at Saint Gall in Switzerland he found, dirty and neglected, an old manuscript of the complete text of Quintilian's *Institutio Oratoria*, as well as a manuscript of some of Asconius's commentaries on speeches of Cicero and other works.[9] Since the early Middle Ages, available texts of Quintilian had contained significant gaps, specifically the beginning of Book 1, the end of Book 5, all of Books 6 and 7, portions of 8, 9, 10, and 11, and the end of Book 12. Quintilian's work enjoyed an enormous popularity in the fifteenth and sixteenth centuries as an authority both on technical rhetoric and on education. His educational theory profoundly affected schools of the liberal arts, such as that of Vittorino da Feltre in Mantua (founded in 1423), and his rhetorical theory is reflected in many writers.[10] Not surprisingly, given the enthusiasm for Quintilian, some reactions were negative—sometimes against his identification of the orator with the good man, sometimes against his definition of rhetoric as knowledge of speaking well, sometimes against his neglect of dialectic.[11] The canon of major Latin rhetorical treatises was completed in 1421 when Gerardo Landriani, bishop of Lodi, found a complete manuscript of Cicero's *On the Orator*, *Orator*, and *Brutus*. The first two works had been known for centuries only in mutilated versions; the *Brutus* was totally unknown. *On the Orator* inspired a series of dialogues on eloquence during the next two centuries.[12] It would be possible to write a history of Renaissance rhetorical thought in terms of the successive impact of rediscovered works: Quintilian, Cicero, and the Greek treatises, especially Dionysius of Halicarnassus's *On Composition*, Hermogenes, Demetrius's *On Style*, and finally Longinus's *On the Sublime*. Several Greek treatises not before known in the West were printed, together with Aristotle's *Rhetoric* and *Rhetoric for Alexander*, in a popular edition by Aldus Manutius in Venice in 1508.

Knowledge of Greek was acquired by the humanists primarily from Greeks who came to Italy in the fourteenth and early fifteenth centuries. This process was complemented by westerners' travels to Greece in search of manuscripts: Giovanni Aurispa (1376–1459) and Guarino of Verona (1374–1460) were among the most important travelers. The increasing threat to Constantinople, ending with the fall of the city to the Turks in 1453, gave a sense of urgency to the effort to preserve and translate into Latin all that could be found of Greek writing.

Knowledge of Hebrew was preserved through the Middle Ages by Jewish scholars. In the Renaissance, some Jews learned in the liberal arts began to apply classical rhetoric to interpretation of the Old Testament and to write works on Jewish preaching and letter writing. The most important work is *The Book of the Honeycomb's Flow*, by Judah Messer Leon (1475), a handbook of Ciceronian rhetoric in Hebrew with application to and examples from Scripture.[13]

Women in the Humanist Movement

Women participated actively in the society of Renaissance Italy.[14] Some, primarily from wealthy families, attended schools together with boys or were tutored at home, learned Latin, and studied the other liberal arts. Women also attended the public lectures of the famous humanists mentioned above. No women is known to have written an account of rhetoric, but several gave epideictic speeches on public occasions that showed knowledge of rhetoric, and some of these were published. Speeches by Battista Malatesta, Constanza Varani, and Ippolita Sforza in the fifteenth century and by Cassandra Fedele in the sixteenth have been translated into English.[15] In 1487 Fedele addressed the students and faculty of the University of Padua on the value of humanistic learning. Other women humanists included the two Nogarola sisters, Isotta and Ginevra,[16] and Laura Cereta, author of a spirited letter to an imaginary male opponent in defense of the liberal education of women.[17]

The most famous woman humanist in France was Christine de Pisan (1363–1431), daughter of the court physician to King Charles V. She wrote lyric poetry, corresponded with intellectual leaders on literary controversies, composed a eulogy of Joan of Arc, and wrote treatises on government. In her most famous work, known in English as *The Treasure of the City of Ladies*, she touches on rhetoric in discussing the appropriate speech by queens, princesses, and women at court.[18]

In England in the sixteenth century royal princesses were given the best available education to prepare them for dealing with public affairs and speaking in public. The future Queen Mary was tutored in the liberal arts by Juan Luis Vives, the greatest humanist scholar then in the country, and Lady Jane Grey and the future Queen Elizabeth were taught by Roger Ascham, the leading educator of the time. Elizabeth acquired an excellent knowledge of Greek and Latin and continued to read the classics all her life. Among her speeches are three in Latin, one delivered at Cambridge University in 1564 and two at Oxford in 1566 and 1592. In the speech at Cambridge she quotes Demosthenes and refers to an anecdote about Alexander the Great.[19]

George Trebizond

Of the Greek emigrants to Italy, the most important for the history of rhetoric is George Trebizond (1395–1472), who introduced the writings of Hermogenes and the Byzantine rhetorical tradition to the West.[20] Surnamed Trebizond from a grandfather who came from the Greek city of that name on the Black Sea, George himself was born in Crete and came to Italy in 1416 to work in the library of the Venetian humanist Francesco Barbaro. The patronage of influential Venetians continued to be important to him throughout his career. A few details about his life may help to make clear the kinds of rhetorical activities practiced by fifteenth-century humanists.

Trebizond had been well educated in classical Greek grammar and rhetoric, but on arrival in Italy had to begin by learning Latin. He soon distinguished himself and became one of the best Latin stylists of his time. As early as 1421 he delivered Latin orations at Vicenza—*In Praise of Eloquence*[21] and *In Praise of Cicero*. He probably taught Greek privately at this time and completed a Latin synopsis of Hermogenes' work *On Ideas*. In 1426 he published a Latin treatise *On Sweetness of Speaking*, based on Hermogenes' discussion of *glykytês*, and was appointed to the public chair of Latin in Vicenza. Discharged at the end of the following year for unknown reasons—he could be very difficult in personal relations, and like many others of his time was quick to engage in acrimonious debate—he devoted himself to private teaching and to the composition of his greatest work, *Rhetoricorum Libri V*, or *Five Books of Rhetoric*, published in 1433 or 1434. This is the first new full-scale rhetoric of the Renaissance; it integrated the Greek tradition of Dionysius of Halicarnassus and Hermogenes into the standard Latin sources with examples from Cicero and Virgil. Trebizond himself apparently thought of it as a rival to Quintilian's treatise, which was then at the peak of its popularity. He also dared to criticize the Latin style of others, including the humanist Guarino of Verona, author of a major commentary on *Rhetoric for Herennius*. This involved him in extended disputes. In 1437 he issued his *Reply to the Invective of Guarino and Defense of His Own Rhetoric*. Meanwhile he had delivered the *Funeral Oration for Fantino Michiel* before the doge and senate of Venice and had completed his *Compendium*, a treatise on the parts of speech based on the grammar of Priscian. This became a popular work for the teaching of Latin grammar throughout the rest of the century.

In 1437 Trebizond moved to Bologna, where he may have lectured on rhetoric at the university and where he delivered his *Oration in Praise of Pope Eugenius IV* before Eugenius himself and the papal court, then in residence there. He also published a letter in Greek to the Byzantine emperor, which is the opening document in what became an obsessive apocalyptic vision of the union of the eastern and western Churches under a Turkish sultan converted to Christianity. In 1440 he published his *Isagoge Dialectica*, or *Introduction to Dialectic*, which is the first humanist textbook on logic. Trebizond regarded dialectic as a minor subject, useful for one entering into the greater field of rhetoric; from it one could learn something about reasoning processes as a basis for study of invention. Ironically, the *Isogage* became popular in northern Europe in the sixteenth century with those interested in removing invention from rhetoric. By 1440 Trebizond was in Florence, where he taught poetry at the university and lectured privately on Greek and Latin, logic, rhetoric, and philosophy. The papal court was now also in Florence, and Trebizond began work there as a secretary. He also wrote a commentary on Cicero's speech *For Ligarius* and completed a translation of Basil's *Against Eunomius*. The latter was done at the request of Cardinal Bessarion, another Greek immigrant, who was, however, to become one of Trebizond's most bitter opponents.

In 1443 Trebizond moved on to Rome and the following year was sworn in as a secretary in the apostolic court. This association, with some interruptions, lasted much of the rest of his life. His time went largely into the translation of Greek works not yet available in Latin, an activity in which the new pope, Nicholas V, was much interested. Trebizond worked on scientific writings of Aristotle, Plato's *Laws*, sermons by John Chrysostom and Gregory of Nazianzus, and other works. He thus made available to the West the classic models of Greek Christian epideictic. He also made new translations of Demosthenes' speech *On the Crown*, one of at least six done in the fifteenth century, and of Aristotle's *Rhetoric*, introducing the chapter divisions still used in modern texts. In 1452, after a nasty brawl with Poggio, he left for Naples but in 1455 returned to serve under a new pope, Calixtus III.

In 1457 Trebizond became involved in the dispute between Platonists and Aristotelians that raged at this time. The humanists in general despised scholasticism as vain and arid, and Aristotle suffered because he had been the favored philosophical authority of the scholastics. Works of Plato were now available in Greek and partially in Latin and evoked humanists' enthusiasm. Trebizond entered the dispute on the side of Aristotle and published *A Comparison of the Philosophers Plato and Aristotle*, to which Cardinal Bessarion replied in a work entitled *Against the Calumniator of Plato* (that is, against Trebizond). Trebizond claimed that his dislike of Plato originated with Plato's treatment of Gorgias in the dialogue of that name, and his own views of rhetoric as seen in his oration *In Praise of Eloquence* and the preface to his *Five Books of Rhetoric* partly echo those of the Greek sophist. Although he translated Aristotle's *Rhetoric* and admired its author, his rhetorical theory was more indebted to Hermogenes and other late Greek writers.

In 1460 Trebizond left Rome to become professor of rhetoric and humanities at Venice, but returned to the papal court in 1464 when his former pupil, Pietro Barbo, was elected Pope Pius II. Constantinople had fallen in 1453, which reawakened Trebizond's hope of converting the Turkish sultan to Christianity and eventually led him to ill-advised activities. In 1465–66 he paid a secret visit to Constantinople but failed to see the sultan, much less to persuade him of the religious destiny that Trebizond envisioned. Church authorities strongly disapproved of Trebizond's efforts at personal diplomacy. On his return he made matters worse by publishing an address to the sultan entitled *The Eternal Glory of the Autocrat*, and as a result was imprisoned for four months in Castel Sant'Angelo in Rome. After his release he remained in Rome, continued his involvement in the Plato-Aristotle debate and other controversial matters, and died in 1472 or 1473. It would be a mistake to describe his career as typical; his apocalyptic religious enthusiasm was unique, but the activities of this indefatigable rhetorician and sophist included almost every aspect of the professional life of a Renaissance humanist, with the exception of discovery of new Latin manuscripts. That effort had been largely completed by others. Trebizond, however, played a major role in bringing the Greek classics to the West.

When Trebizond arrived in Italy, teachers of rhetoric had already begun to make significant improvements in understanding classical rhetoric in the form of commentaries or monographs, but solely within the Ciceronian tradition. Antonio Loschi's commentary on eleven orations of Cicero and Gasparino Barzizza's Ciceronian treatise *On Composition* are examples.[22] Trebizond adopted the framework of the Ciceronian tradition in the full form of all five parts of rhetoric. The structure of his *Rhetoric* is that of *Rhetoric for Herennius*, but with one additional book. He expanded this framework with considerable material from other Roman writers including Quintilian, though Trebizond names Quintilian only to criticize him, and by Greek material; little comes from Aristotle, though he is repeatedly named.

Book 1 begins with a short preface on the utility of oratory in society, reminiscent of the sophistic tradition of antiquity or the famous preface of Cicero's *On Invention*.[23] Rhetoric is then defined as "a science of civic life in which, with the agreement of the audience insofar as possible, we speak on civil questions." Trebizond defines what he means by questions and the kinds of oratory and then takes up the parts of an oration: exordium, narration, and "contention," or proof, which he subdivides into division, confirmation, and refutation. This leads to the question of *status*, which completes Book 1. Book 2 is largely a paraphrase of Hermogenes' *On Stases*, though Trebizond fails to adopt Hermogenes' method of division. Book 3 is entitled "On Argumentation"; here Trebizond incorporates into rhetoric a considerable amount of material on dialectic, including twenty-two dialectical topics derived from Themistius, Boethius, and Peter of Spain. The book ends with an account of the peroration. Book 4 discusses deliberative oratory, demonstrative oratory, the orator's intent, arrangement, memory, and delivery. Book 5 is devoted to style. It begins with a preface in which Trebizond explains that style, unlike invention, can be easily taught to the young—the view of Dionysius of Halicarnassus in the preface to his work *On Composition*. In what follows, he treats both the three kinds of style of the Ciceronian tradition, which he regards as a broad view of the subject, and Hermogenes' "ideas," translated as *formae*, which he treats as a more advanced and subtle analysis of the subject. Trebizond's treatise is firmly in the classical tradition of technical rhetoric. It is written in good, classical Latin; its examples are classical, drawn from Cicero in the earlier books but expanded to include Greek and Latin poetry and historical writing in the last book. Trebizond's own contribution was his knowledge of the Greek sources, his ability to organize the material into a consistent whole, and his polished Latin style, which won the confidence of humanist readers. He himself had no original ideas about rhetoric, but as one who had frequent occasion to speak in public, he had a sound instinct for what was important. His work was widely studied throughout western Europe, first in manuscripts and then in a series of printed editions, and often quoted by others for a century after his death, by which time many other rhetorics and the Greek sources upon which he had drawn were easily available.

As seen in the career of Trebizond and other humanists, rhetoric in Italy had become again a feature of education in the liberal arts analogous to what it had been in antiquity and rivaling grammar and dialectic, which had overshadowed it in the Middle Ages. Trebizond taught rhetoric at various times to young boys, to university students, and occasionally to adults, as did others in his time; but once humanist excitement about rhetoric began to fade, it was in the schools, in company still with grammar and dialectic, and in the introductory stages of university arts courses, that most instruction in rhetoric was given. It must be stressed that students of rhetoric in the Renaissance were largely young boys; even university students at the time were considerably younger than today. Thus a typical rhetorical treatise aimed at being simple, clear, and capable of rote memorization. A good example is Philipp Melanchthon's somewhat later *Elementorum Rhetorices Libri II*, the major source for Leonard Cox's *Arte or Crafte of Rhethoryke*, the first rhetoric handbook in English. Though written by one of the major intellectuals of the sixteenth century, it is addressed to two adolescents who have been studying dialectic for two years and now need a simple introduction to rhetoric.

The elementary nature of most rhetorical studies in the Renaissance contributed to the failure of Aristotle's *Rhetoric* to become a major text. New translations of it into Latin and vernacular languages were made, and university professors sometimes lectured on the text. An important example of the latter are the lectures given by John Rainolds at Oxford in the 1570s.[24] Parts of the *Rhetoric* influenced theories of poetics or politics or moral philosophy, but no true Aristotelian rhetoric was composed in the Renaissance.[25] Cicero, *Rhetoric for Herennius*, and Quintilian remained the ultimate authorities, and when university professors lectured on rhetorical texts it was usually one of these they chose. Further, Plato enjoyed great popularity in Renaissance Italy, and opposition to Aristotle was often involved in love of Plato. The Italian dialogues on rhetoric by Francisco Patrizi (published in 1562) are Platonic and vigorously anti-Aristotelian; they advance a version of the views of Socrates in *Gorgias* without attempting any development of the concepts of *Phaedrus*.[26] Sperone Speroni, though more moderate, preferred modern expression to ancient rhetoric in his *Dialogo della retorica* of 1542 and asked whether the training of the Latin orator was really a suitable discipline for expression in other languages. The increasing importance of the vernacular languages seemed to many to add point to these inquiries.

Enthusiasm for rhetoric thus waned in Italy after 1500, except in the case of preaching. Political conditions were now quite unfavorable for deliberative oratory, and the tendency of rhetoric to take on a literary cast reasserted itself. This trend was reinforced by a keen interest in developing Italian literature to a level rivaling the classics, which produced an important body of literary criticism that became influential as well in France and England. Aristotle's *Poetics* had been known in the later Middle Ages in a Latin version, but like the *Rhetoric*, exercised rather little influence until brought to public attention in a new translation by Gorgio Valla in 1498. Subsequently, a series of works examined critical questions and laid down rules for composition in the classical genres, especially epic and drama, in Italian. Among the more important writers on poetics were Trissino, Minturno, and Castelvetro.[27]

Fichet and Traversagni

The popularity of Trebizond's treatise on rhetoric inspired other approaches in the second half of the fifteenth century. The *Rhetorica* of Guillaume Fichet was the first treatment of the subject to be printed in France (1471) and a direct challenge to the influence of Trebizond. Fichet was in charge of the Sorbonne library from 1468 to 1471 and sponsored the introduction of printing in France by bringing three printers from the Rhineland to Paris. One of the first books printed was a version of the lectures on rhetoric that Fichet had been giving over many years, first in Avignon, later in Paris.[28] In a letter to Cardinal Bessarion, Fichet reported his alarm at discovering certain *Georgiani* in Paris who were setting up Trebizond as a second Cicero and threatening to teach rhetoric from manuscript copies of Trebizond's treatise. It seems likely that a factor in Fichet's interest in printing was the desire to circulate his own work and counteract Trebizond's influence.[29]

Certainly Fichet's *Rhetorica* is very different.[30] It consists of a *Praefatio* and three books, one on judicial rhetoric, one on deliberative and demonstrative rhetoric, and a final book on style. The content is derived largely from the Ciceronian tradition of *On Invention*, *Rhetoric for Herennius*, and Victorinus, with additions from medieval discussions of dialectic. Without acknowledgement, Fichet does include some ideas from Hermogenes known to him through Trebizond.[31] The material is, however, recast into the systematic, logical form of medieval scholasticism, congenial to the French academic setting. The work consists almost entirely of a series of definitions, divisions, definitions of subordinate categories, and often further division and definition. Many new logical relationships are constructed and many new technical terms introduced. The effect is very arid, since no examples of rhetorical techniques are provided, but there is reason to believe that Fichet illustrated his oral lectures with citations from the classics. In the preface he complains of the poor understanding of rhetoric in Paris, a city that should be, he says, the modern Athens or Rome, and indicates that his teaching is intended to be practical. Eloquence will open up offices and rewards to a student and will make possible the propagation of the Christian religion abroad. In Book 2 he gives an unusually full discussion of deliberative and demonstrative oratory.

Soon after the printing of his work Fichet left for Rome. Guillaume Tardiff then emerged as the leading teacher of rhetoric in Paris. He published two short compendia of rhetoric that continued Fichet's emphasis on civic oratory but dropped his elaborate scholastic definitions and divisions and owed a debt to the Italian humanist Lorenzo Valla, which was not the case with Fichet.[32]

A second person who taught and published a new approach to rhetoric in the fifteenth century was Lorenzo Guglielmo Traversagni, an Italian who visited England and completed his *Margarite Castigate Eloquentie* there in 1478. The title can be translated "The Pearls of Purified Rhetoric," and the work is also known as his *Nova Rhetorica*. He later taught in Paris and there composed his *Epitome* of the longer treatise.[33] Traversagni differs from other humanist writers on rhetoric discussed above in that his major objective was to adapt Ciceronian rhetorical teaching to the needs of Christian readers, writers, and speakers in his own time. He illustrated theory from sacred writings and favored a chaste and modest style with little ornamentation.

Ciceronians and Anti-Ciceronians

Late medieval Latin prose shows two contrasting styles.[34] One is characterized by the use of classical figures of speech, but is not very classical in composition and freely employs words found only in medieval Latin.

This is the prose style of homiletic preaching, saints' lives, devotional treatises, and speeches in chronicles. Use of this style survived into the Renaissance in elementary instruction and influenced poetry and prose in the vernacular languages. The other late medieval Latin style is the style of the chanceries and law schools, associated with the dictamen. In this tradition tropes and figures were avoided as poetic and artificial, but other aspects of rhetoric, especially rules for the structure of an oration, were applied.

The humanists, taken as a whole, reacted against both these late medieval Latin styles as inelegant and sought to bring spoken and written Latin back to a classical standard of eloquence as an international medium of communication.[35] They varied among themselves, however, in the extent to which they insisted on Cicero as the touchstone. Humanists of the early fifteenth century, including Leonardo Bruni, Poggio Bracciolini, George Trebizond, Guarino of Verona, and Lorenzo Valla, belonged to the classicizing movement without regarding Cicero as the single model of correctness. The late fifteenth and early sixteenth centuries are the period of the most doctrinaire Ciceronians, of whom Pietro Bembo and his student Christopher Longolius are probably the best examples. They sought to use no Latin word that could not be found in Cicero, as well as to imitate his composition of sentences. Mario Nizzoli (Nizolius) published his *Lexicon Ciceronianum* in 1535, providing a reference work in which usage could be checked to maintain pure Ciceronian diction.

There were reactions against this extreme Ciceronianism in style. Erasmus's *Ciceronianus* of 1528 is the most famous plea for a classical but flexible Latin style. Erasmus drew his Latin vocabulary from a wide variety of ancient authors and sought to keep Latin a vigorous, living, useful tongue. J. C. Scaliger and others attacked Erasmus, but his views had great influence.

A more general reaction against Ciceronianism in style appeared in the mid-sixteenth century. The central figure in this development was Justus Lipsius (1547–1606). He was strongly attracted to the Latin prose writers of the early empire, who were in their own age Anti-Ciceronians. The clipped, epigrammatic but simple Latin of Seneca the Younger was one such model; the more complex, sometimes pregnantly obscure style of Tacitus was another. These and other Latin prose writers, including

Sallust, became the models of some Latin writers of the late sixteenth and early seventeenth centuries, and their influence then extended from Latin over into the baroque prose of the vernacular languages, as seen, for example, in the writings of Montaigne in French. The terms "Atticist" and "Asianist," borrowed from the literary disputes of the first century B.C. to describe the Anti-Ciceronians and Ciceronians, respectively, do not seem suitable descriptions of Renaissance style.[36]

Since rhetoric, even if only in an elementary form, was a standard part of education in the Renaissance, it is not surprising that it sometimes found applications other than in speaking and writing. Plato, Aristotle, Cicero, Quintilian, and other ancient writers sometimes drew analogies between oratory, painting, and sculpture, and Renaissance writers on art often borrowed rhetorical concepts of style and imitation and adapted rhetorical terms to their aesthetic theories. Rhetoric provided them a convenient and widely understood tool of criticism. Among these writers were Paoli Pini, author of *Dialogue on Painting* (1548), Lodovico Dolce, author of a similarly entitled work (1557), and Franciscus Junius, author of *Painting of the Ancients* (1638). Junius was the brother-in-law of the Dutch classical scholar Gerhard Vossius, author of several works on rhetoric to be discussed later in this chapter and of a long treatise *On the Nature and Creation of the Arts and Sciences*, which includes discussion of painting in terms of rhetoric.

The analogy between rhetoric and music was not much discussed in antiquity, though Quintilian devoted a chapter to music (1.10) in terms of ethos and pathos. Renaissance writers took up the matter and elaborated it. Nicola Vicentino in 1555 compared the musician to the orator who speaks loudly or softly, slowly or quickly, to move the souls of his audience. In Germany, Joachim Burmeister produced an introduction to musical composition; the second edition of 1601, under the title *Musicus Autoschediastike*, eulogizes music as a higher form of oratory. In 1601 he expanded this in his *Musica Poetica*, which makes use of rhetorical divisions and identifies a series of musical figures based on figures of speech studied in schools. Other writers of the sixteenth century continued this approach to music as secondary rhetoric.[37] Johann Sebastian Bach was familiar with these theories, and there is some evidence to suggest that he applied his knowledge of Quintilian in composing one of his works.[38]

Rhetoric and Dialectic

Philosophical rhetoric in the Renaissance is represented by continued efforts to describe appropriate methods of preaching and by the efforts of teachers of dialectic to reassert the supremacy of their discipline and to limit the field of rhetoric. The latter movement, found chiefly in Germany and France, parallels the reduction of rhetoric to style in Italy and thus leads to similar results, but for entirely different reasons. It is somewhat reminiscent of Plato's criticism of rhetoric, to which some Renaissance dialecticians refer, but is primarily concerned with method and with logical validity, not with philosophical or scientific truth. Its formulators, however, were doctrinaire classicists who found their concepts and authorities for rearrangement of the system of teaching dialectic and rhetoric in classical sources and who represented their teachings as a return to the classics after the scholasticism of the later Middle Ages.

In Italy in the second quarter of the fifteenth century there arose an apparent interest in restating the relationship of dialectic and rhetoric in the liberal arts on the part of those whose primary interest was in rhetoric. In the Middle Ages rhetoric generally fell between the two more important arts of grammar and dialectic. As interest in rhetoric increased in Italy in the fourteenth and fifteenth centuries a new educational structure seemed needed. Trebizond's solution to the problem was both to produce a simple, introductory work on dialectic, which was to be preliminary to serious study of rhetorical invention, and to include a book on argumentation in his large treatise on rhetoric. The humanist Giovanni Tortelli seems also to have sought to redefine the relationship of dialectic to rhetoric about this time,[39] but the most extreme view was that of the distinguished humanist Lorenzo Valla.

Lorenzo Valla and Rudolphus Agricola

Lorenzo Valla (1407–57) was a rival of Trebizond, overshadowed him in popularity as a teacher of rhetoric in Rome, and like him served the pope as secretary.[40] He did major scholarly work on the texts of the Roman historian Livy and the New Testament, translated Thucydides' history into Latin, and wrote a series of studies called *Elegantiae Latini*

Sermonis, perhaps the most influential work of its time in rediscovering the grammatical and lexical standards of classical Latin. Valla was the most enthusiastic admirer of Quintilian to be found in the Renaissance and a critic of Aristotelianism and scholasticism. In addition to his philological works, he wrote on philosophy and religion. His *Dialectica* was written in the 1430s, a short time before Trebizond's *Introduction to Dialectic*.[41] In this work Valla took the view of logical demonstration found in Quintilian (5.10) and absorbed dialectic entirely into the discipline of rhetoric. "What else is dialectic," he asked, "than a species of confirmation and refutation? These are parts of invention; invention is one of the five parts of rhetoric. Logic is the use of the syllogism. Does not the orator use the same? Certainly he does, and not only that, but also the enthymeme and the epicheireme, in addition to the induction."[42] He further argued that of the three duties of the orator—to teach, to please, and to move—the dialectician's task was only the first, to teach.

The next stage in the redefinition of the relationship between dialectic and rhetoric came a generation later in the work of the Dutch scholar Roelof Huusmann, usually known by the Latin version of his name, Rudolphus Agricola (1444–85).[43] After studying in Erfurt, Louvain, Cologne, and Paris he went to Italy about 1468 to study law, but became converted to the way of life of an Italian humanist, with its emphasis on the study of the classics. While in Italy he began *De Inventione Dialectica*, in three books, and completed it on his return to Germany in 1479. In addition to this influential work, Agricola translated Aphthonius's *Progymnasmata* into Latin. As noted in Chapter 8, this had been the major schoolbook of rhetorical composition for centuries in Byzantium. Agricola did for Aphthonius what Trebizond did for Hermogenes, and for the next two hundred years the schoolboys of western Europe found themselves studying Agricola's text.[44]

Agricola's *De Dialectica Inventione*[45] opens with a short prologue in which Agricola makes immediately clear that rhetoric, which he does not mention by name but which is represented by the Ciceronian duties of the orator, is in his view a subordinate part of dialectic. The first and proper objective of speech is to teach. Teaching involves exposition and argumentation, and argumentation involves probable reasoning from something that is well-known to something that is less well-known. In doing so, it is most useful to understand the seats of arguments, called *loci* (i.e., dialectical topics). Chapter 2 then proceeds to define a *locus* and show how one is used in argument: "This part of the subject, which involves thinking out the middle term or argument, is what dialecticians call invention; there is another part which is called judging," or judgment, whose function is to evaluate all forms of syllogism used in invention and to reject those that are not in accord with reality. In the following chapters of Book 1 Agricola considers the loci discussed by Aristotle, Cicero, and Themistius (as known from Boethius) and describes his own list of twenty-four: definition, genus, species, property, whole, part, etc. There is considerable similarity in lists of topics by different authors but no agreed-upon canon. Although Agricola's three books are concerned only with invention, not with judgment, he returns to the matter of judgment in the introduction to the second book and indicates that the content is drawn from Aristotle, Cicero (especially *Topics* 6), and Quintilian (3.3.5).

Book 2 is devoted to dialectic in a broader sense and the place of rhetorical invention in it. The end of dialectic is to speak with probability about the subject proposed. To please and to move are subordinate to this. The material of dialectic is the question, and its divisions are discussed. Among them is stasis theory. The instrument of dialectic is speech, and Agricola considers the parts of an oration, for which he prefers a four-part division: exordium, narration, confirmation, and peroration. Agricola presents this material with liberal illustration from Cicero and other classical sources.

The third and shortest book is given over to *affectus*, that by which the mind is impelled to seek and avoid something. It deals with the emotions and with what in a more traditional ordering would have been found in rhetorical discussions of arrangement and some parts of style. Agricola does not discuss the ornaments of style, which are thus left to be the subject of a much more limited art of rhetoric. A major contribution of the work is its advice about how to read and understand texts.[46]

Agricola's work was very influential. Philipp Melanchthon (1497–1560), the Protestant leader and friend of Luther, adopted Agricola's division of dialectic and rhetoric in his popular *Elementorum Rhetorices Libri II* (1946),[47] although his earlier *Institutiones Rhetoricae* had treated judgment and arrangement as part of rhetoric.[48] Erasmus approved

Agricola's views, and they are an important precedent for the work of Peter Ramus, to be discussed later in this chapter.

In the later stages of the Renaissance in Germany, the most important treatise on rhetoric was the *Systema Rhetoricae* by Bartholomew Keckermann, a work of over seven hundred pages published in Danzig in 1606.[49] Keckermann reverted to the Ciceronian tradition, giving much attention to invention, especially in the second half of the work entitled *Rhetorica Specialis*, which contains an extended and unusual discussion of arousing the emotions as central to the rhetorical act. Keckermann's work was much studied in northern Europe and in England, where it was a textbook in dissenting schools until the end of the century.

Erasmus

A major figure who contributed his authority to teaching rhetoric from a literary rather than dialectical point of view was Desiderius Erasmus (1469–1536). Born in Rotterdam, he studied in Paris, lived several years in England, paid an extended visit to Italy, and spent the last quarter of his life largely in Basel, Switzerland, and nearby in Freiburg, Germany. He was thus the most international of the humanists and rightly called himself a "citizen of the world." His life's work was the revival of Christian piety through study of the classics, and his greatest achievement was his edition of the Greek New Testament. He also did much for the study of the Fathers of the Church, editing several whose names have appeared in this history—Origen, Chrysostom, Jerome, and Augustine—as well as several classical authors, among them Demosthenes. He was, moreover, a major writer in his own right: His *Praise of Folly* and the *Colloquies* deserve to be regarded as the last great works of Latin literature. Although Erasmus knew thoroughly the whole system of classical rhetoric, the only part of the discipline to which he made a major contribution was style. His objective was the achievement and teaching of a sound knowledge of Latin as a flexible and subtle tool of communication and education.[50] Here his standards were based on good sense and utility, as can be seen in his influential *Ciceronianus* of 1528.[51] Among other important publications by Erasmus were his works on letter writing, *De Conscribendis Epistulis*,[52] and on preaching, *Ecclesiastes sive de Ratione*

Concionandi, which turned back from late medieval preaching theory to classical rhetoric and homiletics.

Most influential was Erasmus's treatise of 1511, *De Duplici Copia Rerum et Verborum*, or *De Utraque Verborum ac Rerum Copia*. It is usually called simply *On Copia*.[53] The word *copia* may be translated "abundance." The major classical source for the concept is the first chapter of the tenth book of Quintilian's *Institutio*, where two kinds are identified, abundance of matter or ideas and abundance of words. Erasmus discusses how to attain this facility in writing Latin prose. In Book 1 he discusses abundance of words, which is secured chiefly by imaginative use of tropes and figures, for which he cites examples from classical Latin sources, including but not restricted to Cicero, and by the study of formulae, which shows how the same idea can be differently expressed. Some of this is a tour de force, as when Erasmus shows (1.33) one hundred and fifty ways to say (in Latin) "Your letter pleased me very much" and two hundred ways to say "I shall remember you as long as I live." Book 2 deals with abundance of thought, of which ten methods are cited; for example, taking something that can be expressed briefly and in general terms and expanding it and separating it into constituent parts, or exploring the causes, or enumerating accompanying circumstances. Erasmus expanded the work in three revisions, and partly as a result the structure of the discussion is confused; but schoolmasters immediately saw the utility of the treatise for teaching composition, and it continued to be reprinted until the early nineteenth century. It was also the subject of commentaries and was translated into vernacular languages.

Many other texts on style were written in the sixteenth century. Among handbooks of tropes and figures that had repeated printings and were used in schools over a long period of time and in many countries were the *Tabulae de Schematibus et Tropis* by Petrus Mosellanus, first published about 1529, and the *Epitome Troporum ac Schematum* of the German schoolmaster Joannes Susenbrotus, from around 1540.[54]

Juan Luis Vives

Vives (1492–1540) was born in Spain but left at the age of seventeen out of fear of the Inquisition and never returned. He studied in Paris with

Erasmus, taught at Louvain and Oxford, served as tutor to the future Queen Mary of England, and died at Bruges. In an encyclopedic work *De Tradendis Disciplinis*, or *On the Transmission of Knowledge*, he attacked scholasticism as a corrupting influence on all humanistic disciplines and rejected the classical conception of rhetoric as irrelevant.[55] In short compass, Vives brought out well the importance traditionally assigned to rhetoric, the authority of the classical writers (chiefly the Romans, but also the Greeks as introduced by Trebizond), and the moral and philosophical issues involving rhetoric as understood at the time, but he sought to make a new beginning appropriate to the needs of the times. Following Agricola, he regarded invention as properly a part of dialectic, and, indeed, all the traditional parts of rhetoric except for style (*elocutio*) seemed to him to be shared with other arts.[56] He also wrote a treatise on rhetoric in three books, *De Ratione Dicendi* (1532), which contains a detailed and systematic investigation of style, beginning with diction and composition in Book 1, discussing ornamentation in Book 2, and providing exercises in rhetorical composition in Book 3. Vives also broke with tradition in his work on letter writing, *De Scribendis Epistolis*,[57] in which he rejected the rhetorical structure taught in the dictamen, recommended a return to the model of Cicero's letters, and urged simplicity and brevity in letter writing.[58]

English Rhetorics of the Sixteenth Century

In the early sixteenth century the teaching of rhetoric in English grammar schools, such as Saint Paul's, Westminster, or Eton, continued in the Ciceronian tradition of the medieval trivium, but gradually new handbooks in Latin from the continent began to exert an influence. These included Erasmus's *On Copia* and writings by Agricola, Melanchthon, Mosellanus, and Susenbrotus as texts became available. The earliest work in English to discuss rhetoric is perhaps the allegorical poem *The Pastyme of Pleasure* (1509) by Stephen Hawes.[59] Allegorical treatment of rhetoric began with Martianus Capella in the fifth century, and "Lady Rhetoric" makes an occasional appearance in medieval literature and art. Chapters 7–13 of Hawes's work give a version of the five parts of rhetoric of the Ciceronian tradition in rhyming verse, with an attack in chapter 9 on those who detract from her reputation.

By the mid-sixteenth century, practical handbooks of rhetoric began to appear in English.[60] That such works were written is an indication that some English schoolmasters for the first time recognized a need to train students in the composition and appreciation of English.[61] This feeling was contemporary with assertions of nationalism under the Tudor kings, including the independence of the Anglican Church from Rome and its substitution of an English liturgy for the Latin mass. The new English rhetorics were derivative, based on continental sources, and their main interest today is that collectively they show how rhetoric was taught when the great writers of the Elizabethan Age, including Shakespeare, were young students.

The first rhetoric book in English was *The Arte or Crafte of Rhethoryke* by Leonard Cox, published about 1535. Cox was at the time a master in the Reading grammar school but had traveled widely in central Europe, knew Erasmus and Melanchthon, and at different times taught Greek and Latin grammar in Prague, Cracow, and elsewhere. Since Latin was not only the international language of scholarship but the medium of all education, a teacher could hope to find employment in different countries. Cox's *Rhethoryke* is partly a translation of Melanchthon's *Institutiones Rhetoricae* of 1521 and partly commentary by Cox on aspects of rhetoric following a study guide compiled by one of Melanchthon's students.[62] The handbook by Melanchthon that he used was an early work (1521), written before Melanchthon adopted Agricola's view that invention was not a proper part of rhetoric. Following Melanchthon's early account, Cox identified four parts of rhetoric—judgment, invention, disposition, and style—and dealt principally with invention, setting out a method based on dialectical topics such as definition, cause, division, similarity, and difference. Although he identifies four classes of orations—logical, demonstrative, deliberative, and judicial—he subsumes logical oratory into the other classes. The rest of the work is concerned with arrangement in terms of the traditional parts of an oration.

Cox did not discuss style, but Richard Sherry met that need a few years later in *A Treatise of Schemes and Tropes, Gathered out of the Best Grammarians and Oratours* (1550), with a translation of Erasmus's work *On the Education of Children* appended. A second edition in 1555 was a bilingual Latin-English version with a different subtitle, *Profitable for All*

That Be Studious of Eloquence, and in Especial for Such as in Grammar Scholes Doe Reede Most Eloquent Poets and Orators.[63] The two editions contain different examples of a declamation using tropes and figures. Sherry's sources included Erasmus and Mosellanus. He discusses figures and tropes first from a grammatical, then from an oratorical perspective, with contemporary English examples of each. In 1577 Henry Peachem published a more elaborate work, *The Garden of Eloquence,* which defines many types of figurative language, with classical, biblical, and contrived examples.[64] It is heavily indebted to Susenbrotus's Latin handbook of figures and tropes and to Sherry's *Treatise.*

The first full-scale English rhetoric book was Thomas Wilson's *Arte of Rhetorique,* eight editions of which were published between 1553 and 1585.[65] Wilson also authored the first English logic, *The Rule of Reason,* published in 1551. Born about 1523 and educated at Eton and Cambridge, he had an eventful life that included exile in Italy during the reign of Queen Mary, trial and torture by the Inquisition in Rome, and triumphant return to England under Elizabeth, who sent him on embassies to Portugal and the Low Countries and made him a privy counselor and secretary of state. He died in 1581.

Wilson's *Arte of Rhetorique* is not a textbook for use in school. He wrote for people like himself: young adults entering public life or the law or the church,[66] for whom he sought to provide a better understanding of rhetoric than they were likely to get from their grammar school studies and at the same time to impart some of the ethical values of classical literature and the moral values of Christian faith. His Protestant religious views are often vigorously expressed, especially in the "Prologue to the Reader" added to the 1560 and later editions and in the preface, where he recasts the opening of Cicero's *On Invention* in a Christian form to argue that eloquence was first given by God but lost by man and then "repaired" by God in the form of the gift of the art of rhetoric. The rhetoric he describes is the full-scale Ciceronian tradition of invention, arrangement, style, memory, and delivery, set out in a lively, readable way with examples and practical advice. His sources include *Rhetoric for Herennius,* Quintilian, Agricola, Melanchthon, Sherry, and others. Several other works by Wilson were printed. One of the most interesting is his *Three Orations of Demosthenes* of 1576, a translation of Demosthenes' *Philippics,* in which Philip of Macedon becomes a figure for Philip II of Spain and Demosthenes' call for intervention in Macedon becomes an allegory urging England's intervention against Spain in the Low Countries.

Other English rhetorics of the mid-sixteenth century include Richard Rainolde's *Foundacion of Rhetorike* (1563), a collection of declamations with comparative analysis, intended for imitation by students, and Angel Day's *The English Secretary* (1586), which classifies types of letters, with examples, gives an account of tropes and figures based on the handbook of Susenbrotus, and discusses the duties of a secretary.

Rhetoric as taught in schools, and especially that part of it devoted to style, was applied to composition in all the languages of Europe. The influence of classical rhetoric on English literature has been recounted in a number of fine books.[67] It is an important subject for understanding the art of almost all great writers from the sixteenth through the eighteenth centuries, not the least of which is that of Shakespeare, whose works are in a concrete way one of the achievements of classical rhetoric. From his early education Shakespeare was not only fully conscious of the rules and conventions of rhetoric, to which he sometimes directly alludes or which he sometimes satirizes, but he fully exploits them in his composition for artistic purposes.[68] Until the romantic movement, poetry was not a matter of free expression but an application and development of the thought of the poet within the arts of grammar, rhetoric, and dialectic as understood at the time.

In the last quarter of the sixteenth century all the works described above lost ground to Ramist rhetorics. Roland MacIlmaine had translated Ramus's handbook of logic into English in 1574. In 1577 Gabriel Harvey published (in Latin) his *Ciceronianus*, an oration in which he describes how he had been a slavish follower of Cicero, more interested in ornamental style than in substance, and how he has been converted to Ramism.

Peter Ramus

The person whose teachings most influenced the history of rhetoric in the sixteenth and seventeenth century was Peter Ramus (1515–72).[69] In his native French, and in many library catalogs, his name is Pierre de la Ramée. Ramus spent most of his life in Paris, where he became head of the Collège de Presles and professor of eloquence and philosophy on royal appointment at the Collège de France. He had been a student of Johannes Sturm in Paris, and learned from him the concept of "method," derived from Hermogenes' treatment of stasis and style. Ramus took up the question of the relationship of rhetoric to dialectic where Agricola had left it, reduced it to a method of teaching, and further decreased the realm of rhetoric. His dialectic, like Agricola's, is divided into invention and judgment. The former is based on the theory of *loci* (topics). The later includes *dispositio*, or arrangement, traditionally the second part of rhetoric but here transferred to dialectic, and apparently absorbs memory also, though that part of rhetoric is largely abandoned.

In his *Institutiones Dialecticae* of 1543 Ramus says that a complementary work on rhetoric will be provided by Omer Talon. Talon, in Latin, Talaeus (ca. 1510–62), was a teacher in colleges of Paris and closely associated with Ramus for most of his life. In 1545 he published his *Institutiones Oratoriae* under his own name, but he was clearly dependent on Ramist principles. The title is derived from Quintilian, who probably exercised more influence on Ramist rhetoric than any other authority, but it is ironic in that Quintilian's meaning was "The Education of an Orator," and neither Ramus nor Talon can be said to have been seriously interested in training an orator. They wanted to train young boys to write Latin with tropes and figures in the most efficient way they could find. Yet Ramus himself was apparently famous as a colorful and eloquent lecturer.

In addition to the 1545 version there is a 1548 *Rhetorica* in one book, a 1562 *Rhetorica* in two books, and 1567 and 1569 editions, written after Talon's death.[70] Talon's name was dropped, and Ramus's part in the work increased in each edition, parallel to his writings on dialectic. In seeking a "method" he seems first to have tried to divide up the subject in accordance with classical categories that can be found in Quintilian, including nature, art, and practice, but in the edition of 1548 and later editions rhetoric is divided, like other arts in Ramist method, into two parts: in this instance, *elocutio*, or style, and *pronunciatio*, or delivery. Each of these is then divided into two parts: *elocutio* into tropes and figures (the latter itself divided into figures of speech and figures of thought), and *pronunciatio* into voice and gesture. These subjects are of course to be found in Quintilian, though much else there is omitted by

Ramus, including the virtues of style, *sententiae*, amplification, and copia. Ramus's definition of rhetoric, *doctrina bene dicendi*, is an adaptation of Quintilian's *scientia bene dicendi*, but speaking well meant far less to Ramus than to Quintilian. Ramus's hostility to Quintilian, for the latter's failure to understand that rhetoric was only a matter of style and delivery, was carried to the extreme when Ramus wrote an attack on him entitled *Arguments in Rhetoric against Quintilian* (1549).[71] It is an ill-tempered, self-serving work that shows a lack of historical understanding or critical judgment.

Ramus, Talon, and others taught rhetoric to boys at about the age of American junior high school students; clarity, simplicity, and a content that could be memorized were desirable features in such teaching. It would have been a logical application of Ramus's theory to study dialectic first and then learn rhetoric, as suggested by Agricola's handbook, but Ramus and most of his successors continued to teach rhetoric before dialectic. The concepts, definitions, and materials of style as taught by Ramus, and much of what he says about dialectic, are drawn from classical authorities; his works are written in good classical Latin, and the objective of his pedagogical works is to teach how to write logical and eloquent Latin. In this sense, Ramist rhetoric was firmly in the classical tradition. Critics of Ramus and his followers, however, have noted several features of Ramism that negate or vitiate the principles on which classical rhetoric was based. Classical rhetoric was essentially civic and oral; Ramism is neither. The attempt of the Italian humanists to recreate a civic rhetoric of public address that would be useful in courts and assemblies was of no interest to Ramus. For all his classicizing, what he described was an elementary course that is a continuation of the trivium of the Middle Ages. Delivery in theory remained a part of his system, but he had little to say about it and his successors usually omitted it. More fundamentally, his whole way of looking at dialectic and rhetoric was not in terms of speech and debate, but in terms of writing and visual images.

The appeal of Ramism was considerable to teachers in England and early America; it had some influence in France and Spain, less in Italy and Germany. Ramus became a Protestant near the end of his life and was killed in the Saint Bartholomew's Day massacre of Hugonauts in 1572, thus elevating him to the stature of a kind of Protestant saint. Perhaps more important, his emphasis on dialectic was consistent with Puritan sentiments about preaching and plain thinking.[72] The rhetoric course at Harvard College (founded 1636) was based on the Ramist approach. Many editions of Ramus's works were published, and other rhetorics were written in Latin or vernacular languages adapting his views. In England these included Gabriel Harvey's *Rhetor* and *Ciceronianus* of 1548,[73] Abraham Fraunce's *Arcadian Rhetorike* of 1588,[74] and Charles Butler's *Rhetoricae Libri Duo* of 1598, which was reprinted throughout the seventeenth century.[75] An attraction of Ramism for teachers, in addition to any religious implications, was its "neatness"; the objection to it was its superficiality and the continued appeal of the Ciceronian tradition, which remained strong in many schools and universities.[76]

Rhetoric in Spain and Mexico

Some study of the trivium as described by Isidore of Seville continued sporadically throughout the Middle Ages in Spain. The first Spanish rhetoric of the Renaissance was *Retórica nueva de Tulio* by Enrique de Aragon (1384–1434), a translation of *Rhetoric for Herennius*. In the fifteenth century Trebizond's new rhetoric was introduced by his student Alfonso de Palencia, and in 1511 a Spanish edition was published by Hernando Alonso de Herrera for use by students at the University of Alcalá de Henares; the debate between Ciceronians and Anti-Ciceronians engaged some Spanish scholars in the sixteenth century; and Ramism had an early influence there as well.[77]

At the end of the sixteenth century the Society of Jesus adopted a *Ratio Studiorum*, or plan of education, which gave a significant place to the study of rhetoric. The approved rhetorical textbook was *De Arte Rhetorica Libri Tres* by the Spanish Jesuit Cypriano Soarez, first published in 1562.[78] Students in Jesuit schools began with study of Latin grammar and then continued in a course in "humanities," readings in Latin, leading to study of rhetoric. In a preface, Soarez explains that standard texts on rhetoric—*On Invention*, *Rhetoric for Herennius*, etc.— were too difficult for these students and that he could find no books that led students *gradually* to understand the principles of oratory. Thus his objective was to supply a textbook for beginners in rhetoric. In Book 1 he discussed invention, supplying sixteen topics for arguments and rules for amplification. Book 2 deals with arrangement, status theory, judgment, conflicts of letter and intent, syllogisms, enthymemes, induction, examples, epicheiremes, sorites, and dilemma. Book 3 is devoted to embellishment, the different kinds of words, prose rhythm, memory, and delivery. The work is a digest of classical rhetorical theory, written in a simple way and with a continuity of thought throughout. Aids to understanding Soarez's work were composed later in the sixteenth century: a *Compendium*, or summary, and *Tabulae*, or lists of rules and definitions. In 1688 materials for study of rhetoric in Jesuit schools were amplified with the *Manuale Rhetorum*, a kind of commentary and expansion of Soarez's original work with more detailed explanations and examples. These textbooks were often reprinted, and Jesuit schools continued to teach rhetoric from them for another century. Another authoritative work was *De Eloquentia Sacra et Humana*, first published in 1619 by the French Jesuit Nicolas Caussin, and reprinted on numerous occasions in France and Germany. It is an enormous treatise of over a thousand pages, of which there is no modern edition. It is said to be unusual in its extensive treatment of the emotions.[79]

Christianization of the native inhabitants of the New World was a part of Spanish imperial policy almost from the beginning of conquests there. Luis de Granada (1504–88), the author of a long work on preaching for the Counter Reformation in Europe, also compiled a *Breve tratado*, a short handbook on how to adapt the Christian message to non-Christians in America.[80] Franciscan friars in New Spain originally attempted a fusion of European and native American cultural features in their preaching and teaching in the second quarter of the sixteenth century, but this was disapproved by the Church and abandoned. The University of Mexico, founded in 1553, adopted the standard European curriculum of the arts, taught in Latin, and promoted the creation of a Spanish American cultural elite that dominated society for centuries. The Jesuits founded a college on their arrival in Mexico in 1572 and stipulated that rhetoric should be taught based on Aristotle, Cicero, and Quintilian. Early in the next century Bernardino de Llanos compiled an anthology of rhetorical and poetical texts for Jesuit teaching, *Illustrium Auctorum Collectanea*, which included the now official rhetoric of Soarez. Several Jesuits in Mexico composed new rhetorical treatises in Spanish or in Latin; examples include *Breve Instrucción y Suma Re-*

thórica de Predicadores by Domingo Velázquez (1625) and *De Arte Rhetorica* (1646) by Tomás González.[81]

G. J. Vossius

The great Dutch classical scholar Gerhard Johann Vossius published several works on rhetoric in the early seventeenth century that were widely used in Europe and Britain and often reprinted. The earliest (1606) was his enormous *Institutiones Rhetoricae*, revised and abridged (still over four hundred pages long) in *Rhetorices Contractae* (1621), and further revised and abridged (to about one hundred pages) in *Elementa Rhetoricae* (1626).[82] Vossius was a vigorous opponent of Ramism who had much to do with the survival of the full classical tradition in rhetoric and who utilized Aristotle's *Rhetoric* to a greater degree than any others of his time, seeking to reconcile Aristotelian and Ciceronian rhetorical theory. He cites Aristotle's definition of rhetoric, discusses ethos, logos, and pathos as means of persuasion, and has much to say about the emotions along Aristotelian lines, but he also discusses stasis theory and tropes and figures at length.

Francis Bacon

The most important figure in the history of rhetoric at the beginning of the seventeenth century in England was Francis Bacon (1565–1621), Lord Chancellor and the herald of the new age of science.[83] Bacon was a distinguished orator in the House of Commons and the lawcourts, a position that gave him an understanding of primary rhetoric similar to that of Thomas Wilson but unknown to most of the other writers discussed earlier. Ben Jonson said of him: "He commanded where he spoke, and had his judges angry and pleased at his devotion. No man had their affections more in his power. The fear of every man that heard him was lest he should make an end."[84] He served in the House of Commons at a time when real political debates on important issues produced major orations for the first time in English, and thus in modern history. The subjects included the religious policy of the crown, the privileges of the House of Commons, and the control of finance.

Bacon discussed aspects of rhetoric in several of his works, but the account here can be limited to what he says in *The Advancement of Learning* of 1605 and its expanded Latin translation of 1623, *De Dignitate et Augmentis Scientarum*.[85] *The Advancement of Learning* is an ambitious and imaginative attempt to restructure human knowledge on rational principles useful for the modern world with its emerging new interest in science. His work became the basis of the organization of knowledge in the *Encyclopédie française* in the eighteenth century, and its influence is still seen in encyclopedias and library catalogs. There are similarities in Bacon's system to Aristotle's theory of knowledge and to the medieval systems of learning of Hugh of Saint Victor and Bonaventura, but a restatement of the role of rhetoric was badly needed with the great expansion of learning in the Renaissance. Aristotle's account of the relationship of rhetoric to dialectic was not entirely clear, reflecting different stages in his thinking and not worked out in detail, and this issue had become divisive by Bacon's time, confused especially by Ramism with its facile solution of the problem of rhetoric and dialectic. Although the one reference to Ramus by name in *The Advancement of Learning* (2.17.12) is complimentary, Bacon clearly criticizes Ramism in his discussion of "method" (2.17.1) as "weakly inquired," and, in fact, he provided a much more satisfactory answer to Ramus than did those who simply reverted to the Ciceronian tradition in the seventeenth century.

Bacon divided human learning into three parts: history, which is based on memory; poetry, based on imagination; and philosophy, based on reason. He takes these up in turn. Philosophy is given the most attention and is divided into divine, natural, and human. Human philosophy is either segregate (dealing with human beings as individuals) or congregate (dealing with social groups). The study of individuals involves either the body (medicine, cosmetics, athletics, or sensual arts) or the mind. Bacon's approach to mind is functional, and here he distinguishes intellectual and moral functions. The intellectual functions include four arts: invention, judgment, custody (by writing or memory), and tradition or transmission. The art of tradition (from Latin *tradere*, "to hand over") is broken down into three parts: study of the organ of transmission, which is speech and grammar; study of the method of transmission, which is logic; and study of the illustration of transmission, which is rhetoric, discussed in the eighteenth chapter of Book 2. Rhetoric is, Bacon says, "a science excellent and excellently well laboured." Though in the abstract inferior to wisdom, as God said to Moses in Exodus 4:16, it is "more mighty," for which the authority of Solomon in Proverbs 16:21 is also cited. Bacon continues:

> Eloquence prevaileth in an active life. And as to the labouring of it, the emulation of Aristotle with the rhetoricians of his time, and the experience of Cicero had made them in their works of rhetoric exceed themselves. Again, the excellency of examples of eloquence in the orations of Demosthenes and Cicero, added to the perfection of the precepts of eloquence, hath doubled the progression of this art; and therefore the deficiencies which I shall note will rather be in some collections, which may as hand-maids attend the art, than in the rules or use of the art itself. (2.28.1)

Rhetoric is here given a secure place in the structure of knowledge, equal in importance to logic, because of its great practical utility. Nothing is said about style, which is not central to rhetoric in Bacon's scheme. The fundamental work on the discipline is attributed to classical authorities, especially to Aristotle; Cicero contributed "experience," and the art is best illustrated by the achievements of Demosthenes and Cicero, that is, by political oratory, whether deliberative or judicial. Throughout his work Bacon goes directly to classical sources and most of his illustrations are classical, though there are occasional contemporary references. He gives special weight to the Greek sources as more primary, and in Book 1 (2.9) had referred to Cicero as "the best, or second orator," correcting himself at the thought of Demosthenes. Bacon believed his own contribution to rhetoric would be to fill in "deficiencies," that is, "lacks," not errors, in the fundamental system of Greek rhetoric, which remained valid.

Bacon them proceeds to define "the duty and office of rhetoric" as "to apply reason to imagination for the better moving of the will" (2.18.2).[86] The definition focuses on the *function* of rhetoric, its primary purpose, not on its secondary manifestations in literature. It also makes clear that the element of purpose is essential to rhetoric and introduces the concept of imagination as rhetorically significant. Plato, Aristotle, Quintilian, Longinus, and other ancient writers had had something to say about the role of imagination in rhetoric, and it was discussed by writers on poetics in almost all periods; Bacon brings it back as an important rhetorical concept, and with it attention to the role of the audience. The orator's imagination, supported by logical arguments, moves the audience's will to act or believe. The audience was to remain important in neoclassical rhetorical theories.

Bacon goes on to explain that the very factors that disturb the judgment of reason—sophism, impression, and affection—are the very factors that are equally used "to establish and advance it": "The end of rhetoric is to fill the imagination to second reason, and not to oppress it" (2.18.2). Bacon then continues with a brief criticism of Plato's objections to rhetoric in *Gorgias* and quotes with approval an observation from *Phaedrus*, showing that these works are in his mind as he writes. Rhetoric can no more be charged with making the worse seem the better cause than can dialectic. Aristotle was right in placing rhetoric between logic on the one hand and ethics and politics on the other, "for the proofs and demonstrations of logic are towards all men indifferent and the same; but the proofs and persuasions of rhetoric ought to differ according to the audience" (2.18.5). As Plato had demanded, "If a man should speak of the same thing to several persons, he should speak to them all respectively and in several ways," a matter Bacon recommends "to better inquiry."

Bacon makes no reference to the five parts of Ciceronian rhetoric or to most other categories as taught in the schools. They are secondary considerations to the essence of philosophical rhetoric. In the last part of chapter 18, greatly expanded in *De Augmentis Scientiarum* (6.3), he considers the specific "deficiencies" of Aristotle. These are slightly disappointing at first sight, but their utility to a practicing orator like Bacon was considerable, and they are elaborations of topics described by Aristotle or Cicero.[87] The first are the "colours of good and evil, both simple and comparative, which are the sophisms of rhetoric." An example of a comparative sophism is "What men praise and celebrate is good; what they criticize and reprehend is bad." This truism can be refuted because, Bacon says, men may praise the bad out of ignorance, bad faith, zeal for a cause, or weakness of character. Second are "antitheta," or arguments for or against something, such as the conflict between the letter and intent of a law. The Latin edition details forty-seven such arguments. Third are commonplaces to be used within a speech in the preface, conclusion, digression, transition, or excuse. Bacon says they are of special ornament and effect, but they are also useful to an extempore orator in maintaining the flow and structure of a speech.

Bacon's work exercised some influence on rhetorical theory during the next two hundred years, but his general influence on later thinkers in encouraging philosophical speculation about rhetoric was more important than any of his specific doctrines. In his work, the philosophical strand of rhetoric, the slenderest thread since antiquity, was recovered, and a new maturity began to emerge in an age of enlightenment.

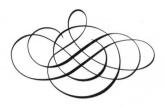

CHAPTER 11

Neoclassical Rhetoric

In the seventeenth and eighteenth centuries rhetoric experienced new developments that were both classical and nonclassical, both a return to a better understanding of classical rhetoric and a more radical departure from the philosophical and civic assumptions of classical rhetoric. These developments are often viewed in terms of the influence of the new science, especially the new logic of Descartes and Pascal in France and of Locke and the British Empiricists, upon the understanding and exposition of rhetoric. Through the work of the Port Royalists, the schools of France, Britain, and America were directly affected in the teaching of logic, but new conceptions of rhetoric only slowly influenced teaching at elementary levels, which frequently kept to the Ciceronian tradition or to the lists of tropes and figures of Ramist rhetoric. Thomas Farnaby's *Index Rhetoricus* of 1625, originally a handbook of Ciceronian rhetoric, was frequently reprinted and much used in British and American schools for over a century, but the later editions reduced it to a Ramist rhetoric of tropes and figures.[1]

It is also possible, however, to approach the new developments in terms of the neoclassical movement that flourished in France in the reign of Louis XIV (1643–1715) and reached England after the restoration of Charles II in 1660.[2] This approach is appropriate in a study of the tradition of classical rhetoric, for the history of the discipline in this period is analogous to a renewed classicism in literature and to the neoclassical movement in architecture, sculpture, and painting. Knowledge of Greek, recovered by the humanists of the fourteenth and fifteenth centuries, first produced Latin translations of Greek works, but in the sixteenth and seventeenth centuries Italian, French, and English translations of literary merit became popular, and awareness of the aesthetic superiority and originality of Greek literature was widely diffused. This new knowledge made possible the classicizing literature of the seventeenth and eighteenth centuries, seen in the dramatic works of Corneille and Racine in France and of Dryden and Addison in England, which imitate Greek models, in contrast to Shakespeare's greater reliance on Roman and medieval forms. In the case of rhetoric, neoclassical Hellenism can be seen in the preference among intellectuals for Plato and Demosthenes over Cicero and Quintilian, already evident in Bacon, and in a new role for primary rhetoric in French and English oratory. At the same time, Latin lost ground to French and English in education, since rhetorical studies increasingly focused on training for speech and writing in the vernacular, but Latin continued to be used throughout the eighteenth century for advanced scholarship and in some reference works. Ernesti's dictionaries of technical terms, published in Leipzig in 1795 and 1797 and still in some use today, are good examples.[3]

Seventeenth-century classicism received official sponsorship from the French Academy, established in 1635. The goals of the Academy from the start included the publication of authoritative works on French language, rhetoric, and poetics.[4] The most essential part of the program, a French dictionary, finally appeared in 1694. Oliver Patru, who became a member of the Academy in 1640, was apparently expected to produce the rhetoric and was occasionally referred to as "the French Quintilian," but he never got beyond an informal prospectus. At least two treatises did eventually appear under the title *La Rhétorique française*, one by René Bary in 1659 and one by sieur Le Gras in 1671. Although both sought to take a broad view of the subject and to adapt it to the French language and the circumstances of seventeenth-century life—for example, by the division of rhetoric into the two contemporary forms of preaching and judicial oratory—neither was an imaginative or creative expression of the new classicism. More influential were two treatises by René Rapin of 1684, which represent the tendency of rhetoric to slip into literary composition in their development of the concept of belles lettres and which cling to the Latin tradition.[5] Consideration of belles lettres became a standard part of discussions of rhetoric in seventeenth-century France, as seen in the writings of Lamy, Fénelon, Rollin, and others to be discussed below, and was brought to Britain in the next century, where it is a major subject of discussion by Blair and others.[6] Ultimately, belles lettres became "literature" as studied in modern universities.

During the seventeenth century important developments were taking place in logic that had an effect on rhetoric. The starting point of these developments was the *Discourse on Method* of René Descartes (published 1637), of whom more will be said later in this chapter, and their most specific manifestation was the *Port-Royal Logic* of 1662, largely the work of Antoine Arnauld, a member of the Jansenist group that had formed a college outside of Paris.[7] Another writer who contributed to the new program was Pascal, in the work called *De l'Esprit géométrique*, also known as *L'Art de persuader* (1664).[8] The effect of these works was to challenge traditional rhetoric. Put in an extreme form, the new logic claimed that the only sound method of inquiry is that of geometry, proceeding from self-evident axioms to universally accepted conclusions. The "topics" of dialectic and rhetoric are useless in discovering truth or in demonstrating it. The role of an orator seeking to dominate communication is inappropriate, and to stir the emotions of an audience is unacceptable. The positive side of the new logic was the establishment of a method of communication needed for the emergence of modern science; its negative side was its apparent ignorance of psychological realities in politics, law, and religion, and of the existence of a special kind of rhetoric evident in philosophical and scientific writing in contradiction to its claims of certainty and objectivity.

Women's Rhetoric in the Seventeenth and Eighteenth Centuries

There was considerable opposition to women's study of the liberal arts in the period under discussion, but there is also evidence that some upper-class women acquired a knowledge of rhetoric. Women constituted a significant part of the audience for fashionable preachers; they often read sermons and were discriminating judges of the eloquence of the pulpit. In seventeenth-century Paris some independent-minded women began to hold elegant salons at which they entertained friends and admirers of both sexes and encouraged conversation on literature, the arts, and ideas of the time, while promoting reforms in family law to give women greater control over their lives. It was in this setting that a distinctive women's rhetoric emerged in the salons and in literature and was given the name *préciosité* by male detractors.[9]

As a linguistic movement, *préciosité* encouraged purity of language at the same time that it exploited metaphors to avoid specifically naming anything regarded as unseemly in reference to the body or society, provoking criticism as being prudish. Molière's farce *Les Précieuses ridicules* (1659) is a scathing satire of the language and ideas about love and society current in women's salons. But the *style précieuse* strongly influenced Corneille and other dramatists and is found in many passages where love or moral virtue are treated in metaphorical language.

As a literary movement, *préciosité* was responsible for the creation of new literary forms by women, often produced by the collaboration of several individuals. The most important of these are the portrait, the conversation, and the maxim, but some women also collaborated in writing novels that employed the linguistic style of *préciosité*. Most famous are the novels of Madeleine de Scudéry, especially *Clélie, histoire romaine*, an enormous work published in ten installments between 1654 and 1660, utilizing the style of *préciosité*, and dealing with many of the issues discussed by women in the salons.

In anticipation of women's future intellectual role in society, some fathers provided their daughters as well as their sons with instruction in literature and rhetoric and in Latin grammar and modern languages. One documented case is that of Beata Rosenhane (1638–74), daughter of a Swedish diplomat who moved in intellectual circles in Sweden, Germany, and France. Her exercise books survive, showing her acquiring an understanding of rhetorical invention, including traditional *loci*, and style.[10] In Italy, women were sometimes allowed to study in universities, and one woman, Elena Lucrezia Carnaro Piscopia, earned a doctor of philosophy degree, awarded in 1678 by the University of Padua.

In England, a few seventeenth-century women began to demand the right to speak in public. The most famous is Margaret Fell, a Quaker who in 1666 while in prison for her religious activities published a tract entitled *Women's Speaking Justified, Proved, and Allowed by the Scriptures*.[11] An early discussion of rhetoric by an English woman is found in *A Serious Proposal to the Ladies, Part II* (1697) by Mary Astell. She devotes some twenty-five pages to showing how women can train themselves in speaking and writing even without the kind of education given males. She recommends that women read Lamy's *Art of Speaking* and shows a knowledge of the Port Royalists.[12] A third woman with good rhetorical skills was Margaret Cavendish, Duchess of Newcastle. In addition to other works, she published *Orations of Divers Sorts, Accommodated to Divers Places* in 1662. This is a kind of novel consisting of speeches by men and women in an imaginary city, illustrating the power of eloquence and the separation of the sexes. Seventeenth-century English women published plays and poetry and argued for their right to do so in prefaces. Examples include Aphra Behn's prefaces to her comedies *The Lucky Chance* and *The Dutch Lover*, and the preface to her *Poems* by Anne Finch, Countess of Winchelsea.[13]

Bernard Lamy

The most original rhetorical treatise to appear in France in the seventeenth century was *De l'Art de parler*, or *On the Art of Speaking*, published anonymously by Bernard Lamy in 1675. Anonymity was probably sought to protect Lamy and the religious order to which he belonged from charges of the influence of Descartes, whose religious views had come under scrutiny by the Church. In 1676 an English version of Lamy's book, with some departures from the French text, was published in London.[14] The translators, who have not been identified with certainty, attributed the original to "Messieurs du Port Royal." Lamy was not a member of the Port Royal group, but he had benefited from some of their thinking about language and logic, and readers easily accepted the new rhetoric as the counterpart of the well-known *Port-Royal Logic* and grammars, thus greatly increasing its sale. The English edition was repeatedly reprinted in the eighteenth century but without inclusion of revisions that Lamy later made in the French text.

Although Lamy admired and quoted Cicero, Quintilian, and Augustine, his handbook is not a traditional work. Aristotle is dismissed with little notice. The influence of Ramism is slight, that of Cartesian method strong, and there are many points of contact with the *Port-Royal Logic*. Lamy reorganized the structure of rhetoric to begin with an account of language: the organs of voice and speech; the parts of speech;

the need to use words in their proper sense. But language, he recognized, is not rich enough to supply terms for all ideas; thus in the second part he proceeds to consideration of tropes and then to figures as expressive of the emotions. The third part of the work discusses sounds, pronunciation, and delivery. The fourth part examines style in a larger sense: imagination, memory, and judgment as the basis of a good style; the three levels of style: the lofty, the simple, and the middle; and the differences between the styles of an orator or preacher, a historian, and a poet. Only in the final section of the work does he come to the means of persuasion, the invention of proofs, dialectical topics, and the arrangement of a speech into parts. Although speech is the subject of the work, Lamy has much to say about poetry, including versification.

In one passage Lamy briefly states what might be called the dogma of neoclassical aesthetics. In the English version, the text reads:

> A discourse is beautiful when it is compos'd according to the Rules of Art; it is great when it is more than ordinary [*sic*] perspicuous; when there is not one equivocation; no sentence unintelligible; no expression ambiguous; when it is well-disposed, and the mind of the Reader led directly to the end of the design, without the *remora* or impediment of impertinent words. Such clearness like a Torch dispels all obscurity and makes every thing visible.[15]

Boileau and "The Sublime"

Shortly after the passage just quoted Lamy refers with approval to the treatise *On the Sublime*, attributed to Longinus. This work had been known for a century but was little noticed until, in 1674, the French poet and critic Nicolas Boileau-Despréaux translated it into French with an introduction and notes. In 1694 he followed this up with a series of essays, *Réflexions critiques sur quelques passages du Rhéteur Longin*.[16] Familiarity with *On the Sublime* brought to neoclassical rhetorical criticism an element it badly needed: a theory of genius and inspiration to rise above pedantic rules of composition without contradicting them. This was particularly valuable to those critics, like Boileau, who sought to defend the greatness of the classics in the debate between the Ancients and Moderns, what Jonathan Swift later called "The Battle of the

Books," a dispute hotly contended in the late seventeenth and early eighteenth centuries.[17]

Interest in "the sublime" grew in France, England, and Germany and finally burst its neoclassical limits completely into the aesthetic of romanticism.[18] The major treatment in English was the work of the parliamentary orator Edmund Burke, entitled *A Philosophical Enquiry into the Origin of Our Ideas of the Sublime and Beautiful* (1757).[19] Burke equated the sublime with the strongest emotions that the mind can feel and saw its sources in ideas of pain and danger, whatever is in any sort terrible, is concerned with terrible objects, or operates in a manner analogous to terror, and he further associated it with vastness, obscurity, infinity, and magnificence, both in nature and art. In contrast, the beautiful is that which causes love or a passion similar to love, like smallness in size, proportion, smoothness, and grace. Some of these concepts are reminiscent of Hermogenes' "ideas" of "grandeur" and "beauty."

Preaching

The history of Christian rhetoric in the Renaissance and early modern period is too complex a subject to attempt to discuss in any detail in this book.[20] Thousands of sermons in Latin and in all the vernacular languages were not only delivered but also published and avidly read; most general works on rhetoric have something to say about preaching, and hundreds of other works are primarily devoted to preaching. Any general account of the subject needs to consider differences between Catholic and Protestant preaching, and, within each group, differences between conservatives and liberals, Jesuits and Jansenists, Lutherans and Calvinists, and Anglicans and Dissenters. Augustine's *On Christian Learning* continued to be an inspiration to many theorists of preaching. The thematic method of the medieval scholastics fell into disrepute. Agricola, Melanchthon, and especially Erasmus made major contributions. Among theoretical questions was the extent to which preaching should seek to stir the emotions of the audience and the related question of the extent to which ornamentation, and thus the classical tropes and figures, had an appropriate use in preaching. Calvinists generally favored a plain style but at the same time one imbued with the passion of the Holy Spirit. Catholic thinkers of the Counter Reformation were more inclined to combine the tradition of Ciceronian rhetoric with Old Testament prophecy to create a Christian grand style. Christian epideictic reached its greatest level of eloquence in the second half of the seventeenth century in France when ecclesiastical orators, including Louis Bourdaloue and Jean-Baptiste Massilon, achieved enormous fame. The greatest of all was Jacques-Bénigne Bossuet (1627–1704) in whose dramatic sermons sin wars with righteousness and death with life, and whose preaching combined rhetorical features of the Old Testament, Cicero, and the Church Fathers.[21]

Fénelon

Fashionable preaching in seventeenth-century France is the background for a fine statement of philosophical rhetoric by François de Salignac de la Mothe Fénelon, entitled *Dialogues sur l'éloquence en général et celle de la chaire en particulier*, written in the late 1670s (but published posthumously in 1718).[22] As the title suggests, Fénelon treats rhetoric in general but gives particular attention to the eloquence of the pulpit (*la chaire*). As archbishop of Cambrai, he had a special interest in the subject, but preaching was the single most important oratorical form in seventeenth-century France. In the fashion for elaborately ornamented preaching Fénelon saw dangers analogous to those Plato had seen in sophistry, and his *Dialogues* are a neoclassical version of the *Phaedrus*. The interlocutors are called A, B, and C. A corresponds to Socrates and states what are apparently the views of Fénelon himself; he is knowledgeable and authoritative, but not much individualized. B is a young man passionately interested in hearing fashionable preachers and, like Phaedrus, is easily taken in by meretricious adornments. C plays only a small role in the first two books, which are chiefly devoted to rhetoric in general, but pushes A hard in the third dialogue to achieve an understanding of early Christian rhetoric and its relevance for the modern preacher. The work has elegance and unity and brings out the issues very well, but it lacks the charm of an original Platonic dialogue. The sources from which A and C draw are primarily Plato, Aristotle, and Augustine. The models of noble eloquence cited are Demosthenes, Cicero, some other Greeks and Romans, biblical orators, and Fathers of the Church. Vitiated contemporary sophist-preachers are not named, but Isocrates is repeatedly taken as the classic model of their faults. References to recent discussions are disguised or indirect, as when A seems to use Cicero and Augustine against Ramist rhetoric in Book 2 (p. 92). Boileau's translation of Longinus is, however, favorably mentioned, and admiration for *On the Sublime* throughout the work is clearly derived from Boileau.

Rhetoric as understood by Fénelon is primary rhetoric: it is spoken and persuasive; his focus is on function, on the effect on the audience. "Why should you speak," asks A, "if not to persuade, to instruct, and to proceed in such a fashion that the listener remembers what you say?" (p. 58). B thinks that simple persuasion is all right for the common people but that "gentlemen have more refined ears" (p. 61). A admits that there are two goals of speaking, to persuade and to please, which is more reminiscent of Horace's statement of the goal of poetry, to teach and to charm (*Art of Poetry* 333–44), than of Cicero's duties of the orator. "But," says A,

> when they seek to please, they have another, more distant, aim, which is nevertheless the principal one. The good man seeks to please only that he may urge justice and the other virtues by making them attractive. He who seeks his own interest, his reputation, his fortune, dreams of pleasing only that he may gain the bow and esteem of men able to satisfy his greed or his ambition. Thus, even his case can be reduced like that of the good man to persuasion as the single aim which a speaker has; for the self-interested man wishes to please in order to flatter, and he flatters in order to inculcate that which suits his interest. (pp. 61–62)

Fénelon's concept of the orator is similar to Plato's: he is to lead a simple life, to be free of passion and self-interest. The people give him honor and accept him as an authority:

> In the dialogue where he makes Socrates speak with Phaedrus, Plato shows that the great defect of the rhetoricians is that they strive for the art of persuasion before they understand, by the principles of philosophy, what are the things which they ought to seek to convince men of. . . . The speaker will be obliged to know what man is, what is his destiny, what are his true interests; of what he is made, that is to say, body and soul; what is the true way to make him happy; what are

his passions, what excesses they may have, how they may be regulated, how they may be usefully aroused in order to make him live in peace and to keep society together. . . . Thus does Plato show that the role of true orator belongs only to the philosopher. It is with this in mind that we must interpret everything he says in the *Gorgias* against the rhetoricians; that is to say, against the kind of person who devises his own art of speech and persuasion, without putting himself to any trouble to know in terms of principles what one ought to seek to convince men of. . . . Cicero has virtually said the same things. (pp. 82–83)

On this note the dialogue of the first day ends.

In Book 2 Fénelon touches on matters of invention, arrangement, style, memory, and delivery, taking truth and nature and the persuasion of the audience as the criteria of excellence in each case without any fondness for rigid rules of composition. A claims that "all eloquence can be reduced to proving, to portraying, and to striking" (i.e., to logos, ethos, and pathos). "Every brilliant thought that does not drive toward one of these three things is only a conceit" (p. 92). The heart of rhetoric is neither in dialectic nor in style, but in persuasion. Delivery, often neglected in rhetorical handbooks, is thus given some prominence: "The entire art of the good orator consists only in observing what nature does when she is not hampered. Do not do what bad speakers do in striving always to declaim and never to talk to their listeners. On the contrary, each one of your listeners must suppose that you are speaking particularly to him" (p. 104). The common system of thematic preaching, with its multiple arid divisions, is scorned: "The ancients did not divide a discourse. But they carefully distinguished therein all the things which needed to be distinguished; they assigned each thing to its place; and they carefully considered in what place each thing must be put to make it most likely to have an effect" (p. 112).

In Book 3 Fénelon discusses preaching. The argument is built on what Augustine had said in *On Christian Learning*. The history of early Christian rhetoric is perceptively reviewed, the influence of vitiated style on Tertullian and some other writers is recognized, and the homiletic preaching of the Fathers of the Church is strongly recommended as a model in content, arrangement, and style.

Fénelon made constructive use of the insistence of the Port Royalists on the logical integrity of the thought of a speech, but without sacrificing an important role for the speaker and audience in the speech situation. He shows no interest in the old system of topics as the basis of oratorical invention. Not only does he not mention them, he insists that the speaker must have a deep knowledge of his subject. In the case of preaching, this knowledge can be a matter of certainty, though in the case of other forms of oratory it must be one of probability. In contrast to the Ramists, he thinks rhetoric is first of all a matter of invention. Style and delivery are important in performing its function, and Fénelon's concept of rhetoric extends to all literature, including poetry, but rhetoric itself is something other than literary technique. The autocratic rule of Louis XIV did not permit much opportunity for deliberative oratory in France, and it is thus largely overlooked by Fénelon. Like most other writers on rhetoric before modern times, he thinks of an orator giving a set speech and does not envision a situation in debate in which exchange leads to compromise or consensus; yet that is what he pictures as resulting from the questions and answers of the characters in his dialogue.

Fénelon's *Dialogues* appeared after his death in numerous French editions and were translated into German, Spanish, Dutch, and English. The influence of the work in Britain was considerable. William Stevenson published a free English translation in 1722, reprinted several times later, and two new translations appeared in the nineteenth century. The ideas of Fénelon entered into the work of several British writers who made major contributions to rhetoric.[23]

Philosophy and Rhetoric:
Descartes, Hobbes, Locke, Vico, Hume, and Kant

The relationship of rhetoric, as understood at the time, to the new science was much debated in the seventeenth century. Bacon had acknowledged a valuable role for rhetoric in human affairs. Descartes, in pursuit of philosophical certainty, was more doubtful. In Part I of *Discourse on Method* (1637) he speaks of his early esteem for eloquence and his subsequent conclusion that those with the strongest powers of reasoning, and who most skillfully arrange their thoughts to render them clear and intelligible, have the best power of persuasion even if they have never studied rhetoric. His adoption of a mathematical model of knowledge caused him to reject probable argument, and thus both dialectic and rhetoric as traditionally understood. In practice, however, like many philosophers, and with some apparent embarrassment, he found it necessary to utilize rhetorical methods to communicate with a general audience. Among his techniques were the use of French instead of Latin, the use of autobiographical narrative of the development of his thinking, and the use of imagery and the dialogue form.[24]

Thomas Hobbes might be said to have moved in the opposite direction from Descartes. Early in his career, while tutoring a young nobleman, he made a Latin translation of Aristotle's *Rhetoric* and later revised it into an English version, published anonymously in 1637 under the title *A Brief of the Art of Rhetorique*.[25] This is the first appearance of the *Rhetoric* in English, though it is more a running outline of the contents, with omissions and additions, than a translation. Later, in his major works, Hobbes came to see rhetoric as a threat to society, stirring up the passions of the crowd, and in the fifth chapter of his most famous work, *Leviathan* (1651), he attacked metaphorical language in particular as senseless, ambiguous, and a cause of contention, sedition, or contempt.[26]

The British counterpart of the French Academy was the Royal Society of London, which began as an informal group shortly before the middle of the seventeenth century and received a charter from Charles II in 1662. In contrast to the linguistic and literary interests of the French Academy, the Royal Society was much more concerned with science; but fundamental to that interest was the development of a new logic—inductive reasoning and scientific method, and discussion of logic in the seventeenth century necessarily involved the question of the province of rhetoric. Several members of the Royal Society had something to say about rhetoric,[27] including the most famous philosopher of the time, John Locke. Locke had given lectures on rhetoric at Oxford in 1663, but what he said then is not known. In his most famous work, *An Essay Concerning Human Understanding*, he seems at first to allow for something like Plato's philosophical rhetoric as described in *Phaedrus*. It would have three legitimate functions: "First, to make known one man's thoughts or ideas to another. Second, to do it with as much ease and quickness as is possible; and Thirdly, thereby to convey the knowledge of things" (3.10.3). Turning, however, to "the abuse of Words," he concludes (3.10.34) with a stinging invective against rhetoric, reminiscent of Plato's *Gorgias*:

> Since wit and fancy find it easier entertainment in the world than dry truth and real knowledge, figurative speeches and allusion in language will hardly be admitted as an imperfection or abuse of it. I confess, in discourses where we seek rather pleasure and delight than information and improvement, such ornaments as are borrowed from them can scarce pass for faults. But yet if we would speak of things as they are, we must allow that all the art of rhetoric, besides order and clearness; all the artificial and figurative application of words eloquence hath invented, are for nothing else but to insinuate wrong ideas, move the passions, and thereby mislead the judgment; and so indeed are perfect cheats; and therefore, however laudable or allowable oratory may render them in harangues and popular addresses, they are certainly, in all discourses that pretend to inform or instruct, wholly to be avoided; and where truth and knowledge are concerned, cannot but be thought a great fault, either of the language or person that makes use of them. What and how various they are, will be superfluous here to take notice; the books of rhetoric which abound in the world, will instruct those who want to be informed; only I cannot but observe how little the preservation and improvement of truth and knowledge is the care and concern of mankind; since the arts of fallacy are endowed and preferred. It is evident how much men love to deceive and be deceived, since rhetoric, that powerful instrument of error and deceit, has its established professors, is publicly taught, and has always been had in great reputation; and I doubt not but it will be thought great boldness, if not brutality, in me to have said thus much against it. Eloquence, like the fair sex, has too prevailing beauties in it to suffer itself ever to be spoken against. And it is in vain to find fault with those arts of deceiving, wherein men find pleasure to be deceived.

The reader might find amusement in identifying the dozen or more tropes and figures to be found in a passage where Locke denounces their use!

Neoclassicism appears in Italian art and architecture, and archaeological excavations began on a serious scale in the eighteenth century, but civic and intellectual life was then in general decay in Italy. One extraordinary figure, however, emerged and has a place in the history of rhetoric. This is Giambattista Vico (1668–1744), who was professor of Latin eloquence at the University of Naples. His lectures, preserved in student notes, have been published under the title *Institutiones Rhetoricae*; they set out the older classical tradition in reaction to views of other rhetorical authorities of his time.[28] He also delivered epideictic addresses on civic and academic occasions in Naples and wrote epideictic poetry. One of his academic orations, expanded into a book, was published in 1709 and is known in English as *On the Study Methods of Our Time*.[29] Here, in opposition to Descartes and the Port Royalists, he argues that the study of logic destroys the minds of the young because it prevents them from developing original thoughts; it should only be undertaken after they have been exercised in the use of metaphors, memory, and imaginative rhetorical composition.

Vico's most important work is *Scienza Nuova*, or *The New Science* (1725, with later revisions), intended to counteract what was regarded as the "new science" in France and England.[30] Here, arguing against Descartes and Locke, he explains that speech precedes thought; since speech is the subject of rhetoric, rhetoric is foundational and the basis of any understanding of human culture. He outlines a series of stages in the development of civilizations, beginning with the poetic wisdom of myth, through which experience of the world is ordered, leading to a later stage of abstract thought. This approach anticipated views of modern anthropologists. He also distinguishes four dominant tropes in social development: first metaphor or fable,[31] then metonymy, synecdoche, and finally irony, when thought becomes philosophical and reflective.[32] Vico's work was ignored by rhetoricians of his own time and had no influence on others until it was rediscovered in the nineteenth and twentieth centuries.

The great Scottish philosopher David Hume was an admirer of classical rhetoric and himself one of the most eloquent of philosophers. In his essay *Of Eloquence* (1743) he laments the state of oratory in his own time:[33] "If we be superior in philosophy, we are still, notwithstanding all our refinements, much inferior in eloquence." This is strange, he thought, since "of all the polite and learned nations, England alone possesses a popular government, or admits into the legislature such numerous assemblies as can be supposed to lie under the dominion of eloquence. But what has England to boast of in this particular?" Ancient eloquence, he thought, "was infinitely more sublime than that which modern orators aspire to." On the lips of "our temperate and calm speakers" Demosthenes' oath by those who fell at Marathon or the pathetical passages of Cicero's speeches against Verres would sound absurd. Equally absurd would seem the vehement delivery of the ancient orators.

Hume examines three reasons to explain this failure in eloquence and finds each unsatisfactory. It is true, he admits, that modern legal procedure and rules of evidence put constraints on judicial oratory, but it was deliberative oratory in antiquity that most elevated genius and gave full scope to eloquence. It is also true that modern customs, "or our superior good sense, if you will, make our orators more cautious and reserved than the ancient, in attempting to inflame the passions, or elevate the imagination of their audience." But in Hume's view modern customs should not have this effect. Ancient orators "hurried away with such a torrent of sublime and pathetic, that they left their hearers no leisure to perceive the artifice by which they were deceived." "Of all human productions," he continues, "the orations of Demosthenes present to us the models which approach the nearest to perfection." Some people claim that the disorders of antiquity gave ampler matter for eloquence, to which Hume replies, "It would be easy to find a Philip in modern times; but where shall we find a Demosthenes?"

These reasons thus rejected, the only conclusion is that modern speakers simply do not make the effort or they lack the genius and judgment of the past: "A few successful attempts of this nature might rouse the genius of the nation, excite the emulation of the youth, and accustom our ears to a more sublime and more pathetic elocution, than what we have been hitherto entertained with." As it is, "we are satisfied with our mediocrity, because we have had no experience of anything better." Hume concludes with a specific observation about modern orators: "Their great affectation of extemporary discourses has made them reject all order and method, which seems so requisite to argument, and without which it is scarcely possible to produce an entire conviction on the mind."

Hume's essay, though not so cogently argued as many of his writings, is an interesting medley of themes of classical and eighteenth-century rhetoric, echoing some of what could be found in Tacitus's *Dialogue on Orators*. Combined here are aspects of the debate of the Ancients and Moderns; the sophistic strand of classical rhetoric, with its admiration of the orator; the effect of the new logic on rhetoric; interest in the sublime and the equation of genius with the grand style; and the appeal of elocution.

The improvement in public speaking that Hume desired took place in English oratory in the second half of the eighteenth and early nineteenth centuries. The challenge of great issues arising from acquisition of a vast empire, and from the American and French Revolutions, brought the response of the most eloquent political debates since antiquity, and important cases in the lawcourts inspired oratorical display. It may well be that there was in fact an effort by speakers to achieve a higher level of eloquence, helped by greater attention to rhetoric in education and by rivalries among leaders of different factions. A French visitor, Amédée Pichot, in 1825 published his observations of British eloquence of the eighteenth and early nineteenth centuries, distinguishing three styles heard in the lawcourts: the English style, simple and devoted to discussion of technical issues; the Irish, florid, emotional, and poetic; and the Scottish, which combined the styles of the other two.[34] The great orators of this period include Thomas Erskine, James Macintosh, Edmund Burke, Charles James Fox, William Pitt the Younger, and in the early nineteenth century, George Canning and Lord Brougham.[35] Burke's speech *On Conciliation with the Colonies* and the series of speeches in prosecution of Warren Hastings for corruption as governor of India are classic works of English literature.

In Germany, rhetoric became the victim of romantic aestheticism and the idealization of poetry. Immanuel Kant, whose influence dominated German philosophy throughout the nineteenth century, expressed the relation as follows:

> The arts of speech are rhetoric and poetry. Rhetoric is the art of transacting a serious business of the understanding as if it were a free play of the imagination; poetry that of conducting a free play of the imagination as if it were a serious business of the understanding. Thus the orator announces a serious business, and for the purpose of

entertaining his audience conducts it as if it were a play with ideas. The poet promises merely an entertaining play with ideas, and yet for the understanding there inures as much as if the promotion of its business had been his one intention.[36]

Kant then describes oratory as exploiting the weakness of hearers and dismisses the art of rhetoric as worthy of no respect.

Major European Rhetorical Treatises of the Eighteenth Century

Before moving on to discuss the important developments of the second half of the eighteenth century in Britain, a subject of special interest to American readers, it is desirable to give brief mention to some major treatises written on the continent. Most are long works, written in vernacular languages, intended for teachers of speech and writing and as a contribution to the development of the national literature of their authors, and adapting the classical tradition to the perceived needs of the time.

France continued to dominate the international scene in the first half of the century. *Traité de l'éloquence* by Claude Buffier, published in 1728, is the work of a Jesuit priest who was familiar with ideas of Descartes and Locke and wished to preserve a place for rhetoric in human affairs.[37] It focuses on the nature and attainment of true eloquence in contrast to what only appears to be eloquent, and emphasizes natural talent and practice more than observation of rules. Invention and arrangement are touched on, but most of the work is devoted to style, by which the soul can be moved to belief and action. The discussion includes some remarks on vivacity, a topic taken up later by British rhetoricians. Toward the end of the work, Buffier discusses judicial rhetoric and preaching, with French examples of different genres and critical observations on Aristotle, Cicero, and Quintilian. Buffier was also the author of a treatise on memory systems, which was frequently reprinted.

Much more widely known was *Traité des études: De la manière d' enseigner et d'étudier les Belles-Lettres*, by Charles Rollin, first published in 1726 with many later printings and repeated translations into English, German, Italian, and even Russian.[38] Rollin was an educational reformer who sought to reduce the role of rote memorization in schools and encourage study of French side by side with Latin, and was also the author of a textbook of ancient history widely used in Europe, Britain, and America as late as the nineteenth century. His treatise on rhetoric, like Lamy's, relates rhetoric closely to language study and illustrates how to analyze exemplary French texts. It thus was a further step toward a primarily literary approach to the subject, encouraged by the need to teach composition in schools and by the relatively limited role of public address in autocratic France.

A crucial further step in the understanding of rhetoric in France began with the treatise *Des Tropes*, published by César-Chesneau Du-Marsais in 1730. Its subtitle can be translated, "Some Different Senses in Which One Can Take a Word in the Same Language." This culminated the tendency toward regarding rhetoric as the study of literary devices of style, begun in France with Ramus, and became the standard approach to the subject in French schools until replaced by Pierre Fontanier's *Traité générale des figures du discours* after 1821.[39] Although DuMarsais's work was translated into English, rhetoricians in Britain in the later eighteenth century, where oratory had a significant role in public life, viewed rhetoric in something closer to the classical sense, with a secondary application to literary composition. The result has been a division between the European understanding of rhetoric as primarily a matter of the use of tropes and figures, taken up by teachers of English in Britain and America, and an American tradition among teachers of speech viewing rhetoric as civic discourse, derived from classical sources and other eighteenth-century British rhetoricians. This split has continued into the twentieth century, although new approaches have begun to find ways to bridge the gap.

The most important German treatise on rhetoric in the eighteenth century was probably Johann Christof Gottsched's *Ausführliche Redekunst*, or "Complete Art of Rhetoric," first published in 1736.[40] It presents rhetoric as understood in the classical tradition, but with ideas from Lamy, Rollins, and others to bring it up-to-date, and with special attention to the speaking and writing of German. The second part of this long work consists of German translations and imitations of classical and other speeches and letters. It was much read in Germany and eastern Europe throughout the eighteenth century.[41]

In Spain the most significant new rhetorical treatise of the eighteenth century was the work of Gregorio Mayáns y Siscar, professor of jurisprudence at the University of Valencia. His *Rhetórica* of 1757 devotes books to invention, including stasis theory and dialectical topics, to arrangement, to style, and to delivery, with a fifth book on framing questions and answers, conversation, letters, dialogues, inscriptions, and historical writing.[42] As Rollin in French and Gottsched in German sought to improve composition in their national languages, so Mayáns was much concerned with the development of literary Spanish. He illustrates his doctrines with Spanish proverbs and the nondramatic literature of the Spanish Golden Age, as well as ancient sources, and criticizes seventeenth-century mannerism. Although Mayáns corresponded frequently with intellectual leaders in other countries, his *Rhetórica* does not seem to have been much known outside of Spain and Latin America.[43]

Rhetorical Theory in Eighteenth-Century Britain: Ward, Sheridan, Lawson, Smith, and Campbell

During the eighteenth century in Britain, five different approaches to rhetoric are evident. One of these is the revival of the technical, largely Ciceronian, tradition. A second was the peculiar Elocutionary Movement, which shares some of the features of sophistry. A third was neoclassical philosophical rhetoric somewhat like that expounded by Fénelon, with roots in Plato. A fourth was belletristic rhetoric, adapting some features of traditional rhetoric to study of literature. A fifth, in contrast to the third, was the attempt to create a new philosophical rhetoric based on the new logic, with the addition to it of a new psychology as developed by the British Empiricist philosophers, paying some lip service to classical rhetoric but differing from it in fundamental ways.

The first approach is seen in the teaching of rhetoric at the elementary level, which continued much as it had throughout the Renaissance, sometimes in the full Ciceronian tradition, sometimes limited to study of tropes and figures.[44] At the more advanced level it is exemplified by the lectures of John Ward at Gresham College, London, which were published in 1759 under the title *A System of Oratory*.[45] Ward's fifty-four lectures set forth Ciceronian rhetoric in a thorough, rather pedantic way. Although he had read Fénelon, he was untouched by his spirit, and although he knew of attacks on the system of topics, he described it in the old way. Ward's rhetoric was praised at the time of publication and was used as a textbook in American colleges, but it was soon overshadowed by newer approaches and not reprinted.

A second approach to rhetoric in the eighteenth century was the Elocutionary Movement.[46] *Elocutio* was the Latin word for style, but it literally means "speaking out," and its English derivative, "elocution," was adapted as a term for delivery or reading aloud. Delivery, divided into control of the voice and use of gestures, was the fifth part of classical rhetoric but had often been neglected by medieval and Renaissance rhetoricians. Interest in it began to revive with the effort to achieve high standards of delivery in preaching and in the theater in the seventeenth century. Early works on rhetorical gestures in English are John Bulwer's *Chirologia, Or the Natural Language of the Hand* and *Chironomia, Or the Art of Manual Rhetoric* (1644).[47]

The French Jesuit Louis de Cressoles wrote a Latin treatise on delivery early in the century. But more influential was the work of a French Protestant, Michel Le Faucher, entitled *Traité de l'action de l'orateur, ou de la pronunciation et du geste*, published soon after his death in 1657. Fénelon also discussed delivery as an important feature of rhetoric, but interest in elocution flourished most in the British Isles, where its leading proponent was the Irishman Thomas Sheridan, father of the dramatist Richard Brinsley Sheridan. The elder Sheridan tried to establish a school of correct English speech, which he hoped would attract students from England, Ireland, Wales, Scotland, and the British colonies and would contributed to the cultivation of a standard English. He lectured widely and published several works, of which his *Course of Lectures on Elocution* (1762) was the best known.[48] To Sheridan, the only part of ancient rhetoric that really mattered was delivery. He attracted much attention, and the resulting Elocutionary Movement has a history in Britain and America that stretches even into the early twentieth century. Demonstrations of elocution are a part of the sophistic strand of classical rhetoric. Plato's *Menexenus* is supposed to have been recited annually in Athens in the Hellenistic and Roman periods, and Greek orators of the Second Sophistic repeated their best speeches with appropriate gestures all over the Roman Empire. Sheridan gave little attention to gesture, as important as it was for elocutionists. An exhaustive treatment of that subject, complete with a system of written notation to be used to "score" a speech, was published in 1806 by Gilbert Austin under the title *Chironomia: or a Treatise on Rhetorical Delivery*.[49]

The third approach, along the lines of the philosophical rhetoric of Fénelon, is best represented by the work of John Lawson, who taught rhetoric at Dublin and in 1758 published his *Lectures Concerning Oratory, Delivered in Trinity College*.[50] Lawson regarded rhetoric as "the Handmaid of Truth" and sought to answer the objections of Locke by taking up Bacon's view that rhetoric, though inferior to wisdom in excellence, was superior in common use: to impart truth, Lawson asserted, it is necessary to "soften the severity of her aspect" and thus to "borrow the embellishments of rhetoric." In approaching the parts of rhetoric, Lawson sought to reconcile Bacon and Aristotle, and in treating the topics he noted the objections to them but felt they were useful for beginners. He viewed the study of rhetoric in his own time as aiming primarily at the improvement of eloquence in English, and especially in preaching. Style was an important part, but Lawson rather scorned the artifices of tropes and figures, and he disapproved of the growing interest in elocution. Most interesting, perhaps, is his eighteenth lecture. Here he turns from Aristotle's *Rhetoric* and Cicero's *On the Orator* as his main sources to Plato's *Phaedrus*, of which he gives a summary. He says that *Phaedrus* contains "the fundamental precepts of rhetoric, enlarged afterwards and reduced into a regular system by Aristotle, to which succeeding writers have added little new; even the eloquence and experience [Bacon's word] of Tully [the common neoclassical name for M. Tullius Cicero] did not much more than adorn these." Lawson ended his lecture with enthusiastic praise of Plato's "poetic" style and a poem of his own composition, modeled on the popular myth of the choice of Heracles, in which the young Plato is faced with a choice between the two allegorical figures of Philosophy and Poetry. He chooses Philosophy but is rewarded with the gift of Poetry as well. Lawson's *Lectures* went rapidly through four printings, but the work did not have as much use as it deserved and was soon overshadowed by others.

In 1958 two sets of student notes of lectures by Adam Smith on rhetoric and belles lettres were discovered in a library in Scotland. Smith, later to become famous for his pioneering work on capitalism, *The Wealth of Nations* (1776), had delivered the lectures while teaching moral philosophy at the University of Glasgow in 1762–63, probably elaborating lectures he had given in Edinburgh earlier.[51] Smith's lectures are the earliest known statement in English of belletristic rhetoric, the fourth of the approaches to rhetoric mentioned above. The lectures were not published until 1963, but they exerted an influence on those who had heard them, including Hugh Blair, who later lectured on the same subject in Edinburgh.

Smith begins, like Lamy, with observations on the nature and history of language. He describes books on figures of speech as generally "very silly." Beauty does not consist in the use of figures; style is beautiful when a thing is neatly and properly described and the sentiment of the author is conveyed. The influence of Locke is evident here. The English prose styles of Jonathan Swift, Joseph Addison, and Lord Shaftesbury are then discussed, followed by appraisals of other authors, ancient and modern, with special attention first to writers of history, then to poets. At this point in the lecture series the student should have an understanding of language, style, narrative, characterization, and literary genres. The last ten lectures are devoted to oratory. Although it was one of Smith's announced objectives to prepare students for activity in public address, he concentrates on giving them an understanding of great classical oratory, especially works of Demosthenes and Cicero, and does not provide a systematic discussion of invention or arrangement. The manuscripts break off at this point. Smith may have continued with observations about British oratory of the recent past.

The fifth approach to rhetoric was the systematic effort to think out a new theory on the basis of the work of the British Empiricist philosophers, and especially that of Hume. Locke had thought of the mind as an empty page on which experience (Greek *empeiria*) writes; knowledge comes partly from experience, partly from reflection on experience. Hume and others added to this the principle of association: the mind draws its conclusions from the association of resemblances, contiguities, or causes and effects. Passions arise in the mind either from direct affections (joy and sorrow, desire and aversion, hope and fear) or from indirect affections associated with objects and their causes. These concepts and others related to them constitute a theory of human nature and human knowledge that has implications for rhetoric. In *Elements of Criticism* (1762) Henry Homes (Lord Kames) applied the new learning to rhetorical style. Contemporary thinking about psychology also influenced Joseph Priestley's *A Course of Lectures on Oratory and Composition* (1777).[52] More significant, however, were the studies of George Campbell, professor of divinity at the University of Aberdeen, who attempted "to explore human nature and find herein the principles which underlie and explain the art of rhetoric."[53] The result was *The Philosophy of Rhetoric*, published in 1776. Book 1 is entitled "The Nature and Foundations of Eloquence," Book 2 "The Foundations and Essential Properties of Elocution," by which Campbell meant style, and Book 3 "The Discriminating Properties of Elocution," which develops Campbell's theory of "vivacity," or liveliness of ideas, the quality, in his theory, primarily responsible for attention and belief.

Campbell departed radically from the traditional structure and terminology and many of the ideas of classical rhetoric, though others, including the roles of speakers and hearers and the stylistic virtues of purity and perspicuity, are discussed.[54] He occasionally cites examples from classical literature or classical rhetoricians, including Aristotle, Cicero, and Quintilian, but at least as often he refers to modern writers. Nevertheless, he thought of his work as directly linked to the classical tradition in rhetoric. In the introduction (pp. L–LI) he outlines the empirical sources of the rhetorical art. The first step, he says, is nature: there were orators before there were rhetoricians. The second is observation, the beginnings of the critical science of discovering modes of arguing or forms of speech. The third step is comparing the various effects, favorable or unfavorable, of those attempts at speech,

> to discover to what particular purpose each attempt is adapted, and in which circumstances only to be used. The fourth is to canvass those principles in our nature to which the various attempts are adapted, and by which, in any instance, their success or want of success may be accounted for. . . . The observations and rules transmitted to us from these distinguished names in the learned world, Aristotle, Cicero, and Quintilian, have been for the most part only translated by later critics, or put into a modish dress and new arrangement. And as to the fourth and last step, it may be said to bring us into a new country, of which, though there have been some successful incursions occasionally made upon its frontiers, we are not yet in full possession.

Campbell thus comes not to deny classical rhetoric, but to go beyond and fulfill understanding of it. When he gives his definition of eloquence in the opening of Book 1, "that art or talent by which the discourse is adapted to its end," he immediately cites Quintilian's support in a note and goes on to say that he chose this definition for two reasons: "it exactly corresponds to Tully's [Cicero's] idea of a perfect orator; and it is best adapted to the subject" of his own work.

Campbell's work was widely studied, not the least in America, where over thirty editions were printed and where it was frequently used as a college text. Its long-term effect was to supply a modern rhetoric that satisfied many teachers and students and reduced their dependence on classical sources, not necessarily on classical statements of rules such as those in Quintilian, but on the more speculative discussions of rhetoric by Plato and Aristotle and by Cicero in *On the Orator*. It was widely believed in the eighteenth century, even by defenders of "the Ancients," that modern philosophy had made remarkable strides beyond that of the past. The reputation of both Plato and Aristotle suffered at this time, and Campbell seemed to be providing a basic theory of rhetoric built on the best of modern thought.

Hugh Blair

The most definitive statement of neoclassical rhetoric, combining features of the approaches just discussed, came from Hugh Blair (1718–1800). Blair, like Hume, Smith, and Campbell, was a part of the Scottish Enlightenment, a group of intellectuals who brought a note of dispassionate common sense and reason to philosophy and literature in the eighteenth century and a note of liberal imagination to the dour Calvinism of the North.[55] Blair was a Presbyterian minister who also served as Regius Professor of Rhetoric and Belles Lettres at the University of Edinburgh. (A "regius" professor is one whose position is funded by the king.) The *Lectures on Rhetoric and Belles Lettres*, which Blair published in 1783, had been repeatedly delivered over more than twenty years, apparently with little revision.[56]

Blair is known today almost solely from his lectures on rhetoric, but he had earlier published an edition of the works of Shakespeare in eight volumes and other literary studies. The title, *Lectures on Rhetoric and*

Belles Lettres, reflects the title of his professorship, but "Lectures on Belles Lettres and Rhetoric" would be a better description. His literary interests are clearly seen from the outset when he begins with belletristic topics important to his contemporaries: taste, criticism, genius, sublimity, and beauty. He then turns to the history of language, with special attention to the development and possibilities of English, culminating in a discussion of style, including classical tropes and figures. He focuses on a small number of devices of style, which he discusses in depth, and avoids the pedantry of meaningless lists. He cites examples from Greek, Latin, and English poetry and concludes the first half of his course with four lectures on the style of Addison, analyzing specific *Spectator* papers, and with one lecture on Jonathan Swift. These are the same two authors that Adam Smith, whose lectures Blair had attended, took as models of good style.

The second volume of the lectures as published then turns to primary rhetoric—its history, its kinds, the oratory of the senate, the bar, and the pulpit, the parts of an oration and its argumentation, and delivery. These subjects take up nine out of a total of forty-seven lectures. Selections from Demosthenes, part of Cicero's speech for Cluentius, and a sermon by Bishop Atterbury are analyzed. "Philosophical rhetoric" is seen in Blair's emphasis on the importance of truth in oratory: "True eloquence," he says, "is the art of placing truth in the most advantageous light for conviction and persuasion" (vol. II, p. 104). "Conviction" is the term used by the British rhetoricians to mean logical demonstration, while "persuasion" includes ethical and emotional factors. The doctrine of topics, or *loci*, is dismissed as of little practical help (II, p. 180).

The philosophical strand in the rhetorical tradition is thus evident in Blair's teaching, but so is the sophistic strand. Consider the following passage in Lecture 34, "Means of Improving Eloquence":

To be an Eloquent Speaker, in the proper sense of the word, is far from being either a common or an easy attainment. Indeed, to compose a florid harangue on some popular topic, and to deliver it so as to amuse an Audience, is a matter not very difficult. But though some praise be due to this, yet the idea, which I have endeavored to give of Eloquence, is much higher. It is a great exertion of the human powers. It is the Art of being persuasive and commanding: the Art, not of pleasing the fancy merely, but of speaking both to the understanding and to the heart; of interesting the hearers in such a degree, as to seize and carry them along with us; and to leave them with a deep and strong impression of what they have heard. How many talents, natural and acquired, must concur for carrying this to perfection? A strong, lively, and warm imagination; quick sensibility of heart, joined with solid judgment, good sense, and presence of mind; all improved by great and long attention to Style and Composition; and supported also by the exterior, yet important qualifications, of a graceful manner, a presence not ungainly, and a full and tuneable voice. How little reason to wonder, that a perfect and accomplished Orator should be one of the characters that is most rarely to be found? Let us not despair, however, between mediocrity and perfection, there is a very wide interval. (II, pp. 226–27)

This is Blair's version of the praise of the orator by Gorgias, Isocrates, Cicero, and Quintilian. He turns then to the question of how to improve oratory. Nature must bestow talent; art must cultivate it. Personal character and disposition are important. Only a good man can be a good orator, as Quintilian maintained. Next in importance is a fund of general knowledge, including poetry and history. Then follows imitation of good models and exercise in composing and speaking, and finally the study of criticism. Here the ancient writers on rhetoric are useful, but they tried to do too much, to form an orator by rule. "Whereas, all that can, in truth, be done, is to give openings for assisting and enlightening Taste, and for pointing out to Genius the course it ought to follow" (II, p. 243). "Of all the antient [sic] writers on the subject of oratory, the most instructive and most useful" is Quintilian, "though some parts of his work contain too much of the technical and artificial system then in vogue" (II, pp. 244–45).

In the thirty-fifth lecture Blair turns from oratory back to belles lettres to discuss the comparative merits of the Ancient and the Moderns— he takes the view that the Ancients are the superior or equals of the Moderns in genius, or creative imagination, but that there have been remarkable developments in modern science—and to discuss the major genres of modern literature. The result is to imbed the discussion of primary rhetoric into the middle of a larger account of language and literature in written form, to integrate rhetoric into belles lettres.

Blair's lectures were widely studied on both sides of the Atlantic. More than fifty editions of the full text are known to have been published in Britain, and the work was translated into German, French, Spanish, Italian, and Russian. Many other editions were published in America, where the work was the most commonly used rhetoric textbook during the first half of the nineteenth century.[57]

Richard Whately

What might arguably be called the last important British neoclassical rhetorical treatise is Richard Whately's *Elements of Rhetoric*, first published in 1828 when Whately was teaching political economy at Oxford and extensively revised in later editions after he became Anglican archbishop of Dublin in 1831. Discussion here relates to the fullest version, the seventh edition of 1846.[58]

Whately's subtitle, *Comprising an Analysis of the Laws of Moral Evidence and of Persuasion, with Rules for Argumentative Composition and Elocution*, gives an indication of the contents and tendency of the work. In an extended introduction Whately says that the "province" of rhetoric at its extreme limits includes all composition in prose, and at its narrowest limits persuasive speaking. He proposes "to adopt a middle course between these two extreme points; and to treat of 'Argumentative Composition' *generally* and *exclusively*, considering Rhetoric (in conformity with the very just and philosophical view of Aristotle) as an offshoot from Logic" (Intro. 1, p. 4). The main body of the work is divided into four parts: I, "Of the Address to the Understanding, with a View to Produce Conviction (Including Instruction)"; II, "Of the Address to the Will, or Persuasion"; III, "Of Style"; and IV, "Of Elocution or Delivery." Whately had earlier published *Elements of Logic*. Logic's function, he thought, was to judge the validity of arguments, whereas rhetoric invented (that is, found arguments to prove a proposition) and arranged them. Appeal to the emotions he described as shared with poetry. His discussion of style considers three virtues: perspicuity, energy or vivacity (from Campbell), and elegance or beauty. In discussing elocution he dismisses the artificial systems of Sheridan and Austin and seeks to train a natural delivery.

In his introduction to Whately's *Elements of Rhetoric* editor Douglas Ehninger made a series of important points about the work. First, it is predominantly an ecclesiastical rhetoric. Whately has nothing to say about civic rhetoric; the chief business of rhetoric in his view is to arm a preacher for the task of conveying the indisputable doctrines of Christianity to his congregation and to arm the Christian controversialist to defend the evidences of religion against the attacks of agnostics and deists. Second, the work persistently focuses on oral argument, although Whately does give practical advice on training in written composition, especially in the introductions to the later editions. Third, the *Elements* was intended as an introductory college text, not a philosophical treatise. Ehninger also stressed the growth of the book over six revisions and its uneven quality, agreeing with other critics that the best parts are the introduction and the discussions of "conviction" and "delivery."

Whately's *Elements of Rhetoric* had some use as a textbook in Britain but was especially popular in America, replacing the works of Blair and Campbell in some colleges. His observations on composition in the introduction, influenced by the romantic movement of his time, encouraged teachers to abandon set themes, imitations, and amplifications as practiced earlier and to assign free composition based on the student's experience: Whately seems to have been the first to propose the essay topic, "What I did on my summer vacation."

The First American Rhetoric Books

Puritans introduced Ramist rhetoric to the Harvard curriculum in the seventeenth century. In the mid-eighteenth century the published lectures of John Ward, discussed above, became the approved texts at several of the new colonial colleges. Study of Ward's lectures brought Ciceronian rhetoric to the colonies at a time when oratory and public debate were about to experience remarkable development during the great events that created the American Republic. The first original teaching of rhetoric in America was the series of lectures on rhetoric given by John Witherspoon at Princeton as part of a course on moral philosophy and eloquence required of all students beginning in 1769.[59]

Witherspoon was born in Scotland in 1722 and was a classmate of Hugh Blair, but they became opponents in controversy over education and church government. Both were Presbyterian ministers, but Blair, a theological moderate, sought to bring English culture to the rougher world of Scotland and to impose an intellectually enlightened clergy on local congregations. Witherspoon stood for a stricter Calvinism, for local influence in choosing ministers, and for individual freedom of conscience. Blair's approach to rhetoric was elitist, belletristic, and concerned with literary criticism; Witherspoon's civic, populist, and connected with politics and ethics. Though he admired literature and learning, Witherspoon conceived of rhetoric as practical training in composition, argumentation, and public speaking. Called to become president of the College of New Jersey (Princeton) in 1768, he found America in political ferment. He trained Madison, Burr, and other leaders of the Revolution, took up the cause of American independence, and signed the Declaration of Independence as a delegate from New Jersey.

The word "rhetoric" appears only rarely in Witherspoon's lectures. His preferred term was "eloquence." He cites Aristotle, Cicero, Longinus, Ward, Lamy, Fénelon, Rollin, Burke, and other sources (Blair's lectures had not yet been published), and his approach throughout is broadly classicizing, but his teaching was original in a number of respects. In Lecture VI, for example, he criticizes Ward's division of style into low, middle, and sublime and prefers to speak of three kinds of eloquence and composition: sublime, simple, and mixed. In Lecture XIII he makes a useful division of eloquence on the basis of the different ends or objects of the writer or speaker, identifying them as information, demonstration, persuasion, and entertainment. Lecture XIV then takes up the subjects of oratory, divided into the eloquence of the pulpit, the bar, and what he calls "promiscuous" (that is, mixed) assemblies. Throughout his lectures, Witherspoon shows sensitivity to the special needs of American students in studying composition and public speaking under the conditions of the times.

Witherspoon's lectures were given, at least intermittently, over a period of about twenty years. He died in 1794. The lectures were published in his collected *Works* in 1800–1801 and in editions with his lectures on moral philosophy in 1810 and 1822, but they never became popular texts.

Blair's lectures were preferred by most teachers as more polished, and, with the end of the revolutionary period, belletristic rhetoric was regarded as an important study in improving taste in a culturally underdeveloped country.

The most classical early American rhetoric is that described in lectures given in 1806 by John Quincy Adams, the first holder of the Boylston Professorship of Rhetoric and Oratory at Harvard. "A subject which has exhausted the genius of Aristotle, Cicero, and Quintilian," said the future president, "can neither require nor admit much additional illustration. To select, combine, and apply their precepts, is the only duty left for their followers of all succeeding times, and to obtain a perfect familiarity with their instructions is to arrive at the mastery of the art."[60] In the following lectures Adams turns most often to Quintilian as his source; he dismisses Plato in Lecture 3 as "intellectual chaos." Although he was familiar with Blair and other Moderns, his presentation is based on classical authorities and even expounds the theory of the topics (Lecture 9).

In contrast, later nineteenth-century reference to classical authority by American teachers of rhetoric is often window dressing. As Professor John McVikar of Columbia complained in 1833, the study of classics and the study of rhetoric drifted apart: "The present junior class knows nothing of Cicero's *De Oratore*," he lamented.[61] Romanticism rejected the belief that artistry should be based on rules and imitations of canonical models, the Elocutionary Movement drew student and public attention, and rhetorical theory became an aspect of belles lettres and English composition. In the course of the century the Boylston Professorship, despite the founder's intention, was converted first into a chair of belles lettres and ultimately into a professorship of poetry.

Philology and Rhetoric

At the same time, however, classical philology advanced rapidly, first in Germany, then in Britain and America. Important publications of the nineteenth century included the collected *Rhetores Graeci* of Christian Walz, published in nine volumes from 1832 to 1836; Richard Volkmann's reference book *Rhetorik der Griechen und Römer in Systematische Übersicht*; E. M. Cope's *Introduction to Aristotle's Rhetoric*, followed by a commentary on the Greek text, edited by J. M. Sandys after Cope's death; and R. C. Jebb's *The Attic Orators*.

The German philosopher Friedrich Nietzsche began his career as a teacher of classical philology at the University of Basel; among the subjects on which he lectured in the period between 1872 and 1874 were Greek oratory and Greek and Roman rhetoric. Some of his lecture notes survive and have been translated into English.[62] In them Nietzsche defends rhetoric against the criticisms of Plato, Kant, and other philosophers and gives an account of the subject based on the classical sources and recent German surveys.[63]

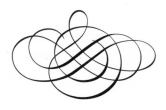

CHAPTER 12

Classical Rhetoric in the Twentieth Century

Classical rhetoric has continued to influence the study and teaching of rhetoric in the twentieth century. New editions, translations, commentaries, and studies of the classical texts have been published, with significant advances in understanding of their contents and influence, and the classical tradition throughout western history has been explored in greater and greater detail. An Institute for the Classical Tradition now exists at Boston University, sponsoring congresses, a journal, and other publications. Two major changes mark the role of classical rhetoric in modern thought: a shift from the practical to the theoretical, and from focus primarily on public address to a wide variety of oral and written genres of discourse. But both of these changes have met with some resistance.

From the earliest handbooks of rhetoric in Greece until the Renaissance, classical handbooks and treatises on rhetoric were studied directly as practical aids to oral and written composition. This is particularly evident in reliance on the handbooks *On Invention* and *Rhetoric for Herennius* in western Europe, and on the Hermogenic corpus in Byzantium. For a thousand years these were authoritative textbooks on which teachers in schools and universities lectured and wrote commentaries and that provided the rules for composition practiced by students and applied in speaking and writing later in life. Even in the early modern period, when Aristotle, Cicero, Quintilian, and other classical authorities were studied as supplementary sources of skills for public speaking, lectures on rhetoric continued to refer frequently to classical sources for practical advice, and the new rhetoric texts that were published were often heavily indebted to their approach. In addition, as long as Greek and Latin remained required studies in the curriculum of schools and colleges, many students read orations of Lysias, Demosthenes, Cicero, and other orators as examples of eloquence, and their influence can be traced in public address. The use of the "topics" or *loci* of classical inventional theory had been attacked in the seventeenth century, and the romantic movement of the nineteenth century rejected composition on the basis of traditional rules of invention, arrangement, style, and memory and the use of rote exercises as found in the *progymnasmata*; free composition, extemporaneity, and individual expression were encouraged instead. The Elocutionary Movement, however, kept alive a classicizing theory of delivery, and students of composition and literature continued to learn the names of tropes and figures as ways of identifying forms of expression.

In the twentieth century classical rhetoricians continue to be studied for their contributions to a theory of discourse and as the basis of analysis of classical, medieval, Renaissance, and modern texts composed by writers who had studied classical rhetoric and were addressing audiences familiar with its conventions. Classical rhetoric is today a common tool of biblical interpretation, illustrated in Chapter 7, and of the interpretation of Renaissance literature in the vernacular languages. Heinrich Lausberg's widely consulted *Handbook of Literary Rhetoric* supplies students of European literature with classical concepts for the analysis of postclassical literature. Histories of rhetoric by the present author and others provide students with an understanding of the historical role of speech and speech studies in western society.

The twentieth century has witnessed a vast development of new forms of communication, resulting from the technological advances of radio, television, and electronic media. The development of this "secondary orality," as it is sometimes called, has been accompanied by the creation of new theory to describe communication to mass audiences, within organizations and small groups, and across cultural lines, often dealing with issues of politics, propaganda, marketing, gender, and other social phenomena. Parallel to this has been the emergence of new linguistic, semiotic, literary, and cultural criticism and theory, some of which can be said to be seeking a general theory of rhetoric. Classical rhetoric, as a theory of discourse, has sometimes directly contributed to these developments, sometimes been an unacknowledged substratum in them, and sometimes been a foil against which writers of new approaches are reacting. A recent book by Richard A. Lanham suggests that technological changes may actually mark a return to some of the conditions under which classical rhetoric flourished, giving it new relevance in the electronic age.[1]

Rhetoric and English Composition

For some teachers of English, classical rhetoric has continued to supply a useful theoretical and practical basis for the teaching of written composition. Probably the best known textbook using this approach is *Classical Rhetoric for the Modern Student* by Edward P. J. Corbett.[2] Kathleen E. Welch has explored the reemergence of rhetoric in the twentieth century, as well as modern applications of classical rhetoric to teaching composition in *The Contemporary Reception of Classical Rhetoric: Appropriations of Ancient Discourse*. She distinguishes two "schools." The "Heritage School," whose assumptions she finds in rationalism and pragmatism, separates classical rhetoric from the historical circumstances in which it arose to elevate it to a universally applicable theory; it relies on the use of formulas and categories, such as the three species of rhetoric and the traditional parts of an oration, and it may seem elitist in its efforts to maintain standards of formal language use. It is a descendant of technical rhetoric as earlier described but values Aristotle's *Rhetoric* as the best statement of rhetorical theory. In contrast, what Welch calls the "Dialectical School" relies "not on discovering a palpable rhetorical 'reality' out there," but concentrates instead "on contemporary epistemological constructions that in turn are capable of producing an interpretation of classical rhetoric."[3] It too values Aristotle's *Rhetoric*, but as a description of a flexible, practical, and productive rather than purely theoretical art. The "Dialectical School" distrusts traditional canons, includes television, film, and "secondary orality" within its area of study, and seeks to be pro-active by engaging students in the reading, listening, and writing process. It can be thought of as a modern descendant of the sophistic strand in the history of rhetoric with its relativism, its love of experimentation, and its concern for oral and visual performance. Journals in composition studies, English, rhetoric, and speech continue to carry articles debating the application of classical rhetoric for modern students. The battlefield is largely within English departments where research and teaching, whether of literature or composition, has been affected by issues of politics, race, and gender.

The Renaissance of Rhetoric

Rhetorical studies have enjoyed a renaissance in the last third of the twentieth century. This can be seen in numerous ways: in the publication of a very large number of books and articles with the word "rhetoric" in the title, though using it in many different senses; in the appearance of new professional societies that hold annual or biennial meetings, including the International Society for the History of Rhetoric and the Rhetoric Society of America, as well as interest groups within the major professional organizations in English and communication studies; and the appearance of new journals, including *Philosophy and Rhetoric*, *Rhetoric Review*, *Rhetoric Society Quarterly*, and *Rhetorica*, which publish many articles and reviews relating to classical rhetoric, its tradition, and its applications. Two recent reference works make accessible a great deal of information about rhetoric, historical and theoretical. The most extensive is the *Historische Wörterbuch der Rhetorik*, projected to run to eight volumes, edited by Gert Ueding and others from offices in Tübingen. A more compact work is *Encyclopedia of Rhetoric and Composition: Communication from Ancient Times to the Information Age*, edited by Theresa Enos. Among recent books that assess the revival of rhetorical studies are *The Rhetorical Turn: Invention and Persuasion in the Conduct of Inquiry*, edited by Herbert W. Simons,[4] and *The Recovery of Rhetoric: Persuasive Discourse and Disciplinarity in the Human Sciences*, edited by R. H. Roberts and J. M. M. Good.[5]

The "New" Rhetorics

Among the new approaches to rhetoric in the twentieth century, a few theoretical works not written as textbooks have achieved special recognition among teachers of rhetoric, though these works have been rather less appreciated by contemporary literary critics and philosophers. All can be described as nonclassical, in that they focus on modern discourse and construct a new theory of rhetoric, but they show some debt to the classical tradition, and their authors were thoroughly trained in Greek, Latin, and classical rhetoric.

The least classicizing, and in many ways the least satisfying, of these three approaches is found in *The Philosophy of Rhetoric* by I. A. Richards, which originated as a series of lectures at Bryn Mawr College in 1936. Richards claimed that rhetoric should be "a study of misunderstanding and its remedies,"[6] and rejected Campbell, Whately, and others who approached the subject philosophically, but he never developed the philosophical, political, or psychological implications of his definition. Richards' book is almost entirely a discussion of "misunderstanding" at the linguistic level, especially as resulting from metaphor. Perhaps the most influential innovation of Richards' study was his introduction of the terms "tenor" and "vehicle" to describe the workings of metaphor: the "tenor" is what is meant by the comparison inherent in the metaphor; the "vehicle" is what is literally said by the words used. Since Richards wrote, many scholars from a variety of fields, especially linguistics, have tried to describe the workings of metaphor and its relationship to other tropes, and all have in varying degrees become victims of *letteraturizzazione*. Roman Jakobson, a great linguist with little knowledge of rhetoric, was responsible for the view that there are only two basic tropes: metaphor, based on a relationship of equivalence, and metonomy, based on a relationship of contiguity.[7] In 1970, six scholars at the University of Liège, calling themselves *Groupe μ*, published a work rather presumptuously entitled *Rhétorique générale*, which is a complex, scientific study of troping, utilizing the term "rhetoric" in its narrowest sense.[8] A voice of sanity in the field of rhetorical linguistics was that of Gérard Genette in *Figures of Literary Discourse*, working in the French tradition from DuMarsais,[9] but probably the finest modern discussion of metaphor, and certainly the one most heavily indebted to classical rhetoric, is Paul Ricoeur's *The Rule of Metaphor: Multi-disciplinary Studies of the Creation of Meaning in Language*.[10]

A broader understanding of rhetoric is found in the writings of Kenneth Burke, especially in *Counterstatement* (1931), with its "Lexicon Rhetoricae," *Grammar of Motives* (1945), and *Rhetoric of Motives* (1950). Burke is a difficult, sometimes quirky writer, whose ideas developed over a long lifetime, but his work is more deserving of being called a "philosophy of rhetoric" than are some other writings with that title in that it has strong dialectical, political, ethical, and psychological foundations. His most classicizing book is probably *The Rhetoric of Religion: Studies in Logology*,[11] which is a rhetorical analysis of Augustine's *Confessions* and chapters of the Book of Genesis. In *Grammar of Motives*[12] Burke describes his best known critical tool, the pentad of act, scene, agent, agency, and purpose, concepts that go beyond Aristotle's original identification of speaker, speech, and audience, though Aristotle is the authority most cited by Burke in this work. In *Rhetoric of Motives*[13] (p. 43) Burke defines the "realistic" function of rhetoric as "the use of language as a symbolic means of inducing cooperation in beings that by nature respond to symbols." This, he thought, was "rooted in an essential function of language itself, a function that is wholly realistic, and is continually born anew." Whereas Richards saw rhetoric as a source of misunderstanding, Burke saw it as the hope of understanding, working through "identification," and a potential basis of peace.

A third innovative writing on rhetoric in the mid-twentieth century was *La Rhétorique nouvelle*, by Chaim Perelman and Lucie Olbrechts-Tyteca, first published in 1958.[14] Perelman was a student of jurisprudence and he approached rhetoric from a philosophical and legal position rather than as a purely linguistic and literary phenomenon. Both in this sense and in the details of its presentation this is the most classicizing, primarily Aristotelian, of the works discussed in this section. Perelman distinguished argumentation, which is always addressed to an audience, from formal proof, which is not, and unlike most modern rhetoricians he makes significant use of a theory of *loci*, or "topics," as sources of argument, divided into those of quantity and quality and those that help to identify and exemplify facts. Figures of speech, in his theory, are not only literary devices of vividness and variety but have a cognitive function in establishing connections between things. Like Burke, he saw rhetoric as a force for better understanding in a world that suffered from bigotry, oppression, and war: "The theory of argumentation will help to develop . . . the justification of the possibility of a human community in the sphere of action" (p. 514).

The rhetorics of Richards, Burke, and Perelman and Olbrechts-Tyteca are all strong reactions to the circumstances of the 1930s and 1940s: economic depression, fascism, and the Second World War. Whether they will continue to be regarded as rhetorical classics is unclear, but it should be remembered that the rhetoric of Plato, Aristotle, Cicero, and Quintilian and those of the French and British rhetoricians of the neoclassical period were also very much products of the circumstances of the time of their composition.

Twentieth-Century Critical Theory

A few words can be said here about some other critical movements of the twentieth century that influence modern approaches to rhetoric. Most have some roots or analogies in Greco-Roman thought.

Semiotics is the study of signs, primarily linguistic signs, but any system of codes that convey meaning. The modern founders of semiotics at the beginning of the century were an American philosopher, Charles Sanders Pierce, and a Swiss scholar of linguistics, Ferdinand de Saussure. The study of signs, however, began in Greece, where Plato's *Cratylus* is an important early text, and where interest in the subject was continued by Aristotle and Hellenistic and later philosophers. Semioticians have always been aware of the history of their discipline and have often included some discussion of classical approaches in their writings.[15] Their interests, however, have been primarily linguistic and cognitive, and they rarely provide for rhetoric in their semiotic systems. One exception is Umberto Eco. In *A Theory of Semiotics* he describes rhetoric as "over-coding," that is, a network of associations invoked by linguistic usages or by the switching of codes, and he discusses "rhetorical labor" in terms of the classical concepts of invention, arrangement, and style.[16] What his discussion lacks is a consideration of how rhetorical "over-coding" as he understands it can accomplish ethical and emotional persuasion.

Semiotics is concerned with structures and codes, or systems of signs, and has been applied by anthropologists, of whom Claude Lévi-Strauss is the best known, to the study of the structures that can be discovered below the surface in society, for example in systems of kinship or taboo as well as in language. *Structuralism* is certainly a feature of classical rhetoric, though not so labeled. The conceptualization of rhetoric in Greece was characterized by the identification and naming of codes and structures of speech as social and political functions, seen, for example, in the species of judicial, deliberative, and epideictic rhetoric, in the parts of the oration, and in the kinds of style appropriate to different contexts. Another example of ancient structuralism is allegorical criticism, which interpreted literary and religious texts in terms of certain fundamental ideas symbolized by images in the text, thus explaining obscurities or answering objections raised by a literal reading. Allegorical interpretation in Greece began as early as the sixth century B.C. and often took the form of identifying the actors in Greek epic with the forces of nature, so that the *Iliad* could be read as a struggle between light and dark, sun and moon, fire and water, rather than between Greek and Trojans, Achilles and Hector; Athene stands for personified wisdom, Aphrodite for sex.[17] Allegorical interpretation then became a major tool in Christian exegesis of the Bible, as described in chapter 7, and remained popular throughout the Middle Ages.

Two other modern critical movements that can be connected with structuralism are *Marxist criticism*, as it has emerged in the twentieth century, and Anglo-American *New Criticism*. Marxist criticism is structuralist in that it finds in literature signs of class struggle. Ancient historians have much to say about class struggles and slavery, and some modern scholars have applied Marxist principles to the interpretation of classical literature, but ancient critics did not read *literature* in terms of class struggle. New Criticism, with which both Richards and Burke had some connections and of which the authoritative textbook was Brooks and Warren's *Understanding Poetry*, first published in 1938,[18] had a dominant interest in discovering structures of imagery that give unity to a work of literature. It has been applied extensively to the interpretation of classical literature by modern scholars, but it was not a form of interpretation practiced by the Greeks and Romans themselves, for all their interest in tropes and figures. New Criticism can be described as *formalist*; that is, in contrast to Marxism it had more interest in aesthetic forms in texts than in political or social meaning. In this sense it is a descendent of ancient criticism as seen in Aristotle's *Poetics*. Aristotle was interested primarily in matters of genre, plot, and language, and had nothing to say about the political, social, or religious meaning of the literature he discussed. *Neo-Aristotelianism*, which flourished especially at the University of Chicago, applied Aristotelian principles to the study of later literature.[19] Wayne C. Booth's much admired books *The Rhetoric of Fiction* and *A Rhetoric of Irony* are a later, more eclectic stage of this approach.

New Criticism was opposed to *biographical criticism* as it had come to be practiced in the nineteenth and twentieth centuries, interpreting texts on the basis of the circumstances and life experience of their authors and conversely reconstructing biographies of writers from hints in their texts. Biographical criticism in the latter sense was practiced in the Hellenistic period in Greece by adherents to the Peripatetic School. Satyrus's biography of Euripides, only partially extant, reconstructed the life of the poet on the basis of incidents in his plays. New Criticism also objected to interpretation on the basis of the intent of the author on the ground that this intention could rarely if ever be known and was in fact irrelevant; the meaning of the work is the meaning found by an intelligent, educated reader in a text. This principle has been further developed in what is called *reader-reception theory*. Ancient *literary* critics rarely fell victim to blind application of the "intentional fallacy." Aristotle, in the *Poetics*, found the sources of tragedy or comedy within the text of a play, not in the intent of the authors, and other ancient critics seem to follow his lead. This may result from the feeling that poetic texts are in some sense "inspired," as understood, for example, by Longinus, and thus not altogether the conscious product of a writer's art. But ancient *rhetorical* criticism worked with the assumption that rhetorical techniques found in a speech were all a part of the conscious art of the orator in accomplishing persuasive intent.

Critical theory in the second half of the twentieth century is often referred to as "post-structural," found in its most extreme form in *deconstruction* as practiced by Jacques Derrida, Paul de Man, and their imitators. De Man had much to say about rhetoric in his books and essays, but Brian Vickers has revealed how misinformed and misleading his discussions are.[20] Derrida, in contrast, is a powerful thinker, well versed in classical Greek language, literature, and rhetoric. In "Plato's Pharmacy," a long section in his book *Dissemination*,[21] he provides a brilliant reading of *Phaedrus*, deconstructing Plato's argument against writing by showing that writing is "always already" inscribed in speech, while playing with the meanings of *pharmakon* in the dialogue as both "cure" and "poison." The closest analogies to this in classical rhetoric and philosophy are found in sophistry and skepticism—in Gorgias's argument that "nothing exists," for example, or in sophistic experiments in making "the worse seem the better cause," and in sophistic love of paradox and play.

New Historicism, developed by Stephen Greenblat and others in studying Renaissance literature, resembles Marxist criticism in its exploration of political and social issues, to which it adds issues of gender. There are only a few examples of this in antiquity. Augustine uses historicism in Books 2 and 3 of *On Christian Learning*, including (3.20) an explanation of polygamy in the Old Testament on the basis of practical needs in the age of the patriarchs.

There is a great deal of social criticism in classical literature, including Plato's attacks on democracy and Tacitus's critique of the autocracy of the Roman Empire. Slavery was endemic in the classical world and was justified by Aristotle (*Politics* 1.4) as natural. It was, however, rarely if ever racially based, since most Greek and Roman slaves were racially indistinguishable from the rest of the population. There were some attacks on the institution of slavery as inhumane, for example in the forty-seventh *Epistle* of Seneca the Younger. Cultural prejudice against foreign groups, especially Asiatics, is evident in Isocrates' calls for Greek union against barbarians, and even more blatantly in the *Satires* of the Roman poet Juvenal.

The most striking examples of ancient criticism of the treatment of women are in drama, especially in Euripides' *Hecuba* and *Medea*. There is almost no feminist *literary* criticism from antiquity; something can be read between the lines in Sappho's allusions to the Homeric poems, and the sixty-first oration of Dio Chrysostom approaches a feminist reading of the *Iliad*. Feminist literary criticism emerges in the Renaissance, in the writings of Christine de Pisan, for example, and modern feminists have been exploring women's voices in ancient, medieval, Renaissance, and modern literature in works cited throughout this book.

Comparative Rhetoric

Comparative studies have been pursued in a number of disciplines—in anthropology, literature, physiology, and politics, for example—as a method of identifying what is common and what is unique to particular physical or social phenomena. Comparative literature, as a distinct humanistic discipline, began in the 1920s in Europe and has developed in American and foreign universities in the second half of the twentieth century. Its fundamental assumption is that features of literature that would not necessarily be clear to a reader from study of a single text or author or literary movement in one national language can be discovered by comparing texts or movements in two or more national literatures. It has had an interest in the history of criticism, and has usually been eclectic in its utilization of critical methods, depending on what seems to bring the best insights to the texts under scrutiny. Students of rhetoric in recent years have begun to realize that *comparative rhetoric* has similar possibilities and may be especially important in the rapidly developing world today of cross-cultural communication. There is, of course, a comparative element within the study of Greek and Roman, or ancient and modern rhetoric, but rhetoric as it has been studied in Europe and America is rhetoric as it has been defined and described in Europe and America. What similarities and differences are there to the rhetorical traditions of the rest of the world, in particular to the rich cultural traditions of China, Japan, India, and the Near East, but also to rhetorical practices in traditionally oral cultures in Africa and the South Pacific and among indigenous Australians or Americans? *Comparative Rhetoric* by George A. Kennedy seeks to provide a starting point for this study, complementing the present work on the western tradition, and seeking to test the general application of concepts of classical rhetoric and revise them as needed for a general theory of rhetoric. Articles and books on nonwestern rhetoric are beginning to increase in number, and professional students of rhetoric are showing increased awareness that there is more to be learned about rhetoric than is found strictly within the western tradition.[22]

NOTES

CHAPTER ONE

1. See Kennedy, *New History of Classical Rhetoric*, pp. 12–13.

2. See Kennedy, *Comparative Rhetoric*, pp. 1–28.

3. See ibid., pp. 128–31.

4. See ibid., pp. 162–64.

5. See ibid., pp. 183–85.

6. On rhetoric in early Greek literature, see Enos, *Greek Rhetoric before Aristotle*; Kennedy, *New History of Classical Rhetoric*, pp. 11–15; John T. Kirby, "The 'Great Triangle' in Early Greek Rhetoric and Poetics," *Rhetorica* 8 (1992): 213–28; and Richard P. Martin, *Language of Heroes: Speech and Performance in the Iliad* (Ithaca: Cornell University Press, 1989).

7. See Lord, *Singer of Tales*, and J. M. Foley, *Theory of Oral Composition*.

8. The early Greeks projected this attitude onto their gods, both male and female. Mortal women in early Greek literature, for example Andromache in *Iliad* and Penelope in *Odyssey*, do not show this inclination.

9. See Ochs, *Consolatory Rhetoric*.

10. See Harris, *Ancient Literacy*.

11. See Ong, *Orality and Literacy* and *Presence of the Word*; Havelock, *Literate Revolution*; and Havelock and Hershbell, *Communication Arts*.

12. Translated in Matson et al., eds., *Readings from Classical Rhetoric*, pp. 38–42.

13. For further discussion of the effects of writing and additional bibliography, see Kennedy, *Comparative Rhetoric*, pp. 116–17 and 191–92.

14. There are many modern translations of some of Sappho's poetry, the most complete of which is that by David A. Campbell in the Loeb Classical Library, *Greek Lyric*, vol. 1; poetic translation by Mary Barnard, *Sappho* (Berkeley: University of California Press, 1958). For a general study of Sappho, see Williamson, *Sappho's Immortal Daughters*.

15. For discussion of Corinna and bibliography, see Easterling and Knox, eds., *Cambridge History of Classical Literature*, 1:239–41 and 749–50.

16. See Pomeroy, *Women in Hellenistic Egypt*.

17. See Waithe, *History of Women Philosophers*.

18. Translated in ibid., 1:20–21.

19. See ibid., 169–95.

20. E. R. Sewter, trans., *The Alexeid of Anna Comnena* (New York: Viking Penguin, 1979).

21. See C. Jan Swearingen, "A Lover's Discourse: Diotima, Discourse, and Desire," in Lunsford, ed., *Reclaiming Rhetorica*, pp. 26–76.

22. See Susan Jarratt and Rory Ong, "Aspasia: Rhetoric, Gender, and Colonial Ideology," in ibid., pp. 9–24.

23. See esp. Blundell, *Women in Ancient Greece*; H. Foley, *Reflections of Women in Antiquity*; Keuls, *Reign of the Phallus*; and Lefkowitz and Fant, *Women's Life in Greece and Rome*. Special issues on women in antiquity were published in the journals *Arethusa* 11, no. 1–2 (1978), and *Helios* 13, no. 2 (1987).

24. For further discussion of women in the history of rhetoric, see Glenn, *Rhetoric Retold*, and Lunsford, ed., *Reclaiming Rhetorica*.

CHAPTER TWO

1. See Cicero *Brutus* 46–48. The full evidence for the beginnings of rhetoric in Greece can be found in Radermacher, "Artium Scriptores"; see also Kennedy, *New History of Classical Rhetoric*, pp. 30–35, and W. M. A. Grimaldi, "How Do We Get from Corax-Tisias to Plato-Aristotle in Greek Rhetorical Theory," in Johnstone, ed., *Theory, Text, Context*, pp. 19–43.

2. See Thomas Cole, "Who Was Corax?" *Illinois Classical Studies* 16 (1991): 65–84.

3. See Cole, *Origins of Rhetoric*, pp. 71–94.

4. Translated by H. Rackham in the Loeb Classical Library volume of Aristotle, *Problems*, 2:266–449.

5. For detailed discussion, see Manfred Fuhrmann, *Das systematische Lehrbuch: Ein Beitrag zur Geschichte der Wissenschaften in der Antike* (Göffingen: Vandenhoeck & Ruprecht, 1960).

6. See Kennedy, *New History of Classical Rhetoric*, pp. 103–6.

7. For more detailed discussion, see ibid., pp. 202–8.

8. Edited, with French translation, introduction, and notes, by Marcel Patillon, *Aelius Théon, Progymnasmata* (Paris: Les Belles Lettres, 1997).

9. Translated in Miller et al., eds., *Readings in Medieval Rhetoric*, pp. 52–68.

10. Translated in Matson et al., eds., *Readings from Classical Rhetoric*, pp. 266–88.

CHAPTER THREE

1. See Schiappa, *Protagoras and Logos*, pp. 54–59.

2. Little of the original work of early Greek sophists has survived; they are primarily known from their appearances in dialogues of Plato and from quotations in other works of Greek writers; what is known is translated in Sprague, ed., *Older Sophists*. See also Cassin, *L'Effet sophistique*; Jarratt, *Rereading the Sophists*; Kennedy, *New History of Classical Rhetoric*, pp. 17–21; Kerford, *Sophistic Movement*; J. Poulakos, *Sophistical Rhetoric*; de Romilly, *Grands sophistes*; and Untersteiner, *Sophists*.

3. See Kennedy, *Comparative Rhetoric*, pp. 158–61 and 179–80.

4. Works by or attributed to Antiphon are translated by K. J. Maidment in the Loeb Classical Library volume of the *Minor Attic Orators*, 1:2–309, and by J. S. Morrison in Sprague, ed., *Older Sopists*, pp. 106–240. See also Michael Gagarin, *Antiphon, Speeches* (Cambridge: Cambridge University Press, 1997).

5. See Edwin Carawan, "The *Tetralogies* and Athenian Homicide Trials," *American Journal of Philology* 114 (1993): 235–70, and *Rhetoric and the Law of Draco*, pp. 171–215.

6. See Sprague, ed., *Older Sophists*, pp. 203–4.

7. See, e.g., Solmsen, *Intellectual Experiments of the Greek Enlightenment*.

8. Translation of the whole speech by Kennedy, *Aristotle on Rhetoric*, pp. 284–88. See John Poulakis, "Gorgias' *Encomium to Helen* and the Defense of Rhetoric," *Rhetorica* 1 (1983): 1–6, and Edward Schiappa, "Toward a Prediscsiplinary Analysis of Gorgias' *Helen*," in Johnstone, ed., *Theory, Text, Context*, pp. 65–88.

9. The figures expressly attributed to Gorgias by Diodorus Siculus (12.53.4) are antithesis, isocolon, parison, and homoeoteleuton. Figures discussed in the *Rhetoric to Alexander* are antithesis, parisos (= isocolon) and paromoeosis (= homoeoteleuton and other similarities of sound). See also Aristotle *On Rhetoric* 3.9.9.

10. See de Romilly, *Magic and Rhetoric*, pp. 3–22.

11. See, e.g., Untersteiner, *Sophists*, pp. 194–205; see also Bruce McComiskey, "Gorgias and the Art of Rhetoric: Toward a Holistic Reading of the Extant Gorgianic Fragments," *Rhetoric Society Quarterly* 27 (1997): 5– 24, and the six articles in the "Panel on Gorgias" published in *Philosophy and Rhetoric* 30, no. 1 (1997).

12. Translation in Sprague, ed., *Older Sophists*, pp. 42–46.

13. See Richard L. Enos, "The Epistemology of Gorgias' *Rhetoric*: A Re-examination," *Southern Speech Communication Journal* 42 (1979): 49.

14. See, e.g., the essays in Vitanza, ed., *Writing Histories of Rhetoric*.

15. Cf., e.g., Mailloux, ed., *Rhetoric, Sophistry, Pragmatism*.

16. There are translations of Isocrates' speeches by George Norlin and LaRue Van Hook in the Loeb Classical Library. Discussion by Jaeger, *Paideia*, 3:46–155; Kennedy, *New History of Classical Rhetoric*, pp. 43–49; T. Poulakos, *Speaking for the Polis*; and Yun Lee Too, *Rhetoric of Identity in Isocrates*.

17. For further discussion, see Terry L. Papillon, "Mixed Unities in the *Antidosis* of Isocrates," *Rhetoric Society Quarterly* 27 (1997): 47–62.

18. See Kimball, *Orators & Philosophers*, pp. 17–21, and Marrou, *History of Education*, pp. 119–36.

19. Translated by Michael Winterbottom in the Loeb Classical Library. See Bonner, *Roman Declamation*; Fairweather, *Seneca the Elder*; and Sussman, *Elder Seneca*.

20. Translation by Lewis A. Sussman, *The Major Declamations Ascribed to Quintilian* (Frankfurt: Lang, 1987) and *The Declamations of Calpurnius Flaccus* (Leiden: Brill, 1994).

21. See Russell, *Greek Declamation*, pp. 21–39.

22. See Dilts and Kennedy, eds. and trans., *Two Greek Rhetorical Treatises*, pp. 77–239.

23. Translated by Wilmer C. Wright in the Loeb Classical Library. See Anderson, *Second Sophistic* and *Sage, Saint, and Sophist*.

24. See Kennedy, *New History of Classical Rhetoric*, pp. 230–56.

25. See de Romilly, *Magic and Rhetoric*, pp. 75–88.

26. Translated by Wilmer C. Wright in the Loeb Classical Library volume with Philostratus.

27. See Russell and Wilson, eds. and trans., *Menander Rhetor*, and Burgess, "Epideictic Literature."

28. See, e.g., Dio's four speeches *On Kingship* and Aristides' *Roman Discourse*. Translated in volumes of the Loeb Classical Library.

CHAPTER FOUR

1. See Guthrie, *History of Greek Philosophy*, 3:349–55.

2. See Karl R. Popper, *The Open Society and Its Enemies*, vol. 1: *The Spell of Plato*, 5th ed. (Princeton: Princeton University Press, 1991). It should be remembered, however, that Plato's ideas are largely attributed to Socrates and expressed in dialogues in which he avoids personal responsibility for what is said, and that many dialogues are "aporetic," that is, lacking a definitive conclusion.

3. For the political factors in the trial, see Mogens H. Hansen, *The Trial of Socrates—from the Athenian Point of View* (Copenhagen: Royal Danish Academy of Sciences and Letters, 1995); for the religious factors, see Richard Parker, *Athenian Religion* (Oxford: Clarendon Press, 1996), pp. 199– 207.

4. See Guthrie, *History of Greek Philosophy*, 4:71–72.

5. See James May, *Trials of Character: The Eloquence of Ciceronian Ethos* (Chapel Hill: University of North Carolina Press, 1988), pp. 28–31.

6. Commentary by E. R. Dodds, *Plato, Gorgias* (Oxford: Clarendon Press, 1983). For further discussion, see Guthrie, *History of Greek Philosophy*, 4:284–312.

7. See Edward Schiappa, "Did Plato Coin *Rhetorike?*" *American Journal of Philology* 111 (1990): 457–70, and the discussion of terms in Chapter 1.

8. See Swearingen, *Rhetoric and Irony*.

9. See Guthrie, *History of Greek Philosophy*, 4:396–97.

10. See G. R. F. Ferrari, *Listening to the Cicadas: A Study of Plato's "Phaedrus"* (Cambridge: Cambridge University Press, 1987).

11. The structure of the second half of the dialogue thus consists of:

A. Discussion of writing (257c–258e); digression (258e–259d)
   B. The orator's need for knowledge (259d–261a)
      C. Is rhetoric an art? (261a–272c)
   B^1. The orator's need for knowledge (272d–274b)
A^1. Discussion of writing (274b–278b); conclusion (278b–279c)

For a slightly different symmetrical arrangement, see Paul Friedlander, *Plato* (Princeton: Princeton University Press, 1969), 3:230–42.

12. This passage is one of the bases of deconstruction of *Phaedrus* in Jacques Derrida's "Plato's Pharmacy," in *Dissemination*, trans. Barbara Johnson (Chicago: University of Chicago Press, 1981), pp. 63–171.

13. See Anton-Herman Chroust, "Aristotle's First Literary Effort: *The Gryllus*, a Lost Dialogue on the Nature of Rhetoric," *Revue des études grecques* 78 (1965): 576– 91, reprinted in Erickson, ed., *Aristotle*, pp. 37– 51.

14. On the chronology, see Kennedy, *Aristotle on Rhetoric*, pp. 299– 305, and John M. Rist, *The Mind of Aristotle* (Toronto: University of Toronto Press, 1989), pp. 135–44. Rist dates the last revision to after Aristotle's return to Athens.

15. See Abraham Edel, *Aristotle and His Philosophy* (Chapel Hill: University of North Carolia Press, 1982), and Anfinn Stigen, *The Structure of Aristotle's Thought* (Oslo: Universitetsforlaget, 1966).

16. See Carol Poster, "Aristotle's *Rhetoric* against Rhetoric," *American Journal of*

Philology 118 (1997): 219–49. Poster concludes (p. 244) that the work is "a manual for the student trained in dialectic who needs, particularly for purposes of self-defense . . . , to sway an ignorant or corrupt audience or to understand the functioning of rhetoric within the badly ordered state. The techniques described are dangerous, potentially harmful to both speaker and audience, and ought not to be revealed to the general readership of Aristotle's dialogues, but only taught within the controlled environment of Aristotle's school, as part of an esoteric corpus of Platonic-Aristotelian teaching."

17. Standard works for study of the *Rhetoric* include Cope, *Introduction to Aristotle's Rhetoric* and *Aristotle's Rhetoric with a Commentary*; and William M. A. Grimaldi, *Aristotle, Rhetoric I: A Commentary* and *Rhetoric II: A Commentary* (New York: Fordham University Press, 1980, 1988). See also Erickson, ed., *Aristotle* (a collection of important essays) and *Aristotle's Rhetoric* (bibliography to 1970); Furley and Nehamas, eds., *Aristotle's Rhetoric*; and Rorty, ed., *Essays on Aristotle's Rhetoric* (with bibliography). Translated by Kennedy, *Aristotle on Rhetoric* (with bibliography, notes, and supplementary texts and essays).

18. See Friedrich Solmsen, *Die Entwicklung der Aristotelischen Logik und Rhetorik* (Berlin: Weidmann, 1929), and William W. Fortenbaugh, "On the Composition of Aristotle's *Rhetoric*," in *Lenaika: Festschrift für Carl Werner Müller* (Stuttgart: Teubner, 1996), pp. 165–88.

19. See Kapp, *Greek Foundations of Traditional Logic*, pp. 60–74.

20. See Gerard A. Hauser, "The Example in Aristotle's *Rhetoric*: Bifurcation or Contradiction?" *Philosophy and Rhetoric* 1 (1968): 78–90, reprinted in Erickson, *Aristotle*, pp. 156–68.

21. See Lloyd F. Bitzer, "Aristotle's Enthymeme Revisted," *Quarterly Journal of Speech* 45 (1959): 399–408, reprinted in Erickson, *Aristotle*, pp. 141–55.

22. See Walter H. Beale, "Rhetorical Performative Discourse: A New Theory of Epideictic," *Philosophy and Rhetoric* 11 (1978): 221–46.

23. See William W. Fortenbaugh, *Aristotle on Emotion* (London: Duckworth, 1975) and "Aristotle on Persuasion through Character," *Rhetorica* 10 (1992): 207–44.

24. See Wisse, *Ethos and Pathos*, pp. 38–39.

25. See William W. Fortenbaugh, "Theophrastus on Delivery," *Rutgers University Studies in Classical Humanities* 2 (1985): 269–85.

26. See McCall, *Ancient Rhetorical Theories of Simile and Comparison*, pp. 24–53.

27. See Kennedy, *New History of Classical Rhetoric*, pp. 85–87.

28. Evidence for Theophrastus's writings on rhetoric are collected and translated in William W. Fortenbaugh et al., eds., *Theophrastus of Eresus* (Leiden: Brill, 1992), 2:508–59.

29. See Friedrich Solmsen, "The Aristotelian Tradition in Ancient Rhetoric," *American Journal of Philology* 62 (1941): 35–50 and 169–90, reprinted in Erickson, ed., *Aristotle*, pp. 278–309.

30. A new edition and translation of Philodemus's *On Rhetoric* is being prepared by Robert Gaines. For rhetoric in other Hellenistic philosophical schools, see Fortenbaugh and Mirhady, eds., "Peripatetic Rhetoric," and Kennedy, *Art of Persuasion*, pp. 290–99 and 321–30.

31. See Kennedy, *Greek Rhetoric under Christian Emperors*, pp. 52–132.

32. See Cole, *Origins of Rhetoric*, pp. 88–89.

CHAPTER FIVE

1. See Robert S. Reid, "Hermagoras' Theory of Prose *Oikonomia* in Dionysius of Halicarnassus," in *Advances in the History of Rhetoric*, ed. Richard L. Enos (Fort Worth: Texas Christian University, 1996), 1:9–24.

2. For a more detailed discussion, see Kennedy, *Art of Persuasion*, pp. 303–21, and Dieter Matthes, "Hermagoras von Temnos," *Lustrum* 3 (1958): 58–214 and 262–87.

3. See Kennedy, *New History of Classical Rhetoric*, pp. 102–17, and for a more detailed account, Kennedy, *Art of Rhetoric*, pp. 3–102.

4. For the date of composition, see Kennedy, *Art of Rhetoric*, pp. 103–11. Translation of *On Invention* by H. M. Hubbell in the Loeb Classical Library.

5. See Patrick Sinclair, "A Study in the Sociology of Rhetoric: The *Sententia* in *Rhetorica ad Herennium*," *American Journal of Philology* 114 (1993): 561–80.

6. See G. M. A. Grube, "Theodorus of Gadara," *American Journal of Philology* 80 (1959): 337–65.

7. See Blum, *Antike Mnemotechnik*, and Yates, *Art of Memory*.

8. The only translation currently available is that by E. W. Sutton and H. Rackham in the Loeb Classical Library. It is unsatisfactory in a number of ways. A new version is being prepared by James May and Jakob Wisse under contract from Oxford University Press.

9. See Wisse, *Ethos and Pathos*, pp. 233–36.

10. Translated by H. E. Butler in the Loeb Classical Library, currently being revised by Donald Russell. For more detailed discussion, see Kennedy, *Art of Rhetoric*, pp. 487–514, and *New History of Classical Rhetoric*, pp. 177–86.

11. Translated by William Peterson in the Loeb Classical Library and by Herbert W. Benario in the Bobbs-Merrill Library of the Liberal Arts (Indianapolis, 1967).

12. See J. P. V. D. Balsdon, *Roman Women* (Oxford: Clarendon Press, 1962), and Richard A. Bauman, *Women and Politics in Ancient Rome* (London: Routledge, 1992). On Cornelia, see Plutarch's lives of the Gracchi; on Livia, Suetonius's biographies of Augustus and Tiberius and the early books of Tacitus's *Annals*; and on Agrippina, Suetonius's biographies of Claudius and Nero and the later books of Tacitus's *Annals*.

13. Translation of *On Stases* by Malcolm Heath, *Hermogenes on Issues* (Oxford: Clarendon Press, 1995), with commentary; translation of *On Ideas* by Cecil W. Wooten, *Hermogenes on Types of Style* (Chapel Hill: University of North Carolina Press, 1987).

14. See Patterson, *Hermogenes and the Renaissance*.

15. Halm, ed., *Rhetores Latini Minores*.

16. See Michael Leff, "The Material of the Art in Latin Handbooks of the Fourth Century A.D.," in Vickers, ed., *Rhetoric Revalued*, pp. 71–76.

17. See Kaster, *Guardians of Language*.

CHAPTER SIX

1. See Williams, *Keywords*, pp. 150–54.

2. The Italian term *letteraturizzazione* for this phenomenon originated with Florescu, *Retorica*, p. 43 and passim.

3. Translated by W. Rhys Roberts, revised by Doreen C. Innes, in the Loeb Classical Library volume with Aristotle's *Poetics*. A commoner word for style in Greek is *lexis*, but that word is often restricted to mean "diction, word choice." Demetrius may have wanted a term including both diction and composition.

4. For further discussion, see Kennedy, *New History of Classical Rhetoric*, pp. 88–90; G. M. A. Grube, *A Greek Critic: Demetrius on Style* (Toronto: University of Toronto Press, 1961); Doreen C. Innes, "Demetrius," in Kennedy, ed., *Cambridge History of Literary Criticism*, 1:196–98; and D. M. Schenkeveld, *Studies in Demetrius* (Amsterdam: Hakkert, 1964).

5. Julius Victor, in Halm, ed., *Rhetores Latini Minores*, pp. 447–48; see also p. 589.

6. Translated by Abraham J. Malherbe, "Ancient Epistolary Theorists," *Ohio Journal of Religious Studies* 5 (1977): 3–77.

7. Translation by Stephen Usher in the Loeb Classical Library. For discussion, see Doreen C. Innes, "Dionysius of Halicarnassus," in Kennedy, ed., *Cambridge History of Literary Criticism*, 1:267–71.

8. Translated by D. A. Russell, *'Longinus' On Sublimity* (Oxford: Clarendon Press, 1965; a revised version in Russell and Winterbottom, eds. *Ancient Literary Criticism*, pp. 460–503); also by W. Hamilton Fyfe, revised by D. A. Russell, in the Loeb Classical Library volume with Aristotle's *Poetics*. Text and commentary by D. A. Russell (Oxford: Clarendon Press, 1964); discussion by Russell in Kennedy, ed., *Cambridge History of Literary Criticism*, 1:306–11.

9. On Hellenistic poetics, see Kennedy, ed., *Cambridge History of Literary Criticism*, 1:200–219.

CHAPTER SEVEN

1. In addition to works cited below, see Cochrane, *Christianity and Classical Culture*; Dodds, *Pagan and Christian*; Goodspeed, *History of Early Christian Literature*; Jaeger, *Early Christianity*; and Norden, *Agnostos Theos*, and *Antike Kunstprosa*, 2:451–79.

Quotations from the Bible are from the Revised Standard Version, copyrighted 1946, 1952 © 1971, 1973, as printed in the *Oxford Annotated Bible* (New York: Oxford University Press, 1962), with permission of the publisher and the Division of Christian Education of the National Council of Churches.

2. See Hayes, ed., *Old Testament Form Criticism*.

3. See Warner, ed., *Bible as Rhetoric*; Watson, ed., *Persuasive Artistry*; and Watson and Hauser, *Rhetorical Criticism of the Bible*.

4. See Joshua Gitay, "Rhetorical Criticism and the Prophetic Discourse," in Watson, ed., *Persuasive Artistry*, pp. 13–24, and Margaret D. Zulick, "The Agon of Jeremiah: On the Dialogic Invention of Prophetic Ethos," *Quarterly Journal of Speech* 78 (1992): 125–48.

5. See W. Eugene March, "Prophecy," in Hayes, ed., *Old Testament Form Criticism*, pp. 157–75.

6. See Whitman, *Allegory*, pp. 58–68.

7. See Kennedy, *Comparative Rhetoric*, pp. 128–31 and 133–35. There was also some influence of classical ideas on Jewish concepts of wisdom; see Wilken, ed., *Aspects of Wisdom*.

8. Rabinowitz, ed. and trans., *Book of the Honeycomb's Flow*.

9. See Lieberman, *Hellenism in Jewish Palestine*; Stowers, *Diatribe*; and Thyen, *Stil der judisch-hellenistische Homilie*.

10. See Kinneavy, *Origins of Christian Faith*.

11. See Kennedy, *New Testament Rhetoric*; Watson, ed., *Persuasive Artistry*; and Watson and Hauser, *Rhetorical Criticism of the Bible*.

12. See Burton L. Mack and Vernon K. Robbins, *Patterns of Persuasion in the Gospels* (Sonoma, Calif.: Polebridge, 1989), and Vernon K. Robbins, *Jesus the Teacher: A Socio-Rhetorical Interpretation of Mark* (Philadelphia: Fortress Press, 1984).

13. See Frederick F. Bruce, *The Speeches in the Acts of the Apostles* (London: Tyndale Press, 1942); Bertil Gärtner, *The Areopagus Speech and Natural Revelation*, trans. Carolyn H. King (Uppsala: Gleerup, 1955); and Ned B. Stonehouse, *The Areopagus Address* (London: Tyndale Press, 1950).

14. See Johannes Weiss, *Beiträge zur paulinischen Rhetorik* (Göttingen: Vandenhoeck & Ruprecht, 1897), and Rudolf Bultmann, *Der Stil der paulinischen Predigt und die cynisch-stoiche Diatribe* (Göttingen: Vandenhoeck & Ruprecht, 1910). For a more negative assessment of Paul's debt to classical sources, see C. Joachim Classen, "St Paul's Epistles and Greek and Roman Rhetoric," *Rhetorica* 10 (1992): 392–44, and R. Dean Anderson, *Ancient Rhetorical Theory and Paul* (Kampen, Netherlands: Kok Pharos, 1996).

15. See Brown, *Power and Persuasion*, and Cameron, *Christianity and the Rhetoric of Empire*.

16. The earliest instance is Pliny the Younger when governor of Bithynia; see his correspondence with the emperor in *Epistles* 10.96–97.

17. There are translations of patristic works discussed in this chapter in volumes of the *Ancient Christian Writers* series (New York: Newman Press) and in the *Fathers of the Church* series (Washington, D.C.: Catholic University of America Press).

18. See Robert D. Sider, *Ancient Rhetoric and the Art of Tertullian* (London: Oxford University Press, 1971), and Timothy D. Barnes, *Tertullian: A Historical and Literary Study* (Oxford: Clarendon Press, 1971), pp. 186–232.

19. See Campbell Bonner, *The Homily on the Passion by Melito, Bishop of Sardis* (London: Christophers, 1940), and A. Wifstrand, "The Homily of Melito on the Passion," *Vigiliae Christianae* 2 (1948): 201–23.

20. See C. W. Macleod, "Allegory and Mysticism in Origen and Gregory of Nyssa," *Journal of Theological Studies* 22 (1971): 362–79; R. W. Smith, *Art of Rhetoric in Alexandria*, pp. 92–94; and Whitman, *Allegory*, pp. 58–77.

21. See Henri Crouzel, *Grégoire le Thaumaturge: Remerciement à Origène suive de la lettre d'Origène à Grégoire* (Paris: du Cerf, 1969).

22. Translated by J. E. L. Oulton and H. J. Lawlor in the Loeb Classical Library volume of Eusebius, *Ecclesiastical History*, 2:398–445.

23. See Harold A. Drake, *In Praise of Constantine: A Historical Study and New Translation of Eusebius' Triennial Oration* (Berkeley: University of California Press, 1976).

24. See Kennedy, *Greek Rhetoric under Christian Emperors*, pp. 135–49.

25. See Rosemary R. Ruether, *Gregory of Nazianzus: Rhetoric and Philosopher* (Oxford: Clarendon Press, 1969).

26. Adopted from McCauley, trans., *Funeral Orations*, pp. 37–38.

27. Translated by Fernand Boulenger, *Saint Basile, aux jeunes gens sur la manière de tirer profit des lettres helléniqus* (Paris: Les Belles Lettres, 1952).

28. See Thomas E. Ameringer, "The Stylistic Influence of the Second Sophistic on the Panegyrical Sermons of Saint John Chrysostom," *Catholic University of America Patristic Studies* 2 (1922); Harry M. Hubbell, "Chrysostom and Rhetoric," *Classical Philology* 19 (1924): 261–76; and Mary A. Burns, "Saint John Chrysostom's Homilies *On the Statues*: A Study of Their Rhetorical Form," *Catholic University of America Patristic Studies* 22 (1930).

29. *On the Obscurity of the Prophecies* (56, p. 165 Migne), as translated by Ameringer (above, n. 28), p. 28.

30. Translated by Augustine Fitzgerald, *The Essays and Hymns of Synesius of Cyrene*, 2 vols. (London: Oxford University Press, 1930). See Kennedy, *Greek Rhetoric under Christian Emperors*, pp. 35–45, and Momigliano, *Conflict between Paganism and Christianity*, pp. 126–50.

31. See Gerald L. Ellspermann, "The Attitude of the Early Christian Latin Writers towards Pagan Literature and Learning," *Catholic University of America Patristic Studies* 82 (1949): 23–42.

32. Translated by McCauley, in *Funeral Orations*.

33. Translated by F. A. Wright in the Loeb Classical Library volume of Jerome, *Select Letters*, pp. 52–129. See also Arthur S. Pease, "The Attitude of Jerome toward Pagan Literature," *Transactions of the American Philological Association* 50 (1919): 150–67.

34. Translated by Mary Francis McDonald, *Lactantius, The Divine Institutes* (Washington, D.C.: Catholic University of America Press, 1964).

35. On Augustine's life, see Brown, *Augustine of Hippo*. Works on Augustine and rhetoric, in addition to those cited below, include Wilfrid Parsons, "A Study of the Vocabulary and Rhetoric of the Letters of Saint Augustine," *Catholic University of America Patristic Studies* 3 (1923), and Joseph Finaert, *Saint Augustin rhéteur* (Paris: Les Belles Lettres, 1939).

36. See Otto A. L. Dieter and William C. Kurth, "The *De Rhetorica* of Aurelius Augustinus," *Speech Monographs* 35 (1968): 90–108, and Miller et al., eds., *Readings in Medieval Rhetoric*, pp. 6–24.

37. The best edition of the Latin text is by Guilelmus M. Green, *Sancti Aureli Augustini Opera*, Corpus Scriptorum Ecclesiasticorum Latinorum, LXXX, 6.6 (Vienna: Hoelder-Pichler-Tempsk, 1963). Quotations are from the translation by D. W. Robertson Jr., *Saint Augustine, On Christian Doctrine*, Library of Liberal Arts (Indianapolis and New York: Bobbs-Merrill, 1958), with permission of the publisher. The best discussion of the work is by Marrou, *Saint Augustin*.

38. See Chamberlin, *Increase and Multiply*, pp. 34–43.

39. Commentary by Sister Theresa Sullivan, "S. Aureli Augustini Hipponiensis Episcopi *De Doctrina Christiana Liber Quartus*," *Catholic University of America Patristic Studies* 23 (1930).

40. See W. R. Johnson, "Isocrates Flowering: The Rhetoric of Augustine," *Philosophy and Rhetoric* 9 (1976): 217–31.

41. Brown, *Augustine of Hippo*, pp. 259–60.

42. See ibid., p. 266.

43. See, e.g., C. S. Baldwin, *Medieval Rhetoric*, p. 51.

CHAPTER EIGHT

1. For more a detailed account of Byzantine rhetoric, see Kennedy, *Greek Rhetoric under Christian Emperors*, pp. 265–303. Other valuable discussions include Thomas Conley, "Byzantine Teaching on Figures and Tropes: An Introduction," *Rhetorica* 4 (1986): 335–74; Hunger, "Aspekte der griechischen Rhetorik von Gorgias bis zum Untergang von Byzanz," Akademie der Wissenschaften, Wien, philosophische-historische Klasse, *Sitzungsberichte* 277, no. 3 (1977): 3–27; George L. Kustas, *Studies in Byzantine Rhetoric* and "Function and Evolution"; and Maguire, *Art and Eloquence in Byzantium*. Texts of Byzantine rhetoricians can be found in Walz, *Rhetores Graeci*; some other editions are cited below, but very little is available in English. Standard works on Byzantine literature include Hunger, *Hochsprachliche profane Literatur*, and Beck, *Kirche und theologische Literatur*. See also Ostrogorsky, *History of the Byzantine State*; Hussey, ed., *Cambridge Medieval History, IV*; Norwich, *Byzantium*; and Kazhdan, ed., *Oxford Dictionary of Byzantium*.

2. See Georgina Buckler, "Byzantine Education," in Baynes and Moss, *Byzantium*, pp. 200–220, and Browning, *Studies in Byzantine History, Literature, and Education*.

3. See Clarke, *Higher Education*, p. 133.

4. Translation in Matson et al., eds., *Readings from Classical Rhetoric*, pp. 266–88.

5. Italian translation by Marcella Gigante, *Theodorus Metochites: Saggio critico su Demostene ed Aristide* (Milan: Istituto Editoriale Cisalpino, 1969).

6. See Kustas, "Function and Evolution," p. 59; Karlsson, *Idéologie et cérémonial*; and A. R. Littlewood, "An 'Ikon of the Soul': The Byzantine Letter," *Visible Language* 10 (1976): 197–226.

7. Translated by Dewing and Downey in the Loeb Classical Library edition of Procopius, vol. 7.

8. See Glanville Downey, "The Christian Schools of Palestine," *Harvard Library Bulletin* 12 (1951): 297–319.

9. Cyril Mango, ed. and trans., *The Homilies of Photius, Patriarch of Constantinople* (Cambridge, Mass.: Harvard University Press, 1958).

10. Hugo Rabe, ed., *Syriani in Hermogenem Commentaria* (Leipzig: Teubner, 1892).

11. See Kustas, *Studies in Byzantine Rhetoric*, pp. 20–22.

12. See Hugo Rabe, ed., *Prolegomenon Sylloge* (Leipzig: Teubner, 1931).

13. See Kustas, *Studies in Byzantine Rhetoric*, pp. 63–100.

14. See Coulter, *Literary Microcosm*.

15. For the texts, see Hermias, *In Platonis Phaedrum Scholia*, ed. P. Couvier (Paris, 1901; reprint, New York: Olms, 1971), and Olympiodorus, *In Platonis Gorgiam Commentaria*, ed. L. G. Westerink (Leipzig: Teubner, 1970).

16. See Thomas Conley, "Aristotle's *Rhetoric* in Byzantium," *Rhetorica* 8 (1990): 29–44.

17. See Hussey, *Church and Learning*, pp. 51–72, and Speck, *Kaiserliche Universität*.

18. See Wanda Wolska-Conus, "Les écoles de Psellos et de Xiphilinus," *Travaux et Mémoires* 6 (1976): 223–43.

19. See Kustas, "Form and Evolution," p. 69.

20. See Robert Browning, "The Patriarchal School of Constantinople in the Twelfth Century," *Byzantion* 32 (1962): 167–202, and 33 (1963): 11–40.

21. See Lindberg, *Studies in Hermogenes and Eustathios*, and Wirth, "Untersuchungen zur byzantinischen Rhetorik."

22. See R. M. Dawkins, "The Greek Language in the Byzantine Period," in Baynes and Moss, *Byzantium*, pp. 252–67.

23. Ibid., p. 257.

24. See Beck, *Kirche und theologische Literatur*, p. 546. Beck discusses panegyrical sermons and homilies from each period.

25. For detailed discussion, see Hunger, *Hochsprachliche profane Literatur*, pp. 120–45.

26. Ibid., pp. 145–57.

CHAPTER NINE

1. Important works for the study of western medieval rhetoric include C. S. Baldwin, *Medieval Rhetoric*; Bolgar, *Classical Heritage* and "The Teaching of Rhetoric in the Middle Ages," in Vickers, ed., *Rhetoric Revalued*, pp. 79–86; Copeland, *Rhetoric, Hermeneutics, and Translation*; Curtius, *European Literature and the Latin Middle Ages*; Haarhoff, *Schools of Gaul*; Laistner, *Intellectual Heritage* and *Thought and Letters*; McKeon, "Rhetoric in the Middle Ages"; Miller et al., eds., *Readings in Medieval Rhetoric*; Murphy, *Rhetoric in the Middle Ages*; Paetow, "Arts Course at Medieval Universities"; F. J. E. Raby, *A History of Secular Latin Poetry in the Middle Ages*, 2 vols. (Oxford: Clarendon Press, 1957); Rand, *Founders of the Middle Ages*; Reynolds, *Medieval Reading*; Riché, *Education and Culture*; Taylor, *Medieval Mind*; and Ward, *Ciceronian Rhetoric*. See also the many relevant articles, with bibliography, in *The Dictionary of the Middle Ages*, 13 vols., ed. Joseph R. Strayer (New York: Scribners, 1982).

2. On the history of the liberal arts, see Kimball, *Orators & Philosophers*, pp. 13–42.

3. Detailed discussion by Stahl et al., *Martianus Capella*, vol. 1; English translation in vol. 2.

4. Jones, ed. and trans., *Introduction to Divine and Human Readings*. The following quotation is from Jones, p. 127.

5. Translation and discussion by Stump, *Boethius' De Topicis Differentiis* (Ithaca: Cornell University Press, 1978). Stump also published a translation of Boethius's commentary *In Ciceronis Topica* (Ithaca: Cornell University Press, 1988). Boethius's

Speculatio on the Knowledge of Rhetoric is a short version of *De Topicis Differentiis*, vol. 4; translation in Miller et al., eds., *Readings in Medieval Rhetoric*, pp. 69–76. See further, Michael C. Leff, "Boethius' *De Differentiis Topicis*, Book IV," in Murphy, ed., *Medieval Eloquence*, pp. 3–24, with extensive bibliography.

6. Translation of Isidore's section on rhetoric in Miller et al., eds., *Readings in Medieval Rhetoric*, pp. 79–95. For discussion, see Fontaine, *Isidore de Séville*.

7. See Ward, *Ciceronian Rhetoric*, pp. 84–85.

8. See Murphy, *Rhetoric in the Middle Ages*, pp. 292–97.

9. Translated by Ernest Brehaut, *History of the Franks by Gregory, Bishop of Tours* (New York: Norton, 1969), and by Lewis Thorpe, *A History of the Franks* (New York: Viking Penguine, 1976).

10. Discussion by George Kennedy, "Forms and Functions of Latin Speech," *Medieval and Renaissance Studies*, ed. G. M Masters (Chapel Hill: University of North Carolina Press, 1984), 10:45–73.

11. Translation of Priscian's *Preliminary Exercises* in Miller et al., eds., *Readings in Medieval Rhetoric*, pp. 52–68; on its common use, see D. L. Clark, "Rhetoric and Literature of the English Middle Ages," *Quarterly Journal of Speech Communication* 45 (1959): 24, and Ward, *Ciceronian Rhetoric*, p. 79.

12. See Judith W. George, *Venantius Fortunatus* (Oxford: Clarendon Press, 1992).

13. Translated in Miller et al., eds., *Readings in Medieval Rhetoric*, pp. 96–122. On later influence, see Veronica Fraser, "The Influence of the Venerable Bede on the Fourteenth-Century Occitan Treatise *Las Leys d'Amors*," *Rhetorica* 11 (1993): 51–61.

14. Bertram Colgrace and R. A. B. Mynors, eds. and trans., *Bede's Ecclesiastical History of the English People* (Oxford: Clarendon Press, 1969).

15. See Luke M. Reinsma, "Rhetoric in England: The Age of Aelfric, 970–1021," *Communication Monographs* 44 (1977): 388–403.

16. See Luitpold Wallach, "Charlemagne's *De Litteris Colendis* and Alcuin: A Diplomatic-Historical Study," *Speculum* 26 (1951): 288–305.

17. Wilbur S. Howell, trans., *The Rhetoric of Charlemagne and Alcuin* (Princeton: Princeton University Press, 1941).

18. See Wallach, *Alcuin and Charlemagne*, pp. 73–82.

19. On memory in the Middle Ages, see Carruthers, *Book of Memory*.

20. Rhetorical theories of delivery influenced medieval drama; see Judy Enders, *Rhetoric and the Origin of Medieval Drama* (Ithaca: Cornell University Press, 1992).

21. Translation of 3.19 in Miller et al., eds., *Readings in Medieval Rhetoric*, pp. 125–27. For discussion, see Murphy, *Rhetoric in the Middle Ages*, pp. 82–87.

22. There is at present no published translation of Notker's work, but there is a good account of it in three articles that quote some passages in English: Otto A. L. Dieter, "The Rhetoric of Notker Labeo," *Papers in Rhetoric*, ed. Donald C. Bryant (Iowa City: University of Iowa Press, 1965), pp. 27–33; Jaffe, "Antiquity and Innovation"; and Bennett, "Function of Adaptation in Notker's *Rhetorica*," 171–84. For the Latin text, see Paul Pier, ed., *Die Schriften Notkers und seiner Schule* (Freiburg: J. C. B. Mohr, 1882), 1:643–84.

23. See Jaffe, "Antiquity and Innovation," 172.

24. See Bennett, "Function of Adaptation in Notker's *Rhetorica*," 183.

25. See Charles H. Beeson, *Lupus of Ferrières: Scribe and Textual Critic* (Cam-

bridge, Mass.: Harvard University Press, 1930). Lupus's letters (see esp. *Ep.* 62 and 103) describe his teaching; see Gordon W. Reginos, *The Letters of Lupus of Ferrières* (The Hague: Mouton, 1966).

26. See Harriet P. Lattin, trans., *The Letters of Gerbert, with His Papal Privileges* (New York: Columbia University Press, 1961); see also Henri Focillon, *The Year 1000* (New York: Ungar, 1969), pp. 127–61.

27. See Beth S. Bennett, "The Significance of the *Rhetorimachia* of Anselm of Besate to the History of Rhetoric," *Rhetorica* 5 (1987): 231–50. There is no English version; the Latin text is to be found in volume 2 of the Monumenta Germaniae Historiae: *Gunzo, "Epistola ad Augienses," und Anselm von Besate, "Rhetorimachia,"* ed. Karl Manitius (Weimar: Hermann Böhlaus, 1958).

28. See Abraham J. Malherbe, "Ancient Epistolary Theorists," *Ohio Journal of Religious Studies* 5, no. 2 (1977): 3–77.

29. See Camargo, *Ars Dictaminis*; Murphy, *Rhetoric in the Middle Ages*, pp. 194–268; and Wieruszowski, *Politics and Culture*. A standard study is that by Rockinger, *Briefsteller und Formelbücher*.

30. See Martin Camargo, "Si Dictare Velis: Versified *Artes Dictaminis* and Late Medieval Writing Pedagogy," *Rhetorica* 14 (1996): 265–82.

31. Translation of Alberic's *Flowers of Rhetoric* in Miller et al., eds., *Readings in Medieval Rhetoric*, pp. 131–61; an anonymous Bolognese treatise of the twelfth century is translated by Murphy, ed., *Three Medieval Rhetorical Arts*, pp. 1–25.

32. See Ward, *Ciceronian Rhetoric*, pp. 69–70. Bartolinus's commentary to *Rhetoric for Herennius*, based on his lectures, survives; see Ward, *Ciceronian Rhetoric*, pp. 70–72.

33. See Paetow, "Arts Course," pp. 80–87.

34. See Martin Camargo, ed., *Medieval Rhetorics of Prose Composition: Five English Artes Dictandi and their Tradition* (Binghamton, N.Y.: Medieval and Renaissance Texts and Studies, 1995).

35. See A. C. Clark, *Cursus*; Croll, *Style, Rhetoric, and Rhythm*, pp. 303–59; and Janson, *Prose Rhythm*.

36. See Ward, *Ciceronian Rhetoric*, pp. 316–17.

37. See Charles B. Faulhaber, "The *Summa Dictaminis* of Guido Faba," in Murphy, ed., *Medieval Eloquence*, pp. 85–111.

38. See Hertter, *Poetasliteratur Italiens*; Kristeller, *Renaissance Thought*, pp. 105 and 155–56; and N. Rubenstein, "Political Rhetoric in the Imperial Chancery," *Medium Aevum* 14 (1945): 21–43.

39. See Murphy, *Rhetoric in the Middle Ages*, pp. 253–55, and Ward, *Ciceronian Rhetoric*, pp. 126–29, 291–92, and 317.

40. See André Wilmart, "*L'Ars arengandi* de Jacques de Dinant avec un appendice sur ses ouvrages *De dictamine*," *Studi e Testi* 59 (1933): 112–51; Emil J. Polak, *A Textual History of Jacques de Dinant's "Summa Dictaminis"* (Geneva: Droz, 1975); and Ward, *Ciceronian Rhetoric*, pp. 316–17. On the development of *ars arengandi* in fourteenth- and fifteenth-century Spain, see Mark D. Johnston, "Parliamentary Oratory in Medieval Aragon," *Rhetorica* 10 (1992): 99–117.

41. Translation of the section on refutation in Miller et al., eds., *Readings in Medieval Rhetoric*, pp. 253–64.

42. See esp. Haskins, *Renaissance of the Twelfth Century*.

43. See Faulhaber, *Latin Rhetorical Theory*.

44. See Taylor, *Medieval Mind*, pp. 298–307.

45. See Bliese, "Study of Rhetoric in the Twelfth Century.".

46. See Gillian Evans, "The Uncompleted 'Heptateuch' of Thierry of Chartres," *History of Universities* 3 (1983): 1–13.

47. See C. S. Baldwin, *Medieval Rhetoric*, pp. 169–72.

48. See Ward, *Ciceronian Rhetoric*, pp. 121–22.

49. See Karen M. Fredborg, *Latin Rhetorical Commentaries by Thierry of Chartres* (Toronto: Pontifical Institute of Mediaeval Studies, 1988).

50. The major account of this subject is the work of Ward, *Ciceronian Rhetoric*.

51. Ward, *Ciceronian Rhetoric*, pp. 65 and 279–305.

52. See H. Silvestre, "Dix plaidoires inédits du XIIᵉ siècle," *Traditio* 10 (1954): 373–97, and Ward, *Ciceronian Rhetoric*, pp. 118–19.

53. See Ward, *Ciceronian Rhetoric*, pp. 107–16.

54. Translation of portions of this work in Miller et al., eds., *Readings in Medieval Rhetoric*, pp. 222–27.

55. See Bliese, "Study of Rhetoric in the Twelfth Century"; P. Osmund Lewry, "Rhetoric at Paris and Oxford in the Mid-Thirteenth Century," *Rhetorica* 1 (1983): 45–63; and Murphy, *Rhetoric in the Middle Ages*, pp. 94–95.

56. See Murphy, *Rhetoric in the Middle Ages*, pp. 97–101.

57. See Ward, *Ciceronian Rhetoric*, p. 289.

58. See Yates, *Art of Memory*, pp. 50–81.

59. See Faral, *Arts poétiques*; C. S. Baldwin, *Medieval Rhetoric*, pp. 183–205; Murphy, *Rhetoric in the Middle Ages*, pp. 135–93; Kelly, *Arts of Poetry and Prose*; and Purcell, *Ars Poetriae*.

60. Translated by Ernest Gallo, in "Matthew of Vendome: Introductory Treatise on the Art of Poetry," *Proceedings of the American Philosophical Society* 118 (1974): 51–92.

61. Translated by Margaret F. Nims, *The Poetria Nova of Geoffrey of Vinsauf* (Toronto: Pontifical Institute of Medieval Studies, 1967), reprinted in O. B. Hardison Jr. et al., eds., *Classical and Medieval Literary Criticism* (New York: Ungar, 1974), pp. 383–404; also translated by Jane B. Kopp, "Poetria Nova," in Murphy, ed., *Three Medieval Rhetorical Arts*, pp. 27–108; see also Marjorie C. Woods, "A Medieval Rhetoric Goes to School—and to the University: The Commentaries on the *Poetria Nova*," *Rhetorica* 9 (1991): 55–65. Geoffrey also wrote a dictaminal treatise; see Martin Camargo, "Toward a Comprehensive Art of Written Discourse: Geoffrey of Vinsauf and the *Ars Dictaminis*," *Rhetorica* 6 (1988): 167–94.

62. Translated by Traugott Lawler, *The Parisiana Poetria of John of Garland* (New Haven: Yale University Press, 1974); see Murphy, *Rhetoric in the Middle Ages*, pp. 175–80.

63. See William M. Purcell, "Eberhard the German and the Labyrinth of Learning; Grammar, Poesy, Rhetoric, and Pedagogy in *Laborintus*," *Rhetorica* 11 (1993): 95–118, and the books cited in note 59, above.

64. See C. S. Baldwin, *Medieval Rhetoric*, pp. 228–57, and Murphy, *Rhetoric in the Middle Ages*, pp. 269–355.

65. A version of the speech was written down by Archbishop Baldric and can be

found in J. M. Watterich's *Pontificorum Romanorum Vitae* (Leipzig, 1862; reprint, Aalen: Scientiae, 1966), 2:599–603.

66. See Caplan, *Of Eloquence*, p. 42.

67. Translated in Miller et al., eds., *Readings in Medieval Rhetoric*, pp. 162–81.

68. See Harry Caplan, "The Four Senses of Scriptural Interpretation and the Mediaeval Theory of Preaching," *Speculum* 4 (1929): 282–80, reprinted in Caplan, *Of Eloquence*, pp. 93–104.

69. Translation of part in Caplan, *Of Eloquence*, pp. 228–39.

70. See Murphy, *Rhetoric in the Middle Ages*, pp. 310–26, and Georgina Donavin, "De Sermone Sermonem Fecimus: Alexander of Ashby's *De Artificioso Modo Prae-dicandi*," *Rhetorica* 15 (1997): 279–96.

71. See Davy, *Sermons univérsitaires*.

72. Translated by Leopold Krul in Murphy, ed., *Three Medieval Rhetorical Arts*, pp. 109–215; selections reprinted in Bizzell and Herzberg, eds., *Rhetorical Tradition*, pp. 439–60.

CHAPTER TEN

1. Publications about Renaissance rhetoric have greatly increased since the first edition of this book was published, although there is no single work covering all aspects of the subject. Studies of specific aspects are cited below. Bibliographical tools include Don P. Abbott, "The Renaissance," in Horner, ed., *Present State of Scholarship*, pp. 84–113; Murphy, *Renaissance Rhetoric: A Short-Title Catalogue*; and Plett, *English Renaissance Rhetoric and Poetics*. See also C. S. Baldwin, *Renaissance Literary Theory*; Bolgar, *Classical Heritage*; Fumaroli, *L'Age de l'éloquence*; Howell, *Logic and Rhetoric in England*; Mack, ed., *Renaissance Rhetoric*; Murphy, ed., *Renaissance Eloquence*; Plett, ed., *Renaissance Rhetorik*; Sonnino, *Handbook to Sixteenth-Century Rhetoric*; and Vickers, *In Defence of Rhetoric*, pp. 254–93. A number of sixteenth-century works are available in microform in *British and Continental Rhetoric and Elocution* and in Murphy, ed., *Renaissance Rhetoric: A Microfiche Collection of Key Texts*.

2. See Eisenstein, *Printing Press as an Agent of Change*.

3. For this definition of humanism, see Kristeller, *Renaissance Thought*, p. 9. On humanism in general, see Garin, *Italian Humanism*, and Seigel, *Rhetoric and Philosophy*. On individual humanists, see Pfeiffer, *Classical Scholarship: From 1300 to 1850*, with bibliography.

4. On the French antecedents, see Kristeller, *Renaissance Thought*, p. 94; on eloquence as an ideal, see Hannah H. Gray, "Renaissance Humanism: The Pursuit of Eloquence," *Journal of the History of Ideas* 24 (1963): 497–514.

5. See Hardison, *Enduring Moment*.

6. On political oratory, see Baron, *Crisis of the Early Italian Renaissance*; on epideictic in the Church, see McManamon, *Funeral Oratory*, and O'Malley, *Praise and Blame*.

7. See Seigel, *Rhetoric and Philosophy*; Scaglione, *Classical Theory of Composition*, pp. 143–44; and Ronald G. Witt, *Coluccio Salutati and His Public Letters* (Geneva: Droz, 1976).

8. On the recovery of texts, see Pfeiffer, *Classical Scholarship: From 1300 to 1850,* pp. 3–66.

9. For Poggio's description of his discovery of Quintilian, see Phyllis G. Gordan, ed. and trans., *Two Renaissance Book Hunters: The Letters of Poggius Bracciolini to Nicolaus de Niccolis* (New York: Columbia University Press, 1966), pp. 193–96.

10. See F. H. Colson, "Knowledge and Use of Quintilian after 1416," in his edition of *M. Fabii Quintiliani Institutionis Oratoriae Liber I* (Cambridge: Cambridge University Press, 1924), pp. lxiv–lxxviii.

11. Among writers discussed in this chapter, critics of Quintilian included Trebizond, whose domination of rhetorical teaching in Italy was threatened by the admirers of Quintilian; Ramus, who attacked him for his neglect of dialectic; and Vives, who rejected his definition of the orator. See John Monfasani, "Episodes of Anti-Quintilianism in the Italian Renaissance: Quarrels on the Orator as *Vir Bonus* and Rhetoric as the *Scientia Bene Dicendi*," *Rhetorica* 10 (1992): 119–38.

12. For a partial list, see Bernard Weinberg, ed., *Tratti di poetica e retorica del conquecento,* 4 vols. (Bari: Giuseppe Laterza, 1970–74), 1:566–81.

13. Rabinowitz, ed. and trans., *Book of the Honeycomb's Flow.* For other Jewish writings on rhetoric, see Isaac Rabinowitz, "Pre-Modern Jewish Study of Rhetoric: An Introductory Bibliography," *Rhetorica* 3 (1985): 137–44.

14. See esp. their role in *Il Libro der Cortegiano,* by Baldesar Castiglione; Charles Singleton, trans., *The Book of the Courtier* (New York: Anchor, 1959). On the subject in general, see Glenn, *Rhetoric Retold,* ch. 4; Levin and Sullivan, eds., *Political Rhetoric*; and the works listed in the following notes.

15. See Margaret L. King and Albert Rabil Jr., eds., *Her Immaculate Hand: Selected Works by and about the Women Humanists of Quattrocento Italy* (Binghampton, N.Y.: Medieval and Renaissance Texts and Studies, 1983), pp. 35–50 and 77.

16. See Margaret L. King, *Women of the Renaissance* (Chicago: University of Chicago Press, 1991), pp. 195–98.

17. Translated in Bizzell and Herzberg, eds., *Rhetorical Tradition,* pp. 495–98.

18. Translated by Sarah Lawson, *The Treasure of the City of Ladies* (New York: Viking Penguin, 1985); excerpted in Bizzell and Herzberg, eds., *Rhetorical Tradition,* pp. 488–93. See Jenny R. Redfern, "Christine de Pisan and *The Treasure of the City of Ladies*: A Medieval Rhetorician and Her Rhetoric," in Lunsford, ed., *Reclaiming Rhetorica,* pp. 73–92.

19. See George P. Rice, ed., *The Public Speeches of Queen Elizabeth: Selections from Her Official Addresses* (New York: Columbia University Press, 1951), pp. 47–48 and 72.

20. The account here is based on Monfasani, *George of Trebizond.*

21. Text in ibid., pp. 365–69.

22. See Scaglione, *Classical Theory of Composition,* pp. 134–35.

23. See Monfasani, *George of Trebizond,* pp. 370–72.

24. See Green, *Rainolds's Oxford Lectures.* The one surviving manuscript contains only lectures on the first nine chapters of Book 1.

25. A possible instance is *De Natura Logicae* of Jacopo Zabarella (1533–89); see W. F. Edwards, "Jacopo Zabarella: A Renaissance Aristotelian's View of Rhetoric and Poetry and Their Relation to Philosophy," in *Arts libéraux et philosophique au Moyen Age,* pp. 843–54.

26. See Eugenio Garin, "Note su alcuini aspetti delle retoriche rinascimentali e sulla *Retorica* del Patrizi," *Testi umanistici su la retorica: Archivo di filosofia* 3 (1953): 7–53. The article includes some discussion of Speroni as well.

27. See Weinberg, *History of Literary Criticism in the Italian Renaissance*.

28. See Jacques Monfrin, "Les lectures de G. Fichet et de J. Heynlin," *Bibliothèque d'humanism et renaissance* 17 (1955): 7–23 and 143–53.

29. See Eisenstein, *Printing Press as an Agent of Change*, p. 399n.

30. For a more detailed description, see George Kennedy, "The *Rhetorica* of Guillaume Fichet," *Rhetorica* 5 (1987): 411–18. The work has never been reprinted and survives only in one manuscript and a few of the original printed copies.

31. See Monfasani, *George of Trebizond*, p. 322.

32. See Franco Simone, "Robert Gaguin ed il suo cenaculo umanistica," *Aevum* 13 (1939): 410–76.

33. Translated by Ronald H. Martin, *The Epitoma Margarite Castigate Eloquentie of Laurentius Gulielmus Traversagni de Saona* (Leeds: Leeds Philosophical and Literary Society, 1986).

34. See Croll, *Style, Rhetoric, and Rhythm*, pp. 255–85.

35. See Scott, *Controversies*, part 1, and M. L. Clarke, "Non Hominis Nomen, Sed Eloquentiae," in Dorey, ed., *Cicero*, pp. 89–95.

36. The term "baroque," borrowed from art criticism, is acceptable as a description of non-Ciceronian prose style, but there is no baroque rhetorical theory; see Wilbur S. Howell, "Baroque Rhetoric: A Concept at Odds with Its Setting," *Philosophy and Rhetoric* 15 (1982): 1–23.

37. See Claude Palisca, "Ut Oratoria Musica: The Rhetorical Basis of Musical Mannerism," in *The Meaning of Mannerism*, ed. F. W. Robinson and S. G. Nichols Jr. (Hanover, N.H.: University Press of New England, 1972), pp. 37–65; G. J. Buelow, "Music, Rhetoric, and the Concept of the Affections: A Selective Bibliography," *Music Library Notes* 31 (1973): 250–59; and Brian Vickers, "Figures of Rhetoric/ Figures of Music," *Rhetorica* 2 (1984): 1–44.

38. See Ursula Kirkendale, "The Source of Bach's *Musical Offering*: The *Institutio Oratoria* of Quintilian," *Journal of the American Musicological Society* 33 (1980): 88–141, and Warren Kirkendale, "On the Rhetorical Interpretation of the Riceror and J. S. Bach's *Musical Offering*," *Studi Musicali* 26 (1997): 331–76.

39. See Monfasani, *George of Trebizond*, p. 38.

40. See Pfeiffer, *Classical Scholarship: From 1300 to 1850*, pp. 35–41, and Nancy Struever, "Lorenzo Valla: Humanist Rhetoric and the Critique of the Classical Languages of Morality," in Murphy, ed., *Renaissance Eloquence*, pp. 191–206.

41. Valla's treatise on dialectic is also known as *Dialectical Disputations against the Aristotelians* and as *Repastinatio* (i.e., "Revision") *Dialectice et Philosophe*. The 1540 Basel edition of Valla's *Opera Omnia* has been reprinted (2 vols. Turin: Bottega d'Erasmom 1961).

42. Quoted from Monfasani, *George of Trebizond*, pp. 304–5.

43. See Mack, *Renaissance Argument*, and John Monfasani, "Lorenzo Valla and Rudolph Agricola," *Journal of the History of Philosophy* 28 (1990): 181–200.

44. See Donald L. Clark, "The Rise and Fall of Progymnasmata in Sixteenth and Seventeenth Century Grammar Schools," *Speech Monographs* 19 (1952): 259–63.

45. Lothar Mundt, ed., *Agricola, De Inventione Dialectica* (Tübingen: Niemeyer, 1992). The original edition (Cologne: Gymnicus, 1539) has been reprinted in *Monumenta Humanistica Belgica*, vol. 2 (Nieuwkoop: de Graff, 1967). The text is also available on microfilm in *British and Continental Rhetoric and Elocution*, reel 8, item 92.

46. See Mack, *Renaissance Argument*, p. 120. For discussion of other early German writing on rhetoric, see Helmut Schanze, "Problems and Trends in the History of German Rhetoric to 1500," in Murphy, ed., *Renaissance Eloquence*, pp. 105–25.

47. Text in *British and Continental Rhetoric and Elocution*, reel 14, item 126.

48. See James R. McNally, "Melanchthon's Earliest Rhetoric," in Fisher, ed., *Rhetoric*, pp. 33–48.

49. There is no modern edition or translation; for an account of the work, see Conley, *Rhetoric in the European Tradition*, pp. 157–59 and 184; see also Joseph S. Freedman, "The Career and Writings of Bartholomew Keckermann (d. 1609)," *Proceedings of the American Philosophical Society* 141 (1997): 305–64.

50. See Marjorie O. Boyle, *Erasmus on Language and Method in Theology* (Toronto: University of Toronto Press, 1977).

51. For a translation, see Scott, *Controversies*, part 2, pp. 19–130.

52. See Judith Rice Henderson, "Erasmus on the Art of Letter-Writing," in Murphy, ed., *Renaissance Eloquence*, pp. 331–55, and "Erasmian Ciceronians; Reformation Teachers of Letter-Writing," *Rhetorica* 10 (1992): 273–302.

53. Translation by Craig Thompson, *Collected Works of Erasmus* (Toronto: University of Toronto Press, 1978), 24:284–659.

54. See T. W. Baldwin, *William Shakespeare's Small Latine*, 2:138–75, and Joseph X. Brennan, "Joannes Susenbrotus: A Forgotten Humanist," *Publications of the Modern Language Association* 75, no. 5 (Dec. 1960): 485–96.

55. Translation by Foster Watson, *Vives on Education* (Cambridge: Cambridge University Press, 1913).

56. See Don Abbott, "La Retórica y el Renacimento: An Overview of Spanish Theory," in Murphy, ed., *Renaissance Eloquence*, pp. 95–104; Emilio Hidalgo-Sema, "Ingenium and Rhetoric in the Work of Vives," *Philosophy and Rhetoric* 16 (1983): 228–41; and "Metaphorical Language, Rhetoric, and *Comprehensio*: J. L. Vives and M. Nizolio," *Philosophy and Rhetoric* 23 (1990): 1–11.

57. Charles Fantazzi, ed. and trans., *Vives, De Conscribendis Epistolis* (Leiden: Brill, 1989).

58. See Judith R. Henderson, "Defining the Genre of the Letter: Juan Luis Vives' *De Conscribendis Epistulis*," *Renaissance and Reformation* 7 (1983): 89–105.

59. See William E. Mead, ed., *The Pastime of Pleasure by Stephen Hawes* (London: Oxford University Press, 1928).

60. See Walter J. Ong, "Tudor Writings on Rhetoric," *Studies in the Renaissance* 15 (1968): 39–68, and Roselyn L. Freedman, "A Bibliography of Sixteenth-Century English Rhetoric," *Rhetoric Society Quarterly* 11 (1981): 118–36.

61. See Crane, *Wit and Rhetoric in the Renaissance*.

62. Frederic I. Carpenter, ed., *Leonard Cox's "The Arte or Crafte of Rhethoryke"* (Chicago: University of Chicago Press, 1899; reprint, New York: AMS, 1973); see Howell, *Logic and Rhetoric in England*, pp. 90–95.

63. Herbert W. Hildebrandt, ed., *A Treatise of Schemes and Tropes* (Gainesville,

Fla.: Scholars Facsimiles and Reprints, 1961); see Howell, *Logic and Rhetoric in England*, pp. 125–31.

64. R. C. Alston, ed., *Garden of Eloquence* (Menston, England: Scolar Press, 1971); see Howell, *Logic and Rhetoric in England*, pp. 132–37.

65. Thomas J. Derrick, ed. *Arte of Rhetorique by Thomas Wilson* (New York: Garland, 1982); see Howell, *Logic and Rhetoric in England*, pp. 98–110.

66. See Richard J. Schoeck, "Lawyers and Rhetoric in Sixteenth-Century England," in Murphy, ed., *Renaissance Eloquence*, 274–91, esp. 285–87, and Mark E. Wildermuth, "The Rhetoric of Wilson's *Arte*: Reclaiming the Classical Heritage for English Protestants," *Philosophy and Rhetoric* 22 (1989): 43–58.

67. See, e.g., Vickers, *Classical Rhetoric in English Poetry*; D. L. Clark, *Rhetoric and Poetry in the Renaissance*; and Crane, *Wit and Rhetoric in the Renaissance*.

68. Shakespeare was apparently acquainted with *Rhetoric for Herennius*, some of Cicero's works, Susenbrotus's handbook of figures, Erasmus's *On Copia*, and perhaps Quintilian's *Institutio*; see T. W. Baldwin, *William Shakespeare's Small Latine*, 2:69–238.

69. See Ong, *Ramus, Method, and the Decay of Dialogue*; Meerhoff, *Rhétorique et poétique au XVIᵉ siècle en France*; and Peter Sharratt, "Recent Work on Peter Ramus (1970–1986)," *Rhetorica* 5 (1987): 7–58.

70. On the rhetorical writings of Talon and Ramus, see Ong, *Ramus, Method, and the Decay of Dialogue*, pp. 270–92. Texts can be found in *British and Continental Rhetoric and Elocution*, reel 15, item 140, and in Murphy, ed., *Renaissance Rhetoric: A Microfiche Collection of Key Texts*.

71. Carole Newlands, trans., *Arguments in Rhetoric against Quintilian*, with an extended introduction and bibliography by James J. Murphy (Dekalb, Ill.: Northern Illinois University Press, 1986).

72. See John C. Adams, "Alexander Richardson's Puritan Theory of Discourse," *Rhetorica* 4 (1986): 255–74, and "Ramist Conceptions of Testimony, Judicial Analogies, and the Puritan Conversion Narrative," *Rhetorica* 9 (1991): 251–68.

73. The text of Harvey's *Rhetor* is in *British and Continental Rhetoric and Elocution*, reel 4, item 39. Translation of *Gabriel Harvey's Ciceronianus* by Harold S. Wilson and Clarence A. Forbes in *University of Nebraska Studies in Humanities*, vol. 4 (Lincoln: University of Nebraska Press, 1945).

74. See Ethel Seaton, ed., *The Arcadian Rhetorike by Abraham Fraunce* (Oxford: Basil Blackwood, 1950), and Howell, *Logic and Rhetoric*, pp. 247–81.

75. For Butler's work, see *British and Continental Rhetoric and Elocution*, reel 2, item 17; see also Howell, *Logic and Rhetoric*, pp. 318–41.

76. See Joseph S. Freedman, "Cicero in Sixteenth- and Seventeenth-Century Rhetoric Instruction," *Rhetorica* 4 (1986): 227–54. Lanham, *Electronic Word*, pp. 157–59, attributes the modern specialization of academic disciplines to the influence of Ramism. This is something of an exaggeration; Aristotle had begun the project and Ramus was largely forgotten by the nineteenth century when specialization emerged as part of an effort to apply scientific method to humanistic studies.

77. See Luisa López-Grigera, "Introduction to the Study of Rhetoric in Sixteenth-Century Spain," *Disposition: Revista Hispánica de Semiótica Literaria* 8 (1983): 1–18, and her book *La retórica en España*. Ramism was introduced by Francisco Sanchez in

his *Organum Dialecticum et Rhetoricum* of 1579; see Alfonso Martín Jiménez, "Rhetoric, Dialectic, and Literature in the Work of Francisco Sanchez," *Rhetorica* 13 (1995): 43–59. For a brief account of other Spanish writers on rhetoric, see Robert W. Smith, "Retórica España: A Checklist in the History of Spanish Rhetoric," *Central States Speech Journal* 26 (1975): 221–36. See also Harry Caplan and Henry H. King, "Spanish Treatises on Preaching: A Book List," *Speech Monographs* 17 (1950): 161–70.

78. See Lawrence J. Flynn, "The *De Arte Rhetorica* of Cyprian Soarez, S.J.," *Quarterly Journal of Speech* 42 (1956): 367–74, and "Sources and Influence of Soarez' *De Arte Rhetorica*," *Quarterly Journal of Speech* 43 (1957): 257–65.

79. For an account of the contents, see Conley, *Rhetoric in the European Tradition*, pp. 155–57 and 182–83.

80. See Abbott, *Rhetoric in the New World*, pp. 9–15.

81. See Don Paul Abbott, "Aztecs and Orators: Rhetoric in New Spain," *Texte: Revue de Critique et de Théorie Littéraire* 8/9 (1989): 353–65, and for further detail, see Abbott's *Rhetoric in the New World*.

82. There are no modern editions or translations of Vossius's rhetorical works. For discussion, see C. S. M. Rademaker, *Life and Work of Gerhardus Johannes Vossius* (Assen: Van Gorcum, 1981), and Conley, *Rhetoric in the European Tradition*, pp. 159–62 and 185–86.

83. See Marc Cogan, "Rhetoric and Action in Francis Bacon," *Philosophy and Rhetoric* 14 (1981): 212–33; Vickers, *Francis Bacon and Renaissance Prose*; and Wallace, *Francis Bacon* and "Bacon, Rhetoric, and Ornament of Words," in Fisher, ed., *Rhetoric*, pp. 49–65.

84. Quoted by Wallace, *Francis Bacon*, p. 4.

85. There are numerous modern editions of *The Advancement of Learning* and an English translation of *De Dignitate et Augmentis* in John M. Robertson, ed., *The Philosophical Works of Francis Bacon* (London: Routledge, 1905), pp. 413–638.

86. More fully stated in the Latin edition: "munus rhetoricae non aliud quam ut rationis dictamina phantasiae applicet et commendet ad exercitandum appetitum et voluntatem," or "the duty of rhetoric is nothing other than to apply and recommend the dictates of reason to imagination for the moving of emotion and the will."

87. See Wallace, *Francis Bacon*, pp. 205–18.

CHAPTER ELEVEN

1. See Ray Nadeau, "Talaeus versus Farnaby on Style," *Speech Monographs* 21 (1954): 59–62.

2. Two basic works for rhetoric in this period are Fumaroli, *L'Age de l'éloquence* (an English translation is in preparation), and Howell, *Eighteenth-Century British Logic and Rhetoric*.

3. J. C. T. Ernesti, *Lexicon Technologiae Graecorum Rhetoricae* (Leipzig, 1795) and *Lexicon Technologiae Latinorum Rhetoricae* (Leipzig, 1797), both reprinted (Hildesheim: Olms, 1962).

4. See Davidson, *Audience, Words, and Art*.

5. See Howell, *Eighteenth-Century British Logic and Rhetoric*, pp. 503–35.

6. See Warnick, *Sixth Canon*.

7. See Howell, *Logic and Rhetoric in England*, pp. 342–63, and Davidson, *Audience, Words, and Art*, pp. 57–108.

8. See Davidson, *Audience, Words, and Art*, pp. 109–40, and Kathleen M. Jamieson, "Pascal vs. Descartes: A Clash over Rhetoric in the Seventeenth Century," *Communication Monographs* 43 (1976): 44–50.

9. See Roger Lathuillère, *La Préciosité: Étude historique et linguistique* (Geneva: Droz, 1966), and Dorothy A. L. Backer, *Precious Women* (New York: Basic Books, 1974).

10. See Stina Hansson, "Rhetoric for Seventeenth-Century Salons: Beata Rosenhane's Exercise Books and Classical Rhetoric," *Rhetorica* 12 (1994): 43–65.

11. See Bizzell and Herzberg, eds., *Rhetorical Tradition*, pp. 670–85.

12. See Christine M. Sutherland, "Outside the Rhetorical Tradition: Mary Astell's Advice to Women in Seventeenth-Century England," *Rhetorica* 9 (1991): 147–63, and "Mary Astell: Reclaiming Rhetorica in the Seventeenth Century," in Lunsford, ed., *Reclaiming Rhetorica*, pp. 93–116.

13. For these texts, see R. C. Davis and Laurie Finke, eds., *Literary Criticism and Theory* (New York: Longman, 1989), pp. 290–97 and 315–20.

14. For the text of the English version, see Harwood, ed., *Rhetorics of Thomas Hobbes and Bernard Lamy*, pp. 131–377. See also Warnick, *Sixth Canon*, pp. 18–34.

15. Harwood, ed., *Rhetorics of Thomas Hobbes and Bernard Lamy*, p. 329.

16. See Monk, *Sublime*, ch. 1, and Warnick, *Sixth Canon*, pp. 74–94.

17. See Highet, *Classical Tradition*, pp. 261–88.

18. See Abrams, *Mirror and the Lamp*, pp. 70–78.

19. Modern edition by J. T. Boulton (London: Routledge, 1958).

20. For a good survey in English, see Shuger, *Sacred Rhetoric*, esp. pp. 55–117.

21. See Jacques Truchet, *La Prédication de Bossuet* (Paris: du Cerf, 1960). Bossuet discussed his theory of preaching in his *Panégyrique de Saint Paul*; see J. Lebarq, ed., *Oeuvres oratoires de Bossuet* (Lille: Desclée de Brouwen, 1891), pp. 302–4.

22. Edited and translated by Wilbur S. Howell, *Fénelon's Dialogues on Eloquence* (Princeton: Princeton University Press, 1951). Page references in the text are to Howell's translation. See Warnick, *Sixth Canon*, pp. 50–57.

23. See Howell, *Eighteenth-Century British Logic and Rhetoric*, pp. 518–19.

24. See Carr, *Descartes and the Resilience of Rhetoric*, and Dalia Judovitz, *Subjectivity and Representation in Descartes* (New York: Cambridge University Press, 1988).

25. Harwood, ed., *Rhetorics of Thomas Hobbes and Bernard Lamy*, pp. 33–128. As noted in Chapter 10, John Rainolds had lectured on Aristotle's *Rhetoric* at Oxford in the previous century, and in 1619 Thomas Goulston published *Versio Latina et Paraphrasis in Aristotelis Rhetoricam*.

26. See James P. Zappen, "Aristotelian and Ramist Rhetoric in Thomas Hobbes's *Leviathan*: Pathos versus Ethos and Logos," *Rhetorica* 1 (1983): 65–91, and Denis Thouard, "Hobbes et la rhétorique: Un cas complexe," *Rhetorica* 14 (1996): 333–39.

27. See Howell, *Eighteenth-Century British Logic and Rhetoric*, pp. 448–502.

28. For the text, see Fausto Nicolini, ed., *G. B. Vico Opere*, vol. 8 (Bari: Latega, 1941).

29. See Donald P. Verene, *Vico on the Study Methods of Our Time* (Ithaca: Cornell University Press, 1990).

30. Translation by Thomas G. Bergin and Max H. Fisch, *The New Science of Giambattista Vico* (Ithaca: Cornell University Press, 1948).

31. See Daniel M. Gross, "Metaphor and Definition in Vico's *New Science*," *Rhetorica* 14 (1996): 359–81.

32. There is now an extensive bibliography relating to Vico; see especially Michael Mooney, *Vico in the Tradition of Rhetoric* (Princeton: Princeton University Press, 1985), and Donald P. Verene, *Vico's Science of Imagination* (Ithaca: Cornell University Press, 1981).

33. T. H. Green and T. H. Grose, eds., *Philosophical Works of David Hume* (Aalen: Scientia Verlag, 1964), 3:163–74; see Adam Potkay, *The Fate of Eloquence in the Age of Hume* (Ithaca: Cornell University Press, 1994), chs. 1–2.

34. See the review of Pichot's *Voyage historique et littéraire* by the great French critic C.-A. Sainte-Beuve in the latter's *Oeuvres* (Paris: Gallimard, 1956), 1:122–34.

35. Chauncey A. Goodrich, professor of rhetoric at Yale, compiled in 1852 an anthology of speeches by these and other orators, accompanied with critical essays, a work much studied in America; see A. Craig Baird, ed., *Essays from Select British Eloquence* (Carbondale: Southern Illinois University Press, 1963).

36. Kant, *Critique of Judgement*, trans. James C. Meredith (Oxford: Clarendon Press, 1961), pp. 184–85.

37. There is no modern edition. For discussion, see Conley, *Rhetoric in the European Tradition*, pp. 194–97 and 229–30, and Kathleen S. Wilkins, *A Study of the Works of Claude Buffier* (Geneva: Institut et Musée Voltaire, 1969).

38. There is no modern edition. For discussion, see Conley, *Rhetoric in the European Tradition*, pp. 201–3 and 230–31, and Barbara Warnick, "Charles Rollin's *Traité* and the Rhetorical Theories of Smith, Campbell, and Blair," *Rhetorica* 3 (1985): 45–65.

39. See Gérard Genette, *Figures of Literary Discourse*, trans. Alan Sheridan (New York: Columbia University Press, 1982), pp. 103–26.

40. See Joachim Birke, ed., *Ausgewälte Werke Hrsg. von J. C. Gottsched* (Berlin: de Gruyter, 1987), 7:59ff.

41. On the history of rhetoric in Germany from the sixteenth to the twentieth century, see Schanze, *Rhetorik*.

42. See Antonio Mestre Sanchis, ed., *Obras Completas de Gregorio Mayáns y Siscar*, vol. 3 (Valencia: Consellería de Cultura, 1984); there is a valuable review describing the contents of the work by Rosalind J. Gabin in *Rhetorica* 5 (1987): 198–206. For additional discussion, see Donald P. Abbott, "Mayans' *Rhetórica* and the Search for a Spanish Rhetoric," *Rhetorica* 11 (1993): 157–79.

43. For a list of other Spanish rhetorics, see Don P. Abbott, "A Bibliography of Eighteenth- and Nineteenth-Century Spanish Treatises," *Rhetorica* 4 (1986): 275–92.

44. A popular Ciceronian rhetoric was John Holmes's *The Art of Rhetoric Made Easy* (1755); an example of a text on figures is Nicolas Burton's *Figurae Grammaticae et Rhetoricae Latina Carmina Donatae* (1702); see *British and Continental Rhetoric and Elocution*, reel 2, item 15; see also Anthony Blackwell's *Introduction to the Classics* (1718), in ibid., reel 1, item 7.

45. John Ward, *A System of Oratory Delivered in a Course of Lectures Publicly Read at Gresham College* (1759; reprint, Hildesheim: Olms, 1969).

46. See Howell, *Eighteenth-Century British Logic and Rhetoric*, pp. 145–256, and Frederick W. Haberman, "English Sources of American Elocution," in Wallace, ed., *History of Speech Education*, pp. 105–26.

47. James W. Cleary, ed., *Chirologia and Chironomia by John Bulwer* (Carbondale: Southern Illinois University Press, 1974).

48. Reprinted, New York: Benjamin Bloom, 1968.

49. Mary M. Robb and Lester Thomssen, ed., *Chironomia by Gilbert Austin* (Carbondale: Southern Illinois University Press, 1966).

50. E. Neal Claussen and Karl R. Wallace, eds., *Lectures Concerning Oratory by John Lawson* (Carbondale: Southern Illinois University Press, 1972). See Howell, *Eighteenth-Century British Logic and Rhetoric*, pp. 616–31.

51. John M. Lothian, ed., *Lectures on Rhetoric and Belles Lettres Delivered in the University of Glasgow by Adam Smith* (Carbondale: Southern Illinois University Press, 1971); also J. C. Bryce, ed., *Glasgow Edition of the Works and Correspondence of Adam Smith*, vol. 4 (New York: Oxford University Press, 1983). See Miller, *Formation of College English*, pp. 178–204.

52. Vincent M. Bevilacqua and Richard Murphy, eds., *A Course of Lectures on Oratory and Criticism by Joseph Priestley* (Carbondale: Southern Illinois University Press, 1965).

53. See Lloyd F. Bitzer, editor's introduction to *The Philosophy of Rhetoric*, by George Campbell (Carbondale: Southern Illinois University Press, 1963), p. xxviii. See Miller, *Formation of College English*, pp. 205–26.

54. See Warnick, *Sixth Canon*, pp. 62–68 and 116–20.

55. See Horner, *Nineteenth-Century Scottish Rhetoric*.

56. Harold F. Harding, ed., *Lectures on Rhetoric and Belles Lettres by Hugh Blair*, 2 vols. (Carbondale: Southern Illinois University Press, 1965). For discussion of Blair's lectures, see Howell, *Eighteenth-Century British Logic and Rhetoric*, pp. 648–74; Miller, *Formation of College English*, pp. 227–52; and Warnick, *Sixth Canon*, pp. 68–71 and 111–16.

57. See Warren Guthrie, "The Development of Rhetorical Theory in America, 1635–1850," *Speech Monographs* 15 (1948): 61–71.

58. Douglas Ehninger, ed., *Elements of Rhetoric by Richard Whately* (Carbondale: Southern Illinois University Press, 1963).

59. See Thomas Miller, ed., *The Selected Writings of John Witherspoon* (Carbondale: Southern Illinois University Press, 1990), pp. 38–47 and 231–318, and "John Witherspoon and Scottish Rhetoric and Moral Philosophy in America," *Rhetorica* 8 (1992): 381–403; see also Howell, *Eighteenth-Century British Logic and Rhetoric*, pp. 671–91.

60. See J. Jeffrey Auer and Jerald L. Banninga, eds., *John Quincy Adams: Lectures on Rhetoric and Oratory*, 2 vols. (New York: Russell and Russell, 1962), 1:28–29.

61. See Wallace, ed., *History of Speech Education*, p. 164.

62. See Carole Blair, "Nietzsche's Lecture Notes on Rhetoric: A Translation," *Philosophy and Rhetoric* 16 (1983): 94–129, and Sander L. Gilman, Carole Blaire, and David Parent, eds., *Friedrich Nietzsche on Rhetoric and Language* (New York: Oxford University Press, 1989).

63. See Vickers, *In Defence of Rhetoric*, pp. 459–64. Vickers takes special pains to refute Paul de Man's misinterpretations of Nietzsche's views on rhetoric.

CHAPTER TWELVE

1. See Lanham, *Electronic Word*, esp. ch. 2.

2. Originally published in New York at Oxford University Press, 1965, and often reprinted.

3. Welch, *Contemporary Reception*, p. 11. Welch identifies examples of textbooks representative of each school and a bibliography of relevant books.

4. Published in Chicago by the University of Chicago Press, 1990.

5. Published in Charlottesville by the University Press of Virginia, 1993.

6. See I. A. Richards, *The Philosophy of Rhetoric* (London: Oxford University Press, 1936), p. 3.

7. See Roman Jakobson, "Two Aspects of Language and Two Types of Aphasic Disturbances," in Jakobson and M. Halle, eds., *Fundamentals of Language* (The Hague: Mouton, 1956), pp. 53–82. Cf. the criticism of Jakobson as one who contributed to the "atrophying" of rhetoric by Vickers, *In Defence of Rhetoric*, pp. 442–48.

8. Published in Paris by Larousse, 1970.

9. Alan Sheridan, trans., *Figures of Literary Discourse* (New York: Columbia University Press, 1982).

10. Translation by Robert Czerny (Toronto: University of Toronto Press, 1977).

11. Published in Boston by Beacon Press, 1961; reprinted in Berkeley at the University of California Press, 1970.

12. Originally published in New York by Prentice-Hall, 1945; reprinted in Berkeley at University of California Press, 1969.

13. Originally published in New York by Prentice-Hall, 1950; reprinted in Berkeley by the University of California Press, 1969.

14. John Wilkinson and Purcell Weaver, trans., *The New Rhetoric: A Treatise on Argumentation* (Notre Dame, Ind.: Notre Dame University Press, 1969).

15. See, e.g., Tzetan Todorov, *Theories of the Symbol*, trans. Catherine Porter (Ithaca: Cornell University Press, 1982), and Roy Harris and Talbot J. Taylor, *Landmarks in Linguistic Thought: The Western Tradition from Socrates to Saussure* (London: Routledge, 1989).

16. See Umberto Eco, *A Theory of Semiotics* (Bloomington: Indiana University Press, 1979), pp. 134 and 276–88.

17. See Whitman, *Allegory*, pp. 14–57.

18. Cleanth Brooks Jr. and Robert Penn Warren, *Understanding Poetry* (New York: Henry Holt, 1938 and later).

19. See, e.g., Elder Olson, ed., *Aristotle's Poetics and English Literature* (Chicago: University of Chicago Press, 1965).

20. Vickers, *In Defence of Rhetoric*, pp. 453–70.

21. Translation by Barbara Johnson (Chicago: University of Chicago Press, 1981), pp. 63–171.

22. A valuable earlier book is Oliver, *Communication and Culture in Ancient India and China*.

BIBLIOGRAPHY

This Bibliography lists books and a few studies in journals that are cited by short title in the notes, as well as some general works useful for study of the history of rhetoric. Other books, including modern editions and translations, and articles relating to single authors or works are fully identified in the notes.

Abbott, Don P. *Rhetoric in the New World: Rhetorical Theory and Practice in Colonial Spanish America*. Columbia: University of South Carolina Press, 1996.

Abrams, M. H. *The Mirror and the Lamp: Romantic Theory and the Critical Tradition*. New York: Oxford University Press, 1953.

Anderson, Graham. *Sage, Saint, and Sophist: Holy Men and Their Associates in the Early Roman Empire*. London: Routledge, 1994.

———. *The Second Sophistic: A Cultural Phenomenon in the Early Roman Empire*. London: Routledge, 1993.

Arts libéraux et philosophie au Moyen Age: Actes du Congrès international de philosophie médiévale, Montréal, 1967. Paris: J. Vrin, 1969.

Backman, Mark, ed. *Rhetoric: Essays in Invention and Discovery*. Woodridge, Conn.: Ox Bow Press, 1987.

Baldwin, Charles S. *Ancient Rhetoric and Poetic*. New York: Macmillan, 1924.

———. *Medieval Rhetoric and Poetic (to 1400) Interpreted from Representative Works*. New York: Macmillan, 1928.

———. *Renaissance Literary Theory and Practice*. Edited by Donald L. Clark. New York: Macmillan, 1939.

Baldwin, T. W. *William Shakespeare's Small Latine and Lesse Greeke*. 2 vols. Urbana: University of Illinois Press, 1944.

Baron, Hans. *The Crisis of the Early Italian Renaissance: Civic Humanism and Republican Liberty in the Age of Classicism and Tyranny*. Princeton: Princeton University Press, 1966.

Baynes, Norman H., and H. St. L. B. Moss. *Byzantium: An Introduction to East Roman Civilization*. Oxford: Clarendon Press, 1948.

Beck, Hans-Georg. *Kirche und theologische Literatur im byzantinischen Reich*. Handbuch der Altertumswissenschaft 12, no. 2, part 1. Munich: Beck, 1959.

Bennett, Beth S. "The Function of Adaptation in Notker's *Rhetorica*," *Rhetorica* 7 (1989): 171–84.

Bizzell, Patricia, and Bruce Herzberg, eds. *The Rhetorical Tradition: Readings from Classical Times to the Present*. Boston: Bedford Books, 1990.

Bliese, John. "The Study of Rhetoric in the Twelfth Century." *Quarterly Journal of Speech* 63 (1977): 364–83.

Blum, Herweg. *Die antike Mnemotechnik*. Hildesheim: Olms, 1969.

Blundell, Sue. *Women in Ancient Greece*. Cambridge, Mass.: Harvard University Press, 1995.

Bolgar, R. R. *The Classical Heritage and Its Beneficiaries*. Cambridge: Cambridge University Press, 1954.

———, ed. *Classical Influences on European Culture, A.D. 500–1500: Proceedings of an International Conference Held at King's College, Cambridge, April 1969*. Cambridge: Cambridge University Press, 1971.

Bonner, S. F. *Education in Ancient Rome*. Berkeley: University of California Press, 1977.

———. *Roman Declamation in the Late Republic and Early Empire*. Berkeley: University of California Press, 1949.

British and Continental Rhetoric and Elocution. Sixteen microfilm reels containing 143 items. Ann Arbor: University Microfilms, 1953.

Brown, Peter. *Augustine of Hippo: A Biography*. Berkeley: University of California Press, 1969.

———. *Power and Persuasion in Later Antiquity: Towards a Christian Europe*. Madison: University of Wisconsin Press, 1992.

Browning, Robert. *Studies in Byzantine History, Literature, and Education*. London: Variorum Reprints, 1977.

Burgess, Theodore C. "Epideictic Literature." *University of Chicago Studies in Classical Philology* 3 (1902): 89–261.

Camargo, Martin J. *Ars Dictaminis, Ars Dictandi*. Typologie des sources du Moyen Age occidental. Turnhout, Belgium: Brepols, 1991.

Cameron, Avril. *Christianity and the Rhetoric of Empire: The Development of Christian Discourse*. Berkeley: University of California Press, 1991.

Caplan, Harry. *Of Eloquence: Studies in Ancient and Medieval Rhetoric*. Ithaca: Cornell University Press, 1970.

Carawan, Edwin. *Rhetoric and the Law of Draco*. Oxford: Clarendon Press, 1998.

Carr, Thomas M., Jr. *Descartes and the Resilience of Rhetoric*. Carbondale: Southern Illinois University Press, 1990.

Carruthers, Mary J. *The Book of Memory: A Study of Memory in Medieval Culture*. New York: Cambridge University Press, 1990.

Cassin, Barbara. *L'Effet sophistique*. Paris: Gallimard, 1995.

Chamberlin, John S. *Increase and Multiply: Arts of Discourse Procedure in the Preaching of Donne*. Chapel Hill: University of North Carolina Press, 1976.

Clark, A. C. *The Cursus in Medieval and Vulgar Latin*. Oxford: Clarendon Press, 1910.

Clark, Donald L. *Rhetoric and Poetry in the Renaissance*. New York: Columbia University Press, 1922.

Clarke, M. L. *Higher Education in the Ancient World*. London: Routledge and Kegan Paul, 1972.

———. *Rhetoric at Rome: A Historical Survey*. London: Cohen and West, 1953.

Cochrane, Charles N. *Christianity and Classical Culture: A Study of Thought and Action from Augustus to Augustine*. London: Oxford University Press, 1957.

Cole, Thomas. *The Origins of Rhetoric in Ancient Greece*. Baltimore: Johns Hopkins University Press, 1991.

Conley, Thomas M. *Rhetoric in the European Tradition*. New York: Longman, 1990. Reprint, Chicago: University of Chicago Press, 1993.

Cope, E. M. *Aristotle's Rhetoric with a Commentary*. Revised and edited by John E. Sandys. 3 vols. Cambridge: The University Press, 1877. Reprint, Hildesheim: Olms, 1970.

——. *An Introduction to Aristotle's Rhetoric with Analysis, Notes, and Appendices*. London: Macmillan, 1867. Reprint, New York: Olms, 1970.

Copeland, Rita. *Rhetoric, Hermeneutics, and Translation in the Middle Ages*. New York: Cambridge University Press, 1991.

Corbett, Edward P. J. *Classical Rhetoric for the Modern Reader*. 3rd ed. New York: Oxford University Press, 1990.

Corvino, William A., and David A. Joliffe. *Rhetoric: Concepts, Definitions, Boundaries*. New York: Allyn & Bacon, 1995.

Coulter, James A. *The Literary Microcosm: Theories of Interpretation of the Later Neoplatonists*. Leiden: Brill, 1976.

Crane, William G. *Wit and Rhetoric in the Renaissance: The Formal Basis of Elizabethan Prose Style*. New York: Columbia University Press, 1937.

Croll, Morris W. *Style, Rhetoric, and Rhythm*. Edited by J. Max Parick and Robert O. Evans. Princeton: Princeton University Press, 1966.

Curtius, Ernst R. *European Literature and the Latin Middle Ages*. Translated by Willard R. Trask. Princeton: Princeton University Press, 1953.

Davidson, Hugh M. *Audience, Words, and Art: Studies in Seventeenth-Century French Rhetoric*. Columbus: Ohio State University Press, 1965.

Davy, M. M. *Les Sermons univérsitaires parisiens de 1230–31: Contribution à l'historie de prédication médiévale*. Paris: J. Vrin, 1931.

Dilts, Mervin R., and George A. Kennedy, eds. and trans. *Two Greek Rhetorical Treatises from the Roman Empire*. Leiden: Brill, 1997.

Dodds, E. R. *Pagan and Christian in an Age of Anxiety: Some Aspects of Religious Experience from Marcus Aurelius to Constantine*. Cambridge: Cambridge University Press, 1965.

Dominik, William J., ed. *Roman Eloquence: Rhetoric in Society and Literature*. London: Routledge, 1997.

Dorey, T. A., ed. *Cicero*. London: Routledge and Kegan Paul, 1964.

Dzielska, Maria. *Hypatia of Alexandria*. Translated by F. Lyra. Cambridge, Mass.: Harvard University Press, 1995.

Easterling, P. E., and B. M. W. Knox, eds. *The Cambridge History of Classical Literature*, vol. 1: *Greek Literature*. Cambridge: Cambridge University Press, 1985.

Eisenstein, Elizabeth L. *The Printing Press as an Agent of Change: Communications and Cultural Transformations in Early-Modern Europe*. 2 vols. New York: Cambridge University Press, 1979.

Enos, Richard L. *Greek Rhetoric before Aristotle*. Prospect Heights, Ill.: Waveland Press, 1993.

——. *The Literate Mode of Cicero's Legal Rhetoric*. Carbondale: Southern Illinois University Press, 1988.

Enos, Theresa, ed. *Encyclopedia of Rhetoric and Composition: Communication from Ancient Times to the Information Age*. New York: Garland, 1996.

Erickson, Keith, ed. *Aristotle: The Classical Heritage of Rhetoric*. Metuchen, N.J.: Scarecrow Press, 1974.

———. *Aristotle's Rhetoric: Five Centuries of Philological Research*. Metuchen, N.J.: Scarecrow Press, 1975.

Fairweather, Janet. *Seneca the Elder*. Cambridge: Cambridge University Press, 1981.

Faral, Edmond. *Les Arts poétiques du XVIIe et du XIIIe siècle: Recherches et documents sur la technique littéraire du Moyen Age*. Bibliothèque de l'école des hautes études, 238. Paris: Champion, 1924.

Faulhaber, Charles B. *Latin Rhetorical Theory in Thirteenth and Fourteenth Century Castile*. Berkeley: University of California Press, 1972.

Fisher, Walter R., ed. *Rhetoric: A Tradition in Transition*. East Lansing: Michigan State University Press, 1975.

Florescu, Vasile. *La Retorica nel suo sviluppo storico*. Bologna: Il Mulino, 1971.

Foley, Helene P. *Reflections of Women in Antiquity*. New York: Gordon and Beach, 1981.

Foley, John M. *The Theory of Oral Composition: History and Methodology*. Bloomington: Indiana University Press, 1988.

Fontaine, Jacques. *Isidore de Séville et la culture classique dans l'Espagne wisigothique*. 2 vols. Paris: Etudes Augustiniennes, 1959.

Fortenbaugh, William W., and David Mirhady, eds. "Peripatetic Rhetoric after Aristotle." *Rutgers University Studies in Classical Humanities* 6. New Brunswick, N.J.: Rutgers University Press, 1993.

Fumaroli, Marc. *L'Age de l'éloquence: Rhétorique et res litteraria de la Renaissance au seuil de l'époque classique*. Geneva: Droz, 1980.

Furley, David J., and Alexander Nehamas, eds. *Aristotle's Rhetoric: Philosophical Issues*. Princeton: Princeton University Press, 1994.

Garin, Eugenio. *Italian Humanism: Philosophy and Civic Life in the Renaissance*. Translated by Peter Munz. New York: Harper and Row, 1965.

Glenn, Sheryl. *Rhetoric Retold: Regendering the Tradition from Antiquity through the Renaissance*. Carbondale: Southern Illinois University Press, 1997.

Golden, James L., and Edward P. J. Corbett. *The Rhetoric of Blair, Campbell, and Whately*. New York: Holt, Rinehart, and Winston, 1990.

Goodspeed, Edgar J. *A History of Early Christian Literature*. Revised and enlarged by Robert M. Grant. Chicago: University of Chicago Press, 1966.

Green, Lawrence D., ed. *John Rainolds's Oxford Lectures on Aristotle's Rhetoric*. Newark: University of Delaware Press, 1986.

Grube, G. M. A. *The Greek and Roman Critics*. London: Methuen, 1965.

Guthrie, W. K. C. *A History of Greek Philosophy*. 6 vols. Cambridge: Cambridge University Press, 1969–81.

Guy, Henry. *L'École des rhétoriqueurs*. Bibliothèque littéraire de la Renaissance, n.s., 4. Paris: Champion, 1910.

Haarhoff, Theodore. *Schools of Gaul: A Study of Pagan and Christian Education in the Last Century of the Western Empire*. London: Oxford University Press, 1920.

Halm, Karl, ed. *Rhetores Latini Minores*. Leipzig, 1863. Reprint, Frankfurt: Minerva, 1964.

Hardison, Osborne B., Jr. *The Enduring Monument: A Study of the Idea of Praise in Renaissance Literary Theory and Practice*. Chapel Hill: University of North Carolina Press, 1962.

Harris, William V. *Ancient Literacy*. Cambridge, Mass.: Harvard University Press, 1989.

Harwood, John T., ed. *The Rhetorics of Thomas Hobbes and Bernard Lamy*. Carbondale: Southern Illinois University Press, 1986.

Haskins, Charles H. *The Renaissance of the Twelfth Century*. Cambridge, Mass.: Harvard University Press, 1927.

Havelock, Eric A. *The Literate Revolution in Greece and Its Cultural Consequences*. Princeton: Princeton University Press, 1982.

Havelock, Eric A., and Jackson Hershbell. *Communication Arts in the Ancient World*. Mamaroneck, N.Y.: Hastings House, 1978.

Hayes, John H., ed. *Old Testament Form Criticism*. San Antonio: Trinity University Press, 1974.

Hellwig, Antje. *Untersuchungen zur Theorie der Rhetorik bei Platon und Aristotles*. Hypomnemata, 38. Göttingen: Vandenhoeck & Ruprecht, 1973.

Hertter, F. *Die Poetasliteratur Italiens im 12. and 13. Jahrhundert*. Leipzig: Teubner, 1910.

Highet, Gilbert. *The Classical Tradition: Greek and Roman Influences on Western Literature*. New York: Oxford University Press, 1949.

Horner, Winifrid B. *Nineteenth-Century Scottish Rhetoric: The American Connection*. Carbondale: Southern Illinois University Press, 1993.

———, ed. *The Present State of Scholarship in Historical and Contemporary Rhetoric*. Rev. ed. Columbia: University of Missouri Press, 1990.

Howell, Wilbur S. *Eighteenth-Century British Logic and Rhetoric*. Princeton: Princeton University Press, 1971.

———. *Logic and Rhetoric in England, 1500–1700*. Princeton: Princeton University Press, 1951.

Hubbell, Harry M. *The Influence of Isocrates on Cicero, Dionysius, and Aristides*. New Haven: Yale University Press, 1913.

Hunger, Herbert. *Die hochsprachliche profane Literatur der Byzantiner*, vol. 1: *Philosophie, Rhetorik, Epistolographie, Geschichtsschreibung, Geographie*. Handbuch der Altertumswissenschaft 12, no. 5, part 1. Munich: Beck, 1978.

Hussey, J. M. *Church and Learning in the Byzantine Empire, 867–1185*. London: Oxford University Press, 1937.

———, ed. *The Cambridge Medieval History, IV: The Byzantine Empire*. Cambridge: Cambridge University Press, 1966.

Ijsseling, Samuel. *Rhetoric and Philosophy in Conflict: An Historical Survey*. The Hague: Nijhoff, 1976.

Jaeger, Werner. *Early Christianity and Greek Paideia*. Cambridge, Mass.: Harvard University Press, 1961.

———. *Paideia: The Ideals of Greek Culture*. Translated by Gilbert Highet. 3 vols. New York: Oxford University Press, 1939–44.

Jaffe, Samuel. "Antiquity and Innovation in Notker's *Nova Rhetorica*: The Doctrine of Invention." *Rhetorica* 3 (1985): 165–81.

Janson, Tore. *Prose Rhythm in Medieval Latin from the 9th to the 13th Century*. Stockholm: Almqvist and Wiksell, 1975.

Jarratt, Susan C. *Rereading the Sophists: Classical Rhetoric Refigured*. Carbondale: Southern Illinois University Press, 1991.

Jebb, R. C. *The Attic Orators from Antiphon to Isaeos*. 2 vols. London: Macmillan, 1893.

Jenkyns, Richard, ed. *The Legacy of Rome: A New Appraisal*. Oxford: Oxford University Press, 1991.

Johnstone, Christopher L., ed. *Theory, Text, Context: Issues in Greek Rhetoric and Oratory*. Albany: State University of New York Press, 1996.

Jones, Leslie W., ed. and trans. *An Introduction to Divine and Human Readings by Cassiodorus Senator*. Records of Civilization: Sources and Studies, 40. New York: Columbia University Press, 1946.

Kapp, Ernst. *Greek Foundations of Traditional Logic*. New York: Columbia University Press, 1946.

Karlsson, Gustave. *Idéologie et cérémonial dans l'épitolographie byzantine*. Uppsala: Studia Graeca Upsaliensia, 1962.

Kastely, James L. *Rethinking the Rhetorical Tradition: From Plato to Postmodernism*. New Haven: Yale University Press, 1997.

Kaster, Robert. *Guardians of Language: The Grammarians and Society in Late Antiquity*. Berkeley: University of California Press, 1988.

Kazhdan, A. P., ed. *The Oxford Dictionary of Byzantium*. New York: Oxford University Press, 1991.

Kelly, Douglas. *Arts of Poetry and Prose*. Typologie des sources du Moyen Age occidental, 59. Turnhout, Belgium: Brepols, 1991.

Kennedy, George A. *The Art of Persuasion in Greece*. Princeton: Princeton University Press, 1963.

——. *The Art of Rhetoric in the Roman World*. Princeton: Princeton University Press, 1972.

——. *Comparative Rhetoric: An Historical and Cross-Cultural Introduction*. New York: Oxford University Press, 1997.

——. *Greek Rhetoric under Christian Emperors*. Princeton: Princeton University Press, 1983.

——. *A New History of Classical Rhetoric*. Princeton: Princeton University Press, 1994.

——. *New Testament Interpretation through Rhetorical Criticism*. Chapel Hill: University of North Carolina Press, 1984.

——, ed. *The Cambridge History of Literary Criticism*. Vol. 1: *Classical Criticism*. Cambridge: Cambridge University Press, 1989.

Kerford, George B. *The Sophistic Movement*. Cambridge: Cambridge University Press, 1981.

Keuls, Eva C. *The Reign of the Phallus: Sexual Politics in Ancient Athens*. New York: Harper & Row, 1985.

Kimball, Bruce A. *Orators & Philosophers: A History of the Idea of a Liberal Education*. New York: Teachers College Press, 1986.

Kinneavy, James I. *Greek Rhetorical Origins of Christian Faith*. New York: Oxford University Press, 1987.

Kristeller, Paul O. *Renaissance Thought: The Classic, Scholastic, and Humanist Strains*. New York: Harper, 1961.

Kroll, Wilhelm. "Rhetorik." *Paulys Real-Encyclopädie der classicischen Altertumswissenschaft*, Supplementband 7, colls. 1039–138. Stuttgart: Metzler, 1940.

Krumbacher, Karl. *Geschichte der byzantinische Literatur*. Munich: Beck, 1897. Reprint, New York: B. Franklin, 1970.

Kustas, George L. "The Function and Evolution of Byzantine Rhetoric," *Viator: Medieval and Renaissance Studies* 1 (1970): 55–73.

———. *Studies in Byzantine Rhetoric*. Thessaloniki: Pontifical Institute for Patristic Studies, 1973.

Laistner, M. L. W. *Intellectual Heritage of the Early Middle Ages*. Ithaca: Cornell University Press, 1957.

———. *Thought and Letters in Western Europe, A.D. 500 to 900*. Ithaca: Cornell University Press, 1957.

Lanham, Richard A. *The Electronic Word: Democracy, Technology, and the Arts*. Chicago: University of Chicago Press, 1993.

Lausberg, Heinrich. *Handbook of Literary Rhetoric: A Foundation for Literary Study*. Translated by Matthew T. Bliss et al., edited by David E. Anton and R. Dean Anderson. Leiden: Brill, 1998.

Lefkowitz, Mary, and Maureen B. Fants, eds. *Women's Life in Greece and Rome: A Source Book in Translation*. 2nd ed. Baltimore: Johns Hopkins University Press, 1992.

Levin, Carole, and Patricia A. Sullivan, eds. *Political Rhetoric: Power and Renaissance Women*. Albany: State University of New York Press, 1995.

Lieberman, Saul. *Hellenism in Jewish Palestine: Studies in the Literary Transmission, Beliefs, and Manners of Palestine in the Ist Century BCE–IVth Century CE*. New York: Jewish Theological Seminary of America, 1962.

Lindberg, Gertrude. *Studies in Hermogenes and Eustathios: The Theory of Ideas and Its Application in the Commentaries of Eustathios on the Epics of Homer*. Lund: Lindell, 1977.

The Loeb Classical Library. Cambridge, Mass.: Harvard University Press.

Lopez-Grigera, Luisa. *La Retórica en la España del Siglo de oro: Teoría y practica*. Salamanca: Ediciones Universidad, 1994.

Lord, Albert B. *The Singer of Tales*. Cambridge, Mass.: Harvard University Press, 1960.

Lunsford, Andrea, ed. *Reclaiming Rhetorica: Women in the Rhetorical Tradition*. Pittsburgh: University of Pittsburgh Press, 1995.

McAlister, Linda L. *Hypatia's Daughters: Fifteen Hundred Years of Women Philosophers*. Bloomington: Indiana University Press, 1996.

McCall, Marsh. *Ancient Rhetorical Theories of Simile and Comparison*. Cambridge, Mass.: Harvard University Press, 1969.

McCauley, Leo P., trans. *Funeral Orations by Saint Gregory Nazianzus and Saint Ambrose*. Washington, D.C.: Catholic University of America Press, 1955.

Mack, Peter. *Renaissance Argument: Valla and Agricola in the Traditions of Rhetoric and Dialectic*. Leiden: Brill, 1993.

——, ed. *Renaissance Rhetoric*. New York: St. Martin's Press, 1994.

McKeon, Richard. "Poetry and Philosophy in the Twelfth Century." *Modern Philology* 43 (1946) 217–34. Reprinted in Backman 1987, 167–93.

——. "Rhetoric in the Middle Ages." *Speculum* 17 (1942) 1–32. Reprinted in Backman 1987, 121–66.

McManamon, John M. *Funeral Oratory and the Cultural Identity of Italian Humanism*. Chapel Hill: University of North Carolina Press, 1989.

Maguire, Henry. *Art and Eloquence in Byzantium*. Princeton: Princeton University Press, 1981.

Mailloux, Steven. *Rhetoric, Sophistry, Pragmatism*. New York: Cambridge University Press, 1995.

Manitius, Max. *Geschichte der lateinischen Literatur des Mittelalters*. Handbuch der Altertumswissenschaft, IX, 2. 3 vols. Munich: Beck, 1911–31.

Marrou, Henri-Irenée. *A History of Education in Antiquity*. Translated by George Lamb. New York: Sheed and Ward, 1956. Reprint, Madison: University of Wisconsin Press, 1997.

——. *Saint Augustin et la fin de la culture antique*. Paris: de Boccard, 1938. Reissued with "Retractatio," 1949.

Martin, Josef. *Antike Rhetorik: Technik und Methode*. Handbuch der Altertumswissenschaft II, 3. Munich: Beck, 1974.

Matson, Patricia P., Philip Rollinson, and Marion Sousa, eds. *Readings from Classical Rhetoric*. Carbondale: Southern Illinois University Press, 1990.

Meerhoff, Kees. *Rhétorique et poétique au XVIᵉ siècle en France: Du Bellay, Ramus, et les autres*. Leiden: Brill, 1986.

Miller, Joseph M., Michael H. Prosser, and Thomas W. Benson, eds. *Readings in Medieval Rhetoric*. Bloomington: Indiana University Press, 1973.

Miller, Thomas P. *The Formation of College English: Rhetoric and Belles Lettres in the British Cultural Provinces*. Pittsburgh: University of Pittsburgh Press, 1997.

Momigliano, Arnaldo, ed. *The Conflict between Paganism and Christianity in the Fourth Century*. Oxford: Clarendon Press, 1963.

Monfasani, John. *George of Trebizond: A Biography and a Study of His Rhetoric and Logic*. Leiden: Brill, 1976.

Monk, Samuel H. *The Sublime: A Study of Critical Theories in 18th Century England*. New York: Modern Language Association, 1935.

Murphy, James J. *Medieval Rhetoric: A Select Bibliography*. Toronto: Center for Medieval Studies, 1971.

——. *Renaissance Rhetoric: A Short-Title Catalogue of Works on Rhetorical Theory from the Beginning of Printing to A.D. 1700*. New York: Garland, 1981.

——. *Rhetoric in the Middle Ages: A History of Rhetorical Theory from Saint Augustine to the Renaissance*. Berkeley: University of California Press, 1974.

——, ed. *Medieval Eloquence: Studies in the Theory and Practice of Medieval Rhetoric*. Berkeley: University of California Press, 1978.

——, ed. *Renaissance Eloquence: Studies in the Theory and Practice of Renaissance Rhetoric*. Berkeley: University of California Press, 1983.

——, ed. *Renaissance Rhetoric: A Microfiche Collection of Key Texts, A.D. 1455–1600, from the Bodlean Library, Oxford*. Oxford Microform Publ., n.d.

——, ed. *Three Medieval Rhetorical Arts*. Berkeley: University of California Press, 1971.

Murphy, James J., and Martin Davies. "Rhetorical Incunabula: A Short-Title Catalogue of Texts Printed to the Year 1500." *Rhetorica* 15 (1997): 355–470.

Norden, Eduard. *Agnostos Theos: Untersuchungen zur Formgeschichte religiöser Rede*. Stuttgart: Teubner, 1956.

——. *Die antike Kunstprosa vom VI. Jahrhunderts vor Christus bis in die Zeit der Renaissance*. Leipzig: Teubner, 1909.

Norwich, John J. *Byzantium*. 3 vols. New York: Knopf, 1989–95.

Ochs, Donovan J. *Consolatory Rhetoric: Grief, Symbol, and Ritual in the Greco-Roman Era*. Columbia: University of South Carolina Press, 1993.

Oliver, Robert T. *Communication and Culture in Ancient India and China*. Syracuse: Syracuse University Press, 1971.

O'Malley, John W. *Praise and Blame in Renaissance Rome: Rhetoric, Doctrine, and Reform in the Sacred Orators of the Papal Court, c. 1450–1521*. Durham, N.C.: Duke University Press, 1979.

Ong, Walter J. *Orality and Literacy: The Technologizing of the Word*. London: Methuen, 1982.

——. *The Presence of the Word: Some Prolegomena for Cultural and Religious History*. New Haven: Yale University Press, 1967.

——. *Ramus, Method, and the Decay of Dialogue: From the Art of Discourse to the Art of Reason*. Cambridge, Mass.: Harvard University Press, 1958.

Ostrogorsky, Gregory. *History of the Byzantine State*. Translated by J. M. Hussey. New Brunswick, N.J.: Rutgers University Press, 1969.

Paetow, Louis J. "The Arts Course at Medieval Universities with Special Reference to Grammar and Rhetoric." *University of Illinois Studies* 3 (1910): 491–624.

Patterson, Annabel. *Hermogenes and the Renaissance: Seven Ideas of Style*. Princeton: Princeton University Press, 1970.

Perelman, Chaim, and L. Olbrechts-Tyteca. *The New Rhetoric: A Treatise on Argumentation*. Translated by John Wilkinson and Purcell Weaver. Notre Dame, Ind.: Notre Dame University Press, 1969.

Pfeiffer, Rudolph. *History of Classical Scholarship: From the Beginnings to the End of the Hellenistic Age*. Oxford: Clarendon Press, 1968.

——. *History of Classical Scholarship: From 1300 to 1850*. Oxford: Clarendon Press, 1976.

Plett, Heinrich F. *English Renaissance Rhetoric and Poetics: A Systematic Bibliography of Primary and Secondary Sources*. Leiden: Brill, 1995.

——, ed. *Renaissance Rhetorik/Renaissance Rhetoric*. Berlin: de Gruyter, 1993.

Pomeroy, Sarah. *Women in Hellenistic Egypt*. New York: Schochen Books, 1984.

Porter, Stanley E., ed. *Handbook of Classical Rhetoric in the Hellenistic Period, 330 B.C.–A.D. 400*. Leiden: Brill, 1997.

Poulakos, John. *Sophistical Rhetoric in Classical Greece*. Columbia: University of South Carolina Press, 1994.

Poulakos, Takis. *Speaking for the Polis: Isocrates' Rhetorical Education*. Columbia: University of South Carolina Press, 1997.

——, ed. *Rethinking the History of Rhetoric: Multidisciplinary Essays on the Rhetorical Tradition*. Boulder, Colo.: Westview Press, 1993.

Purcell, William M. *Ars Poetriae: Rhetorical and Grammatical Invention at the Margins of Literacy*. Columbia: University of South Carolina Press, 1996.

Rabinowitz, Isaac, ed. and trans. *The Book of the Honeycomb's Flow by Judah Messer Leon*. Ithaca: Cornell University Press, 1983.

Radermacher, Ludwig. "Artium Scriptores (Reste der voraristotelischen Rhetorik)," Akademie der Wissenschaften, Wien, philosophisch-historische Klasse, *Sitzungsberichte* 217, no. 3. Vienna: Rohrer, 1951.

Rand, Edward K. *Founders of the Middle Ages*. Cambridge, Mass.: Harvard University Press, 1928.

Reynolds, Suzanne. *Medieval Reading: Grammar, Rhetoric, and the Classical Text*. Cambridge: Cambridge University Press, 1996.

Riché, Pierre. *Education and Culture in the Barbarian West, Sixth through Eighth Centuries*. Translated by John J. Contreni. Columbia: University of South Carolina Press, 1976.

Rockinger, Ludwig. *Briefsteller und Formelbücher des eilften bis vierzehnten Jahrhunderts*. New York: B. Franklin, 1961.

Romilly, Jacqueline de. *Les Grands sophistes dans l'Athènes de Périclès*. Paris: De Fallois, 1998.

——. *Magic and Rhetoric in Ancient Greece*. Cambridge, Mass.: Harvard University Press, 1975.

Rorty, Amélie O., ed. *Essays on Aristotle's Rhetoric*. Berkeley: University of California Press, 1996.

Russell, Donald A. *Criticism in Antiquity*. Berkeley: University of California Press, 1981.

——. *Greek Declamation*. Cambridge: Cambridge University Press, 1983.

Russell, Donald A., and N. G. Wilson, eds. and trans. *Menander Rhetor*. Oxford: Clarendon Press, 1981.

Russell, Donald A., and Michael Winterbottom, eds. *Ancient Literary Criticism: The Principal Texts in New Translations*. Oxford: Clarendon Press, 1972.

Scaglione, Aldo. *The Classical Theory of Composition from Its Origins to the Present: A Historical Survey*. Chapel Hill: University of North Carolina Press, 1972.

Schanze, Helmut. *Rhetorik: Beiträge zu ihrer Geschichte in Deutschland von 16–20. Jahrhundert*. Frankfurt: Athenaion, 1974.

Schiappa, Edward. *Protagoras and Logos: A Study in Greek Philosophy and Rhetoric*. Columbia: University of South Carolina Press, 1991.

Scott, Izora. *Controversies over the Imitation of Cicero as a Model for Style and Some Phases of Their Influence on the Schools of the Renaissance*. New York: Teachers College, Columbia University, 1908. Reprint, 1972.

Seigel, Jerrold E. *Rhetoric and Philosophy in Renaissance Humanism: The Union of Eloquence and Wisdom, Petrarch to Valla*. Princeton: Princeton University Press, 1968.

Shuger, Debora K. *Sacred Rhetoric: The Christian Grand Style in the English Renaissance*. Princeton: Princeton University Press, 1988.

Sider, Robert D. *Ancient Rhetoric and the Art of Tertullian*. London: Oxford
University Press, 1971.

Smith, Craig R. *Rhetoric and Human Consciousness: A History*. Prospect Heights,
Ill.: Waveland Press, 1998.

Smith, Robert W. *The Art of Rhetoric in Alexandria*. The Hague: Mouton, 1974.

Solmsen, Friedrich. *Intellectual Experiments of the Greek Enlightenment*. Princeton:
Princeton University Press, 1975.

Sonnino, Lee A. *A Handbook to Sixteenth-Century Rhetoric*. London: Routledge
and Kegan Paul, 1968.

Speck, Paul. *Die kaiserliche Universität von Konstantinopol*. Munich: Beck, 1974.

Spengel, Leonard, ed. *Rhetores Graeci*. 3 vols. Leipzig: Teubner, 1853–56. Reprint,
Frankfurt: Minerva, 1966. Vol. 1 reedited by Caspar Hammer. Leipzig: Teubner,
1894.

Sprague, Rosamond K., ed. *The Older Sophists*. Columbia: University of South
Carolina Press, 1972.

Stahl, William H., Richard Johnson, and E. L. Burge. *Martianus Capella and the
Seven Liberal Arts*. 2 vols. New York: Columbia University Press, 1971, 1977.

Stowers, Stanley K. *The Diatribe and Paul's Letter to the Romans*. Chico, Calif.:
Scholars Press, 1981.

Sussman, Lewis A. *The Elder Seneca*. Leiden: Brill, 1978.

Swearingen, C. Jan. *Rhetoric and Irony: Western Literacy and Western Lies*. New
York: Oxford University Press, 1991.

Taylor, Henry O. *The Medieval Mind*. 2 vols. Cambridge, Mass.: Harvard
University Press, 1925.

Thyen, Hartweg. *Der Stil der judisch-hellenistische Homilie*. Göttingen:
Vandenhoeck & Ruprecht, 1955.

Ueding, Gert, et al., eds. *Historisches Wörterbuch der Rhetorik*. 8 vols. Tübingen:
Niemeyer, 1992–.

Untersteiner, Mario. *The Sophists*. Translated by Kathleen Freeman. Oxford: Basil
Blackwell, 1953.

Vickers, Brian. *Classical Rhetoric and English Poetry*. London: Macmillan, 1970.

———. *Francis Bacon and Renaissance Prose*. Cambridge: Cambridge University
Press, 1968.

———. *In Defence of Rhetoric*. Oxford: Clarendon Press, 1988.

———, ed. *Rhetoric Revalued*. Binghampton, N.Y.: Center for Medieval and Early
Renaissance Studies, 1982.

Vitanza, Victor J., ed. *Writing Histories of Rhetoric*. Carbondale: Southern Illinois
University Press, 1994.

Waithe, Mary Ellen, ed. *A History of Women Philosophers*. 4 vols. Dordrecht:
Martinus Nijhoff, 1987–95.

Wallace, Karl R. *Francis Bacon on Communication and Rhetoric*. Chapel Hill:
University of North Carolina Press, 1943.

———, ed. *History of Speech Education in America: Background Studies*. New York:
Appleton-Century-Crofts, 1954.

Wallach, Luitpold. *Alcuin and Charlemagne: Studies in Carolingian History and
Literature*. Ithaca: Cornell University Press, 1959.

Walz, Christian, ed. *Rhetores Graeci.* 9 vols. London, 1832–36. Reprint, Osnabruck: Zeller, 1968.

Ward, John O. *Ciceronian Rhetoric in Treatise, Scholion, and Commentary.* Typologie des sources du Moyen Age occidental, 58. Turnhout, Belgium: Brepols, 1995.

Warner, Martin, ed. *The Bible as Rhetoric: Studies in Biblical Persuasion and Credibility.* London: Routledge, 1990.

Warnick, Barbara. *The Sixth Canon: Belletristic Rhetorical Theory and Its French Antecedent.* Columbia: University of South Carolina Press, 1993.

Watson, Duane F., ed. *Persuasive Artistry: Studies in New Testament Rhetoric in Honor of George A. Kennedy.* Sheffield, England: Sheffield Academic Press, 1991.

Watson, Duane F., and Alan J. Hauser. *Rhetorical Criticism of the Bible: A Comprehensive Bibliography with Notes on History and Method.* Leiden: Brill, 1993.

Weinberg, Bernard. *A History of Literary Criticism in the Italian Renaissance.* 3 vols. Chicago: University of Chicago Press, 1961.

Welch, Kathleen E. *The Contemporary Reception of Classical Rhetoric: Appropriations of Ancient Discourse.* Hillsdale, N.J.: Lawrence Erlbaum, 1990.

Whitman, Jon. *Allegory: The Dynamics of an Ancient and Medieval Technique.* Cambridge, Mass.: Harvard University Press, 1987.

Wieruszowski, Helene. *Politics and Culture in Medieval Spain and Italy.* Rome: Edizione di Storia e Letteratura, 1971.

Wilken, Robert L., ed. *Aspects of Wisdom in Judaism and Early Christianity.* South Bend, Ind.: Notre Dame University Press, 1975.

Williams, Raymond. *Keywords: A Vocabulary of Culture and Society.* New York: Oxford University Press, 1976.

Williamson, Margaret. *Sappho's Immortal Daughters.* Cambridge, Mass.: Harvard University Press, 1995.

Wirth, Peter. "Untersuchungen zur byzantinischen Rhetorik der zwölf Jahrhunderts mit besonderer Berücksightigung der Schriften des Erzbischofs Eustathios von Thessalonike." Inaugural dissertation, University of Munich, 1990.

Wisse, Jakob. *Ethos and Pathos from Aristotle to Cicero.* Amsterdam: Hakkert, 1989.

Yates, Frances A. *The Art of Memory.* London: Routledge and Kegan Paul, 1966.

Yun Lee Too. *The Rhetoric of Identity in Isocrates: Text, Power, Pedagogy.* Cambridge: Cambridge University Press, 1995.

INDEX

Clement, Second Letter of, 155–56
Cleopatra, 18
Commonplaces, 27, 33, 84–85, 160. See also Topics
Comnena, Anna, 18, 185, 192
Comparative rhetoric, 4, 299–300
Composition, 26–27, 41–42, 114, 122, 131–32, 135, 214, 291
Constantine the Great, 152, 163, 169, 184
Constantinople, patriarchal school of, 191–92; "University" of, 190
Controversiae, 46, 211. See also Declamation
Copia, 116, 133, 245
Corax. See Tisias
Corinna, 16
Cornelia, 119
Cornificus. See Rhetoric for Herennius
Covenant speeches, 140–41
Cox, Leonard, 236, 247
Cressoles, Louis de, 278
Cursus, 215
Cyprian, 167–68

Day, Angel, 249
Decembrio, Pier Candido, 228
Declamation, 45–47, 100, 118, 125, 129, 209, 211, 217, 249
Deconstruction, 298–99
Deliberative rhetoric, 7–8, 14, 38, 86, 92, 107, 210, 237, 273
Delivery, 25, 90, 93, 98, 102, 109–10, 209, 248, 250, 253, 264, 268, 278–79
Demetrius: On Style, 122, 130–31, 189, 213
Demetrius of Phaleron, 46, 130, 133
Democracy, 1, 14, 20, 53, 54, 59
Demosthenes, 33, 47, 56, 59, 69, 88, 91, 122, 131–33, 135, 161, 186, 188, 192, 229, 231, 233, 244, 248, 256, 260, 273, 283
Derrida, Jacques, 298
Descartes, René, 259, 260, 263, 269–70, 272, 275
Deuteronomy, 141
Dialectic, 15, 30, 56, 58–59, 71, 79–81, 83–86, 89, 95–97, 145, 151, 175, 181,

198, 202, 212, 232–33, 241–43, 250, 252, 260, 292
Dialogue, 13, 30, 66, 208–9, 266–69
Diatribe, 144, 149
Dictamen, 212–16
Diction (word choice), 22, 42, 90–91, 135, 136, 253
Diêgêsis. See Narration
Digression, 56, 105–6
Dinant, Jacques de, 216
Dinarchus, 133
Dio Chrysostom, 17, 37, 47, 51, 299
Diognetus, Letter to, 154
Dionysius of Halicarnassus, 15, 122, 131–32, 133, 189, 191, 232
Dionysius Thrax, 26, 186
Diotima, 18
Dispositio. See Arrangement
Dolce, Lodovico, 240
Dominicans, 219, 222
Donatus, 124–25, 200
Du Marasais, C.-C., 276
Duties of the orator, 114, 178, 179, 210, 242

Eberhard, 221
Ecclesiastes, 143
Ecphrasis, 27, 162, 186, 187
Elizabeth I of England, 231, 248
Elocutio. See Style
Elocutionary Movement, 277–79, 291
Emotions. See Pathos
Empedocles, 34, 36
Empiricism, 259, 280–81
Encomium. See Epideictic; Panegyric
Encyclopedias, 27–28, 197–201, 203–4
Enrique de Aragon, 252
Enthymeme, 79, 83–84, 89, 105, 140, 202, 253
Epicheireme, 93, 105, 253
Epicureans, 94
Epideictic, 7–8, 14, 29–30, 38, 45, 49, 85–87, 92, 107, 129, 142, 183, 210, 220, 237; Christian, 160–66, 194, 210
Epilogue, 9, 22, 35, 56, 92, 106, 178, 243
Epistle. See Dictamen; Letter writing
Epitaphios. See Funeral oratory

Historiography, 128, 148, 264, 276
Hobbes, Thomas, 270
Homer, 5–12, 16, 132, 136, 153, 161, 165, 186
Homes, Henry, 280–81
Homily, 143–44, 148, 156–57, 160, 175, 180, 194, 223
Homosexuality, Greek, 67–69
Horace, 136, 220
Hortensia, 119–20
Hrabanus Maurus, 182, 209–10
Hugh of St. Victor, 97, 182, 214, 255
Humanists, 117, 226–37, 239, 242
Humbert of Romans, 182
Hume, David, 272–73, 280
Hypatia, 17
Hypereides, 131, 133
Hypothesis, 99

Ideas of style, 122–23, 191
Imitation, 6, 30, 50, 133, 178
Insinuatio, 103–4
Inspiration, 6, 134–35, 139, 145
Invention, 11, 24, 42, 89, 98, 102–8, 180–81, 247, 248, 252
Irenaeus, 155
Irnerius, 212
Irony, 10
Isaeus, 131, 133
Isaiah, Book of, 142, 144
Isidore of Seville, 2, 28, 203–4, 252
Isocrates, 14, 24, 33, 35, 37, 38–45, 50–51, 69, 76, 92, 117, 131–33, 194, 266, 299; Isocratean tradition, 45, 106; and Plato, 66, 73–74

Jerome, 159, 168–69, 171, 244
Jesuits, 252–53, 265, 275, 278
Jesus Christ, 144–47, 224
Jewish rhetoric, 98, 137–44, 149, 230
John, Gospel of, 146, 147
John Chrysostom. *See* Chrysostom, John
John Doxapatres, 188
John Geometres, 186, 189
John of Garland, 221

John of Salisbury, 118, 217
John of Sardis, 186
John Siceliotes, 188
Joshua, Book of, 141
Judah Messer Leon, 230
Judicial rhetoric, 5, 7–6, 14, 20–21, 25, 28, 30–32, 38, 55–58, 86–88, 92, 102–7, 124, 205, 208–9, 210, 237, 275
Julius Rufinianus, 123
Julius Victor, 118, 123, 131, 209, 213
Junius, Franciscus, 240
Justin Martyr, 153

Kant, Immanuel, 274–75, 289
Kautilya, 4
Keckermann, Bartholomew, 244
Kêrygma, 145–46
Koine Greek, 48, 192

Lactantius, 169–70
Lamy, Bernard, 260, 263–64
Landriani, Gerardo, 230
Lanfranc, 216
Latini, Brunetto, 216
Lawcourts and lawyers. *See* Judicial rhetoric
Lawson, John, 279
Le Faucher, Michel, 278
Le Gras, 260
Leontium, 17
Leo the Wise, 194
Letteraturizzazione, 3, 14, 128–29
Letter writing, 23, 33, 131, 149, 197, 212–13, 221, 244, 246, 249. See also *Dictamen*
Libanius, 47, 48, 51, 165, 186, 192, 194
Liberal arts, 43, 172, 173, 197–98, 210, 220, 253, 266
Licymnius, 22
Lipsius, Justus, 239
Literate revolution, 12–13, 45
Livia, 119
Llanos, Bernardino de, 253
Loci. See Topics
Locke, John, 259, 270–71, 275, 286
Logic. *See* Dialectic

Perelman, Chaim, 295–96
Pericles, 17, 65
Periodic style, 91–92, 130, 178
Peroration. *See* Epilogue
Peter Lombard, 182
Peter of Blois, 214
Peter of Spain, 235
Peter the Apostle, 148
Petrarch, 226, 228–29
Petronius, 118
Philodemus, 94, 136
Philo Judaeus, 138, 158
Philostratus, 47
Photius, 188
Piccolomini, Enea Sylvio, 228
Pichot, Amédée, 274
Pico della Mirandola, 228
Pilato, Leonzio, 229
Pini, Paolo, 240
Piscopia, Elena, 262
Pistis. See Proof
Planudes, Maximus, 188
Plato, 14, 18, 24, 29, 41, 49, 54, 113 126,
    131, 133, 135, 161, 163, 186, 192, 260,
    289; Academy of, 17, 76; *Apology*, 4,
    55–58; commentaries on, 190; *Cra-*
    tylus, 296; *Gorgias*, 1, 29, 30, 35, 58–
    66, 69, 71, 75, 79, 93, 94, 190, 257; *Ion*,
    135; *Menexenus*, 18, 278; *Meno*, 58;
    Phaedrus, 13, 21–22, 32, 37, 66–74, 79,
    93, 94, 190, 257, 266–68, 279, 298;
    Protagoras, 29; in the Renaissance,
    233, 236; *Republic*, 30, 59, 65–66, 69;
    Timaeus, 191; translations of, 229
Pletho, Georgius, 189
Pliny the Younger, 49, 131
Plutarch, 133
Poetics, 135–36
Poetry, 90, 128
Poggio Bracciolini. *See* Bracciolini,
    Poggio
Politian, 227
Polus, 22, 61–63
Port-Royalists, 259, 260, 263, 272
Praetextatus of Rouen, 205
Preaching, 23, 143–44, 146, 155–57, 174–

82, 197, 204, 207, 209–10, 244–45,
    253, 264, 265–69, 286; medieval
    handbooks of, 221–25
Préciosité, 262
Priestley, Joseph, 281
Priscian, 27, 205, 232
Probability, argument from, 21–23, 24,
    31–32, 56, 72–73, 105
Procopius of Caesarea, 186, 187
Procopius of Gaza, 187, 194
Prodicus, 29
Proemium, 8, 21, 31, 33, 35, 56, 92, 103–
    4, 160–61, 177, 214, 235, 243
Progymnasmata, 26–27, 28, 129, 136,
    186, 189–90, 205, 220, 291
Prolegomena, 94, 188–89, 214
Proof: as part of a speech, 9, 22, 24, 35,
    92, 104–5, 177, 235, 241. *See also* Argu-
    mentation; Enthymeme; Example
Prophecy, 141–42, 148, 155–56
Proposition, 8, 27, 92
Propriety, 90–91
Prosopopoeia, 9, 27
Protagoras, 22, 37, 50, 53
Proverbs, Book of, 143
Psalms, Book of, 142–43, 185
Psellus, Michael, 185, 189, 190–91, 194
Ptahhotep, The Instruction of, 4, 143
Pythagoreans, 17, 36

Quadratus, 153
Quadrivium, 198
Quintilian, 24–26, 41–42, 46, 66, 75, 95,
    115–19, 125, 128, 132, 133, 180, 197, 201,
    211, 232; in Middle Ages, 205, 211, 217;
    in Neoclassical period, 260, 282, 284,
    288; in the Renaissance, 226, 229, 233,
    242, 245, 251

Ramus, Peter, 249–52, 255, 259, 267, 276
Rainolds, John, 236
Rapin, René, 260
Refutation, 22, 27, 105
Rhetores Latini Minores, 123–24
Rhetoric: definitions of, 1, 59–60, 62,
    70, 77–78, 81–82, 102, 115, 203, 210,

234, 251, 256–57, 268, 271, 274–75,
282, 283; literary, 127–36; philosophi-
cal, 14–15, 53–97, 225, 277; primary, 2;
secondary, 3; sophistic, 14, 29–52,
292, 298–99; technical, 13–14, 20–28,
102–12, 115, 182, 225, 292
Rhetoric for Alexander, 24–25, 26
Rhetoric for Herennius, 14, 25, 26, 28, 99,
108–12, 122, 132, 197; in the Middle
Ages, 214, 216, 217, 219, 223; in the Re-
naissance, 224, 226, 237, 252
Rhythm in prose, 45, 91, 215, 221, 253
Richard of Thetford, 223
Richards, I. A., 294
Robert of Basevorn, 182, 223
Rollin, Charles, 260, 275–76
Rosenhane, Beata, 262
Royal Society of London, 270
Rufinus of Aquila, 159

Salutati, Coluccio, 227, 228
Sappho, 15–16, 132, 299
Scaliger, J. C., 239
Schêma. See Figures of speech
Scholasticism, 219, 223, 238, 246
Scudéry, Madeleine de, 262
Second Sophistic, 47–52, 69, 130, 154, 227
Semiotics, 296
Seneca the Elder, 46, 118
Seneca the Younger, 47, 299
Sententiae, 10, 116, 129
Sermon on the Mount, 144–45
Sermons. *See* Preaching
Servius, 136, 211
Sforza, Ippolita, 231
Shakespeare, 260
Sheridan, Thomas, 278–79, 286
Sherry, Richard, 247–48
Sidonius Apollinaris, 205
Simile, 10, 91
Slavery, 82, 299
Soarez, Cypreano, 252–53
Socrates, 53–57, 102, 266. *See also* Plato
Solon, 102
Sopatros, 47, 188
Sophists and sophistry, 14, 29–52, 102,

114, 117, 128, 181–82, 184, 209, 277, 292,
298–99; Christian, 49, 160–66; Latin,
49. *See also* Second Sophistic
Spain, rhetoric in, 203–4, 277, 285
Speech writers. *See* Logographers
Speroni, Sperone, 236
Stasis theory, 92, 93, 94, 97, 98, 99–100,
102–3, 106–7, 115, 121–22, 193, 201,
203, 205, 235, 253
Stephen the Martyr, 148
Stoics, 93–94, 97, 144, 149, 158
Structuralism, 296–97
Sturm, Johannes, 250
Style, 11, 22, 24, 34–35, 42, 89–92, 94, 98,
102, 111–12, 117, 169, 246, 248, 250, 253,
264, 265, 280, 283; kinds of, 7, 74, 111,
122, 130–32, 179, 181, 210, 220–21, 235.
See also Composition; Figures of
speech; Ideas of style; Virtues of style
Suasoriae, 46. *See also* Declamation
Sublime, The, 134–35, 264–65, 283. *See
also* "Longinus"
Sulpicia, 119
Sulpicius Victor, 123
Susenbrotus, Joannes, 245
Swift, Jonathan, 37, 264, 280, 283
Syllogism, 83–84. *See also* Dialectic;
Enthymeme
Symmachus, Q. Aurelius, 172
Syncrisis, 27, 135, 186
Synesius of Cyrene, 37, 48, 51, 166–67
Syrianus, 188

Tacitus, 117, 118–19, 129, 135, 167, 274
Talon, Omer, 250
Tardiff, Guillaume, 238
Tatian, 153
Tertullian, 154, 167–68
Themistius, 48, 51
Theodorus (archbishop), 206
Theodorus Metochites, 186
Theodorus of Byzantium, 21–22
Theodorus of Gadara, 109
Theon, 26–27
Theophrastus, 17, 72, 74, 76, 91, 92–93,
110, 131